W9-CHY-864

(Continued)

Bridging the Literacy Achievement Gap, Grades 4–12

EDITED BY

Dorothy S. Strickland and Donna E. Alvermann

Foreword by Ronald F. Ferguson

Teachers College
Columbia University
New York and London

Published by Teachers College Press, 1234 Amsterdam Avenue, New York, NY 10027

Library of Congress Cataloging-in-Publication Data

Bridging the literacy achievement gap, grades 4–12 / edited by Dorothy S. Strickland and Donna Alvermann.
   p. cm. — (Language and literacy series)
Includes bibliographical references and index.
ISBN 0-8077-4487-5 (cloth : alk. paper) — ISBN 0-8077-4486-7 (pbk. : alk. paper)
   1. Language arts (Secondary)—United States. 2. English language—Study and teaching (Secondary)—United States. 3. Educational equalization—United States.
I. Strickland, Dorothy S. II. Alvermann, Donna E. III. Language and literacy series (New York, N.Y.)

LB1631.B7644   2004
428.4'071—dc22   2004043965

ISBN 0-8077-4486-7   (paper)
ISBN 0-8077-4487-5   (cloth)

Printed on acid-free paper

Manufactured in the United States of America

11 10 09 08 07 06 05 04   8 7 6 5 4 3 2 1

Contents

Foreword

Closing racial and ethnic gaps in academic achievement is now a focus of public policy and national discourse. News reports on the topic occur with increasing frequency in both print and electronic media. To a degree difficult to imagine as recently as a decade ago, national leaders declare confidently that we *can* close these gaps—and, indeed, they say that we *must*. Racist beliefs challenging the plausibility of ever achieving equality of educational outcomes among groups surely persist in some quarters, but most public discussions are conducted as if they do not. It seems that leaders from the far left to the far right of the political spectrum want to believe that dramatically raising achievement among black and brown children *on a national scale* is possible.

Reasons are not hard to find. Continuing a long-term decline in the market value of physical labor as compared with brainpower, the future prosperity of the society and the quality of life for individuals and families in the United States depend fundamentally on skills learned in schools. Future earnings are destined to be meager for youth lacking adequate literacy and numeracy skill—life will be hard. Moreover, the value of 401K plans, Social Security, and other retirement arrangements that rest on the value of the stock market and the health of the U.S. economy put even the highest-income professionals of today at risk for bad consequences during their retirement years, if today's children are insufficiently skilled as adults to sustain the nation's economic vitality.

A key fact is that a few decades from now, there will be no racial or ethnic majority group in the United States. So along with African Americans, Latinos, Asian Americans, and American Indians, Americans of European ancestry will be a minority. Collectively, non-Whites will constitute the majority in both the electorate and the workforce. It is no exaggeration to say that failure to raise achievement among Black and Brown children may weaken the economic, political, and social stability of the nation. As never before, closing the achievement gap is in everyone's interest, and the nation's leaders know it.

Policymakers' main strategy has been to impose new rules and incentives (some would say "threats"), frequently without sufficient resources to finance the responses they seek from schools and teachers. More resources are needed. Nevertheless, the threats have been, on balance, helpful. New rules and incentives have been catalysts for many new efforts. Admittedly, some of these efforts—for example, teaching to bad tests—are perverse and diversionary. Still, disaggregation of test scores by racial subgroups is causing even upper-income districts to come to terms with underperformance among some segments of the student population. Across the nation, school leaders and many teachers have intensified the search for ideas to raise achievement and narrow gaps. The new pressures are making a difference.

Hence, the critical need for a book such as this. Changing instruction in ways that produce genuine, widespread improvements in literacy and comprehension is no simple task for a society. Ideas do not flow effortlessly from teacher to teacher or from research to practice. The pages of this volume both report and embody the type of work necessary to make the dream of achievement equality come true. The work that the authors in this volume do in their professional practices and report in the chapters of this book provides evidence that many promising ideas are being developed and applied in the emerging national movement to close achievement gaps. I learned a lot from reading them, and I trust that you will, too. Because of such work, I'm guardedly optimistic.

Ronald F. Ferguson
John F. Kennedy School of Government
Harvard University
January 2004

Acknowledgments

We express our thanks to Andrés Henríquez, Program Officer for Education at the Carnegie Corporation of New York, for his deep interest and encouragement and to Carol Collins, publications editor at Teachers College Press, for her help in guiding this project to publication. A special thanks also goes to Rebecca Brittain and Margaret O'Connor, graduate assistant and administrative assistant, respectively, to Dorothy Strickland, and to Joy Fulmer, administrative assistant to Donna Alvermann, for their ongoing help in a variety of ways.

This publication was made possible by a grant from the Carnegie Corporation of New York. The statements made and views expressed are solely the responsibility of the authors.

Learning and Teaching Literacy in Grades 4–12

Issues and Challenges

Dorothy S. Strickland and Donna E. Alvermann

Key Points

- Adolescents engage in multiple literacies that are linked to their particular life experiences in a rapidly changing, technological world.
- Literacy learners are expected to use effective text-processing strategies, to be motivated, and to adopt normative ways of reading and writing.
- Socioeconomic status, home background, linguistic background, and quality of instruction contribute to achievement gaps between groups of students.

This chapter is divided into four sections. First, after a brief word about definitions, we outline what we consider to be key issues related to improving literacy learning among preadolescents and adolescents. Second, we describe how these issues become magnified in importance when working to alleviate the achievement gap among youth who, for a variety of reasons, are not achieving as well as educators, policymakers, and their parents expect. Third, we argue that these issues urgently need addressing if the goal is to close the achievement gap by improving literacy learning among youth from low-income minority neighborhoods. Finally, we outline key points in the forthcoming chapters to provide our readers with both a preview and a bridge to what is to come.

A BRIEF WORD ABOUT ADOLESCENCE AS A CONCEPT

Until recently the term *adolescence* drew little critique from scholars interested in studying the physical, emotional, intellectual, and social development of youths ranging in age from roughly 10 to 18. Its unquestioned acceptance rested largely on the notion that adolescence was a developmental stage through which youngsters passed on their way to becoming adults, or, as Appleman

(2001, p. 1) has wryly described it, "a kind of purgatory between childhood and adulthood." Although this concept of adolescence is by no means obsolete, it has been tempered a bit by work that questions the distinctions thought to separate the adolescent world from the adult world.

For example, the normative view of adolescents—as "not yet" adults and thus less competent and less knowledgeable than their elders—is one that is increasingly being critiqued in the professional literature. Like others (Amit-Talai & Wulff, 1995; Lesko, 2001) before us, we do not subscribe to this view. Instead, we like to think of adolescents as knowing things that have to do with their particular life experiences and the particular spaces they occupy both in and out of school in a quickly changing world. This situated perspective on youth culture recognizes that school literacy, though important, is but one among multiple literacies that young people use daily.

Because students as young as 10 years of age are particularly adept at multitasking, it is not uncommon for them to use their knowledge of traditional print, the Internet, and various forms of multimedia simultaneously. Picture, for example, a youth seated at her computer searching the Internet for information that she can use in writing a report that is due in social studies class tomorrow. Note how she switches her attention momentarily from the class assignment to instant messaging her friends about a newly released music CD. Note, too, how quickly she refocuses her attention on the assignment as she performs the necessary keystrokes to download a visual image that can be inserted into the report she is writing, all the while listening to her favorite music playing in the background.

KEY ISSUES IN IMPROVING YOUNG PEOPLE'S LITERACY LEARNING

Granted, there are problems with the foregoing picture, not the least of which is the issue of access to the Internet, a problem commonly referred to as the *digital divide,* which can lead to inequity in opportunities for youth living in economically depressed conditions. There are also questions concerning students' attention spans and the quality of the homework that they complete while multitasking. These concerns stem primarily from the fact that much of what is known about exemplary literacy instruction for preadolescents and adolescents assumes an equal playing field, one in which attention is duly focused on constructing meaning from and with texts of various kinds by applying common background knowledge. That this assumption is rarely the case, especially given the increasing diversity of students in U.S. schools, will come as no surprise. Nevertheless, it is important to know what is expected of literacy learners at the intermediate, middle, and high school levels *as a group* before considering how these expectations may or may not play out for different subgroups of students. It is also important to understand the issues behind these expectations, several of which are spelled out here.

Expectation #1—Students Will Use Effective Text-Processing Skills and Strategies

A research base summarized by the National Reading Panel (2000) and the RAND Reading Study Group (2002) shows that comprehension monitoring, using graphic organizers, generating self-questions, using text structure as an aid to remembering, and summarizing are effective strategies and lead to improved comprehension. Too few students possess these basic skills.

In the United States, according to the Carnegie Foundation (http://www .carnegie.org/sub/news/sns.html), close to 50% of all incoming ninth graders in this country's comprehensive, public high schools cannot comprehend the texts that their teachers expect them to read in order to complete class assignments. Students who do not comprehend adequately, not surprisingly, end up failing their courses and eventually dropping out of school. Even those who manage to stay in school often have a history of reading difficulties that prevent them from acquiring the requisite background knowledge, skills, and specialized vocabulary needed for learning in the subject areas. Their teachers understandably become frustrated and sometimes resort to what Finn (1999) calls a "domesticating" education. That is, they expect less of these students in exchange for the students' good will and reasonable effort in completing assignments that typically require little, if any, reading. It's an unfortunate case of less leading to less.

Instruction that is effective is embedded in the regular curriculum and makes use of the new literacies (Lankshear & Knobel, 2003), including multiple forms of texts (print, visual, aural, and digital) that can be read critically for multiple purposes in a variety of contexts. For this to become a reality, it will be important to teach students how to use relevant background knowledge and strategies for reading, discussing, and writing about a variety of texts. It will require the support of administrators and policymakers who buy into the idea that all students, including those who struggle to read in subject area classrooms, deserve instruction that is developmentally, culturally, and linguistically responsive to their needs (Alvermann, forthcoming).

Expectation #2—Students Will Be Motivated and Engaged

The cognitive demands of text processing, such as those described in the previous paragraph, are only part of the story, however. At issue here is the additional expectation that students will be motivated to participate in subject matter learning despite the fact that such learning often requires a long-term engagement with difficult concepts that on the surface may seem to have little relevance to adolescents' everyday lives. This expectation is heightened further when factors related to feelings of competency, or self-efficacy, are taken into account.

In adolescence, as in earlier and later life, it is the belief in the self (or lack of such belief) that makes a difference in how competent a person feels. Perceptions of one's competencies are central to most theories of motivation, and the research on self-efficacy bears out the hypothesized connection between feeling competent and being motivated to learn something new. For example, providing adolescents who are experiencing reading difficulties with clear goals for a comprehension task and then giving feedback on the progress they are making can lead to increased self-efficacy and greater use of comprehension strategies (Schunk & Rice, 1993). Likewise, creating environments that make use of multimedia and newer forms of information communication technologies can heighten students' motivation to become independent readers and writers. This is turn can increase their sense of competency as readers (Kamil, Intrator, & Kim, 2000).

What is less clear from the research, however, is why students' motivations to read decline over time. Although decreases in intrinsic reading motivation have been noted as children move from the elementary grades to middle school, explanations vary as to the cause, with a number of researchers attributing the decline to differences in instructional practices (Eccles, Wigfield, & Schiefele, 1998; Oldfather & McLaughlin, 1993). Other researchers (e.g., Wade & Moje, 2000) attribute preadolescents' and adolescents' declining interests in subject matter reading to the transmission model of teaching. This model, with its emphasis on skill and drill, teacher-centered instruction, and passive learning, is viewed as inferior to a participatory model of instruction that actively engages students in their own learning (individually and in small groups) and that treats texts as tools for learning rather than as repositories of information to be memorized and then all too quickly forgotten.

Expectation #3—Students Will Adopt Normative Ways of Reading and Writing

The academic struggles of preadolescents and adolescents who can read but all too frequently choose not to do so is an issue that bears close scrutiny. These individuals are commonly referred to as aliterate, but their situation is no less worrisome than that of readers who struggle to read for lack of adequate skills. Unlike the rather straightforward definition for aliteracy (having the capacity to read but electing not to), the term *struggling reader* is a contested one. A cursory analysis of the reading research literature reveals that *struggling* is used to refer to youth with clinically diagnosed reading disabilities as well as to those who are English learners, "at-risk," low-achieving, unmotivated, disenchanted, or generally unsuccessful in school-related reading.

This smorgasbord of descriptors, when applied to either aliterate students or struggling readers, tells little or nothing about the sociocultural construction of such students. The descriptors also provide little guidance to teachers in terms of how to instruct individuals who can read but won't, or who want to read despite the struggle. According to the anthropologists McDermott and Varenne (1995), it is society at large that produces the conditions necessary for some individuals to succeed, others to struggle, and still others to fail outright. Applied to education, one could interpret this to mean that for some adolescents who have turned their backs on a version of reading and writing commonly referred to as academic literacy, it is the traditional school curriculum that is contributing to their difficulties.

Why might this be the case? One of us has argued elsewhere (Alvermann, 2001) that in an effort to raise the bar by implementing higher standards—a noteworthy goal in most people's minds—some schools are promoting certain normative ways of reading texts that may be disabling some of the very students they are trying to help. The possibility that schools are constructing certain types of readers as "aliterate" or "struggling" is even more problematic when one considers that certain normative ways of reading and writing are losing their usefulness, and perhaps to some extent their validity, in a world increasingly defined by the Internet, hypermedia, e-mailing, instant messaging, and the like (Bruce, 2002). If instruction is to benefit both aliterate and struggling readers, it should take into account their personal and everyday literacies in ways that enable them to use those literacies as springboards for engaging actively in academic tasks that are challenging and worthwhile. It should also make use of the new literacies (Lankshear & Knobel, 2003), including multiple forms of texts (print, visual, aural, and digital) that can be read critically for multiple purposes in a variety of contexts.

Finally, rather than expecting all students to adopt normative ways of reading and writing, preference might be given to rethinking current intervention programs, perhaps along the lines of what Luke and Elkins (2000) have alluded to as re/mediating adolescent literacies. *Re/mediation,* not to be confused with the older term *remediation,* without the slash, involves rethinking or reframing the way we think about intervening in adolescents' reading lives. It calls for moving beyond fruitless searches for some method or "magic bullet" that purportedly will fix their so-called deficits in reading. *Re/mediation,* in the sense that Luke and Elkins (2000) use the term, involves refashioning instructional conditions so as to enable students to use their out-of-school literacies and knowledge of various media forms to learn in the classroom. In a metaphoric sense, re/mediation involves fixing the conditions in which students learn rather than attempting to fix the students per se.

THE ACHIEVEMENT GAP

The key issues we have outlined, regarding preadolescent and adolescent learners, are compounded when the students come from low-income and low-income-minority homes. Specifically, these issues become demonstrably acute when students are members of families that are poor and African American or Latino. Such students are likely to attend schools with high mobility rates, inadequate resources and facilities, and large numbers of children with challenging learning needs. Even when their teachers try hard to make the best of the challenges before them, Knapp (1995, p. 1) suggests, "many wonder why it seems so hard to engage and maintain children's attention to learning tasks, communicate what often appears to be common sense, and show demonstrable achievement gains on conventional measures of learning." However,

Knapp also recognizes that, from the perspective of many of the students these teachers are trying to reach, "[I]t is not always obvious what they have to gain from being in school or from going along with what schools ask of them" (Knapp, 1995, p. 1).

Despite efforts by educators and policymakers during the past several decades, achievement gaps between certain groups of students stubbornly persist. Surveys of student achievement by the National Assessment of Educational Progress (NAEP) (Donahue, Finnegan, Lutkus, Allen, & Campbell, 2001) between 1973 and 1999 showed a persistent although slightly narrowing gap between White and Black students. The score gap between White and Black fourth-graders was smaller in 2002 than in 1994, and the gap between White and Hispanic fourth graders narrowed between 2000 and 2002, but neither was found to differ significantly from 1992. At grades 8 and 12, no significant change in either gap was seen across the assessment years. It is important to note that overall NAEP results for reading in 2002 were not encouraging. Gaps between students of different racial and ethnic backgrounds continue to be of concern (National Center for Education Statistics, 2003).

In 2001, the reauthorization of the Elementary and Secondary Education Act, known as the No Child Left Behind Act (2002), brought greater attention to this problem by requiring individual states, districts, and schools to be accountable for eliminating the achievement gap by the year 2014. States and districts are required to assess all students annually from grades 3 through 8 and disaggregate the results to show adequate yearly progress for their total student population as well as for different demographic groups.

Although a great deal of serious attention has been given to this problem, it is safe to say that, as an educational community, we are far from final answers. The emerging concerns faced by educators and policymakers are extremely complex. Contributing factors rarely stand alone. More often, they are interactive and interdependent and include issues of socioeconomic status, home and linguistic background, and quality of instruction. A brief discussion of these follows.

Socioeconomic Status

Family income and reading achievement are closely linked. Socioeconomic differences are generally indexed by such variables as household income and parents' education and occupation, alone or in some weighted combination. Families rated low in socioeconomic status (SES) not only are less affluent and less educated than other families, but they also tend to live in communities in which the average family SES is low and tend to receive less adequate nutrition and health services. In their discussion of SES as a risk factor, Snow, Burns, and Griffin (1998) describe low SES as both an individual risk factor and a group risk factor. As individuals, poor children attending the same schools as more affluent children are more likely to become poorer readers than children from high-income families. Also as a group, low SES children from low-income communities are likely to become poorer readers than children from more affluent communities. However, when achievement scores and SES are measured individually for all children in a large sample, the strength of the association between SES and achievement is far lower. A low-status child in a generally moderate- or upper-status school or community is far less at risk than that same child in a whole school or community of low-status children (Snow, Burns, & Griffin, 1998, p. 124). The effect of SES is strongest when it is used to indicate the status of a school, a community, or school district, rather than the status of the individual.

School funding plays an important role in the socioeconomic status of schools and communities. Recent studies have reanalyzed the research on school funding and its influence on the SES of schools and school districts. Biddle and Berliner (2003) analyzed the average annual expenditures per student for each of the states and the variation among districts in total revenues per student within each state. They found that while the disparities in funding differ sharply among the states, they were greater within some states than among the states as a group. Some U.S. students who live in wealthy communities or neighborhoods within states that have high levels of funding for public schools are now attending public schools where funding is set at $15,000 or more per student per year, whereas other U.S. students, who live in poor communities or neighborhoods within states that have low levels of funding, must make do with less than $4,000 in per-student funding in their schools for the year (Biddle & Berliner, 2003, p. 3). Unlike the Coleman report (1972), in which school quality (and level of school funding) had little to no impact once home and peer factors were taken into account, Biddle and Berliner state that funding inequities do make a difference and suggest that there were methodological flaws in the Coleman report. For example, according to Biddle and Berliner, "The study included no measures for classroom size, teacher qualifications, classroom procedures, academic pressure, or sense of community associated with schools" (Biddle & Berliner, 2003, p. 8).

Home Background

Research indicates that the achievement gap is already in place before children enter kindergarten. The U.S. Department of Education's Early Childhood Longitudinal Study (ECLS-K) (2000) for the kindergarten class of 1998–99 is a compilation of data from a nationally representative sample of 20,000 children (and their parents and teachers) who entered kindergarten in the fall of 1998. In addition to numerous family background variables, the data include measures of cognitive skills and knowledge. The ECLS shows that by the time children are five years old, there is a gap in school-related skills and knowledge between African American and European American children, even when their mothers have equal years of schooling. Of course, as Ferguson (2000b) points out, "[E]qual years of schooling is not the same as equal quality of schooling. There is no measure in this data of parents' own test scores or the quality of the schools that the parents attended." Nevertheless, the ECLS survey reveals differences in home-learning activities between children whose mothers have different amounts of schooling and also differences between Blacks and Whites within each mother's schooling category. In general, Whites across categories buy more books, records, tapes, and CDs and engage more with their children in reading and academic enrichment activities than do Blacks. Though the study also indicates that Blacks play and sing with their children more than Whites, these activities may not have the long-term benefits for beginning reading achievement that reading to children provides.

Phillips (2000) analyzed several achievement-gap-related surveys in an attempt to describe age related changes in the Black–White gap as children move through the grades. According to Phillips, "Taken together, we estimate that at least half of the black–white gap that exists at the end of twelfth grade can be attributed to the gap that already existed at the beginning of first grade. The remainder of the gap seems to emerge during the school years" (Phillips, 2000, p. 136). While less is known about the child-rearing practices that may affect children's school performance during the middle school and high school years, it may be safe to say that differences (not deficits) in child-rearing practices may contribute to the gap. Explanations such as that offered by Ogbu (2002), who attributed much of the problem to Black youth cultural patterns and behaviors that are counterproductive for academic success, have been disputed by other researchers. Ferguson (2002a) speculates that what Ogbu observed was "a clumsy attempt by Black students to search for a comfortable racial identity." Indeed, as adolescents attempt to find their place in society, their personal goals and behaviors often diverge from what the school expects and demands. When these students come from cultural backgrounds that differ greatly from that of the school, their attempts to "find their place" may be seen as even more divergent and may put them at risk of missing out on important educational experiences offered by the school and expected by society.

Linguistic Background

An increasing number of children enter school speaking a language or a dialect other than standard English. Many of these children and their families immigrated from other countries in order to seek a better life. For a variety of social and economic reasons, these families usually remain within their new communities, thus helping to maintain existing similarities in culture and language. Educators have expressed growing concern about the disparities that exist between home and school language and culture in some communities. The concerns are often expressed in terms of deficits rather than differences. Yet it is clear that students come to the classroom with varied linguistic abilities and educational backgrounds. This is especially true of preadolescent and adolescent learners.

The low achievement of poor African American and Latino children, in particular, has often been associated with their dialect or language. During the

1960s, linguists looked closely at language diversity as a cause of school failure. Those studies revealed key principles of language learning that remain helpful to teachers and curriculum developers: all language varieties are equally valid; all language varieties can accommodate all levels of thought; and any variety of standard English is not intrinsically better than any nonstandard dialect (Gopaul-McNicol, Reid, & Wisdom, 1998). Similarly, research in the language development of children for whom English is a second language supports the belief that the learner's home language should be valued and accepted as part of second language acquisition and learning. In their highly influential report, *Preventing Reading Difficulties in Young Children,* Snow and her colleagues (Snow, Burns, & Griffin, 1998) contend that research has shown that being able to read and write in two languages has cognitive, social, and economic benefits and should be supported whenever possible.

None of this denies the fact that the form language takes has economic, social, and political importance. Nor does it suggest that helping students achieve competence in standard English is not an important goal of the school. It does suggest that much of the low achievement of language-minority students may be pedagogically induced or exacerbated and therefore amenable to change (Rueda, 1991). Perhaps most important is the need to keep in mind that all children learn the language to which they have been exposed. As educators, we must resist the tendency to equate the use of language other than standard English with incompetence or a lack of intelligence (Strickland, Ganske, & Monroe, 2002).

The intermediate grades provide an excellent time in which to guide children in an exploration of various languages and dialects. Preadolescents are capable of comparing and contrasting various ways to express ideas, both orally and in writing. They can also begin to make judgments about when certain forms of language may be more appropriate than others. The notion of expanding children's language repertoires to accommodate a wider range of situations and linguistic capability should be the ultimate goal.

Quality of Instruction

Many researchers have turned their attention to what is increasingly considered to be a key contributing factor to the achievement gap—the differences in the quality of instruction that students receive. According to Haycock (2001), rather than focus on poverty and parental education, we should begin to concentrate on what takes place in the classrooms that minority students attend. The problems listed by Haycock include:

- Students in high-poverty and high-minority schools are not being challenged;
- Minority students are placed in low-level classes with a curriculum that does not prepare them for college;
- No provision is made for students who require more time and instruction to get on grade level;

- Teachers are often not qualified in the subjects that they teach;
- Schools with 90% greater enrollment of minority students have a higher percentage of underqualified teachers than predominantly White schools.

Other researchers (Darling-Hammond & Hudson, 1989; Ferguson, 1998) have linked teacher quality with student achievement and called for a look at both teacher quality and teaching quality, such as competency levels and pedagogical practices. Teacher quality pertains to distinct characteristics of teachers that are believed to predict teaching quality. Teaching quality refers to the effectiveness in teaching students to learn. Poor minority students appear to be at risk when teacher quality and teaching quality are not sufficiently high. High-quality, ongoing professional development geared to the specific needs of the teachers and students in particular schools is a solution offered by many researchers (Haycock, 2001). Special incentives for teachers who work in high-risk schools is another (Christie, 2002).

In summary, recent research in adolescent literacy has shifted away from a primary focus on issues of cognitive processes and teacher instructional practices to acknowledge the importance of the complex intersections among adolescent learners, texts, and contexts (Payne-Bourcy & Chandler-Olcott, 2003). In particular, the importance of multiple literacies has been emphasized, and the impact of culture and societal trends on the students' literacy development has become an important aspect of what educators consider as they tackle hard questions about engaging these learners and keeping them engaged. There is also a growing awareness that these issues begin to surface well before adolescence. For many students, the upper elementary grades may provide the last opportunity to address the prevention of continued failure in reading and writing. As students enter middle schools, increasing emphasis is placed on independent application of literacy skills to content area learning.

This book addresses the issues of learners, texts, and contexts for students from grades 4 through 12, emphasizing issues related to learners who are not achieving as well as expected. The chapters in Part I describe specific issues and possible solutions and new directions. This is followed in Part II by descriptions of promising programs that are authored and co-authored by practitioners and researchers working collaboratively. The result is a valuable resource for those involved in teaching and setting policy for the literacy education of preadolescent and adolescent learners.

OVERVIEW OF *BRIDGING THE LITERACY ACHIEVEMENT GAP, GRADES 4–12*

Bridging the Literacy Achievement Gap, Grades 4–12 is divided into two parts. Part I, Understanding the Literacy Achievement Gap: Learners and Context, provides thoughtful summaries of information about key factors thought to contribute to the achievement gap. Topics surrounding the literacy learning and teaching of Latino and African American students, the working poor, and students with special needs are given careful analysis by established researchers in these areas. In addition to these learner variables, issues related to the learning context, including the implementation of school reform measures and the importance of motivation are addressed. Each chapter provides the reader with the background information needed to understand and address the challenges described and offers some possible solutions and new directions. Part II, Addressing the Literacy Achievement Gap: Promising Practices, consists of a series of rich descriptions of promising programs and practices designed to address the issues raised in Part I. Each chapter represents a joint effort by practitioners and researchers working collaboratively. The result is a practical resource for teachers, administrators, and those setting policy for the literacy education of preadolescent and adolescent learners who are not achieving as well as expected.

Parts I and II exemplify the interrelationship between the thoughtful presentation of issues associated with the literacy achievement gap and the description of approaches that have worked. It is the way in which these two sections complement each other that makes this book unique. We realize that many readers will approach the chapters in this book in the order in which they are organized. Others will choose to enter at various points and impose their own organizational structure on the content. To facilitate either approach, we provide separate introductions to Parts I and II. In addition, at the beginning of each chapter, brief descriptions of its major points are outlined.

We urge our readers to approach this book as a written dialogue between the issues (Part I) and the promising solutions (Part II) that surround a major challenge faced by educators and policymakers today. Questions about the literacy achievement of preadolescent and adolescent learners, particularly those who are poor and members of minority populations, are at the forefront of concern. We are fortunate to have harnessed the efforts of some of the very best and most experienced minds at work on these issues. We believe that this book can provide a basis for reflection and action in the classroom, the boardroom, and the legislature.

REFERENCES

Alvermann, D. E. (2001). Reading adolescents' reading identities: Looking back to see ahead. *Journal of Adolescent & Adult Literacies, 44,* 676–690.

Alvermann, D. E. (2003, April). Exemplary literacy instruction in grades 7–12: What counts and who's counting? Paper presented at the IRA/Urban Partnership Conference, San Diego, CA.

Amit-Talai, V., & Wulff, H. (Eds.). (1995). *Youth cultures: A cross-cultural perspective.* New York: Routledge.

Appleman, D. (2001, April). *Unintended betrayal: Dilemmas of representation and power in research with youth.* Paper presented at the meeting of the American Educational Research Association, Seattle, WA.

Biddle, B. J., & Berliner, D. C. (2003). *What research says about unequal funding for schools in America: Policy perspectives.* San Francisco: WestEd.

Bruce, B. C. (2002). Diversity and critical social engagement: How changing technologies enable new modes of literacy in changing circumstances. In D. E. Alvermann (Ed.), *Adolescents and literacies in a digital world* (pp. 1–18). New York: Peter Lang.

Christie, K. (2002). States address achievement gaps. *Phi Delta Kappan, 84,* 102–103.

Coleman, J. S. (1972). The evaluation of equality of educational opportunity. In F. Mosteller & D. P. Moynihan (Eds.), *On equality of educational opportunity: Papers deriving from the Harvard University Faculty Seminar on the Coleman Report* (pp. 146–167). New York: Vintage Books.

Darling-Hammond, L., & Hudson, L. (1989). Teachers and teaching. In R. J. Shavelson, L. M. McDonnell, & J. Oakes (Eds.), *Indicators for monitoring mathematics and science education* (pp. 67–95). Santa Monica, CA: RAND Corporation.

Donahue, P. L., Finnegan, R. J., Lutkus, A. D., Allen, N. L., & Campbell, J. R. (2001). *NAEP Reading 2000.* Washington, DC: U.S. Department of Education, National Center for Education Statistics.

Eccles, J. S., Wigfield, A., & Schiefele, U. (1998). Motivation to succeed. In N. Eisenberg (Ed.), *Handbook of child psychology: Vol. 3, Social, emotional and personality development* (5th ed., pp. 1017–1095). New York: Wiley.

Ferguson, R. F. (1998). Teacher perceptions and expectations and the Black–White test score gap. In C. Jencks & M. Phillips (Eds.), *The Black–White test score gap* (pp. 160–183). Washington, DC: Brookings Institution Press.

Ferguson, R. F. (2002a). As reported in *New York Times,* November 30, 2002, p. B11.

Ferguson, R. F. (2002b). *Why America's Black–White achievement gap persists.* Unpublished manuscript.

Finn, P. J. (1999). *Literacy with an attitude: Educating working-class children in their own self-interest.* Albany: State University of New York Press.

Gopaul-McNicol, S., Reid, S., & Wisdom, G. (1998). The psychoeducational assessment of Ebonics speakers: Issues and challenges. *Journal of Negro Education, 67,* 16–24.

Haycock, K. (2001). Closing the achievement gap. *Educational Leadership, 58*(6), 6–11.

Kamil, M. L., Intrator, S. M., & Kim, H. S. (2000). The effects of other technologies on literacy and literacy learning. In M. L. Kamil, P. B. Mosenthal, P. D. Pearson, & R. Barr (Eds.), *Handbook of reading research* (Vol. 3, pp. 771–788). Mahwah, NJ: Erlbaum.

Knapp, M. S. (1995). *Teaching for meaning in high-poverty classrooms.* New York: Teachers College Press.

Lankshear, C., & Knobel, M. (2003). *New literacies: Changing knowledge and classroom learning.* Buckingham, UK: Open University Press.

Lesko, N. (2001). *Act your age! A cultural construction of adolescence.* New York: Routledge Falmer.

Luke, A., & Elkins, J. (2000). Re/mediating adolescent literacies. *Journal of Adolescent & Adult Literacy, 43,* 396–398.

McDermott, R., & Varenne, H. (1995). Culture *as* disability. *Anthropology & Education Quarterly, 26,* 324–348.

National Center for Education Statistics. (2003). *The nation's report card: Reading highlights 2002.* Washington, DC: U.S. Department of Education.

National Reading Panel. (2000). *Report of the National Reading Panel.* Washington, DC: National Institute of Child Health and Human Development.

No Child Left Behind Act of 2001. (2002). Public Law No. 107-110, 115 Stat. 1425.

Ogbu, J. U. (2002). As reported in *New York Times,* November 30, 2002, p. B11.

Oldfather, P., & McLaughlin, J. (1993). Gaining and losing voice: A longitudinal study of students' continuing impulse to learn across elementary and middle school contexts. *Research in Middle Level Education, 3,* 1–25.

Payne-Bourcy, L., & Chandler-Olcott, K. (2003). Spotlighting social class: An exploration of one adolescent's language and literacy practices. *Journal of Literacy Research, 35,* 551–590.

Phillips, M. (2000). Understanding ethnic differences in ethnic achievement: Empirical lessons from national data. In D. W. Grissmer & J. M. Ross (Eds.), *Analytic issues in the assessment of student achievement.* Washington, DC: National Center for Education Statistics.

RAND Reading Study Group. (2002). *Reading for understanding: Toward an R&D program in reading comprehension.* Santa Monica, CA: Science & Technology Policy Institute, RAND Education.

Rueda, R. (1991). Characteristics of literacy programs for language-minority students. In E. H. Hiebert (Ed.), *Literacy for a diverse society: Perspectives, practices, and policies.* New York: Teachers College Press.

Schunk, D. H., & Rice, J. M. (1993). Strategy fading and progress feedback: Effects on self-efficacy and comprehension among students receiving remedial reading services. *Journal of Special Education, 27,* 257–276.

Snow, C., Burns, M. S., & Griffin, M. (1998). *Preventing reading difficulties in young children.* Washington, DC: National Academy Press.

Strickland, D. S., Ganske, K., & Monroe, J. (2002). *Supporting struggling readers and writers: Strategies for classroom intervention 3–6.* Newark, DE: International Reading Association.

U.S. Department of Education. (2000). *Early Childhood Longitudinal Study (ECLS-K).* Washington, DC: National Center for Education Statistics.

Wade, S. E., & Moje, E. B. (2000). The role of text in classroom learning. In M. L. Kamil, P. B. Mosenthal, P. D. Pearson, & R. Barr (Eds.), *Handbook of reading research* (Vol. 3, pp. 609–627). Mahwah, NJ: Erlbaum.

Understanding the Literacy Achievement Gap

Learners and Context

PART I gives readers an overview of the research and current thinking in key areas related to the literacy learning and teaching of preadolescent and adolescent learners deemed at risk of not achieving up to their potential. **Robert Jiménez** opens with a research synthesis on what is known about teaching English language learners. Although his focus is on Latino learners, he shares implications for all second language learners and includes recommendations for policy and practice.

Poverty is a major factor associated with poor achievement in school. In her chapter on living below the poverty line, **Deborah Hicks** chronicles the lives and voices of youth growing up in white poverty in an Appalachian community. She provides a vivid picture of the complexities and contradictions of learning to read and coming of age between worlds divided by social class.

The structures and reforms put in place to address the literacy achievement gap are discussed by **Timothy Shanahan**. Focusing on secondary school reform, this chapter describes the key elements that need attention if reading achievement is to improve in the upper grades. Issues such as amount of instruction, curriculum, teacher quality, special programs, and instructional materials are addressed.

The development of motivation to read during adolescence is crucial to long-term reading engagement. **Allan Wigfield** points out that we currently know less about adolescents' reading motivation and the classroom practices influencing it than we know about younger children's motivation. Nevertheless, there is a growing body of literature describing classroom practices that can facilitate (or inhibit) adolescents' motivation to read. Wigfield shares these and provides implications for policy and practice.

The achievement gap between Black and White students remains a perplexing national issue. In her chapter, **Carol Lee** reviews existing studies on the characteristics of learning environments that have promoted achievement in literacy among African American preadolescent and adolescent learners and, by contrast, environments characterized by failure to learn. She concludes with implications for teachers' knowledge required to design and orchestrate environments for productive literacy learning among African American learners, and, by extension, for pre-service teacher preparation.

Don Deshler, **Jean Schumaker**, and **Susan Woodruff** deal with issues related to youth with special needs. They differentiate between "inclusion" and "inclusive teaching." They also describe instructional practices that have been validated for use in inclusive settings in secondary schools as well as the types of instructional conditions that result in the most significant outcomes.

These scholars, whose voices you hear in Part I, take a critical stance toward assumptions that continue to drive content literacy instruction in the upper grades, and they challenge school reformers, professional development experts, and classroom-based teachers and researchers to look for culturally responsive ways of addressing such assumptions.

Reconceptualizing the Literacy Learning of Latino Students

Robert T. Jiménez

Key Points

- A history of neglect of Latino students and educators' loss of control over their profession pose challenges to increased Latino academic achievement.
- Ongoing ecologically valid research is essential in the search for solutions.
- Change can be facilitated through programs sensitive to Latino students, better ESL instruction, and the use of native language for instructional purposes.

The issue of Latino students' literacy has to be one of the most exciting topics today in educational research. As is well known, large gains in student achievement are most likely when and where previous performance has been the poorest. For a variety of reasons, many Latino students have experienced difficulties with their literacy learning, and assessments of their progress have tended to reflect these problems. I argue here that the difficulties these students face are seldom through any fault of their own; nor should their families be blamed. Furthermore, it is not productive to cast their teachers as the villains. Instead, I will examine larger societal structures and ways of thinking concerning Latino students. These entrenched ways of thinking, many of them without merit or foundation, permeate school programs, approaches to literacy instruction, and even the everyday, seemingly inconsequential linguistic interactions between teachers and students. The goal of this chapter is to critically examine these ideas, provide the basis for developing deeper understanding of students' potential, and recommend experiences that include informed reflection concerning the literacy learning of Latino students. These goals are integrated throughout the various sections of this chapter.

Latino students have experienced disproportionate problems with academic achievement throughout their history of contact with Anglo America; 1848 was the year that the United States acquired almost half of Mexico's territory, and 1898 marked the acquisition of the island of Puerto Rico from Spain. These historical events, marked by military conquest and subsequent colonialism, have created multiple unique historical contexts for those groups referred to as Latinos. Other Caribbean island nations and Central American countries also have their own histories and consequent relationships to the United States that are marked by asymmetries in power. Surprisingly, and somewhat paradoxically, few groups believe as strongly in the U.S. educational system as fervently as recent immigrants. Because so many Latino students and their families are first or second generation immigrants, this fact is a potentially significant strength that has yet to be fully appreciated. For example, during a recent sabbatical in Mexico, I met with a returned migrant parent who spoke quite favorably concerning his children's experience in U.S. schools. My colleagues in Mexico confirmed that many Mexican, and other Latino, parents hold U.S. schools in high esteem, as have other researchers in the United States (Nieto, 2000). Even so, the general public in the United States, including many educators, often assumes that Latino parents do not value education. This belief has been used as justification for denying Latino students quality instruction. In my opinion, such unexamined beliefs cause difficulties for many Latino students. Conversations with Latino parents that provide opportunities for them to speak concerning their views of schooling, learning, and their children's futures almost always reveal a deep respect for teachers and learning. So, in spite of the fact that U.S. schools often fail to provide meaningful educational opportunities to Latino students, their families and communities maintain hope that schooling will allow their children to achieve more than the previous generation.

Some theorists, such as Macedo (2000), have argued that the so-called failure of U.S. schools concerning Latino students is not a failure at all but, rather, the intended outcome of a system that was never designed to provide these students with a quality education. While some might question the conspiratorial tone of such a charge, too much effort has gone into finding fault with Latino students, their families, or their teachers rather than into examining how larger systems predetermine and constrain students' opportunity. Deeper questions concerning lack of adequate health care and worthwhile economic opportunity, and the relationships these issues have to instructional quality, have most often been ignored. Yet these issues were raised by Latino educators such as Sánchez (1940) more than 60 years ago. They are now being revived by a new generation of scholars who refuse to separate and disconnect material conditions from schooling (Luke, 2003).

The aforementioned relationships are tangible and visible components of students' lives, however, and could be incorporated into the curriculum by bringing in local professionals, gathering the stories of parents and community members, and providing space for students to discuss how these issues influence and affect their opportunities and motivation for learning. In other words, while it may be beyond the immediate ability of educators to change these conditions, the conditions themselves can be made a part of the curriculum, particularly for middle school and high school students. Strategies for actually changing these conditions could also form a part of the curriculum. For example, Padilla (1985) showed that the larger Latino community in Chicago—Mexican American, Puerto Rican, and Central American—found ways to work together to interrogate large corporations concerning their hiring practices. Using the history of students' communities can provide hope, motivation, and worthwhile goals, particularly in cases where the community has achieved success through joint action.

SIGNIFICANT CHALLENGES

A central argument of this chapter is that a business-as-usual approach will result in literacy failure for Latino students. In other words, as Luke (2003) has argued, simply tinkering with industrial-era school systems, adding an ethnic component, or raising teachers' awareness concerning students from minority communities is insufficient to bring about worthwhile and significant changes. Significant challenges face those who truly desire to bring about these changes. In this section, I will present a brief overview of some of these challenges, and in the following section I will outline some ideas derived from my research and that of others that I believe may be useful to bring about desired changes.

A History of Neglect

The first challenge that needs to be acknowledged and dealt with is the history of neglect of Latino students in the United States. Latino students were segregated both by custom and by law until such segregation was finally declared illegal, in the *Brown v. Board of Education* ruling. As did the African American community, Latinos brought many lawsuits against this practice (San Miguel, 1987). The Latino community won some and lost others, but the basic pattern was established: Latino students were not welcome in U.S. schools in the company of European American children. Separate programs were established ostensibly to "Americanize" students with respect to language and culture. The language and culture of Latino students, of course, found no place within the official curriculum. These programs had the effect of denying Latino students access to the curriculum of power and learning experiences and instruction that might lead to enhanced economic opportunity. Even today, political and economic forces have created residential patterns that result in schools where Latino and other minority students constitute the majority. Segregation continues to affect these students' school performance negatively.

In the new times in which we live, policymakers are making increased demands for student accountability. Culturally and linguistically diverse students are now and will be the workers of tomorrow. The economy depends on these individuals—hence, the renewed interest in their performance—but contradictory forces are at work within our economic system. The demand for cheap labor contrasts with the need for highly skilled, knowledgeable individuals. We are entering a period in which both types of workers are increasingly viewed as expendable, as "raw materials" that exist only to serve economic interests. When the needs of workers clash with those of employers, jobs are often simply exported to locations that provide more profit. Latino students and their families, especially, are seen as a readily available workforce that can be disposed of when no longer wanted through deportation and the denial of the rights of citizenship. These contradictions are embarrassingly evident when states pass special legislation to allow temporary workers into the country because they are necessary to sectors such as agribusiness while, at the same time, measures are legislated into law that deny basic human rights to immigrants such as jobs, health care, education, and the use of their languages.

In the past, the struggles of students from linguistically and culturally diverse backgrounds were simply ignored by the schools. These students were provided with only a watered-down version of the curriculum and the instruction provided to students from mainstream backgrounds, and few worried much when they failed to graduate from high school. Students traditionally performed badly, and not much more than hand-wringing happened as a result. For example, when I was looking for students to include as participants for my dissertation research in 1990, I told an elementary building principal that I wanted to work with successful grade 6 and 7 Latino bilingual readers. His response was, "Do we have any of those?" The assumption appeared to be that being Latino was equivalent to failure. Such thinking has done irreparable harm to many children. What concerns me about this way of thinking is that, if Valencia (1991) is correct when he claims that Latino students have faced difficulties wherever they happen to be found within the United States, then we may be facing a massive new wave of problems. Latino immigrants are moving into places where they traditionally have not resided, such as rural Nebraska, Iowa, and downstate Illinois. Large communities of Latinos can be found in much of the Southeast: in Georgia, North Carolina and South Carolina, and Tennessee. School districts in rural areas seldom are prepared in terms of personnel and materials to support students from linguistically diverse backgrounds. My fear is that many of the ineffective practices employed in a previous era in the Southwest will once again be instituted in these new settings.

This history of neglect can and should become an object of study for Latino students and the educators who work with them. The successes of previous generations need to be celebrated and critiqued by those concerned with the present. The work of writers such as San Miguel (1987) and Donato (1997) are very useful for this purpose. Videos that detail the struggle of the Latino community, such as the *Lemon Grove Incident* and the *Taking Back the Schools* from the *Chicano!* series, dramatize and flesh out the lives of some of the focal participants.

A Loss of Control Over Curriculum and Instruction Decisions

One of the more troubling changes in education in recent times has been the loss of control that educators have experienced with respect to their profession. Moll (1998), a noted researcher and writer at the University of Arizona, has pointed out that political changes can pull the rug out from under decades of work and effort, most notably in the field of bilingual education. Proposition 227 in California and Proposition 203 in Arizona, both of which sought to eliminate bilingual education programs, are examples of what can happen. These simpleminded, politically expedient solutions have been enacted without any real concern for the students affected. These are solutions that appeal to particular segments of the voting population (older, white, male, middle to upper class). In addition, literacy curricula have been mandated in some places because of a few highly influential special interest groups and individuals. These programs leave little room for professional judgment or discretion. We are moving toward the kinds of curriculum and instruction found in countries where everyone does the same thing at the same time. These programs de-skill and demoralize teachers. They serve to deprofessionalize the field of teaching at a time when retention is absolutely critical and dropout rates are approaching crisis proportions. As a result of these programs, students learn to be good low-level workers, not critical thinkers. The emphasis is on proper behavior, reductionistic displays of small bits and pieces of literacy, and carefully constrained patterns of speaking and writing. These outcomes correspond to what business wants from low-paid workers: proper deference to authority, acceptance of dull and repetitive work routines, and availability to work for low wages. Our lack of control over the public agenda is nowhere more evident than in the fact that in good times, money is provided to education sparingly and grudgingly. In bad times, like right now, funds are cut. School districts are told to do a lot more (all the new demands) with a lot less. Politicians and other non-educators determine the agenda, and teachers and other educators are ordered to carry them out.

Again, information concerning control over the field of education is produced daily and appears on the Internet, in newspapers, and in special documentaries devoted to this topic. Here the relationship of the economy is easily discerned and one can trace how funding decisions are made concerning schools and other educational institutions. Educators especially need a deeper understanding of how these decisions affect their professional lives, the opportunities available to their students, and how these in turn are influenced by other important factors such as health care and jobs.

A Presumption That We Know How to Effectively Serve Culturally and Linguistically Diverse Students

Critics on both the right and the left often assume that effective literacy programs and instruction are simply a matter of implementing well-documented practices. I would caution that, although a great deal could be done using what we currently know, a great deal more still needs to be learned. Perhaps the most convincing argument against lapsing into complacency is the fact that the world is changing at an incredible pace. Lo Bianco (2000) points out that the deregulation of the world's economic markets, instantaneous communication, and the unification of monetary systems have created a qualitatively different world from the one for which schools prepared most of us. There is no reason to believe that future changes will be any less dramatic than those already observed. Finding solutions to the literacy learning problems of students from marginalized communities will demand the best thinking we can muster, the use of the most sophisticated theories, the collection of well-defined sources of data, and rigorous analysis that does not rule anything out of bounds. This activity will be needed on an ongoing basis to keep students prepared for future changes.

Of concern, however, is that educational researchers are increasingly pressured to conduct research within a narrowing set of parameters. The research questions, methods, and forms of analysis are prescribed by government funding agencies. Such work can never hope to accomplish more than maintain the status quo. Patton (2002), a recognized methodologist, declared that dictating the methods that researchers must use is only one step removed from dictating the results. The net result of this work generates findings and conclusions that support the political and ideological interests of dominant groups. For example, the U.S. Department of Education is currently requesting research studies that require comparisons of transitional forms of bilingual education and traditional ESL programs, two programs whose goal is to place students as quickly as possible within all English instructional settings. Both of these program models have been critiqued by experts in the field of second language acquisition because they fail to provide students with the necessary cultural and linguistic capital required for academic success (Baker, 2001). Other types of programs, such as dual language immersion models (described later in this chapter), at least hold a glimmer of hope that students will have access to the curriculum of power. I would argue that we still lack deep, satisfying understanding of the populations served by schools, particularly Latino students and recent immigrants. We will not be able to find the most satisfying answers if we hobble ourselves in terms of the questions we ask and the tools we use.

Clearly, rigid prescriptions for instructional practice are not the answer. Yet it would be foolish to ignore what we already have learned. One solution to this problem is to foster greater communication between researchers and teachers. In a project I conducted several years ago (Jiménez, 1997), teachers and administrators revealed to me the need for more information concerning Latino students who were three to four years behind in their literacy development. These students consisted of two distinct groups: the first comprised recent arrivals in the United States who were behind in their Spanish literacy; the second consisted of students who had been in the U.S. educational system since kindergarten or first grade but were not making progress in English literacy commensurate with that of their peers. Both groups needed intensive small group instruction that focused on culturally relevant texts and that provided them with reading strategies grounded in their particular linguistic and cultural strengths. The point I want to make here is that without active collaboration between researchers and educators, the most pressing educational problems will not be recognized, much less addressed, by the field at large.

Research that is ecologically valid and ecological in its approach is needed. Ecologically valid research refers to work that is conducted in real classrooms with real teachers and students, not research conducted by ideologically rigid partisans of a specific approach to literacy instruction or that found in laboratories using university students as subjects. An ecological approach to literacy research refers to placing our understanding and uses of literacy into its historical, sociological, and political context (Barton & Hamilton, 2000). In other words, how do school literacy practices reflect larger societal relationships of power, and how do these practices contribute to and create those same relationships? I hope that the first half of this chapter has provided a sense of the ideas and directions that drive my thinking concerning the literacy learning of Latino students. In what follows, I attempt to demonstrate more specifically a few of the activities I would employ to attain my goals.

FUTURE DIRECTIONS

Perhaps most important for those working with Latino students is to recognize the high degree of diversity with the group. These students come from working-class and middle-class backgrounds; they arrive in U.S. schools at all ages, from preschool through high school; and they come with excellent to almost nonexistent prior schooling. The kind of instruction and program that makes sense for a student from an extremely low-income, rural background will prove completely unacceptable to a student from a middle-class, urban background.

Designing Programs That Are Sensitive to the Many Different Types of Latino Students Served by Our Schools

Good assessment is the key. It is imperative to know where the students come from, how much prior schooling they have had, what they want, and what their parents want for them in terms in schooling in the United States (Jiménez, in press). Perhaps the most damaging aspect of all programs designed for a specific type of student is that they can become academic dead ends. Some bilingual education and ESL programs have become just that (as have many other types of programs, such as special education, remedial reading, and submersion language contexts) for students who are English language learners. Although well-implemented bilingual and ESL programs facilitate the progress of many Latino students, others provide low levels of challenge and shield students from the curriculum necessary for successful placement at the next level of schooling (Valdés, 2001).

One of the assignments I give students in my Foundations of Bilingual Education class is to interview current university students who spent at least two years in bilingual education at some point in their K–12 experience. The interviews they conduct reveal that about 40% of these "successful" graduates of bilingual education are pleased with their experience; about 40% feel that it did not challenge them sufficiently in terms of content or the demands placed on them; and about 20% have somewhat conflicting views about their experience. The following comments from two students provide representative examples of the first two perspectives.

> *Vanessa:* I was placed in bilingual education when I was in the second grade and I stayed there until I was in sixth grade. I didn't speak any English before being enrolled in the program, but I understood a little bit. I think the bilingual program was very effective for me. It gave me the opportunity to learn English in a comfortable setting. I think it is really good because nowadays being a bilingual person allows for many opportunities. I think this definitely had long-term effects on me. I learned English, and I feel good because now I am in college with people who knew English as their native language while I am able to manage two languages. I do value both languages very much. Spanish was my first language, and it is essential for family communication, while English is required for school and the workplace. From my experience, I think bilingual education is very good.

Vanessa pretty much describes a positive experience. She also provides a specific frame for the amount of time she spent in bilingual education. The fact that she entered the program in second grade points to the fact that she completed at least one, maybe two, years of schooling in her home country. In addition, she highlights the fact that she has maintained her bilingualism at least partially because of her experience in a bilingual program, and she communicates the fact that Spanish is an important part of her identity. She does not include any kind of critique of her experience in bilingual education, but her comments only cover language issues: maintenance of Spanish and learning English as a second language. She does not mention content area learning at all. Still, she seems very pleased with the fact that she has maintained her Spanish while learning English well enough to succeed in a demanding university environment.

Another student, Luis, raises the issue of content area learning, and he reaches a conclusion similar to that of the Latina educator Reyes (1992) when he critiques the lack of effective instruction provided to Latino students.

> *Luis:* I feel that those placed in bilingual education are kind of held back. I think that while they're in bilingual education, their peers are surpassing them educationally, and they are being held back and not being challenged enough to explore their skills. In the end, they are not going to be at the same level as their peers, and they might not advance because of it. Think about this: What if while I am learning my *ABCs*, my counterparts are learning advanced math or science concepts? Right away because I participated in bilingual education I got screwed out of going to college.

Luis critiques the program he attended as not providing access to the kind of curriculum necessary to make progress in the school systems with which he is familiar. Although there is a bit of a contradiction here in that Luis is now a student at a prestigious university, his comments probably signal his awareness that he has had to work a lot harder to keep up with his peers from mainstream backgrounds because of deficiencies in his education. Also, he points a finger directly at a school experience that was less than demanding or challenging. Notice, too, that he says nothing concerning language learning—English or Spanish. One might infer that he was pleased—or, at least, satisfied—with this aspect of his education.

The dissatisfaction with content area learning, a charge also forcefully made by Valdés (2001) in her recent book, *Learning and Not Learning English,* is something that all teachers and educators who work with Latino students need to consider. More careful examination of the demands placed on students from linguistically and culturally diverse backgrounds is necessary. The question, "If my child were enrolled in this program, how satisfied would I be with his or her education?" should set the standard for how much to challenge and demand of students.

The university students' comments only hint at the underlying situation: that the task facing them as learners is much more difficult than that of their mainstream peers. That is, they have to learn a new language and culture, as well as master the information found in the curriculum. This fact demands quality language instruction with lots of meaningful opportunities to use and practice the language. An important component of many language learning theories is the need for interaction with native-English-speaking peers and others. Unfortunately, large numbers of Latino students attend schools in which they are the majority. In other words, they attend segregated schools, and the ability to interact with native English speakers can be quite limited.

Providing Much Better Instruction in English as a Second Language

English language instruction needs to be tied to age-appropriate content learning and a rigorous curriculum. This is something that immigrant parents want and that Latino children expect. These students come highly motivated to learn English, but they often become disillusioned. How much opportunity to learn English do English language learner students really have? One could point to the fact that there is a major difference between the kind of English necessary to succeed in everyday conversation and that needed to make progress in age-appropriate curriculum. The bilingual education theorist Cummins (2000) has focused precisely on this problem. But from recent work in this area, I think the problem may be broader than imagined. Researchers such as Valdés (2001) and Norton (2000) are providing evidence that native English speakers often refuse to engage in meaningful exchanges with English language learners. In other words, the power differences that exist between groups are exercised in a manner that disadvantages students who wish to learn English. So when educators evaluate their programs, it is not only the quality of instruction provided to Latino students that needs to be considered, but also opportunities for interaction with native English speakers. Can Latino students be blamed for struggling with English when the teacher is the only contact they have with the English-speaking world? What would careful examination of the language interactions of Latino students in your school reveal about the amount and quality of language input and opportunities for language production?

Schools and school districts have it within their power to structure more interaction between English language learners and native English speakers. Multiple schemes for cooperative learning have been demonstrated to be effective in increasing not only students' achievement but also their social interaction. Finding ways to get students to listen and talk with one another, to read one another's writing, and to write to one another are all well within the scope of what schools should be doing, regardless of the populations they serve. A few bilingual education designs, such as dual language immersion programs, provide highly structured opportunities for native English speakers to interact with English language learners. The design ideally calls for a mix of approximately 50% native English speakers and 50% English language learners (Lindholm-Leary, 2001). The underlying idea is that each group will learn the other's language. This results in instruction that is evenly split between the use of English and use of the non-English language, in this case Spanish (alternating days, weeks, or even semesters have been used). Research has shown that these programs are very effective for both Latino and mainstream students.

Taking Full Advantage of Students' Native Languages for Instructional Purposes

Finally, I would argue that in those school districts where it is still legal and feasible to do so, we should use students' native languages as much and as effectively as possible. Research with Latino students in California is showing just how excruciatingly difficult it is to use only English to teach them science, math, and other content area subjects (Gándara, 2000; Gutierrez, Baquedano-López, & Asato, 2000). This approach, which uses English only to teach all subjects, is often called a sheltered English approach. Students' native languages, however, can be used to present to them the most rigorous and challenging curriculum possible and help keep them on par with their English-speaking peers. Their native language can also be used to review and clarify what they are learning in English, and it can be used to help students actually learn English. Again, Valdés (2001) points out that every native-English-speaking student in the United States who is learning a foreign language receives a textbook with substantial written English to support his or her learning of the new language. There is no reason why students learning English should be denied similar support. Students' native language can be used to show them how to transfer what they know from their native language to English, and we can use the native language to build bridges between students' lives and the curriculum of power.

For example, research is beginning to make clear that the literacy activities in schools look, feel, and are used in qualitatively different ways from the literacy activities in students' communities, homes, and everyday lives. These differences have led some scholars to posit the existence of multiple literacies.

In my estimation, these alternative literacies hold great potential for bringing new meaning into classrooms. In one of my recent projects, preadolescent and young adolescent Latino students told me that they viewed particular forms of literacy, or non-school literacies, as highly necessary and desirable (Jiménez, 2001). Because their parents depend on them for help to negotiate the demands of English language literacy, they often serve as language brokers to translate documents such as rental and lease agreements, income tax forms, and other commercial transactions such as telephone and power bills. Many Latino students take these responsibilities seriously and view the help they provide to their parents and other family members as an important contribution to the family. In addition, parents and other adult family members may depend on their children for oral translation in stressful, high-paced interactions such as purchasing a vehicle or returning merchandise at a retail establishment. All of these activities can be viewed as alternative forms of literacy in contradistinction to school-based literacy. Gregory and Williams (2000) believe that these alternative literacies are "Treasure Troves" of experience and information, with attending benefits for both students and teachers. I propose that these practices, as they become better documented and understood by researchers, could serve as bridges for more effective literacy instruction within schools. Very recent research has demonstrated both quantitatively and qualitatively that the more students engage in language brokering activities, the higher their academic achievement. These literacies hybridize Spanish and English in ways that are new and unique both to the students' parents and to the students themselves. Finding ways to help students see the relationship between the literacy presented to them in school and the literacies they need to function as legitimate members of their communities should receive high priority in any program designed to serve Latino students.

CONCLUSION

A business-as-usual approach to literacy instruction will result in failure for Latino students. Ways of being, thinking, and doing—what Gee (1996) calls *discourses*—that create negative experiences for Latino students need to be challenged and, when possible, replaced with more hopeful and progressive perspectives. The larger political, economic, and sociological context of students' lives needs to be considered when designing instruction and programs for Latino students. This consideration should include what Barton and Hamilton (2000) call an ecological approach to literacy research, as well as instruction. Such an approach might mean interrogating tasks commonly found in U.S. classrooms, such as "put the main idea into your own words" (Orellana, Reynolds, Dorner, & Mesa, 2003). This seemingly self-evident activity is actually quite loaded with assumptions that can be tied to political, economic, and sociological factors. The idea that the student is allowed to isolate the main idea, possess it, and transform it may not be self-evident at all to members of diverse cultural backgrounds. Putting decontextualized ideas into one's "own words" may also be a novel idea to many students, one that conflicts with other ways of thinking about learning and students' responsibilities. Yet both conscious and subconscious assessments of students' thinking, learning potential, and even their overall intelligence is routinely evaluated on the basis of such interactions. An ecological approach calls for consideration of these everyday, taken-for-granted assumptions and working hypotheses about students from diverse backgrounds.

Finally, Latino students need much higher quality ESL instruction that includes frequent opportunities for interaction with native-English-speaking peers, and the language that they know best—in many cases, Spanish—needs to be employed in ways that provide them with a rigorous and challenging curriculum. The curriculum needs to be expanded beyond simply that which has been found useful with mainstream, middle-class, monocultural populations. I have argued here, perhaps counterintuitively, that doing so will provide Latino students with meaningful access to the curriculum as they become aware of how school-based literacy can enhance their mastery of other literacies necessary to their daily lives.

REFERENCES

Baker, C. (2001). *Foundations of bilingual education and bilingualism* (3rd ed.). Philadelphia: Multilingual Matters.

Barton, D., & Hamilton, M. (2000). Literacy practices. In D. Barton, M. Hamilton, & R. Ivanic (Eds.), *Situated literacies* (pp. 7–15). New York: Routledge.

Cummins, J. (2000). *Language, power, and pedagogy.* Clevedon, UK: Multilingual Matters.

Donato, R. N. (1997). *The other struggle for equal schools: Mexican Americans during the civil rights era.* Albany: State University of New York Press.

Gándara, P. (2000). In the aftermath of the storm: English learners in the Post-227 era. *Bilingual Research Journal, 24*(1–2), 1–13, http://brj.asu.edu/v2412/abstractt.html.

Gee, J. P. (1996). *Social linguistics and literacies.* Philadelphia: Routledge.

Gregory, E., & Williams, A. (2000). *City literacies: Learning to read across generations and cultures.* New York: Routledge.

Gutierrez, K., Baquedano-López, P., & Asato, J. (2000). "English for the children": The new literacy of the old world order, language policy and educational reform. *Bilingual Research Journal, 24*(1–2), 1–26, http://brj.asu.edu/v2412/abstractt.html.

Jiménez, R. T. (1997). The strategic reading abilities and potential of five low-literacy Latina/o readers in middle school. *Reading Research Quarterly, 32*(3), 224–243.

Jiménez, R. T. (2001). "It's a difference that changes us": An alternative view of the language and literacy learning needs of Latina/o students. *The Reading Teacher, 54*(8), 736–742.

Jiménez, R. T. (In press). More equitable assessments for Latino students. *The Reading Teacher.*

Lindholm-Leary, K. (2001). *Dual language education.* Buffalo, NY: Multilingual Matters.

Lo Bianco, J. (2000). Multiliteracies and multilingualism. In B. Cope & M. Kalantzis (Eds.), *Multiliteracies: Literacy learning and the design of social futures* (pp. 92–105). London: Routledge.

Luke, A. (2003). Literacy and the other: A sociological approach to literacy research and policy in multilingual societies. *Reading Research Quarterly, 38*(1), 132–141.

Macedo, D. (2000). The colonialism of the English only movement. *Educational Researcher, 29*(3), 15–24.

Moll, L. C. (1998). Turning to the world: Bilingual schooling, literacy, and the cultural mediation of thinking. In T. Shanahan & F. Rodriguez-Brown (Eds.), *47th Yearbook of the National Reading Conference* (pp. 59–75). Chicago: National Reading Conference.

Nieto, S. (2000). Puerto Rican students in U.S. schools: A brief history. In S. Nieto (Ed.), *Puerto Rican students in U.S. schools* (pp. 5–37). White Plains, NY: Erlbaum.

Norton, B. (2000). *Identity and language learning: Gender, ethnicity and educational change.* New York: Longman.

Orellana, M. F., Reynolds, J., Dorner, L., & Mesa, M. A. (2003). In other words: Translating or "para-phrasing" as a family literacy practice in immigrant households. *Reading Research Quarterly, 38*(1), 12–34.

Padilla, F. M. (1985). *Latino ethnic consciousness: The case of Mexican Americans and Puerto Ricans in Chicago.* Notre Dame, IN: Notre Dame University Press.

Patton, M. Q. (2002). *Qualitative evaluation and research methods* (3rd ed.). Thousand Oaks, CA: Sage.

Reyes, M. L. (1992). Challenging venerable assumptions: Literacy instruction for linguistically different students. *Harvard Educational Review, 62*(4), 427–446.

San Miguel, G. (1987). *"Let all of them take heed": Mexican Americans and the campaign for educational equality in Texas, 1910–1981.* Austin: University of Texas Press.

Sánchez, G. I. (1940). *Forgotten people: A study of New Mexicans.* Albuquerque: University of New Mexico Press.

Valdés, G. (2001). *Learning and not learning English.* New York: Teachers College Press.

Valencia, R. R. (1991). *Chicano school failure and success: Research and policy agendas for the 1990s.* New York: Falmer Press.

2

Coming of Age in Working-Poor America

Lessons from Ethnography and Teaching

Deborah Hicks

Key Points

- A broader vision of literacy takes into account how language and cultural identity shape students' reading and writing of texts.

- Cultural practices of high-poverty students can be brought into productive dialogue with those more typical of middle-class schools.

- Adopting a wider vision of literacy includes taking seriously the material and psychological effects of poverty on students' lives and voices.

F our decades ago, a massive population shift occurred as rural families from the Southern states and Appalachia headed north in search of employment and a better future for their children. These rural migrants settled in cities in the Midwest and Northeast, seeking and often finding employment in the burgeoning manufacturing industry of the postwar era. The history of Lower Bond Hill, a working-poor community nestled in a midsize Midwestern city, begins with this migration north—one fueled by risk, gritty work, and hope.[1]

LOWER BOND HILL

With the shift from a manufacturing base to an information- and technology-based global economy, Lower Bond Hill, like many working-class communities, has suffered economic decline.[2] Currently, 56% of families live below the poverty line, marking Lower Bond Hill as an enclave of what urban sociologists call concentrated or ghetto poverty. Young people growing up in Lower Bond Hill today face challenges unlike those faced by earlier generations: a labor market that is unforgiving to high school dropouts or even those with a GED, a growing problem with street drugs such as OxyContin and heroin, and the health threat of HIV and hepatitis C—one Achilles' heel of drug-related needle use.

To one side of the crossroads marking the neighborhood's center are visible the images of everyday life in Lower Bond Hill. There, amid tightly packed brick townhouses, typically broken up into multiple-family apartment units, young people experience the close-knit family life that remains a source of strength for them and their community. The children who live in the center of Lower Bond Hill can walk to their K–8 school, a 1930s school building that some of their parents attended. Others are bused a short distance, often from a stretch of road leading out of the neighborhood and past its largely deserted warehouses and factories. Along this stretch of highway can be found clusters of African American families and a small but growing enclave of Guatemalan and Mexican families. But Lower Bond Hill is distinctive among urban working-poor neighborhoods for its predominant whiteness—an enclave of what hooks (2000) has called the hidden face of poverty. Many residents trace their histories and cultural identities to Appalachia. Youth live out these identities through summer trips to see rural kin, through religion and shared cultural values, and through language—in which traces of rhythm, intonation, grammar, and discourse reveal the once rural histories of these contemporary urban youth.

Historically, rates of high school dropout have been exceedingly high among the youth of Lower Bond Hill, with conservative estimates starting at 57% and more realistic estimates reaching 70%. These high rates of dropout have been tied to low rates of functional literacy among adults and low passage rates among younger students on high-stakes reading and writing proficiency tests. In the first year that I began this research project, for instance, only 6.5% of second-grade students passed the "off-grade" proficiency test in reading. I entered the second-grade classroom of a welcoming teacher at Linden Elementary School, aiming to understand *why* students in this particular school and community were struggling with reading and how responsive pedagogies might change things for the better.

As the project evolved over the next three years, my focus shifted to the educational experiences of girls growing up in Lower Bond Hill. Beginning in the second summer, I designed and have been lead teacher for a summer and after-school literacy project for girls, continuing in my role as ethnographer and sometimes co-teacher in these students' regular fourth- and then fifth-grade language arts classroom. Thus, my discussion of key issues facing literacy educators working with high-poverty students draws on sustained pedagogical and ethnographic work with preadolescent girls. Although the particulars of the examples used might differ in the case of boys, I focus on broad issues that would pertain to the literacy education of high-poverty boys and girls.

The framing of this discussion of literacy in a particular landscape of working-poor America is deliberate, tied to a certain argument about how concerned educational scholars and practitioners might think and act for social change. The thinking of policymakers and some academics has removed the specifics of poverty from decision making. Reductive theories and solutions have been framed around a single dimension of literacy education, what Green (2002) terms *operational* or functional literacy—and a narrow vision of how language functions in literate contexts. It is as though, to quote Coles's prophetic writing from an earlier era, we have embraced "icy reasoning" (Coles, 1961, p. 110)—a detached kind of theory, research, and policymaking that renders complex problems into isolated variables that suit the market-driven norms of a fast capitalist economy. I want to argue for a broader vision of literacy research and practice, one that extends across disciplines and takes seriously the multilayered ways in which poverty shapes thought, feeling, imagination, and material possibility among the vulnerable young people growing up in working-poor America.

KEY ISSUES

In a summer school reading program held in the weeks following the end of fourth grade, Alison (Ali) is reading a horror paperback, *The Haunting* (Philbrick & Harnett, 1995b), Book I in a series that has become one of the hottest reads of the summer. Asked to read aloud a few pages in the text, Ali pauses when she comes to the word *paranoid*. The word appears in the context of some ghoulish events. Twelve-year-old Jason, the book's main protagonist, keeps having freakish experiences: for example, scalding hot water shoots out of the pipes in the bathroom where the door handle has also suddenly and mysteriously fallen off, trapping him inside. After his escape from this ordeal in the summer rental house where he and his family are staying, Jason reflects: "A guy could get paranoid around here, that was for sure!" (Philbrick & Harnett, 1995b, p. 50).

After asking about the meaning of the unknown word, Ali offers her elaboration of what *paranoid* means. One of her aunts, who was pregnant, kept seeing a bird at the window. The bird hovered at the window for about a week until the aunt's baby was born—dead. Ali's mother had explained the meaning of these strange events. When a bird flies through the window, it means someone is going to die. Ali expressed her fear that something bad might happen to her or to her grandparents, with whom she was living. A bird had been hovering at the window of the bedroom Ali shared with her younger brother. Ali used these stories tinged with the supernatural to explain her understanding of the word *paranoid,* which to her meant being nervous that something bad could happen.

Language

Mikhail Bakhtin, a philosopher of language and literacy from the former Soviet lands, argued that language is intonated, drenched, with the concrete histories of its usage by others whom we encounter in the social settings that shape our encounters with language. As he once wrote, "[T]he word does not exist in a neutral and impersonal language (it is not, after all, out of a dictionary that the speaker gets his words!), but rather it exists in other people's mouths, in other people's contexts, serving other people's intentions: it is from there that one must take the word and make it one's own" (Bakhtin, 1981, p. 294).

For Ali—as for all readers—phrases and texts (including books, films, digital texts, and media) take on meanings that come wrapped in the histories and values of the cultural contexts in which reading occurs. New and hybrid meanings are created as the speaking voices constituting a reader's history in specific social and cultural landscapes are brought to bear on her reading of books, films, and media texts. There is no such thing as neutral meaning making.

As teachers of reading, we easily fall into the trap of perceiving meaning to be transparent, for to us—as experienced readers whose language and lives are embedded in middle-class values—texts simply have obvious meanings. For many students growing up in high-poverty communities, reading is more complicated. The seeming transparency of texts occurs in part because literature can reflect cultural and linguistic expectations about how language operates in particular domains of discourse. Take, for instance, the following excerpt from Book III, *The Final Nightmare,* of the same paperback series (Philbrick & Harnett, 1995a, p. 15), in which the hapless Jason encounters a ghost in the attic.

> I was about to yell for my dad. Then I heard something move behind me. A rustling, sneaky sound in the shadows.
> The back of my neck tingled.
> I was slowly turning around to look when a horrible voice spoke right by my ear. A creaky, raspy voice of the undead.
> *"You!"* it shrieked. *"It's all your fault! I'll get you! I'll get you for good!"*

For the preadolescent readers in the summer school project, this kind of text was engaging on a number of levels but partly because, to them, its meaning seemed transparent. The preteen readers in this program were familiar with popular culture horror genres, having encountered them in inexpensive paperbacks purchased at the local supermarket and in made-for-television horror films, such as Stephen King's *Rose Red*. Thus, the recurrent language patterns and particular forms of narration in horror genres made this kind of reading experience familiar, fast, and interesting for the girls. It was different from the "highbrow" literature I preferred—and that they proclaimed *boring*—in which a distinctive set of literary and linguistic techniques is used to convey things like changes in characters' internal states. Who among the girls in my project, surrounded as they were with the boisterous oral traditions of Lower Bond Hill, would find the following kind of language familiar and transparent?

> Ellie's mother had always been quiet. She was a nervous woman with a nervous laugh, and though she had been welcoming with her warm arms when the girls were all small, she had withdrawn those arms more and more as the girls grew. Now Ellie couldn't remember the last time she had been hugged by her mother. And she saw, when she looked at her, a woman with a thin, set mouth and a wall around her. (Rylant, 2001, p. 15)

Even the language of reading pedagogy can seem distancing or *boring*— the latter perhaps a code word among these preadolescent readers for language practices that are unfamiliar and not engaging. In a mocking imitation of a middle-class reading practice, Elizabeth, in the spring of fourth grade, commented that all the middle-class teachers do is "talking, talking, talking." Talking about a book after one has read it is a language practice, a discourse, that is drenched in the meanings, histories, and values connected with middle-class speaking voices.

Cultural Identity

Listen to the voice of a fifth-grade girl, Brandy, who has composed a poem modeled after the poet George Ella Lyon's (1999) "Where I'm From":

> I am from the heroes who died on September 11th.
> I am from New York where the towers fell.
>
> I am from a ghetto neighborhood where people fight in the streets.
> I am from the other end of Main Street where people are always arguing
>   in the streets.
>
> I am from the past who died.
> I am from my Grandpa who died in WWII.
> Underneath my bed is a box full of pictures falling out like old memories,
>   Just coming back to me. . . .
>
> I am from God who made me.
> I am from Jesus who died on the cross for us. . . .
>
> I am from the red, white, and blue, which are the colors of my country.
> I am from the heroes who saved our country and sometimes even died. . . .
>
> I am from my Mom who had me.
> I am from my Grandma who took care of me.

The "I am from" poetic structure based on Lyon's model provides a writing frame (see Wray & Lewis, 1997) that eases the demands of writing poetry, an unfamiliar literary genre for many students in Brandy's fifth-grade classroom. At the same time, it provides a pedagogical opportunity for something that does not always occur for Brandy and her classmates: the strong expression of community values and beliefs within a school-based literacy practice. We hear in Brandy's poem patriotism, a belief in one's country and its heroes, and Christian faith that is a source of both strength and sometimes fundamentalism. We hear the centrality of *family* and the changes in family life and structure that have touched the lives of many youth in Lower Bond Hill. Brandy is being raised by her grandmother as her mother struggles with problems of drug addiction.

Heath (1983) has argued that the focus of ethnographic, linguistic, and pedagogical research should be on the local, place-specific ways in which relations such as class, race, ethnicity, and gender are lived in communities. Each working-poor community in America is connected to wider issues of social, racial, and economic inequality; yet each presents its own landscape in which particular social practices, images, sounds, and language shape the lives and voices of young people. Walking into Lower Bond Hill's local coffee shop, one is struck by familiar images that signal a certain class identity: folks having a smoke, heavyset women sipping Cokes, the strained look on the faces of locals who work swing and graveyard shifts or who do not work at all. From the jukebox emerge the distinctive rhythms of bluegrass music, reminding the ethnographer (or teacher) that this is a working-poor community with a unique cultural and regional identity—an identity of place.

In an ideal pedagogical world, these locally meaningful cultural practices and values would be brought into productive dialogue with those more typical of middle-class schools. This is what the literacy researcher Dyson (1993) refers to as a *permeable curriculum,* in which the language(s), identities, and cultural practices of both teacher and students can inform the shape of classroom literacies. Brandy's "Where I'm From" poem would be an example of this kind of curriculum. In some instances, these dialogic encounters can seem harmonious; they lead to deeper cultural understanding for teachers and a stronger sense of agency for students.

At other times, the tension points between distinctive cultural and class identities become visible in the language arts classroom. In the words of the cultural studies scholar Hall (1980), students produce *negotiated readings* of the texts and textual practices that we hold out to them. Negotiated readings are "shot through with contradictions" (Hall, 1980, p. 137), as they reflect the conflicts that are inherent in living and reading across worlds of cultural and class difference. Nicole's reading of the 1970s film *A Little Romance* (Hill, 1979) has produced one such moment in which a raw, working-class language for sexuality shapes a text that in some pedagogical contexts would be viewed as transgressive. Nicole composed this response to the film in the context of the after-school literacy project that I direct.

> I think that girls should be romantic. If not, they should act like they do at least have a little romance in their life. Well, girls should like boys. Well that would be okay if they don't like boys. If they just like girls that means they are kind of gay. I wouldn't care if my friends were gay. All I care is that they are nice and kind to me. Like I was getting ready to say, girls could be sluts or hoes. Or they could be bitches or [do] tricks. They could do what they want to do. Like I said, "bitches and sluts should have the same respect as other girls do!" Some people say that you shouldn't judge somebody by the way they look. All that matters is that they have respect for you and others. Some whores and sluts have respect for people. But some don't. Some sluts and whores are disrespectful for their elders.

This piece of writing rings with the power of neighborhood *words* for female sexual identity: slut, hoe, bitch, doing tricks. These would, for Freire

(1970/1999), be potential generative words—words connected to local cultural practices and broader systems of oppression. However, these deeply felt words for female sexual identity would not be welcome in many English and language arts classrooms. This raises critical questions about the writing workshop metaphor of nurturing the development of "authentic voice." For students such as Nicole, "voice" can entail contradiction and tension as they try to figure out how to read, write, and speak in a setting that is, for them, fraught with risk.

Fragmentation, Resistance, and Agency

It is all too easy to forget how fragmenting the experience of growing up in poverty can be for young people. Listen to a narrative essay written by Brandy, the fifth grader whose "Where I'm From" poem conveyed the values of her family and community in a positive light. In a piece aptly titled, "My Life as a Girl," we see the pain and confusion associated with growing up on a street where some people (including Brandy herself) fight and where others do freakish things.

> My life as a girl is in [name of city]. My neighborhood is dirty, crazy, and weird. It is dirty because people throw trash on the ground. It's crazy because people talk to the billboards. And it's weird because people give you weird looks or act weird. There is fighting, arguing, and trying to kill people and other things happening.
>
> I'm always getting in arguments with other people. When I argue I feel like going over there and hitting them, but I don't. I let them hit me first. The other day I got in an argument with a girl. She called me a white girl so I went over there and told her I was proud to be a white girl. I always let them hit me first, then I have the right to hit them back.
>
> My life sucks because I always get grounded for coming in late. My life is also kind of cool because I get to stay out in the summer time. We get to eat out instead of my Mom cooking. My life is not all that great, but it's in between. But I love my life!

In a disturbing epitaph to this reflective narrative, Brandy commented in the summer following fifth grade that she lives in hell. It would be easy to understand how she could evoke this strong metaphor. Four generations of family members live in the run-down, wood-frame house where Brandy lives on the road leading out of Lower Bond Hill. Racial tensions run high in this part of Lower Bond Hill, with poor White, African American, and Latino residents sometimes becoming hostile protagonists in a shared economic story of marginalization. Brandy is all too aware of the fundamental poverty that is thwarting her life opportunities. Just outside her home is a huge yellow billboard that beckons those ready to sell: "We Buy Ugly Houses." A stench can fill the air on humid days because of environmental pollution. A former creek, now a ravine, is a dumping ground for sewage. A company that burns off and spits into the air industrial waste—some of it toxic—from barrels, a notorious violator of environmental health standards, is minutes from Brandy's home. All around Brandy—inside the crowded spaces of her home, outside where trash and toxins confront the body, on the street where fighting occurs—are the sights, sounds, smells, and raw emotions that go with living in urban poverty.

It is interesting, then, that Brandy concludes her narrative with the hopeful statement: "But I love my life!" Students like Brandy can sometimes live out a psychological life that entails what the critical psychologist Walkerdine (1990) describes as splitting. One the one hand, she can (and does) express anger about the fact that she is poor and that the world around her is dirty, confusing, and frightening. For Brandy, a Stephen King fan and an avid writer of horror fiction herself, it is indeed the landscapes of Lower Bond Hill that are haunted. On the other hand, Brandy shows a deep attachment to her family and neighborhood identity. What transpires in the English and language arts classroom is something that one might not expect from a student who would be viewed in most contexts as academically gifted. One of the strongest readers and writers in the fifth grade at her school, Brandy invokes the powerful tool that has saturated the pages of writing about education among working-class students: *resistance*. She stays home from school whenever she can (invoking any possible excuse to spend the day in bed, reading) and spends a fair amount of time during reading workshops in a disengaged sulk.

Over the months and years that I have engaged in teaching and ethnography in Lower Bond Hill, I have come to view resistance as an important part of *agency*—something that I view as a central goal for literacy pedagogy. It is easy for students living out their lives in economically and socially marginalized neighborhoods to lose a sense of control and voice within the literacy practices articulated by teachers. They seek power where they can get it—for example, the working-class lads in Willis's (1977) study of adolescent boys in England who tear their teachers apart ideologically; the working-class girls in McRobbie's (1991/2000) youth culture studies who embrace a culture of romance in defiance of academic identities; the youth offenders in Finders's (1998) ethnography who invoke subversive female sexual identity in an English classroom. For things to change, students need to engage in practices in which the endpoint is not just new skills but new forms of consciousness. The summer and after-school literacy project, for example, created a "safe space" where Brandy could bring her complex, disturbing, and textually rich life into her neighborhood school. There, she helped produce a magazine (*A Girl's Word*) and associated website. For our next publishing project, Brandy has announced that she wants to write a book.

Language, cultural identity, psychological fragmentation, resistance—these are complex issues that affect successful literacy education for high-poverty students. The complexity of these issues does not lend itself to reductive analyses or solutions. Rather, what is called for is something more like the flexible ruler in Aristotle's vision of ethics in the social realm. To remove poverty, language, and culture from pedagogical decision making and policy is to turn our gaze away from the very realities that are shaping the futures of youth in working-poor America. Instead, we need pedagogical frameworks that take seriously these realities as they look forward to helping high-poverty youth participate in a world that is increasingly different from the postwar society in which neighborhoods such as Lower Bond Hill were beacons of hope for the rural working-poor.

CONCLUSION: RECOMMENDATIONS FOR POLICY AND PRACTICE

Young people coming of age in Lower Bond Hill today have one foot in the neighborhood's cultural and labor history and one foot in a present and future that could alter the shape of their lives. The girls in my project name Lizzie McGuire, the popular culture film and television screen heroine, as the character with whom they strongly identify. They sing along to music in the rap, pop, and country rock traditions. These fifth graders seek out practices that place them amid a wider media and technological culture, even as they hold on to local, neighborhood values such as the centrality of family and Christian religious belief. At the same time, girls such as Alison, Brandy, Nicole, and Elizabeth live in economic isolation, victims of a widening disparity in America between rich and poor. Changing workforce practices have meant that the professional classes hardly ever come into contact with these girls' lives; in a complementary way, the girls seldom spend extended periods of time in middle-class settings. If there is an increasing geographic isolation of poverty, there is also a symbolic isolation that is in tension with the desires of young people to participate in a changing society.

The relevant policy solutions that have received the most attention in the media hinge on education and job training. Liberal and conservative analysts alike have latched on to the solution that seems the most direct: Give young people the basic skills they need to participate in the new economy.

Thus, inside the English and language arts classroom there has been a resurgent interest in teaching basic reading and writing skills, with the addition of training in technology. Students in Brandy's fifth-grade language arts classroom, for instance, participated in a weekly computer class as they also spent the better part of the school year preparing for the performance assessment widely touted as the measure of literacy skills: proficiency (fourth grade) and off-grade (fifth grade) proficiency tests. In fifth grade, Brandy and her classmates spent two months (January and February) in what was billed as "proficiency boot camp," becoming familiar with the particular kinds of literacy that define the tests and influence policy and funding decisions.

This historical shift to a focus on the achievement of skills that can be measured—cast as part of the "symbolic capital" (Bourdieu & Passeron, 1977/2000) of individuals, schools, and districts—is linked to the heightened status of what the Australian literacy scholar Green (2002) terms *operational* discourses about literacy. The thrust of these pedagogical discourses in the

United States has been the renewed vigor of debates about explicit instruction in reading and writing skills: phonics for the young ones; spelling and grammar for the upper elementary and middle grades students. Progressive educational methods have become the favorite whipping boy of what some social analysts call the New Right.

Historical analyses tell a different story from the one that might be culled from this hopeful projection of high-poverty students entering the workforce ready for the new economy. Close ethnographic analyses of what actually happens inside school buildings have revealed an educational system that is deeply divided by social class. Anyon's (1980) research from the late 1970s is particularly relevant. Through studies that unpacked the day-to-day experiences of fifth graders in four class-specific educational settings, ranging from working class to elite, Anyon reached a conclusion that strongly reflects the realities of social class and pedagogy: Working-class students are educated for working-class jobs. Anyon's study revealed that students in upper-middle-class and elite schools engaged in research projects and critical discussions of ancient Greece while students in working-class schools were taught procedures for completing a worksheet. High-poverty and working-class students have always received education focused on basic skills—training and not *pedagogy* in a deeper sense. In urban neighborhoods such as Lower Bond Hill, little has changed since Anyon conducted her research.

A more effective set of recommendations for policy and practice might come from further reflection on the key issues discussed earlier in this chapter. Recall for a moment how poverty shapes the thoughts, feelings, and imaginations of children such as Brandy, leading to resistance rather than to the deep engagement with literature and the critical analysis of which she and students like her are capable. The problem with the normative emphasis on the functional aspects of literacy, connected as this is in American school systems to a back-to-basics ideology of schooling, is that it is not sufficiently rich as a *theory* of literacy education to offer responsive, transformative directions for *practice*. Rather than Aristotle's flexible ruler, we have a straight-edged tool that can successfully measure certain things but that is less appropriate when applied to the complex web of language, geography, (popular) culture, history, and economic inequity that shapes the voices and lives of young people.

A broader vision can come in part from adapting the model developed by Green (2002), who in his work drew on a growing body of theorizing, research, and practice that some have termed *new literacy studies* (see Collins, 2000). "[T]he most worthwhile, robust understanding of literacy," argues Green, "is one that brings together the 'operational,' 'cultural,' and 'critical' dimensions of literate practice and learning" (Green, 2002, p. 27). Green draws on a tradition of literacy education in Australia in which *operational* perspectives on literacy include a focus on how language functions not only at the word or sentence level but also at the level of discourse. Recall, for instance, the particular *kind* of literary narrative that the girls in my summer and after-school project resisted reading, one that draws on language conventions found in "highbrow" literature—that is, slow, internally focused change versus fast-paced drama. Genre-based pedagogies (see Cope & Kalantzis, 1993) were developed in Australia to address disparities in the experiences of diverse kinds of learners with these more formal or *secondary* (Gee, 1996) literate practices.

If there is a starting point for designing more equitable forms of literate practice, it is, Green argues, with the *cultural* dimension. The unique social and cultural landscapes of Lower Bond Hill shape a certain difference among young learners who do not always share the language and values of middle-class America. Those same differences, however, could be viewed as cultural resources in a literacy curriculum that is inclusive, not restrictive. Such a change would require literacy teachers to assume something of the stance and the techniques of ethnographers—a willingness to learn about the local forms of language and practice that are such formative aspects of students' group identities and individual biographies. Rather than aim toward a single literacy pedagogy, often the approach taken by schools and school districts, the focus should be on designing pedagogies that are, to appropriate a word from Bakhtin's (1990) writings, *answerable* to the particular. As the cultural studies scholar Lusted argues, "What is required . . . is attention to open-ended and specific pedagogies, sensitive to context and difference, addressed to the social position of any learning group and the position of the individuals within it" (Lusted, 1986, p. 10).

In the same essay, Lusted argues for a view of pedagogy focused on the changes in consciousness that must occur if pedagogy is to be engaging and critical rather than simply instrumental. Reading Lusted's description of pedagogy, we can think back to the moments in our own lives when learning occurred—a shift not just in what we *know* but who we can *be*: "Knowledge is produced . . . in the *consciousness*, through the process of thought, discussion, writing, debate, exchange; in the social and internal, collective and isolated struggle for control of understanding; from engagement in the unfamiliar idea, the difficult formulation pressed at the limit of comprehension or energy; in the meeting of the deeply held with the casually dismissed; in the dramatic moment of realisation that a scarcely regarded concern, an unarticulated desire for the barely assimilated, can come alive, make for a new sense of self, change commitments and activity" (Lusted, 1986, p. 4). Designing literacy pedagogies that would move in such critical directions would require a discerning, imaginative engagement with the community and popular culture influences on students' lives and identities, along with a deepened understanding of *language*. In my project, for instance, one could imagine moving from Nicole's honest portrayal of female sexual identity using the language of Lower Bond Hill to a wider discussion of agency and economic opportunity for girls and women.

The social and economic forces that once led to the formation of urban working-poor neighborhoods such as Lower Bond Hill have once again shifted, creating a new generation of vulnerable youth. Without activist educational interventions that are sensitive to context and particularity, these youths are likely to remain outside the new economic order. Projecting ahead to her life as a young adult, Alison says that she wants to have babies and to quit studying after high school. Brandy notes that she wants to be a hair stylist and maybe get a GED. In the meantime, the adult women in their lives—mothers, grandmothers, aunts, sisters—make do on the barest of incomes garnered through service jobs, Supplemental Security Income, and the unregulated economy. For these students, engaging productively in institutional and economic worlds beyond Lower Bond Hill will indeed require new forms of consciousness. Taking on the "speaking voices" that come with new forms of language and literate practice is no easy feat, but it is one worth the struggle. As a teacher and ethnographer, I have seen high-poverty girls struggle and resist and then, in the end, engage in challenging and critical ways with literature, writing, and technology.

The wider vision for which I argue would entail taking seriously the material and psychological effects of poverty on students' lives and voices—the longing of preteen girls to read horror paperbacks, for instance, when outside the school's walls they must confront the anguished faces of addicts. Perhaps what is needed, as Harrington (1962/1993) argued in *The Other America,* is an approach that does not forsake the ability of literature, history, or ethnography to reveal the complex truths of how poverty shapes thought, feeling, imagination, and material possibility. "The poor can be described statistically," he wrote. "[T]hey can be analyzed as a group. But they need a novelist as well as a sociologist if we are to see them" (Harrington, 1962/1993, p. 17). If only some aspects of Harrington's utopian socialist thought of the 1960s could be brought to bear on the creation of new literacies for new economic times—times, however, in which social inequalities still haunt the lives of young people.

NOTES

1. The research and pedagogical project described in this chapter was made possible by an AERA/OERI research grant and funding from the Martha Holden Jennings Foundation, the Sociological Initiatives Foundation, and the University of Cincinnati Friends of Women's Studies. I gratefully acknowledge this funding support, as I also assume full responsibility for the project and any intellectual ideas resulting from it.
2. All place and personal names used in this chapter are pseudonyms.

SUGGESTIONS FOR FURTHER READING

Hicks, D. (2002). *Reading lives: Working-class children and literacy learning.* New York: Teachers College Press.

Rose, M. (1989). *Lives on the boundary.* New York: Penguin Books.

REFERENCES

Anyon, J. (1980). Social class and the hidden curriculum of work. *Journal of Education, 162*(2), 67–92.

Bakhtin, M. M. (1981). Discourse in the novel. In M. Holquist (Ed.), C. Emerson & M. Holquist (Trans.), *The dialogic imagination: Four essays by M. M. Bakhtin* (pp. 259–422). Austin: University of Texas Press.

Bakhtin, M. M. (1990). *Art and answerability: Early philosophical essays by M. M. Bakhtin.* M. Holquist & V. Liapunov (Eds.), V. Liapunov (Trans.). Austin: University of Texas Press.

Bourdieu, P., & Passeron, J. C. (1977/2000). *Reproduction in education, society, and culture* (2nd ed.). Thousand Oaks, CA: Sage.

Coles, R. (1961, July). A young psychiatrist looks at his profession. *The Atlantic,* 108–111.

Collins, J. (2000). Bernstein, Bourdieu, and the new literacy studies. *Linguistics and Education, 11*(1), 65–78.

Cope, B., & Kalantzis, M. (1993). *The powers of literacy: A genre approach to teaching writing.* Pittsburgh: University of Pittsburgh Press.

Dyson, A. H. (1993). *Social worlds of children learning to write in an urban primary school.* New York: Teachers College Press.

Finders, M. (1998, October). *You just gotta be bad: Literacy, schooling, and female youth offenders.* Featured address at the Watson Conference, Louisville, KY.

Freire, P. (1970/1999). *Pedagogy of the oppressed* (20th anniversary ed.). New York: Continuum.

Gee, J. P. (1996). *Social linguistics and literacies: Ideology in discourses* (2nd ed.). Bristol, PA: Falmer Press.

Green, B. (2002, July). A literacy project of our own? *English in Australia, 134,* 25–32.

Hall, S. (1980). Encoding/decoding. In S. Hall, D. Hobson, A. Lowe, & P. Willis (Eds.), *Culture, media, language* (pp. 129–138). Birmingham, UK: Centre for Contemporary Cultural Studies.

Harrington, M. (1962/1993). *The other America: Poverty in the United States.* New York: Simon & Schuster.

Heath, S. B. (1983). *Ways with words: Language, life, and work in communities and classrooms.* New York: Cambridge University Press.

Hill, G. R. (Director). (1979). *A little romance* [Motion picture]. United States: Orion Pictures.

hooks, b. (2000). *Where we stand: Class matters.* New York: Routledge.

Lusted, D. (1986). Why pedagogy? *Screen, 27*(3), 2–14.

Lyon, G. E. (1999). *Where I'm from.* Spring, TX: Absey.

McRobbie, A. (1991/2000). *Feminism and youth culture* (2nd ed.). New York: Routledge.

Philbrick, R. & Harnett, L. (1995a). *The final nightmare.* New York: Scholastic.

Philbrick, R. & Harnett, L. (1995b). *The haunting.* New York: Scholastic.

Rylant, C. (2001). *A blue-eyed daisy.* New York: Aladdin Paperbacks.

Walkerdine, V. (1990). *Schoolgirl fictions.* London: Verso.

Willis, P. (1977). *Learning to labor: How working class kids get working class jobs.* New York: Columbia University Press.

Wray, D., & Lewis, M. (1997). *Extending literacy: Children reading and writing non-fiction.* New York: Routledge.

3

Improving Reading Achievement in Secondary Schools

Structures and Reforms

Timothy Shanahan

Key Points

- The training of principals and other school leaders plays an important part in developing sound literacy leadership.
- Reading achievement can be improved by increasing reading and writing instruction in content area classes, using content area texts.
- Disciplinary-specific professional development of teachers is more effective than generalized training.

Let's face it: Higher reading achievement is not the academic point of high school. High schools—and by extension, middle schools and junior highs—are animated by the somewhat conflicting disciplinary demands of English, mathematics, science, and social studies and the relentless attractions of teen culture. Secondary schools strive to communicate a fundamental body of knowledge and the specialized content of a diverse assortment of electives to teens who are usually more interested in raging hormones and hip-hop than in academic success. In prestigious schools, teachers and principals labor to compel students to the heights of the SATs, ACTs, and advanced placement exams. In less advantaged schools, the goals are less lofty, if not more formidable: to keep kids in school long enough to earn a diploma. In the top schools, bragger's rights go to those with the richest buffet of extracurricular activities—from debate to water polo and from sculpture to aviation. In the struggling schools, pride often resides in a good season for the basketball team. And for all of this, reading achievement is rarely the point.

If you are reading these words, I assume that, for you, high school reading achievement is of some interest. Maybe you are a teacher who toils in the arid fields of high school reading duty—endless special classes for the kids no one else wants to teach. You may be a social studies teacher who has recognized the difficulty of successfully teaching a group of teens who cannot, or will not, read the history book. You may be a counselor who has heard from college admissions officers and local employers about how essential reading skills are to student placement. Or you could be a teacher who understands that developing the specialized knowledge of science—or literature, history, or mathematics—depends on the accomplishment of a high level of literacy. Maybe you are a principal or department head who wants better test scores, and you've figured out the value of improved reading to that goal.

Whatever the reason, how can we arouse secondary schools from their studied neglect of reading? More to the point, what can we do to move high schools and middle schools to higher reading achievement—an aspiration so formidable that American schools have not accomplished it in more than three decades (Grigg, Daane, Jin, & Campbell, 2003)?

This chapter will explore what can be done to improve reading achievement for older students. The advice is based on research on school achievement as well as on my personal experiences as director of reading for the Chicago Public Schools, a job that made me responsible for the literacy development of approximately 80,000 secondary students.

MISGUIDED REFORMS

Before turning to the solutions that work, let's consider some that have not—popular avenues that have done more to distract and deflect than to improve.

1. *Let's avoid the fatuous rhetoric that "all teachers are teachers of reading."* I can think of few things more insulting to professionals who have spent years gaining credentials to teach science, math, literature, or history only to find themselves labeled reading teachers. But this is more than an issue of professional courtesy among colleagues. It is recognition that we can do more to improve literacy skills for students by teaching them to meet the rigorous demands of a challenging content curriculum than by withdrawing to an emphasis on supposedly generalizable reading skills that are decontextualized from subject matter concerns (Bohr, 1994). The teachers who can do the most in improving reading achievement are those most committed to teaching their subject matter, because they can be persuaded to reveal to students the specialized reading demands of their content without retreating from the rigorous content requirements of the disciplines.

2. *Let's resist the gravitational pull of the quick fix,* the silver-bullet solutions that always seem to come up when reading is the topic in secondary schools. Double-block English periods may seem as if they will fix the reading problem, but what they really do is relegate responsibility for reading improvement to the English teacher—letting everyone else off the hook. Doubling English does not necessarily increase reading instruction for anybody. Similarly, various commercial products may claim to provide the needed answer to adolescent reading improvement: Just buy our program, and blah, blah, blah. Show me the research—and I don't mean the shaky evaluation studies from the

companies' marketing departments—that shows these products have ever been the sole or main reason for reading improvement.

3. *Let's stop the blame game.* Blaming the teachers at the local feeder schools (who blame the elementary teachers, who blame the parents) doesn't do much good. Lots of people—including high school educators—seem to believe that reading needs to be taught better during the early years, with the idea that this will solve the high school reading problem. It won't. It certainly is a good idea to upgrade the quality of what happens to children in the preschool and primary grades, but that alone will not help students meet the literacy demands of the disciplines. No early reading program has ever been consistently or credibly proved to improve high school reading achievement (Shanahan & Barr, 1995). Success in high school reading depends on both a good start and a good finish. Even if your feeder schools are doing a great job, you still have to build on the base.

4. *Let's not be fooled into thinking practice is more important than instruction* (Krashen, 2002). A popular notion among upper grade teachers is that the reason high school students are not reading better is simply that they don't read enough on their own; that television, movies, dating, driving, and the Internet don't leave students enough time to read. It seems plausible. Practice matters in reading, as it does in anything else. Adolescents do read somewhat less than younger and older students. And, "It couldn't hurt." The problem is that reading practice solutions (e.g., sustained silent reading periods, Drop Everything and Read times throughout the school day) reduce the amount of instruction available to students—with no reliable evidence that they help (National Reading Panel, 2000). When I came to Chicago, the district had mandated that every high school teacher stop teaching his or her subject for five minutes daily in each class to allow students to read for pleasure. I ended that policy as soon as I arrived.

KEY VARIABLES FOR READING ACHIEVEMENT

With that, let's turn to the changes needed to ensure that secondary students improve at literacy. This chapter will weigh the value of seven key variables in improving reading achievement.

Leadership

Most of the studies of the importance of leadership in school improvement have focused on the role of elementary principals (Brookover & Lezotte, 1979; Hallinger, 1996; Puman, Karweit, Price, Ricciuiti, Thompson, & Vaden-Kiernan, 1997; Weber, 1971; Wilder, 1977). It appears to be safe to generalize from those studies to the secondary schools, however (Ames, 1996). An effective principal might have a relatively greater effect in an elementary school, but only because there is less competition from other potential leaders, and the effects are more quickly seen there because elementary schools are usually smaller. Nevertheless, leadership—whether embodied in the principal, an administrative team of principals and assistant principals, or a corps of department heads—has a big impact on students' success.

Why is leadership so important? Leadership is needed to set goals and to direct resources toward common outcomes. In high schools, leadership is sometimes diffused, and what the common direction is can be unclear. Beyond this, the individuals who observe instruction in the classroom for the purpose of evaluating teachers can have a powerful impact on encouraging teachers to channel their efforts in particular directions. Likewise, hiring policy—and personnel management—can make a big difference in terms of hiring well-prepared professionals, as well as in retaining them. Some schools, particularly those in poor neighborhoods, have difficulty keeping a stable teaching force. Leadership is necessary to manage the educational environment in such a way that good teachers will stay put.

Finally, a common complaint among teachers in struggling schools is the lack of consistent decision making. They come to have a sense that it is possible to wait out any new initiative without improving anything. Leadership is important because it provides a sense of stability and continuity.

To be frank, few principals are prepared to lead when it comes to reading (Jacobson, 1992), and this is especially true in secondary schools. Principals have little preparation in reading (it is almost never a part of their credentialing), and few have much practical experience in teaching it (especially at the secondary level, given that so few high school teachers have taught literacy). In some schools, it might be possible to identify a few teachers who can speak for the school on reading issues by working closely with the administration. I've seen that work in some suburban high schools.

In Chicago, we recognized that leadership would not just emerge. It had to be developed through our efforts at the district level. Not only did few principals have the background to do much more than give encouragement; they had few teachers with reading preparation on whom to depend. Chicago has about 75 high schools, but only 15 high school teachers had a state endorsement or certification in reading. That is just too narrow a knowledge base on which to build sound leadership.

To alter this, we began assembling literacy leadership teams for each school. These teams minimally had to include the principal, one lead teacher from each of the core academic areas (math, science, English, social science), and a reading teacher if the school had one. Some schools went further, including additional professionals. These teams were required to attend training together, to establish goals for their schools, and to develop plans for meeting the students' reading needs and the literacy teaching needs of their teachers. Someone ultimately has to determine that it is essential to raise reading achievement in a school, that other decisions will reflect this need, that resources will be brought to bear on the need, and that the effort will continue until it is successful. That is what sound literacy leadership is about. That kind of leadership can be embodied in a dynamic leader or distributed through a cluster of leaders, but it is essential if real improvement is to happen.

Amount of Instruction

There are no more consistent findings in educational research than those concerning the importance of instructional time (Fisher & Berliner, 1985; Frederick & Walberg, 1980; Frederick, Walberg, & Rasher, 1979; Shanahan & Walberg, 1985; Wang, Haertel, & Walberg, 1993). The more instruction that is provided, the more learning that accrues. That is why in high schools, if you want to raise achievement in math, you start requiring more units of math. There can be diminishing returns to more and more teaching, but most academic subjects, including reading, have high ceilings for the amount that can profitably be provided (Walberg & Tsai, 1984).

The problem with amount of instruction as a key variable in literacy development in high school is that literacy is not a basic academic subject. Unlike English, mathematics, social studies, and science, there are few required reading courses—except for those provided to remedial students. This means that there are few obvious avenues for increasing the amount of instruction in these grade levels. The major solution to the time problem that I have seen over the years is the double-block English period. Many schools, sensing the problem that the students are having with reading, reduce the length of all other classes to allow the students to have two periods of English. I'm certainly not against the double-block period generally (handled right, it can be an effective strategy), but in my experience it rarely leads to an increase in the amount or quality of reading instruction for secondary students.

What are the common problems with the double block? The most basic one is that English teachers usually lack much preparation in the teaching of reading. (They may have more than other secondary teachers but still not much.) Under those circumstances, one usually finds that they do not actually use the extra period to provide reading instruction. What really happens is that the kids get a double dose of English. However, English has its own curriculum, and most of it is not about teaching students how to read. Even when it is about that, the focus of this reading is on literature: how to read novels, poetry, plays, and short stories. Such reading does not provide students with adequate preparation to allow them to do well with a typical biology or world culture text, not to mention the plethora of diverse materials available on the Internet. The vocabulary, text structures, purposes, and strategies of literature reading are simply too different from other kinds of reading to allow for much transfer.

How do we ensure that students get more instruction? One way to do this is to set up special additional instruction for kids in need. A number of high schools that I work with have summer freshman reading academies in which students receive about six weeks of extra instruction before they enter ninth grade. Chicago provides summer school classes at most grade levels to provide this kind of a boost, as well, and after-school programs (so-called Lighthouse programs) keep kids studying after the official end of the school day. Obviously, maintaining orderly schools, keeping after truancy, and discouraging extended visits "home" during the academic year by immigrant students all can help to increase instructional time. However, there are even more central ways to increase teaching.

In my professional practice in schools, I require a minimum of two to three hours per day of reading and writing instruction. (In Chicago, we mandated it.) This typically devolves into two hours of average daily teaching in secondary classrooms. Two hours is more than students typically get now (and an increase in amount of instruction usually leads to an increase in achievement). This amount of time is intentionally greater than the length of two instructional periods. This means that even if a double-block schedule is established, it will not satisfy the instructional time demands without further adjustments to all of the classes.

Framework and Curriculum

Differences in amount of instruction explain the greatest amount of variance in students' achievement, and what is taught in the curriculum delivers the second greatest amount (Good & Brophy, 1986; Purkey & Smith, 1983; Wang et al., 1993). What we teach matters. If your science curriculum emphasizes biology over chemistry, your kids will do well on the life sciences tests but will look like laggards when it comes to chemistry. If your social studies curriculum emphasizes American over European studies, your kids will generally know more about the American fight for independence than the French Revolution. It is the same way with reading. We need to ensure that secondary schools emphasize the things that matter in reading development.

Toward that end, I developed a curriculum framework that emphasizes the kinds of things that need to be taught. It is now used in nearly 100 high schools and junior highs. My framework divides literacy instruction into four parts and argues for relatively equal amounts of teaching time devoted to each component of the framework. Given that I require two hours per day of literacy work, this means that schools would have to devote about 10 hours per week to literacy—roughly 2.5 hours per week devoted to each literacy component.

The four areas of instruction that require attention are word knowledge, fluency, comprehension, and writing. *Word knowledge* refers to both word recognition and word meaning, but at the high school level vocabulary teaching fills the bill. *Fluency* refers to being able to read a text orally with appropriate accuracy, speed, and expression. (If students can read grade-level-appropriate text with fluency, the time devoted to this can be reduced.) *Reading comprehension* refers to the ability to read various types of text with understanding and learning, and *writing* refers to the ability to compose text effectively for a variety of purposes.

To ensure that students have access to this amount of teaching, we induce the major academic departments to agree on a division of responsibility for accomplishing this. The English department might agree that it will provide 45 minutes per week of vocabulary work and another 45 minutes for text comprehension, and so on. What this means is that all academic teachers agree to teach these essentials of literacy for a particular amount of time per week (not per day), and that the amounts total 2.5 hours per component and 10 hours overall for the week across the departments.

What counts as reading instruction? Whatever instruction is delivered by a teacher needs to be relevant to the subject area. A science teacher should not willingly agree to stop teaching science for 45 minutes per week to deal with vocabulary. However, this teacher must recognize the importance of vocabulary to science achievement and therefore be willing to help build science vocabulary with the students for the agreed on time. The connections to more general vocabulary are achieved by making certain that students learn both the technical or scientific meanings of a term and the more general meanings, if it has both. That means that words such as *hybrid* and *eruption* get more thorough attention. Also, English and science teachers often will teach the meaning of combining forms, such as *geo-, poly-, tri-,* and so on without any concerns about loss of focus on their appropriate subject matter—and these do have general value. The key here, however, is that math teachers are always teaching math—even though they may be spending some time teaching students to deal with the specialized vocabulary and text demands of reading and writing within math. It is the same with the teachers from all of the departments.

Also, there is a need to differentiate teaching and practice here. Not long ago, I heard a history teacher remark that meeting the comprehension requirement of my framework is easy—all you have to do is have the kids read the chapters in the social studies book for the prescribed time and answer the questions at the end of the chapter. That, however, does not satisfy my standard at all, and on its own it is unlikely to do much to improve reading achievement. That activity is practice or social studies work or something, but it is not reading or writing instruction. What would count? To meet the requirement, the time has to be spent in a serious effort to teach students how to read and learn from the social studies text effectively. The teacher might, for example, teach students how history reading depends on more than just understanding the individual episodes presented in the history book; it depends on being able to make connections among these episodes to end up with a larger explanation of the event. The teacher then might show students some examples and provide a chart that would encourage them to think that way when they read history independently. In that context, assigning a chapter and having students practice reading it to find those connections would clearly count as instruction by my definition—and would, consequently, satisfy the time requirements. In other words, assignments can be part of instruction, but they cannot replace it. Reading instruction involves teaching the student to master some skill, strategy, or structure that can be used again in the future.

Professional Development

Unfortunately, most secondary teachers know too little about the teaching of literacy. Many states have had severely limited requirements for secondary teachers concerning knowledge of reading instruction until fairly recently (Romine, 1996), and, of course, not all teachers meet all certification standards. Despite the fact that national educational standards in most disciplines explicitly mandate or imply (through the specification of model lessons that involve sophisticated literacy demands) literacy teaching in the high school, the states have often not done enough to guarantee that content teachers know about the textual demands of their subjects or how to build literacy skills appropriate to the requirements of the discipline. This means that the only way a secondary school is likely to improve reading achievement is with a big investment in teachers' knowledge.

In Chicago, our situation was dire. The state did not require any reading preparation for high school teachers (except for those who were specifically reading teachers), though those requirements have recently been changed, which will help in the future. Likewise, the school district did not officially recognize reading certification credentials at these grade levels, and it had not invested much in professional development in reading at the secondary school level. Teachers who had formal knowledge about these issues were few and far between, and typically they had no professional authority or opportunity to share their knowledge with others.

Increasing professional development in this area is an ongoing process in Chicago. The need for teachers with reading preparation is now officially recognized, and principals make more of an effort to hire teachers (when they have a choice) who have this training. More important, the district has started to work with area universities to establish graduate-level programs aimed specifically at providing appropriate reading credentials to high school teachers—particularly those in the four major academic areas—and the district has been paying to enroll its teachers in such programs.

Even more effective, however, have been local district efforts to provide for teachers' professional development needs. We started out by providing a summer Secondary Reading Academy that key teachers and principals from each school were required to attend for two weeks. These sessions dealt with how to provide sound reading instruction in vocabulary, fluency, comprehension, and writing in the various subject areas, and time was set aside for school team meetings to develop their own improvement plans. Throughout the school year these workshops were held monthly to keep people on board and to extend their knowledge of reading instruction.

The key to successful professional development in reading at the secondary level is to carry out the work in disciplinary teams. Unlike at elementary levels, grade-level differences rarely matter much, but subject matter concerns dominate. Remember that the important stress here is on improving reading *within* the disciplines. I prefer grouping teachers together around their disciplinary needs. This can be even more important than having the teachers together with colleagues from their own school. The school groups are useful, of course, for accomplishing various administrative agreements as to which departments will do what, but the disciplinary teams are more central within professional development activities.

This is not to say that there are no teacher training generalizations across subject matter: Vocabulary learning does not differ much between math and English. This means that some training, such as in the basics of the framework itself, are appropriately dealt with while everybody is together. But the best progress comes once all of the examples and language are appropriate to the specific disciplinary requirements of each subject. Professional development activities can be—need to be—rich and varied, but different experiences are likely to be needed at different times. Initially, it is a good idea to have one or more presentations on the framework and each of the four components. Presentations on the components need to provide a sense of what the reading curriculum might look like (understanding that there will be different local choices as to which comprehension strategies or writing elements or vocabulary words are going to be taught) and some sound ways to teach these (relying on methods that have been found to be successful in improving reading achievement by research), and they should provide a clear sense of how well students must understand and be able to perform what is taught (which raises assessment issues).

Presentations of this type are necessary but insufficient for fostering change in a high school classroom. Teachers can benefit from other formats once these lessons have been delivered. These might include being involved in guided lesson planning in which they get help in building lessons that teach the content of the discipline while addressing all four aspects of the framework. (Some of my most effective work with middle school teachers has taken place during unit planning with groups of teachers who were trying to develop effective lessons that would include appropriate reading and writing instruction.) If skilled reading teachers are available who are classroom-savvy, it becomes possible to use them as coaches—sending them into classrooms to give feedback and suggestions to teachers on what they are trying out or providing demonstrations of model lessons. Another type of workshop that can be very successful is one in which students' work is the focus of the discussion. For example, I have often sat with math teachers who were working on the evaluation and feedback routines for use with students' writing from the math classes. No matter what the topics or approaches to professional development, understand that improving reading achievement at the secondary level is unlikely without substantial opportunities for teachers to work together toward improving their knowledge and skills. Making sure that teachers know how to teach reading effectively is essential to success.

Special Learners

There is a need for a multi-tiered response to students' reading needs at the secondary level, with increasingly elaborated responses for students with the greatest problems. Let's face it: Some kids are entering high school so far behind that it is unlikely they will be able to do high school work without a lot of support.

The most important thing that can be done to improve reading is to improve the amount and quality of the daily reading and writing instruction in the regular classroom programs. Making certain that all students—no matter what their level—receive reasonable opportunities to improve their reading and writing skills throughout their school experience is imperative. But even if that is done, some students will still lag. Some may be so far behind that they will have difficulty benefiting from the reading opportunities that are provided.

What can be done for these students? For most, more instruction—beyond that which can be provided in the core courses—is the ticket. I have already mentioned summer academies and after-school programs that can give large numbers of students opportunities to work on their reading when it will not interfere with regular school offerings. Another popular approach is to create reading courses specifically for lower-achieving readers. These courses are offered during the school day and take the place of an elective in the students' schedules, but they do not interfere with the core academic offerings (a student still takes math, science, social studies, and English, but he or she can also pick up a section of reading). The benefit of such courses, whether offered during the summer or during the school year, is that they extend the amount of reading instruction provided but also allow for greater adjustment of the level of teaching. Greater responsiveness to students' needs is possible in this kind of setting.

The kinds of programs noted up to this point are ideal for helping teens who are two or three years below grade level, but some lag much farther behind than that. What about them? Students who are that far behind really are in need of much more intense individualized intervention and are more the province of special education than the regular program. Kids who are this far behind should receive diagnostic testing from highly skilled learning disabilities specialists, and the programmatic responses should be individually tailored to their needs. That might mean using instructional materials written at levels far below a student's grade level. It might mean teaching word recognition skills that typically would not be part of a high school or junior high curriculum. It might mean teaching a student more vocabulary than comprehension or more comprehension than fluency—the idea being that the program plan would be based on the student's needs.

Instructional Materials

Materials—textbooks, computers, instructional programs—often play a big role in determining what happens in high school and middle school classrooms. Secondary teachers are aware of the pivotal role of text, and they often arrive at solutions that are not salutary to students' progress. A teacher might notice that some of the kids—25%, 50%, 75%—are struggling with the textbook. To ensure that the kids don't miss out on learning biology, the teacher hits on a brilliant solution: teaching without text. That is, all lessons are presented by the teacher, meaning that the students are not held back by their limited reading skills. This seems rational. It keeps kids from missing out and so on, but it also means that after a year of not reading science material, the kids are probably in even worse shape for their next science class. Too many teachers make the choice to avoid reading, and the problem snowballs. I insist on starting with a pledge from all secondary teachers that they will use text in their classrooms and that most students will be expected to read the text material.

Even teachers who are willing to do this often would like to see the purchase of a reading program—that is, materials designed specifically to teach reading. Generally, I don't think reading programs per se are particularly useful in most high school settings, except for use with special students who are far behind grade level or in special sections that have been set up for the kids who are behind. Even in many of those situations—depending on how far behind the kids are—I would still argue that their instruction would be better focused on the regular daily classroom text materials.

Think about what that means. The students may be struggling with their science books, but the science teacher is devoting substantial time to helping the students learn the vocabulary from the science text, to read the text fluently and with understanding, and to write about the science content presented in the text. In addition, the struggling readers may have a daily class in reading, and in that class he or she is working with . . . You guessed it, the same science book. The idea here is that more thorough attention to the reading demands of these materials would offer the student the greatest opportunity to improve his or her ability to handle the science book. It is also likely to lead to greater science knowledge—a real benefit to the science teacher. Some reading teachers will even go over the science chapter with the students before its introduction in the science class so things will go more smoothly from the beginning.

Of course, as already noted, some kids are just too far behind for this plan to help enough. Those students really need to have greater opportunity to build their general reading skills, and that is going to take much more individualized work. Instructional materials designed specifically to teach reading to adolescents who are far behind are very appropriate in those cases.

Parent Involvement

The role that parents can play in the educational progress of adolescents is often neglected and misunderstood. I am told by parents and teachers alike that parents have no role to play at this stage because of the strong influence of peers and media on teenagers. There just isn't room for parents to make things happen academically for their children. Some teachers even resist the idea of parents' involvement, as they fear it will discourage independence on the part of the student.

When it comes to raising reading achievement, we should consider all possible sources of improvement. Counter to claims about the peer orientation of teens, research has shown that parents play a much greater role in stimulating student progress than is usually acknowledged (Flouri, Buchanan, & Bream, 2002; Shanahan & Walberg, 1985). For example, an analysis of data from 50,000 high school seniors and sophomores nationwide found that, even when the differences in achievement due to socioeconomic status were controlled, parent influences were sizeable and significant and were greater than comparable statistics for peer and media influences (Shanahan & Walberg, 1985). Kids might look to one another for the latest hair styles and music craze, but they look to the adults for a sense of what matters academically. How much adolescents talked to their parents about school and homework had a clear impact on students' learning.

It is important that secondary schools reach out to parents to get them involved (Feuerstein, 2000). Establishing direct connections between teachers and parents is effective in instigating such involvement. It is also helpful to set clear homework policies and then to work with parents to develop appropriate involvement and responses to this homework. Communicating to parents how they can help and letting them know the value of talking to their teens about school are worthwhile. Even parents who do not understand the academic content of their children's coursework can play an important role by monitoring homework completion and advising students on what to do if they are having trouble ("Talk to the teacher").

One innovative strategy for opening lines of communication with parents was pioneered by a suburban reading teacher. Her school had a career awareness program in which parents—and others in the community—came to tell students about particular occupations. That is common, of course, but the teacher built an unusual component into the program: The workers talked to kids about the reading, writing, and mathematics demands of their work. Often they brought along the reading material that they had to be able to handle. Something that surprised everyone was the huge amount of reading and writing expected in most jobs and how demanding that reading often was, even in blue-collar jobs such as mechanic or truck driver. The school parleyed this community involvement into increased student–parent discussions about the importance of education and the importance of reading in their futures. That's a real winner.

CONCLUSION

This chapter has tried to make the case that reading achievement needs to be a greater focus in secondary schools, and it holds out the possibility of improving reading achievement for adolescents. To make this happen, seven key variables can be addressed. These include secondary school leadership, a generous amount of reading and writing instruction, the curricular focus of that instruction, professional development, special support for struggling students, textbooks and other instructional materials, and parent involvement. There are no magic bullets for improving secondary reading achievement, just lots of hard work. Hard work directed toward the right variables is the key to improved reading achievement.

REFERENCES

Ames, N. L. (1996). Creating secure school environments through total school reform: The Harshman story. *Middle School Journal, 27*(3), 4–13.

Bohr, L. (1994). Courses associated with freshman learning. *Journal of the Freshman Year Experience, 6,* 69–90.

Brookover, W. B., & Lezotte, L. W. (1979). *Changes in school characteristics coincident with changes in student achievement.* (Occasional Paper No. 17). East Lansing: Michigan State University, Institute for Research on Teaching.

Feuerstein, A. (2000). School characteristics and parent involvement: Influences on participation in children's schools. *Journal of Educational Research, 94,* 29–40.

Fisher, C. W., & Berliner, D. C. (Eds.). (1985). *Perspectives on instructional time.* New York: Longman.

Flouri, E., Buchanan, A., & Bream, V. (2002). Adolescents' perceptions of their fathers' involvement: Significance to school attitudes. *Psychology in the Schools, 39,* 575–582.

Frederick, W. C., & Walberg, H. J. (1980). Learning as a function of time. *Journal of Educational Research, 73,* 183–194.

Frederick, W. C., Walberg, H. J., & Rasher, S. P. (1979). Time, teacher comments, and achievement in urban high schools. *Journal of Educational Research, 73*(2), 63–65.

Good, T. L., & Brophy, J. E. (1986). School effects. In M. C. Wittrock (Ed.), *Handbook of research on teaching* (3rd ed., pp. 328–375). New York: Macmillan.

Grigg, W. S., Daane, M. C., Jin, Y., & Campbell, J. R. (2003). *The nation's report card: Reading 2002.* Washington, DC: National Center for Educational Statistics.

Hallinger, P. (1996). School context, principal leadership, and student reading achievement. *Elementary School Journal, 96,* 527–549.

Jacobson, J. (1992). Reading instruction: Perceptions of elementary school principals. *Journal of Educational Research, 85,* 370–380.

Krashen, S. (2002). Defending whole language: The limits of phonics instruction and the efficacy of whole language instruction. *Reading Improvement, 39,* 32–42.

National Reading Panel. (2000). *Report of the National Reading Panel: Teaching children to read.* Bethesda, MD: National Institute for Child Health Development.

Puman, M. J., Karweit, N., Price, C., Ricciuti, A., Thompson, W., & Vaden-Kiernan, M. (1997). *Prospects: Final report on student outcomes.* Washington, DC: Planning and Evaluating Service, U.S. Department of Education.

Purkey, S. C., & Smith, M. S. (1983). Effective schools: A review. *Elementary School Journal, 83,* 427–452.

Romine, B. G. (1996). Reading coursework requirements for middle and high school content area teachers: A U.S. survey. *Journal of Adolescent & Adult Literacy, 40,* 194–198.

Shanahan, T., & Barr, R. (1995). Reading recovery: An independent evaluation of the effects of an early instructional intervention for at-risk learners. *Reading Research Quarterly, 30,* 958–996.

Shanahan, T., & Walberg, H. J. (1985). Productive influences on high school student achievement. *Journal of Educational Research, 78,* 357–363.

Walberg, H. J., & Tsai, S. (1984). Reading achievement and diminishing returns to time. *Journal of Educational Psychology, 76,* 442–451.

Wang, M. C., Haertel, G. D., & Walberg, H. J. (1993). Toward a knowledge base for school learning. *Review of Educational Research, 63,* 249–294.

Weber, G. (1971). *Inner city children can be taught to read: Four successful schools* (Occasional Papers No. 18). Washington, DC: Council for Basic Education.

Wilder, G. (1977). Five exemplary reading programs. In J. T. Guthrie (Ed.), *Cognition, curriculum, and comprehension* (pp. 57–68). Newark, DE: International Reading Association.

4

Motivation for Reading During the Early Adolescent and Adolescent Years

Allan Wigfield

Key Points

- Self-efficacy, intrinsic and extrinsic motivation, the valuing of reading, and mastery goals are associated with reading motivation.
- Secondary school classroom practices and organizational structures are partly responsible for the decline in adolescents' reading motivation.
- Increased motivation can be fostered by building students' reading successes, focusing on improvement rather than comparison, and providing greater student choice.

James is a 10th grader who enjoys reading many different kinds of materials, including classic and modern novels, websites containing information about his favorite hobbies, and informational books about topics that he wants to learn more about. He takes on the challenge of reading difficult material because he has the confidence that he can understand that material. Even if a book contains many words and phrases that are difficult to comprehend, he works hard to ensure his eventual understanding of the material. When he reads a book he really likes, he gets totally immersed in it, often losing track of time and reading until late at night. By contrast, Geneva, also a 10th grader, reads infrequently and does not have much confidence in her reading skills. Her difficulties in reading began in elementary school, and she continues to struggle with reading. When she encounters challenging reading materials in different classes and in situations outside of school, she quickly backs away from them. She tells her teachers that reading is not important to her and that she does not enjoy it. These two students differ in their reading skills but also in their motivation to read, and both of these things have an impact on their engagement in reading. By *reading engagement* I mean the mutual functioning of motivation, knowledge, strategies, and social interactions during reading.

In this chapter I discuss adolescents' motivation to read and how it relates to their engagement in reading. I also look at instructional influences on adolescents' reading motivation and discuss practices that can facilitate adolescents' reading motivation. During adolescence, individuals experience many changes, including the biological changes associated with puberty, important changes in relations with family and peers, and the social and educational changes resulting from transitions from elementary school to junior high school and junior high school to high school. Adolescents also explore and try to come to terms with their identities in meaningful ways and face important issues about the future direction of their lives. Because of these changes and issues, various writers have characterized adolescence as a period of "storm and stress," when there is a great deal of conflict between children, parents, and teachers. Teachers (and parents) have been heard to say, "If we could just lock kids up for those years, things would be fine!" Although some researchers now believe that the characterization of this time period as one of storm and stress is an overstatement, others continue to use the term *crisis* in their description of the state of contemporary American adolescents (see Wigfield & Eccles, 2002, for further discussion).

What role does reading play in adolescents' development? As many writers have discussed, whether or not adolescents become capable, engaged readers has many important implications for their educational and economic futures, the formation of their identities, and their acclimation into society. As illustrated in the experiences of James and Geneva, adolescents' motivation plays an important role in the development of their reading capabilities as well as in their engagement in reading.

Before presenting a definition of reading motivation, I want to make two points about my approach and focus in this chapter. First, I am an educational psychologist by training, so the perspective I take in this chapter is a psychological one. Second, my colleagues and I have focused on reading motivation in our work, so in this chapter I focus primarily on reading rather than on literacy as it is more broadly defined.

DEFINING READING MOTIVATION

For many years, reading researchers focused primarily on the cognitive aspects of reading. This research has contributed much to our understanding of both the nature of reading and how children can be taught to read. But because reading is an effortful activity that often involves choice, motivation is crucial to reading engagement. Even the reader with the strongest cognitive skills may not spend much time reading if he or she is not motivated to read.

Currently, many researchers think of motivation as being determined by the beliefs, values, and goals the individual has. Guthrie and Wigfield defined reading motivation in the following way: "[R]eading motivation is the individual's personal goals, values, and beliefs with regard to the topics, processes, and outcomes of reading" (Guthrie & Wigfield, 2000, p. 405). An important implication of this definition is that the individual is in control of his or her motivation, because it is determined by her beliefs, values, and goals.

BELIEFS, VALUES, AND GOALS

I focus in this section on the beliefs, values, and goals associated with reading motivation: self-efficacy, intrinsic and extrinsic motivation, the valuing of reading, and mastery goals. I chose these because they relate to students' motivation and achievement and have received attention from reading researchers.

Reading Self-Efficacy

Self-efficacy is defined as individuals' assessments of their ability at different activities and their sense that they can accomplish the activity (Bandura, 1997). There are two important parts of this definition: the belief that one is capable, and the explicit connection of that belief to the accomplishment of an activity. An adolescent who believes that he is efficacious at reading not only has that belief but also effectively engages in reading activities.

One of the most important sources of information about one's self-efficacy is previous performance. When individuals do well on an activity such as reading, they develop a positive sense of efficacy for that activity. When they do less well, their sense of efficacy is less positive. An important implication of this point is that children's early experiences with reading in school will have a strong influence on their developing sense of self-efficacy for reading. By adolescence, individuals probably have a fairly clear sense of efficacy as readers, with some adolescents believing they are capable readers, and others doubting this. Other important sources of information about efficacy are watching others do well or poorly and encouragement from others.

Researchers have shown that children with high self-efficacy do better on different achievement activities, choose more difficult activities to try, and persist at them even if they are having trouble completing them. Further, research has shown that children's self-efficacy in subject areas such as reading can be enhanced by providing them with skills necessary to do the activity better as well as with direct feedback that they are capable of doing the activity. Building self-efficacy thus is a key to students' success.

Intrinsic Motivation

When individuals are intrinsically motivated, they do activities for their own sake and out of interest in the activity. Their motivation comes from inside themselves rather than from external sources. When they are intrinsically motivated to learn, students become deeply involved in the activity they are doing and devote much time and energy to it (Ryan & Deci, 2000). They also seek to improve their skills and build on what they know. A substantial body of research indicates that intrinsic motivation relates to long-term engagement in activities, as well as to deeper learning. When intrinsically motivated individuals are in a state of flow, they lose track of time and become totally immersed in what they are doing.

Children's intrinsic motivation develops when they have interesting materials to work with, opportunities to develop their competencies, control of their own learning, and opportunities to collaborate with others. The latter two become especially important during the adolescent years. I will return to this point later.

Extrinsic Motivation

When extrinsically motivated, individuals do activities in order to receive some benefit, such as a reward. Their motivation comes from what they will receive for doing the activity rather than from inside themselves. Examples of rewards are privileges in the classroom, money from parents, and grades. Students often eagerly engage in activities when they are rewarded for doing so. However, there is evidence that when children work solely for extrinsic motivators, they no longer pursue the activity when the rewards are taken away (see Deci, Koestner, & Ryan, 1999). Thus, rewards must be used with some care.

The influence of extrinsic motivation compared with intrinsic motivation on individuals' engagement in different activities continues to be debated, sometimes fiercely (e.g., Cameron & Pierce, 1994; Deci et al., 1999). This debate centers on whether the use of extrinsic rewards undermines intrinsic motivation. There is compelling evidence that this can occur under certain conditions. However, some researchers discuss how intrinsic and extrinsic motivations can coexist and say that students often are motivated for both intrinsic and extrinsic reasons (Lepper & Henderlong, 2000). In general, it appears that both kinds of motivation can increase children's engagement in reading. Many programs designed to increase children's reading focus on providing students with extrinsic motivators to get them to read. However, because of the long-term benefits of intrinsic motivation, it is important to work toward building adolescents' intrinsic motivation to read.

The Valuing of Reading

The subjective value of a task refers to individuals' incentives or purposes for doing an activity. Eccles and colleagues discuss four aspects of subjective task values (see Eccles, Wigfield, & Schiefele, 1998). The first is interest value, which is conceptually similar to intrinsic motivation. When a student values an activity because it is interesting to her, it means she likes the activity and engages in it for the pleasure of it. The second is attainment value, or how important the task is to the individual and how it relates to his or her sense of self. Some tasks or activities are quite salient to the individual and so have great importance to him. The third is utility value, which concerns the usefulness of the activity to the individual. Will this activity help me accomplish my goals? An example is taking a science class to get into medical school rather than because it is interesting.

Cost is the fourth aspect and refers to the individual's understanding that doing one activity (reading) may interfere with doing another (calling a friend).

Cost may be an especially important aspect of value during adolescence, as adolescents have to choose from among many possible activities. Eccles and her colleagues have found that students' valuing of different activities influences their choices of whether or not to continue to do the activity. When adolescents value an activity, they are more likely to continue doing it.

Mastery Goals

When students have a mastery goal orientation, they focus on improving their skills and developing their competencies. Students who have a mastery goal orientation are intrinsically motivated to learn and put a lot of effort into their learning. These students take on challenging tasks in order to improve their skills (Anderman, Austin, & Johnson, 2002). Such goals often are contrasted with performance goals, which reflect students' concern to outperform others, demonstrate that they are able, and focus on getting high grades. Many students, of course, have both kinds of goal orientations. However, a focus on mastery goals has been shown to facilitate children's learning.

I have discussed the motivation beliefs, values, and goals separately, but it is important to understand that they relate to one another. Students with high self-efficacy to read are more likely to be intrinsically motivated to read, and to value reading. When students believe they are capable of doing an activity, they enjoy it more and often pursue it for intrinsic reasons. Mastery goals also relate closely to intrinsic motivation. Students who focus on learning and improvement generally are intrinsically motivated to learn, as well. Thus, the different aspects of motivation operate together and influence one another. There may be an optimal pattern of these motivational characteristics. Students who are efficacious about their reading, intrinsically motivated to read, value reading, and focus on mastery goals are more motivated to pursue reading activities.

MOTIVATION AND READING ENGAGEMENT

As noted earlier, reading engagement refers to the mutual functioning of motivation, knowledge, strategies, and social interactions during reading. There are several specific ways that motivation contributes to reading engagement. First, motivation influences adolescents' choices of which activities to do. If adolescents are motivated to do an activity such as reading, they will more often choose to do it. Second, motivation activates adolescents' behavior. When adolescents are motivated to do an activity, they bring much more energy to it. This is true of individual adolescents and of adolescents working together in groups.

Third, adolescents' motivation influences how committed they are to the activity. Whenever individuals do an activity, they eventually run into challenges or difficulties that they have to overcome to complete the activity successfully. Teachers often hear students say, "This is too hard" and "I can't do this." Some adolescents start saying such things very soon after they start an activity. Such statements mean not only that the adolescents are not confident that they can do the activity but also that they are not strongly committed to completing the activity. Motivation is one of the key factors that helps students persist when these challenges arise. Students' sense of efficacy is especially important here.

Why is reading engagement itself important? There are many answers to this question, but one that I think is important to emphasize is that engaged readers are more likely to enjoy reading and to read frequently. The frequency of reading itself relates strongly to children's achievement in reading, which opens many possibilities for children and adolescents. When children are engaged in reading, many positive things can occur for them.

DEVELOPMENT OF ACHIEVEMENT MOTIVATION

There have been many studies of how children's motivation develops. I highlight two basic findings from this research in this section. First, researchers have found that as children get older, their beliefs about competence, intrinsic motivation, and valuing of different achievement activities become more consistent or stable. This finding means (using intrinsic motivation as an example) that for adolescents, a student who is intrinsically motivated to read one year is more likely to continue to be intrinsically motivated to read the next year. Younger students' intrinsic motivation is more variable from year to year. Thus, children's motivation has the potential to shift more when they are younger.

Second, even with these increases in stability, researchers studying how children's beliefs, goals, and values change during early adolescence and adolescence often have found that they decline. Specifically, early adolescents have lower perceptions of their competence for different school subjects than do elementary-school-age children, who often are quite optimistic about their competence. Students' valuing of different school subjects often suffers a decline as they move through school, with the declines becoming especially marked across the transition to middle school. Their intrinsic motivation for learning in general, and for reading in particular, often decreases. Students often focus more on performance goals as they get older at the expense of task mastery goals.

How do we reconcile the findings that children's motivation is more stable during adolescence but also declines? This apparent paradox occurs because the stability refers to the individual's position within her peer group from year to year. At adolescence, the finding about stability means that adolescents maintain their relative position in the group to a greater extent than do younger children. As noted earlier, a student who is intrinsically motivated to read in one year is more likely to be so in the next year during adolescence than at earlier points in her development. However, even with this stability, the overall *group*'s intrinsic motivation is decreasing each year. So relative position is similar, but overall, motivation goes down.

Self-Comparisons

These changes in children's sense of competence and intrinsic motivation have been explained in two main ways. One explanation focuses on changes that occur within the child. As children go through school, their capacity to understand their own performance increases. They receive more and more feedback about their performance in school and become much more sophisticated at understanding its meaning. Report card grades, feedback about performance on different school projects and tests, and other evaluative information can lead some children to the realization that they are not as capable as other children. The realization that one is not as capable as others can decrease intrinsic motivation to learn.

Children also learn how to compare themselves with others. These comparisons have implications for their own sense of competence. Children compare themselves with others more frequently once they enter school, because they spend all day with same-age peers. At first they do not seem to understand how these comparisons reflect on their judgments about themselves, but they soon begin to figure this out. For instance, even in first grade children are quite aware of which reading groups they are assigned to and what that means regarding their capabilities. Some of these changes in beliefs about competence may be inevitable. Not everyone can be the best at all activities, and students always will compare themselves with others. But it may be possible to help many students maintain a stronger sense of competence and enjoyment of learning.

Grading and Grouping Practices

A second explanation focuses on how teaching practices may contribute to a decline in some children's motivation. As just discussed, children get better at interpreting the evaluative information they receive. They also receive increasing amounts of this information as they go through school. Further, this information gets more specific and focused. For instance, points replace stars, and letter grades replace O for outstanding and S for satisfactory. Practices that emphasize comparison of students and too much competition between them may lead students to focus too much on how their skills compare with those of others. Examples of such practices include public evaluations of students, public displays of students' graded work, teachers' making direct comparisons of how different students are doing, and competitive activities such as spelling bees. Such practices can deflate the competence beliefs of adolescents who are doing less well.

Grouping practices also can have a strong impact. In elementary schools, children are often grouped by ability within classrooms for instruction in subjects such as reading. During middle and high school, students often are tracked and thus are grouped with adolescents of similar ability levels throughout the school day or for at least part of the school day. These practices are controversial and have attracted much attention. A major concern is that children and adolescents in the lower-ability groups will perceive that they are not very able. As mentioned earlier, even during the early elementary school years, children often are very aware of their group membership and what it means, despite the best efforts not to label the groups in obvious ways. Further, the lower-ability groups often have a much higher concentration of minority students in them.

Research on ability grouping's effects on motivation, while not completely clear-cut, shows that it may have benefits for higher-ability students' motivation but may weaken the motivation of children in the lower groups. Because of the potential negative effects of ability grouping, especially on children in the low groups, such grouping should be used with care. Teachers should reevaluate group membership on a regular basis. Adolescents should know that they have the opportunity to move into different reading groups and to read different kinds of materials.

SCHOOL STRUCTURE AND STUDENT MOTIVATION

I have discussed some particular teaching practices that may relate to the decline of students' achievement motivation. Much also has been written about how the organization and structure of middle and high schools may negatively affect students' motivation. Most secondary schools are much larger than elementary schools, as they draw their students from a number of different schools. As a result, students' friendship networks often are disrupted as they attend classes with students from several different schools. Students also are likely to feel more anonymous because of the school's large size.

Instruction often is organized departmentally, especially in high school. Middle and high school teachers typically teach several different groups of students each day and are unlikely to teach any particular students for more than one year. This departmental structure can create a number of difficulties for students. One is that the curriculum often is not integrated across different subjects. A second is that students typically have several teachers each day, with little opportunity to interact with any one teacher on anything except the academic content of what is being taught and disciplinary issues. The middle school teaming concept, when done well, can alleviate some of these difficulties.

Researchers also have discussed how teaching changes in secondary schools away from practices that foster mastery goals and intrinsic motivation to a focus on practices that promote a performance goal orientation in students (see Maehr & Midgley, 1996). Such practices also can contribute to the decline in students' academic competence beliefs, interest, and intrinsic motivation.

Secondary School Teaching Practices

In this section, I briefly discuss some changes in certain key practices that are likely to contribute to declines in motivation. First, there are changes in *authority relationships*. Secondary school classrooms, as compared with elementary school classrooms, are characterized by a greater emphasis on teacher control and discipline and fewer opportunities for student decision making, choice, and self-management. Second, traditional secondary school classrooms, as compared with elementary school classrooms, often are characterized by a *less personal and positive teacher–student relationships* in school. Positive and emotionally warm relations with teachers promote students' motivation and adjustment in the classroom, and these often occur less as students move through school.

Third, the shift to middle school is associated with systematic changes in the *organization of instruction.* For example, teachers often have the entire class work together, and between-classroom ability grouping is used more frequently. Under these learning conditions, adolescents who are doing less well in school increasingly will doubt their capabilities as learners. Fourth, secondary school teachers often feel less effective than elementary school teachers, especially for low-ability students. These are the very students who are likely to need the most efficacious teachers.

In summary, secondary schools have a variety of classroom practices and organizational structures that have negative effects on students' competence beliefs, mastery goals, valuing of learning activities, and intrinsic motivation for learning in general and reading in particular. One important reason that these practices have a negative impact is that they are developmentally inappropriate for early adolescents. At a time when the children are growing cognitively and emotionally, desiring greater freedom and autonomy and focusing on social relations, they experience teaching practices such as these, which do not fit well with the developmental characteristics of adolescents.

Reform Efforts

Middle school reform efforts across the country have implemented changes to deal with some of these organizational issues and to structure middle schools in developmentally appropriate ways. Some of these changes include replacing departmental structures with teams of teachers and students so that teachers get to know students better and can integrate the curriculum more effectively. "School within school" learning communities have been generated to create smaller learning communities in large schools in an attempt to connect better with students. Some schools have moved away from strict ability grouping. Many middle schools now focus on different aspects of early adolescent development along with instruction in the different subject areas. Teachers are given planning time with other teachers so they can work together to enhance the curriculum. These reforms have had an impact on students' motivation and performance, although many school districts still have not implemented such changes. The pace of reform in high schools appears to be even slower.

READING INSTRUCTION AND STUDENT MOTIVATION

How does reading instruction in secondary schools influence adolescents' motivation for reading? This is a complex question that has many answers, as practices vary greatly across different schools. However, several general points can be made with respect to this question. I will focus on three. First, reading is often no longer taught as a separate subject area once children reach middle school, particularly after the first year of middle school. This has strong implications particularly for students entering middle school who still do not read well. Such students often have low self-efficacy for reading, and without specific instruction in reading it may be quite difficult for them to improve their reading skills and develop a sense of efficacy about reading.

Second, content area teachers—even those teaching subjects that require a lot of reading, such as history—often are unprepared to teach reading and do not necessarily want to do so. Again, students struggling with reading in these classes are not likely to receive the instruction they need to become better readers; thus, they will have difficulty comprehending the material they have to read in these classes, particularly as that material becomes more difficult, which it often does during high school. When students continually struggle with reading, their motivation will drop.

Third, students often see the reading materials used in their classes as dry, uninteresting, and perhaps even irrelevant to their lives. This is particularly true of textbooks used in different fields; such books can be sterile and generic. Such materials do little to enhance children's intrinsic motivation for reading in general and for reading within the specific field or subject area. The problem of the perceived irrelevance of textbooks and reading materials may be especially prevalent among students from varying cultural backgrounds, particularly if the books they encounter do little to include their cultural heritage or values. All three of these things can (and have) been changed in schools, but when they are not, they present challenges to the development of children's reading motivation and skills in reading.

CONCLUSIONS: IMPLICATIONS AND RECOMMENDATIONS FOR READING INSTRUCTION

In this section, I draw some implications for reading instruction during the adolescent years, with a focus on ways to enhance students' motivation for reading. I organize this discussion around the different motivation constructs presented in this chapter, particularly self-efficacy, intrinsic motivation, and the valuing of reading.

Fostering Adolescents' Reading Self-Efficacy

As discussed earlier, the strongest influence on students' efficacy for reading (and for other activities) is their previous performance. By adolescence, students have a long history of performance in school in general, and in reading in particular. Some have done consistently well, some consistently poorly, and some have a mixed pattern. Students who have done consistently poorly in reading are likely to have a low sense of their efficacy as readers. This means that they will avoid challenging reading materials; they will not put a lot of effort into their reading (for fear that it will indicate they are poor readers); and they will not persist at reading. Rather than approach reading activities, they will attempt to avoid them. Remember also that students' motivation becomes more stable at adolescence, meaning that it may be more difficult for students to begin to believe they can be good readers.

So what can be done for students with low self-efficacy for reading? The most important thing is for them to experience success in reading so they can begin to develop some confidence in their reading skills. Building these students' confidence in reading may not be an easy process, however. A few successful reading experiences will not be enough to overcome a long history of reading failure or struggle. Students must see a change in their long-standing pattern of struggling as readers in order to begin to develop competence in reading and to develop the belief that they are competent. Encouragement and support from teachers are crucial to this process, but they cannot take the place of being successful at reading different kinds of materials.

Struggling readers often are given simple books or materials that they know are written for children below their grade level. They may be able to read these books and in that sense experience success, but reading simple books may not increase their efficacy. This is particularly true when students focus on comparing their reading skills with others' (I can read this book, but I know that it is a very easy book that everyone else read years ago). Instead of focusing on such comparisons, students need to be encouraged to focus on how they are improving, even if that improvement is gradual. When improvement is the criterion, all students can grow and begin to develop efficacy. By contrast, comparing oneself with others always will leave some students doubting their ability.

Fostering Adolescents' Intrinsic Motivation and Valuing of Reading

Another problem with simple books and reading materials is that they may not be interesting to the students, or they may present things conceptually in such a simple way that adolescent students will think that the material is childish. Even if they can read these materials, they still may not be interested in reading additional materials like them. So along with fostering efficacy, students' interest and intrinsic motivation to read needs attention.

Children's intrinsic motivation to read can be fostered in a number of ways. First and foremost are the kinds of reading materials provided in different classrooms or recommended by teachers if they cannot actually be provided to students. When teachers are able to go beyond textbooks and have students read expository and informational books and other kinds of reading materials of interest to them, their interest in reading can be sparked. They can learn that reading is a way to learn new things about topics of interest to them and therefore become involved in reading and curious to learn more from reading. They may even begin to incorporate reading as an important part of their identity as learners. Going beyond the textbooks in these ways may be especially important for students from different cultural backgrounds, who may not find their culture or heritage represented well in textbooks.

Books are only one kind of reading material, and adolescents are exposed to and use many different kinds of reading materials in their lives. This is especially true of students from cultures in which people engage in reading in ways other than those typical in traditional school settings. When these materials and activities can be incorporated into classrooms and schools, adolescents' motivation to read may be enhanced.

Another way to enhance adolescents' intrinsic motivation to read is to optimize students' choice of reading comprehension activities in the classroom. When students can make meaningful choices around what they read and the assignments that they do, they begin to take control of their own learning, which supports the development of intrinsic motivation. Students who take ownership of their reading and learning are more likely to engage in reading. The sense of autonomy and of ownership become especially crucial at adolescence, when students are establishing independence—an important accomplishment during this developmental period.

Supporting the development of students' autonomy by providing choice and other opportunities for self-directed learning is important for the development of intrinsic motivation. However, care must be taken to structure choice in developmentally appropriate ways. Some adolescents are able to make reasonable choices about materials to read and how to structure assignments and other learning activities. Other adolescents, particularly those who have not had much experience in controlling their own learning, may need help in making meaningful choices so they are not frustrated by choosing reading materials that are too difficult to read or hard to find. As their experience in making meaningful choices grows, they can be given the opportunity to make more complex choices. It is essential that students at all reading levels be given choice, however.

Another way to increase intrinsic motivation is to give students opportunities to interact around their reading. Reading is inherently a social act, but in secondary classrooms students often are not given the chance to interact with other students. Social interactions and opportunities for discussion give students a chance to express their views of reading in classrooms, which is likely to involve them more fully in reading activities.

There are many ways in which students can work together as they read in order to develop their intrinsic motivation for reading. Of course, collaboration and social interaction do not happen automatically. Teachers must structure collaborative groups carefully, shift group membership on a regular basis, and ensure that each member of the group has a meaningful and important role. Contributing in meaningful ways to a group can be especially important for lower-achieving students, whose contributions can be discounted.

Fostering Mastery Goals

When students have a mastery goal orientation, their main focus is on improving their skills and learning new things. Having meaningful learning opportunities helps students develop a mastery goal focus. Teachers also can try to minimize the amount of social comparison that students do by limiting their public evaluation of students and focusing on effort and improvement in their assessments. Maehr and Midgley (1996) provide a rich description of how a middle school changed many instructional and organizational practices in order to promote mastery goals rather than performance goals. Through collaborations with teachers and school administrators, different practices in the school were changed in order to facilitate mastery rather than ability-focused goal orientations. They focused on creating teams of teachers, "schools within the school," and on changing the student recognition patterns so that student improvement rather than just ability was recognized. Other practices were changed as well. These changes were put in place in the schools, though the processes by which that occurred often were challenging (see Maehr & Midgley, 1996, for detailed discussion of the challenges they faced).

In summary, there are many ways in which instructional practices in secondary schools can be changed to help foster adolescents' motivation for reading. Good examples of these practices in operation can be found in some schools across the country. But too often, instructional practices still do not work to enhance children's reading motivation. This needs to change so that more students from all backgrounds can engage fully in reading activities.

SUGGESTIONS FOR FURTHER READING

For discussions of the nature of achievement motivation and its development, see

Pintrich, P. R., & Schunk, D. H. (2002). *Motivation in education: Theory, research, and applications* (2nd ed.). Columbus, OH: Merrill-Prentice Hall.
Wigfield, A., & Eccles, J. S. (Eds.). (2002). *Development of achievement motivation.* San Diego: Academic Press.

For discussion of ways to facilitate children's reading motivation, see

Guthrie, J. T., Wigfield, A., & Perencevich, K. (Eds.). (In press). *Comprehension and engagement in reading: Concept Oriented Reading Instruction.* Mahwah, NJ: Erlbaum.

For discussion of adolescents' reading, including a concern for adolescents' reading motivation, see

Alvermann, D. E., Hinchman, K. A., Moore, D. W., Phelps, S. F., & Waff, D. R. (Eds.). *Reconceptualizing the literacies in adolescent lives.* Mahwah, NJ: Erlbaum.
Moje, E. (2000). *"All the stories that we have": Adolescents' insights about literacy and learning in secondary school.* Newark, DE: International Reading Association.

REFERENCES

Anderman, E. M., Austin, C. C., & Johnson, D. M. (2002). The development of goal orientation. In A. Wigfield & J. S. Eccles (Eds.), *Development of achievement motivation* (pp. 197–220). San Diego: Academic Press.
Bandura, A. (1997). *Self-efficacy: The exercise of control.* New York: W. H. Freeman.

Cameron, J., & Pierce, W. D. (1994). Reinforcement, reward, and intrinsic motivation: A meta-analysis. *Review of Educational Research, 64,* 363–423.

Deci, E. L., Koestner, R., & Ryan, R. M. (1999). A meta-analytic review of experiments examining the effects of extrinsic motivation on intrinsic motivation. *Psychological Bulletin, 125,* 627–668.

Eccles, J. S., Wigfield, A., & Schiefele, U. (1998). Motivation to succeed. In N. Eisenberg (Ed.), *Handbook of child psychology* (5th ed., Vol. 3). New York: Wiley.

Guthrie, J. T., & Wigfield, A. (2000). Engagement and motivation in reading. In M. L. Kamil, P. B. Mosenthal, P. D. Pearson, & R. Barr (Eds.), *Handbook of reading research* (Vol. 3, pp. 403–422). Mahwah, NJ: Erlbaum.

Lepper, M., & Henderlong, J. (2000). Turning play into work and work into play: Twenty-five years of research on intrinsic versus extrinsic motivation. In C. Sansone & J. M. Harackiewicz (Eds.), *Intrinsic and extrinsic motivation: The search for optimal motivation and performance* (pp. 257–307). San Diego: Academic Press

Maehr, M. L., & Midgley, C. (1996). *Transforming school cultures.* Boulder, CO: Westview Press.

Ryan, R. M., & Deci, E. L. (2000). Intrinsic and extrinsic motivation: Classic definitions and new directions. *Contemporary Educational Psychology, 25,* 54–67.

Wigfield, A., & Eccles, J. S. (2002). Children's motivation during the middle school years. In J. Aronson (Ed.), *Improving academic achievement: Contributions of social psychology* (pp. 159–184). San Diego: Academic Press.

5

African American Students and Literacy

Carol D. Lee

Key Points

- Historical legacies of racism continue to limit opportunities to learn for African American students.

- There has been sparse implementation of research documenting how the design of literacy instruction can scaffold the resources based on cultural practices that African American students bring to their school experiences.

- Issues with which researchers, practitioners, and policymakers must grapple revolve around race, ethnicity, language, and assumptions about poverty and resilience.

A ny examination of literacy achievement among African American K–12 students must take into account the unique history of African Americans in the United States. Were it not for this unique history, there would be no reason to focus on African American students. Americans of African descent—with the exception of more recent immigrants from the Caribbean, South America, and Africa[1]—were forcefully removed from their homelands and endured 200 years of bondage that many call the African Holocaust of Enslavement. During this holocaust, indigenous languages, religions, and familial networks were brutally banned. It was illegal for any African to learn to read or write under punishments that included chopping off hands and other inhumane acts. In defiance of this history, the first institutions developed by African Americans after the Civil War were independent schools, more than 500 of which were distributed across the South (Anderson, 1988). During the Jim Crow era that followed Reconstruction, people of African descent were segregated in every area of human life, including in schools that were woefully underfunded in comparison with schools that served white students. Under these most difficult circumstances, the segregated African American schools, particularly in the South, served as anchors for community development and empowerment (Siddle-Walker, 1996). Today, the majority of African American students receiving graduate degrees completed their undergraduate education in historically Black colleges. The legacies of this history that most directly affect African American literacy achievement fall into three areas: (a) attitudes toward African American English; (b) assumptions about Blacks' inferiority; and (c) a continuing history of under-resourced schools serving predominantly African American populations.

In this chapter, I will provide a brief overview of national trends for African American K–12 students in reading and writing; illustrate how these historical legacies continue to limit opportunities to learn for African American students; and conclude with more recent research of proactive efforts to design learning environments that build on students' strengths and result in achievement in literacy for African American students.

NATIONAL TRENDS IN LITERACY ACHIEVEMENT FOR AFRICAN AMERICAN K–12 STUDENTS

Trends on National Assessment of Educational Progress (NAEP) reading comprehension scores for 17-year-olds document gaps in achievement rates between African American students and their White counterparts. The achievement gap decreased significantly between 1970 and 1988, widened between 1988 and 1994, and decreased again between 1994 and 1999, although it never returned to the 1970 levels. Overall, African American 17-year-olds score as well as White 13-year-olds on NAEP reading assessments. Ironically, while Black students in integrated schools tend to outperform Black students in urban districts, these largely middle-class students still tend to score below their White and Asian American peers in the same school. This is reflected in differences in tracking, course taking, and grade point averages. In spite of these national trends, there are schools, districts, and states where these disparities in achievement do not occur. Information on these schools is available at the Education Trust website (http://www.edtrust.org). The examples that counter national trends highlight the importance of variables that directly affect achievement, including quality of instruction; preparation of teachers; school-level organizational features that sustain professional learning communities and promote nurturing relationships with students; and district and state policies that articulate high academic standards aligned with rigorous assessments, as well as generative supports for professional development.

HISTORICAL LEGACIES LIMITING OPPORTUNITIES TO LEARN

The historical legacies of racism that continue to limit opportunities to learn for African American students are

1. Attitudes toward African American English;
2. Assumptions about Blacks' inferiority;
3. A continuing history of under-resourced schools serving predominantly African American populations.

The inequitable distribution of resources in such schools is perhaps most evident in teachers' qualifications and in forms of tracking. Particularly in large urban districts, schools with histories of low achievement serving largely low-income communities are likely to have a significant proportion of African American students. Studies have shown that such schools are most likely to have teachers who are not certified, and that certification levels of teachers do affect achievement. The gross differences in the quality of instruction based on tracking practices and an overall culture of low expectations have been well documented (Oakes, 1990). Teachers' expectations are often triggered by attitudes toward African American English.

A majority of African Americans speak some version of African American English (AAE). The issue of language is central to literacy because language is the medium of literate activities, whether they are oral or written. The recent debate over the decision of the school board in Oakland, California, to highlight explicit instruction regarding AAE sparked enormous controversy. While the Linguistic Society of America put forth a resolution on the Oakland Ebonics issue,[2] the popular media, bolstered by prominent African Americans such as Jesse Jackson (who ironically is known for his masterly use of the African American rhetorical tradition), battered the Oakland board into submission. Linguists have long documented the systematic nature of AAE (Mufwene, Rickford, Bailey, & Baugh, 1998), asserting that differences in valuations of language varieties arise from politics rather than from any inherent superiority or inferiority among the languages themselves. However, differential access to instruction has often been attributed to assumptions that AAE is an inferior language variety. During the 1970s, dialect readers were developed under the false assumption that speakers of African American English Vernacular (AAEV) had difficulty learning to decode because of differences in the phonological systems of AAEV and Academic English (Wolfram, Adger, & Christian, 1999). Under the premise that African American students were restricted in their vocabulary and syntax, direct instruction in the form of commercial programs such as DISTAR provided explicit instruction in vocabulary, syntactical patterns, and decoding to meet the presumed deficits of African American students. That legacy of direct instruction continues today in many districts serving large proportions of African American students from low-income communities. Studies of an activity structure in kindergarten and first-grade classrooms called Sharing Time (Michaels, 1981) documented how some White teachers were unable to provide support for African American students whose oral storytelling styles differed from that of their White peers in the classrooms. Michaels identified the oral stories of the African American students as topic-associative and that of the White students as topic-centered. Subsequent research has documented a wider array of storytelling styles among African American students (Champion, 2003), including a larger proportion of Black students employing the topic-centered style, especially as they move through the grades. Cazden (2001) followed up the sharing time studies, examining how assumptions about language influenced evaluations of students.

Other studies have documented how teachers make negative evaluations of students based on how the students use language that differs from Academic English (Ball & Farr, 2003).

Assumptions about Blacks' inferiority are related to attitudes about AAE and are revealed in low expectations by teachers and institutionally by school districts. These attitudes are further confounded by class. According to 2002 U.S. Census Bureau data, 30% of African American children live in poverty. Any combination of these overt markers—language, color, class—can trigger stereotypes and, consequently, low expectations. Unfortunately, particular combinations of these markers can trigger low expectations from teachers of all racial, ethnic, and class backgrounds. These triggers, particularly language and class, can be very important in the teaching of reading and writing. Language use and world knowledge acquired are the result of experiences that are clearly influenced by class. Both language and world knowledge are central to acts of reading comprehension and composing. In reading instruction, text selection can influence the demands of syntactic knowledge, vocabulary knowledge, and relevant world knowledge. In a 1972 paper presented at the annual meeting of American Psychological Association, Williams and Rivers (1972) found that when the vocabulary was changed to reflect the experiences of Black students, Blacks scored as well as White middle-class children on whom the assessment was standardized. In 1975, Hall and colleagues tested "the effects of racial group membership and dialect on unstructured and probed recall for comprehension of simple stories" (as cited in Hall & Guthrie, 1980, p. 444). They found that "whites performed better than blacks in SE [Standard English]; blacks performed better than whites in VBE [Vernacular Black English]; blacks tested in VBE were equivalent to whites tested in SE; and whites performed better in SE than in VBE" (Hall & Guthrie, 1980, p. 445). Also, a number of studies conducted by the Center for the Study of Reading demonstrated the clear influence of prior knowledge on reading comprehension, including the ways that cultural knowledge can enhance or constrain comprehension (see Lee, 1993, for a review of these studies). Since prior knowledge is such a strong predictor of comprehension, teachers should select texts for which students have significant prior knowledge in the early stages of comprehension instruction. Additionally, teachers should spend significant time in building prior knowledge when teaching texts that are remote from students' experiences. Such an approach can strongly impact students' abilities to develop as independent and competent readers.

INVESTIGATING LEARNING AMONG AFRICAN AMERICAN STUDENTS: THREE ASSUMPTIONS

One can investigate successful learning environments to support literacy learning among African American students from at least three points of view. The first assumes that generically good instruction will benefit African American students. The second assumes that because nearly a third of African American youngsters currently live in poverty, instruction that has proved successful with low-income students will also benefit African American students. The third assumes that because African Americans are a culturally distinct group, culturally responsive teaching will be most beneficial. I agree and take issue with each of these positions.

1. *Generically Good Instruction Will Benefit African American Students*

Generically exemplary literacy instruction can be characterized by the following:

   a. Explicit instruction that addresses decoding and fluency; vocabulary; comprehension strategies, including metacognitive monitoring; general linguistic knowledge (including syntax and grammar); and rich topical knowledge applicable to content area reading;[3]
   b. Students' reading widely across a broad array of genres and topics;
   c. Students' writing widely across subject matters and genres;
   d. Alignment with rigorous standards and external assessments;
   e. Application of literacy skills in contexts that help students understand the usefulness of such skills beyond the classroom, with the aim of socializing lifelong competent readers and writers; and
   f. Meaningful feedback that allows students to understand their areas of weakness and strength in ways that can facilitate continued learning.

What these attributes will look like will differ by grade level. In particular, content area reading at the secondary level in its most rigorous instantiation requires distinct competencies for reading and writing according to disciplinary requirements (Alvermann & Moore, 1991). Reviews of research in reading comprehension by several national panels of experts have affirmed these characteristics of effective literacy instruction (National Reading Panel, 2000; Snow, 2002). In addition, NAEP surveys have consistently found positive correlations between many of these features of good instruction and achievement. Thus, there is every reason to believe that instruction so characterized will be effective with African American students. At the same time, the devil is in the details. In many schools serving low-income African American students in particular, explicit instruction has been mandated as scripted lessons in what is known as Direct Instruction. Direct Instruction has its roots in the early 1970s with the DISTAR program, which was based on studies claiming that speakers of AAEV spoke an inferior language that interfered with their ability to both decode and comprehend. While Direct Instruction has proved very successful in achieving basic skills, there is little evidence to support the claim that it is effective in promoting more complex, rigorous, and nuanced literacy achievement. The evidence is complicated in part by the fact that most of the assessments used to measure the effects of Direct Instruction are basic skills tests.

A second caveat to the claim that generically good instruction is sufficient comes from studies that look at differences in achievement between African American and White students in middle-class, suburban, integrated school districts. The recently formed Minority Student Achievement Network (http://www.msanetwork.org) has taken on the task of trying to understand this phenomenon in suburban districts across the country and to initiate efforts to eliminate this gap. In these districts, where schoolwide achievement scores are generally well above national averages, one assumes that literacy instruction on the whole reflects the generically effective characteristics outlined. If this is the case, then a question arises: Why does this race achievement gap continue? A number of studies by Ronald Ferguson (2002) of Harvard University point to interesting and nuanced possible explanations. On the whole, African American students are less likely to be enrolled in honors and advanced placement classes; they have lower grade point averages; and they report questions about teachers' expectations. These findings are most pronounced for African American males. They suggest that African American students in these schools, especially males, do not experience the same instruction as their mainstream classmates, perceive their teachers as less receptive to them, and appear not to socialize with higher-achieving students who are often in honors-level track courses. There is more to instruction than pedagogical strategies and content. The perceptions of both students and teachers influence the sense each makes of his or her joint activity and the efforts each puts forth.

2. *Effective Instruction for Low-Income Students Will Benefit African American Students*

The second point of view is that instruction that is effective with low-income students will be effective with African American students who are concentrated in large urban districts. The assumptions about literacy instruction and poverty assert that students living in low-income communities enter school with fewer language resources; less intellectual stimulation in the home for literacy tasks; and greater cognitive, developmental, and emotional challenges, which make instruction difficult. This was the reasoning behind the development of Head Start: the belief that a rich preschool experience could compensate for deficits in the home and neighborhoods as children entered school. Socioeconomic status is consistently among the strongest predictors of achievement in literacy in the United States. To wrestle with these assumptions, I refer to the work of Margaret Beale Spencer.

Spencer posits the Phenomenological Variant of Ecological Systems Theory, or PVEST. She argues that many students—including ethnic and racial minorities and low-resource families—face dual sources of risk. First, they struggle with the normal psychosocial developmental tasks that all humans face

(Spencer, 1999). They simultaneously face additional sources of risk because of racism and other forms of social stigmatization. How they experience these dual sources of risk depends on the balance between the nature of the risks themselves and the quality of the social experiences in their immediate environments (family, classrooms, peer social networks, etc.). It is the perception of risk, and the available supports to help one cope with the risks, that determine overall resiliency or lack thereof, as well as overall identity processes in life course development. This is a fundamentally different view from one purporting that the poor are inherently and inevitably at risk and characterized largely by deficits to be overcome by school. The broad findings from research on Head Start highlight the pivotal role played by school—and, by extension, by the proximal socialization that takes place in the face-to-face interactions inside classrooms. Due in part to methodological differences, the short-term findings on the effects of Head Start are mixed, but overall the program has proved effective in promoting literacy achievement from preschool through the primary grades. However, there is little evidence of its long-term impact past the third or fourth grade. I assert that this is so in part because instruction within the primary grades is more closely aligned with the instruction students would have received in an early childhood program such as Head Start. Beyond fourth grade, the content of reading to learn becomes more specialized. The demands of such literacy tasks are fundamentally different. In particular, the role of prior knowledge in reading to learn in the content areas is extremely important. The emphasis in primary grades is on reading narratives; thus, students may become fluent with the syntax, vocabulary, and knowledge of human goals and attendant actions that characterize the world of personal narratives—that is, reading for personal reasons. However, they may not be prepared for the syntax, vocabulary, and specialized kinds of prior knowledge required when reading to learn concepts in the sciences, social studies, and mathematics. The content of reading in the subject matters in the upper elementary grades and high school becomes more and more specialized, more remote from the everyday lives of students. As students progress into the upper elementary grades and high school, the following problems intensify the risks underachieving and low-income African American students face: increased complexity in the demands of reading, the long history of a school culture of low expectations, and teachers' limited knowledge about the teaching of reading in their disciplines, particularly reading comprehension. This spiral of problems increases the likelihood of student disengagement and teacher frustration.

Nevertheless, there is clear evidence that schools can "beat the odds." In a national sample of middle and high schools serving largely low-income students and significant proportions of students of color, Langer (2001) found that schools outperformed district achievement when teachers and curriculum developers in literacy instruction did the following:

- Fostered integrated skills across units of instruction that were intellectually coherent and rigorous;

- Provided students with multiple opportunities to learn, to apply key concepts, and to understand the strategies and self-monitoring needed for both reading and writing; and
- Aligned their instruction to high-stakes assessments but did not engage in long, scripted test preparation.

The Consortium on Chicago School Research (Byrk, Nagaoka, & Newmann, 2000) found positive relationships between the rigor of work assigned and the quality of students' work in Chicago public schools, a system that serves largely low-income African American and Latino students. Unfortunately, the consortium also found that rigorous assignments were not typically assigned in the schools it studied. In a similar vein, small schools in New York that promote intimate and responsive relationships among students, faculty, staff, and parents have shown strong gains in achievement in reading (Ancess, 2003). These schools serve largely low-income African American and Latino student populations. In these schools, teachers work collaboratively in instructional planning that makes the demands of literacy tasks explicit and involves students in authentic work that extends beyond the classroom. Advisory structures include both academic and social counseling, including tutoring. The use of portfolios socializes students into reflecting on the quality of work and the processes or "habits of mind" they engage to carry out their work. The importance of high expectations and supportive relationships with teachers has also been found in studies of teachers who are successful with African American students (Foster, 1997; Ladson-Billings, 1994).

In reading, two problems surface as major transition points and areas where African American students often face many challenges: (a) the transition into learning to read; and (b) the transition to secondary school, where reading to learn is the norm. For African American children who are AAEV speakers and who live in low-income communities, the problems of learning to read have been identified in two areas. One deals with decoding issues that may arise for AAEV speakers. The second involves issues of prior knowledge of topics and of vocabulary.

Learning to Read. Decoding issues can involve phonemes that are captured in the written code but are either not articulated or are articulated in different ways by AAEV speakers. Past-tense markers such as /ed/ may be deleted from oral speech. Problematic phonemes may include consonants, particularly initial and final. For example, an AAEV speaker may pronounce *told* as *toll, mist* as *miss*. Words ending in /th/ are likely to be pronounced as if they end in /f/. These questions were debated hotly in the 1970s (Hall & Guthrie, 1980; Wolfram et al., 1999). However, overall conclusions of that research were that children from many English dialect communities wrestled with these problems in early reading, and that the differences between written code and spoken code were not determining factors in students' abilities to learn to read. In fact, part of the process of learning to read in English for all children involves reconciling differences between the phonetic code and the oral code. Some of the studies involving what were called dialect readers, however, also introduced the second variable of prior knowledge and vocabulary. That is, they explored how reading comprehension is facilitated when students read texts for which they have significant prior knowledge and vocabulary. Several studies highlight interesting findings that, unfortunately, have not been widely addressed since the initial studies. As discussed earlier, Williams and Rivers (1972) found that on texts with familiar vocabulary, African American students comprehended comparably to their middle-class White counterparts. Hall, Reder, and Cole (1975) found that the race of the interviewer, the language of the interview, and the language of the story accounted for similarities and differences between the story recall of African American and White students.

Reading to Learn. The transition to reading to learn specialized content in secondary schools is a second critical area for African American students and others. It is critical in part because the data clearly show that the longer African American students remain in school, the further they lag behind their White counterparts, and in part because the demands of reading in the content areas at the secondary level are highly specialized and very different from the work of reading in elementary schools. That is, the typical student who enters high school as a struggling reader faces a range of decoding problems that does not compare with those of students entering school as non-readers. They are apples and oranges. The Strategic Literacy Project (Greenleaf, Schoenbach, Cziko, & Mueller, 2001) has designed instruction to address the needs of struggling readers who enter high school. In large urban districts, many of these will be African American students. For struggling adolescent readers, problems of prior knowledge and vocabulary become more acute. Concepts in the academic disciplines are often counterintuitive, and forms of argumentation are complex and discipline-specific. For example, reading in science often involves specialized vocabulary in which even everyday words take on specialized meanings (for example, *fruit, dark matter*). Data to support claims in scientific texts often involve mathematical representations and illustrations. Reading primary documents in history involves systematic ways of questioning authenticity.

The challenges that many African American students face when they enter high school are complicated by a number of factors. First, few urban school districts have systems in place to address the needs of such students. Most high school teachers are not trained to diagnose reading difficulties or to teach reading. Second, the normative response in schools and districts serving large numbers of low-income African American students is to raise accountability standards through testing, without comparable intensive efforts to improve the quality of instruction. In many districts, these efforts take the form of scripted lessons and defined courses of study that emphasize rote learning of facts over conceptual understanding and authentic displays of deep reasoning. The routines of instruction socialize students in terms of what literacy means. Rosa, a student from the Strategic Literacy Project, captures the kinds of instructional routines that many African American students and others face:

Um, usually in, like, a regular history class, like the one I had last year? Which was just pretty much all writing? Okay, "read from page so-n-so to so-n-so, answer the red square questions and the unit questions and turn them in." And he corrects them and says, "You did this wrong, you did this right. Okay, here you go." And that was pretty much the basic way every single day was gone. So, from day one to the end of the year, that's pretty much all we did. Answer the red square questions. And pretty much it's been like that since I got to middle school. (Greenleaf et al., 2001, p. 101)

The Strategic Literacy Project designed a special reading course for struggling high school readers that presents explicit comprehension strategies, emphasizing the importance of reading as an effort to make sense, and builds vocabulary and requisite prior knowledge to help students read across subject matters and genres within them. Surveys indicate that, in addition to gains in reading comprehension scores, students double the number of books they read over the year. In one example, the same student, Rosa, explains her thinking processes while reading: "I guess I'd have to start by the title. And them, un, just try to relate the first paragraph, second paragraph . . . [b]ecause it usually explains it in the first paragraph and it just goes on from there" (Greenleaf et al., 2001, p. 102).

3. *Culturally Responsive Instruction Will Benefit African American Students*

The third assumption regarding effective environments for literacy instruction for African American students is based on the assertion that African American culture is unique. This assertion is best interrogated by examining different ways of thinking about culture. The most ecologically valid explanation is that African American culture is both unique and diverse. It is unique—or, at least, bounded—in the sense that people of African descent in the United States have maintained cultural practices that are influenced by their African cultural ancestry (Holloway, 1990). These practices include ways of using language—phonological features, syntactical features, rhetorical features, and speech genres (Mufwene et al., 1998; Smitherman, 2000); ways of structuring musical and dance forms; practices in religious worship; and the social structure of families and intergenerational relationships. These adaptations are historically African (particularly West African) but also represent the unique ways that people of African descent adapted to the historical and contemporary circumstances of their experiences in the United States. African American culture is also diverse in the sense that differences based on generational cohort, developmental age, region, class, and immigrant status (e.g., more recent immigrants from the Caribbean, South America, and Africa) shape different cultural practices. Educators should not assume that all members of an ethnic group equally share in the cultural practices of a community. Instructional decisions should be made based on actual investigation of the routine cultural practices of students. Thus, teachers should assume a critical lens toward blanket instructional approaches based on the presumed learning styles of all African American students. In the examples that follow, culturally responsive instructional design is instead based on observed routine practices of African American students, in some cases defining for whom the design is relevant.

Cultural Modeling is an analytic framework for designing learning environments that makes generative connections between subject matter and students' funds of knowledge constructed within their families, communities, and peer social networks (Lee, 1993, 1995, 2001). While the framework is applicable across subject matter and across ethnic, racial, and language communities, all of the empirical work to date has focused on African American students and literacy. Cultural Modeling calls for a careful analysis of generative tasks within the subject matter. It also calls for analyses of the routine practices of students to determine where they may engage in similar modes of reasoning or with concepts that may be analogies, naive theories, or misconceptions that are relevant to the academic tasks. In addition, Cultural Modeling calls for designing instructional conversations that reflect community-based norms for talk while socializing students into disciplinary norms of reasoning and argumentation. In the domain of response to literature, Lee has identified core categories of problems that readers will face in reading literary works across genres and national literatures. These include interpretive problems such as symbolism, irony, satire, and use of unreliable narration; plot configurations such as mysteries, science fiction, magical realism, allegories, and fables; and character types such as the trickster, the epic hero, and the picaresque hero. The field of English education has not done very much to identify strategies for recognizing these problem types, for using knowledge of these problem types to make predictions and test hypotheses, and for reconstructing inferred meanings beyond the literal. Because of this, in the arena of response to literature it is important to articulate what it means to make explicit to students what Delpit (1986) refers to as the knowledge of power. Delpit speaks of conveying knowledge of ways to use language, particularly in writing instruction, rather than simply assuming that students will somehow construct such understandings through inquiry-based instruction, including the traditional approaches to teaching the writing process that Delpit explicitly critiques. Through what I call metacognitive instructional conversations, and through modeling and sequencing texts, Cultural Modeling makes explicit interpretive strategies for response to literature, drawing on cultural funds of knowledge that many African American students bring to the classroom—funds that have not only traditionally gone untapped, but that in fact have been demonized as deficits to be overcome rather than viewed as resources to be used to scaffold instruction and learning.

This process begins with the organization of units of instruction, the sequencing of texts, and the design of instructional conversations. Units of instruction are organized around interpretive problems, such as symbolism, irony, or satire. This focus provides students with repeated opportunities to apply strategies and to recognize generative patterns in literature. Within each unit, cultural data sets are identified. Cultural data sets are texts, broadly speaking, that students meet in everyday routine practices, the interpretation of which requires the same modes of reasoning as the canonical texts they will meet in the units of instruction. For example, in a unit on symbolism, rap lyrics where symbolism is central become texts for investigation. The focus of metacognitive instructional conversations is to help students make public the strategies that they use tacitly. For example, in a unit on symbolism, students interrogate the symbolism of the mask in the lyrics to the song "The Mask" by the Fugees. No student thinks that any of the characters in the lyrics—workers at Burger King, a friend from Lauryn Hill's old neighborhood—are literally wearing physical masks. They all understand that the mask stands for something. The quality of reasoning that students demonstrate from the very beginning of instruction is complex and rigorous and analogous to the reasoning they will employ with canonical texts that follow (Lee, 2001). The anchor text in the symbolism unit was Toni Morrison's *Beloved,* an extraordinarily complicated novel that is replete with symbolism. Students whose standardized reading scores fell largely in the bottom quartile tackled with vigor and nuance the many challenges this award-winning novel posed from the very beginning of instruction. In Cultural Modeling, texts are sequenced not only according to the kinds of interpretive problems they pose, but also according to the social codes on which characters operate. This means that all of the texts in a unit of instruction will pose comparable interpretive problems. With African American students, the initial texts will be African American texts, where we have reason to assume they are likely to have relevant social knowledge of the subjunctive social worlds of the texts. This approach involves a definition of genre that if different from the typical definition in high school literature curricula and standard literature anthologies. Test data from the Cultural Modeling Project at Fairgate High School show that students who have historically been underachievers demonstrate advanced literary reasoning with very difficult canonical texts across literary traditions. Similar approaches drawing on youth culture have been carried out by Jabari Mahiri of the University of California at Berkeley, Ernest Morell of Michigan State University, and Shuaib Meacham of the University of Delaware.

Studies have also documented ways that cultural knowledge has been taken up in the composing processes of African American students. Ball (1992) has documented preferences identified by African American adolescents for patterns in expository writing. These patterns include narrative interspersion and circumlocution. These patterns differ from the classic patterns taught in school, such as comparison–contrast and problem–solution. These rhetorical patterns are also used by political and religious African American orators. While these patterns were not being taught, the African American students in Ball's sample employed them in their expository writing and were able to identify the patterns they used. In a related body of work, Smitherman (2000) has identified what she calls the African American Rhetorical Tradition. In a study of 867 writing samples of African American students from National Assessments of Educational Progress of 1984 and 1988–89, Smitherman analyzed expository and narrative writing for the presence of African American rhetorical features. Smitherman found a positive correlation between the presence of these features and higher ratings by NAEP scorers. She also discovered that the use of AAEV syntax decreased over the years, and that the African American students in the NAEP samples performed better in narrative writing. Drawing on Smitherman's work, Lee (Lee, Rosenfeld, Mendenhall, Rivers & Tynes, in press) designed a Cultural Modeling intervention in narrative writing with third- and sixth-grade African American students. Using pictures that characterized typical scripts in African American life, storytelling by African American storytellers, and oral narratives situated in the African American rhetorical tradition performed in films such as the adaptation of August Wilson's *The Piano,* these students produced written narratives that creatively used African American rhetorical features. Based on primary trait scoring, the overall ratings were high. Consistent with arguments made by others (see Ball & Farr, 2003, for a review), the incorporation of rhetorical features of African American English discourse appear to enhance the quality of written composition in both narrative and expository genres. Ball (1999) offers a comprehensive overview of research on evaluations of the composition of African American students. The overall recommendations conclude that, with proper support, language variation—including African American English—can be a valuable resource to support writing instruction.

CONCLUSION

This chapter has tried to place the questions about environments to support literacy learning among African American students in their historical context, taking a critical stance on three core assumptions that have driven instructional planning for African American students. There is long-standing research evidence that race, language, and class have severely restricted opportunities to learn for African American students. Responses to these historical and contemporary trends have varied (Ball, 2002), with some of these trends reviewed in this chapter. There is also significant research documenting how the design of literacy instruction can scaffold the resources based on cultural practices that African American students bring to their experiences in schools (Ball, 2002; Ladson-Billings, 1994; Lee, 1993, 1995). However, the application of these findings in public schools has been sparse. Considering the continued achievement gap in reading and writing for African American students, the implications for teachers' preparation and ongoing professional development, textbook design, curriculum design, assessment, and public policy are grave. The most central areas with which researchers, practitioners, and policymakers must grapple revolve around race, ethnicity, language, and assumptions about poverty and resilience. These are enduring and difficult questions that go to the heart of cultural worldviews in the United States.

NOTES

1. It is important to note that people of African descent in the Caribbean and South America share with African Americans a history of forced enslavement, and that most African countries have a similar history in terms of colonial occupation by European countries.
2. The College Composition and Communication Conference of the National Council of Teachers of English took a position in 1974 supporting students' rights to use their own language.
3. By explicit instruction I do not mean scripted instruction. Rather, I mean instruction that uses a variety of methods to make strategies, norms, and modes of reasoning public.

SUGGESTIONS FOR FURTHER READING

Gasden, V., & Wagner, D. (Eds.). (1995). *Literacy among African-American youth: Issues in learning, teaching and schooling.* Cresskill, NJ: Hampton Press.

Irvine, J., & York, D. E. (1995). Learning styles and culturally diverse students: A literature review. In J. Banks & C. M. Banks (Eds.), *Handbook of research on multicultural education* (pp. 484–497). New York: Macmillan.

Lee, C. D. (1997). Bridging home and school literacies: A model of culturally responsive teaching. In J. Flood, S. B. Heath, & D. Lapp (Eds.), *A handbook for literacy educators: Research on teaching the communicative and visual arts* (pp. 330–341). New York: Macmillan.

Lee, C. D., & Slaughter-Defoe, D. (1995). African American education. In J. Banks & C. Banks (Eds.), *Handbook of multicultural education.* New York: Macmillan.

Perry, T., & Delpit, L. (Eds.). (1998). *The real Ebonics debate: Power, language and the education of African-American children.* Boston: Beacon Press.

REFERENCES

Alvermann, D., & Moore, D. (1991). Secondary school reading. In R. Barr, M. Kamil, P. Mosenthal, & P. D. Pearson (Eds.), *Handbook of reading research: Vol. II* (pp. 951–983). New York: Longman.

Ancess, J. (2003). *Beating the odds: High schools as communities of commitment.* New York: Teachers College Press.

Anderson, J. D. (1988). *The education of Blacks in the south, 1860–1935.* Chapel Hill: University of North Carolina Press.

Ball, A. F. (1992). Cultural preferences and the expository writing of African-American adolescents. *Written Communication, 9*(4), 501–532.

Ball, A. F. (1999). Evaluating the writing of culturally and linguistically diverse students: The case of the African American Vernacular English speaker. In C. R. Cooper & L. Odell (Eds.), Evaluating writing: The role of teachers' knowledge about text, learning, and culture (pp. 225–248). Urbana, IL: National Council of Teachers of English Press.

Ball, A. F. (2002). Three decades of research on classroom life: Illuminating the classroom communicative lives of America's at-risk students. In W. Secada (Ed.),

Review of research in education (Vol. 26, pp. 71–112). Washington, DC: American Educational Research Association.

Ball, A. F., & Farr, M. (2003). Language varieties, culture and teaching the English language arts. In J. Flood, D. Lapp, J. Squire, & J. Jensen (Eds.), *Handbook of research on teaching the English language arts* (2nd ed., pp. 435–445). Mahwah, NJ: Erlbaum.

Bryk, S., Nagaoka, J., & Newmann, F. (2000, October). *Chicago classroom demands for authentic intellectual work: Trends from 1997–1999.* Chicago: Consortium on Chicago School Reform.

Cazden, C. (2001). *Classroom discourse: The language of teaching and learning.* Portsmouth, NH: Heinemann.

Champion, T. (2003). *Understanding storytelling among African American children: A journey from Africa to America.* Mahwah, NJ: Erlbaum.

Delpit, L. (1986). Skills and other dilemmas of a progressive Black educator. *Harvard Educational Review, 56*(4), 379–385.

Ferguson, R. F. (2002). *What doesn't meet the eye: Understanding and addressing racial disparities in high-achieving suburban schools.* Oak Brook, IL: North Central Regional Educational Lab.

Foster, M. (1997). *Black teachers on teaching.* New York: The New Press.

Greenleaf, C. L., Schoenbach, R., Cziko, C., & Mueller, F. (2001). Apprenticing adolescent readers to academic literacy. *Harvard Educational Review, 71*(1), 79–129.

Hall, W., & Guthrie, L. (1980). On the dialect question and reading. In R. Spiro, B. Bruce, & W. Brewer (Eds.), *Theoretical issues in reading comprehension: Perspectives from cognitive psychology, linguistics, artificial intelligence and education* (pp. 439–450). Hillsdale, NJ: Erlbaum.

Hall, W. S., Reder, S., & Cole, M. (1975). Story recall in young Black and White children: Effects of racial group membership, race of experimenter, and dialect. *Developmental Psychology, 11,* 828–834.

Holloway, J. E. (Ed.). (1990). *Africanisms in American culture.* Bloomington: Indiana University Press.

Ladson-Billings, G. (1994). *The dreamkeepers.* San Francisco: Jossey-Bass.

Langer, J. A. (2001). Beating the odds: Teaching middle and high school students to read and write well. *American Educational Research Journal, 38*(4), 837–880.

Lee, C. D. (1993). *Signifying as a scaffold for literary interpretation: The pedagogical implications of an African American discourse genre* (Research Report Series). Urbana, IL: National Council of Teachers of English.

Lee, C. D. (1995). A culturally based cognitive apprenticeship: Teaching African American high school students skills in literary interpretation. *Reading Research Quarterly, 30*(4), 608–631.

Lee, C. D. (2001). Is October Brown Chinese: A cultural modeling activity system for underachieving students. *American Educational Research Journal, 38*(1), 97–142.

Lee, C. D., Rosenfeld, E., Mendenhall, R., Rivers, A., & Tynes, B. (in press). *Cultural modeling as a framework for narrative analysis.* In C. Dauite & C. Lightfoot (Eds.), *Narrative analysis: Studying the development of individuals in society.* Thousand Oaks, CA: Sage Publications.

Mahiri, J. (2000, December). Pop culture, pedagogy and the end(s) of school. *Journal of Adolescent & Adult Literacy, 44*(4), 382–386.

Meacham, S. (2001, Summer). Vygotsky and the blues: Re-reading cultural connections and conceptual development. *Theory into Practice, 40*(3), 190–198.

Michaels, S. (1981). "Sharing time": Children's narrative styles and differential access to literacy. *Language in Society, 10,* 423–442.

Morrell, E., & Duncan-Andrade, J. (2002, July). Promoting academic literacy with urban youth through engaging hip-hop culture. *English Journal, 91*(6), 88–93.

Mufwene, S. S., Rickford, J. R., Bailey, G., & Baugh, J. (1998). *African-American English: Structure, history, and use.* New York: Routledge.

National Reading Panel. (2000). *Teaching children to read: An evidence based assessment of the scientific research literature and its implications for reading instruction.* (NIH Publication No. 00-4769). Washington, DC: U.S. Government Printing Office.

Oakes, J. (1990). *Multiplying inequalities: The effects of race, social class and tracking on opportunities to learn mathematics and science.* Santa Monica, CA: RAND Corporation.

Siddle-Walker, E. V. (1996). *Their highest potential: An African American school community in the segregated south.* Chapel Hill: University of North Carolina Press.

Smitherman, G. (2000). African American student writers in the NAEP, 1969–1988/89, and "The blacker the berry, the sweeter the juice." In G. Smitherman, *Talkin that talk: Language, culture and education in African America* (pp. 163–194). New York: Routledge.

Snow, C. (2002). *Reading for understanding: Toward a research and development program in reading comprehension.* (Report of the RAND Reading Research Study Group). Arlington, VA: RAND Corporation.

Spencer, M. (1999). Social and cultural influences on school adjustment: The application of an identity-focused cultural ecological perspective. *Educational Psychologist, 34*(1), 43–57.

Williams, R., & Rivers, W. (1972). *Mismatches in testing from Black English.* Paper presented at the meeting of the American Psychological Association, Honolulu, HI.

Wolfram, W., Adger, C., & Christian, D. (1999). *Dialects in schools and communities.* Mahwah, NJ: Erlbaum.

6

Improving Literacy Skills of At-Risk Adolescents

A Schoolwide Response

Donald D. Deshler, Jean B. Schumaker, and Susan K. Woodruff

Key Points

- A five-level conceptual framework for literacy instruction includes strategies implemented by both general education teachers and supporting specialists.
- Effective literacy instruction is responsive, systematic, and intensive.
- Implementation of the conceptual framework in Muskegon High School resulted in substantial performance gains.

Secondary education is filled with a long list of challenges for both teachers and administrators: creating an environment in which students feel safe, aligning curriculum offerings with state outcome examinations, maintaining an engaging array of extracurricular offerings in times of growing budget constraints . . . and the list goes on. High on this list is the challenge of finding sufficient time to teach the necessary literacy skills to those adolescents who failed to acquire the skills during their elementary years—especially in light of the large amounts of subject matter that must be taught and mastered in each core curricular area.

Figure 6.1 depicts the fact that during the elementary grades, the primary goal of general and remedial education is largely the same. Namely, teachers spend most of their time instructing basic literacy skills to their students (this is especially the case in kindergarten through third grade). If students struggle with mastering these competencies in their general education classes, and remedial assistance is tapped (e.g., remedial reading, special education, etc.), the goal associated with remedial programs is largely the same as the prevailing goal associated with general education: the acquisition of basic literacy skills. However, during the secondary grades, the primary instructional goal associated with general education typically turns to the mastery of critical subject matter. Regrettably, many of the students who struggle with the mastery of subject matter often do so because of a deficiency in foundational literacy skills. Unlike the elementary years, however, when remedial assistance

		Acquisition of Literacy Skills	Acquisition of Subject Matter
Elementary Grades	General Education	X	
	Remedial Education	X	
Secondary Grades	General Education		X
	Remedial Education	X	

FIGURE 6.1. Primary instructional goals across grades.

is sought, the goals of general and remedial education tend to diverge; the focus of general education is subject matter mastery, and the focus of remedial education is literacy acquisition.

The difference in the instructional goals associated with general and remedial education across the elementary and secondary grades has significant instructional implications. As shown in Figure 6.2, because of the similarity of the instructional goals associated with general and remedial education in the elementary grades, there can be considerable overlap in terms of planning and instruction across teachers and settings. If students receive remedial instruction, that instruction can be easily tied to what is being taught in general education classes. In fact, co-teaching arrangements in which remedial and general education teachers work together in the same classroom are quite common. Inasmuch as each teacher is focusing on the acquisition of literacy competencies, there can be a great deal of overlap in conceptualizing and implementing instructional programs.

In contrast, since instructional goals are quite divergent during the secondary grades, general and remedial education teachers have little in common. Because of the high demands on general education teachers to cover large amounts of subject matter, there is very little, if any, time available to them to teach literacy skills. Hence, remedial and general education teachers tend to be more separate than related in what they teach and how they work with students. Not surprisingly, there is little joint planning and coordination between what takes place in general education courses, where subject matter coverage dominates, and what occurs in remedial classes, where literacy tends to be the focus of instruction. In the process, students who have literacy skill deficits struggle in their subject matter classes because of those deficits, and they do not benefit fully from their remedial instruction because the skills and strategies that they are taught in those settings are not sufficiently tied to the demands of their subject matter courses.

In short, teachers and administrators in secondary schools face enormous challenges with regard to helping at-risk students. Clearly, these students need

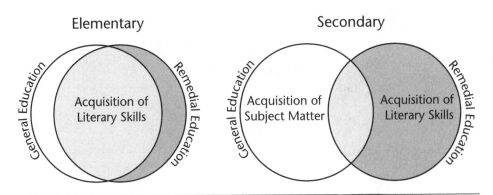

FIGURE 6.2. Relationship of goals.

a sophisticated array of literacy skills in order to succeed in subject matter courses. But because of the shortage of time available to them to learn the skills and strategies that should have been mastered earlier in their school careers, at-risk students struggle in their content classes and, if they stay in school, earn barely passing grades (Hock & Deshler, 2003). More often than not, the instruction that they receive in remedial settings fails to put them in a position to respond successfully to instruction in the general education classroom. As a result, they often are not even enrolled in rigorous general education courses when they enter high school (Schumaker, Deshler, Bulgren, Davis, Lenz, & Grossen, 2002).

The purpose of this chapter is to describe methods that teachers can use to respond to these challenges. First, a conceptual framework for providing literacy instruction in secondary schools, called the Content Literacy Continuum, will be introduced. Second, a set of instructional practices that have been found to promote growth in literacy skills and strategies by at-risk adolescents will be described. Third, a secondary literacy program that is based on the Content Literacy Continuum and the instructional practices will be highlighted. Simultaneously, summaries of student outcome data resulting from this program will be presented.

THE CONTENT LITERACY CONTINUUM— A FRAMEWORK FOR LITERACY INSTRUCTION

The conceptual framework for literacy instruction to be described in this chapter is an optimistic vision of what at-risk adolescents can learn and accomplish. It is based on the notion that adolescents who lack basic literacy skills can learn these skills if they have intensive, focused, and sustained instruction that helps them catch up with their peers. It is also based on the idea that these students need to participate in the general education curriculum so they do not fall behind their peers in content knowledge. Enrolling these students in watered-down courses or in study halls can be counterproductive to helping them eventually succeed because of the content instruction that they miss. In addition, the conceptual framework is based on the notion of shared responsibility for literacy instruction. These students are most likely to realize significant outcomes when a large majority of teachers and administrators feels a sense of responsibility for their literacy competence (Deshler, Schumaker, Lenz, Bulgren, Hock, Knight, & Ehren, 2001). In other words, enhancing the literacy performance of at-risk adolescents occurs when ownership of the problem is shared and when deliberate steps are taken to coordinate instruction across teachers and classes. Finally, the conceptual framework takes into account the idea that individual students have different needs. Because of the broad array of students' needs and the complexity of the problems presented by adolescents with poor literacy skills, no single program or approach can possibly meet the needs of all. Certain students will need more individualized, explicit, intensive instruction of basic reading skills, while other students will need opportunities to practice fluency and comprehension skills within the context of their general education assignments. Others might need tutoring in before- and after-school achievement centers. In short, students must receive instruction appropriate to their needs and literacy development levels (Hock, Schumaker, & Deshler, 1999).

Thus, the conceptual framework for literacy instruction provides a structure for: (a) how secondary teachers and administrators can see their roles with regard to promoting literacy skills; (b) how basic literacy skills can be taught as a part of the secondary school curriculum; (c) how instruction can be coordinated and responsibilities can be shared across settings within a school; and (d) how individual students' needs can be met. This framework, developed by Lenz and Ehren (1999) at the University of Kansas Center for Research in Learning, is known as the Content Literacy Continuum because it has five levels of literacy support, representing a continuum of educational services that can be used in secondary schools (see Figure 6.3). The various levels in this continuum emphasize the importance of infusing literacy instruction throughout the secondary school curriculum *and* of requiring a host of secondary teachers with different types of expertise to address the broad array

Level 1	Ensuring mastery of critical content in all subject area classes
Level 2	Weaving learning strategy instruction within rigorous general education classes
Level 3	Supporting mastery of learning strategies for targeted strategies
Level 4	Developing intensive instructional options for students who lack foundational skills
Level 5	Developing intensive clinical options for language intervention

FIGURE 6.3. Content literacy continuum.

of literacy needs presented by adolescents. In addition, because the challenges facing adolescents with literacy problems are so significant, intervention outside the school day is warranted. Hence, this continuum includes provisions for before- and after-school tutoring programs. The major outcome associated with the Content Literacy Continuum is that students will attain appropriate achievement standards on state assessment tests and demonstrate real-world content literacy. The levels of the continuum (Hock & Deshler, in press) are described in the following sections.

Level 1: Ensuring Mastery of Critical Content in Rigorous Subject Area Classes

Level 1 literacy instruction takes place in general education subject area courses. Because adolescents with poor literacy skills typically have great difficulty understanding much of the content taught in their classes, they need a special kind of instruction to acquire the core knowledge they are expected to learn. To that end, general education teachers participating in Level 1 use teaching methods and devices that help students better understand and remember the content being taught. The use of such tools as graphic organizers, prompted outlines, structured reviews, guided discussions, and active student involvement combined into special "teaching routines" have been shown to promote students' understanding and mastery of secondary content (Schumaker, Deshler, & McKnight, 2002). Thus, these teaching routines are used by Level 1 teachers to enhance their instruction. Although Level 1 interventions are designed to help students with limited levels of literacy, they also have been designed so that their use benefits *all* of the students in academically diverse classes. In other words, in order for teachers to continue to use Level 1 methods, they must see that students from low-, average-, and high-achieving groups in a class are benefiting from their use of these instructional practices.

An example of a Level 1 instructional method is the Concept Comparison Routine, which was developed by Bulgren, Schumaker, Deshler, Lenz, and Marquis (2002) to help students clearly understand the key information involved in conducting a thorough and systematic comparison of two concepts (e.g., democracy and monarchy). Many students have difficulty identifying, categorizing, and systematically comparing the relevant information related to two or more concepts. In order to help these students, a graphic device called the Comparison Table (see Figure 6.4), is associated with the routine on which students record information related to the comparison. Use of the Concept Comparison Routine and the Comparison Table not only guides students in identifying like and unlike characteristics of the concepts being compared. It also gives them structures to prompt their language to facilitate their ability to talk about and use the information derived from the comparison on assignments and tests (Bulgren, Lenz, Deshler, & Schumaker, 1995). By carefully configuring the Comparison Table to display core concepts and important attributes related to each concept, then hav-

② **Overall Concept**
ELEMENTS OF LITERATURE

C Communicate Targeted Concepts
O Obtain the Overall Concepts
M Make Lists of Known Characteristics
P Pin Down Like Characteristics
A Assemble Like Categories
R Record Unlike Characteristics
I Identify Unlike Categories
N Nail Down a Summary
G Go Beyond the Basics

① **Concept**
PLOT

① **Concept**
THEME

③ **Characteristics**

May be one or more in work of literature

Found in narrative literature

Consists of a sequence of events

Provides entertainment

③ **Characteristics**

May be one or more in work of literature

Found in a variety of literature

Consists of a statement about meaning

Delivers a message or idea

⑨ **Extensions**

Investigate the element of "style" in literature, and create a list of characteristics to be compared to plot and theme. Use this information to develop a Multiple-Concept Comparison Table.

④ **Like Characteristics**

May be one or more in a work of literature

⑤ **Like Categories**

Number

⑥ **Unlike Characteristics**

Found in narrative literature

Consists of a sequence of events

Provides entertainment

⑥ **Unlike Characteristics**

Found in a variety of literature

Consists of a statement about meaning

Delivers a message or idea

⑦ **Unlike Categories**

Location

Form

Function

⑧ **Summary**

Two elements of literature are plot and theme. They are alike in terms of number (there may be more than one plot or theme in a piece of literature). They are different in their location in literature, the form they take, and the function they serve.

FIGURE 6.4. Comparison table.

ing students use the tool to study the information, teachers can improve the test scores of students with literacy problems by an average of 17%. Of equal importance, they can also improve the performance of the average- and high-achieving students.

Level 2: Weaving Learning Strategy Instruction Within Rigorous General Education Courses

When Level 1 interventions are insufficient to affect the overall performance of students with literacy problems, teachers can use instructional methods aligned with the next level in the intervention continuum, Level 2. At this level, general education teachers incorporate instruction in selected learning strategies into their classes. Students with literacy problems often have not acquired the learning strategies they need to help them understand and remember the information being taught (e.g., they do not know how to paraphrase important chunks of information to facilitate their comprehension and recall of it; they do not know how to organize information to help them memorize it for tests; etc.). In the midst of teaching their subject matter, and on an ongoing basis, teachers using Level 2 methods look for opportunities to teach students particular strategies that will help them learn the information being taught. They explain how to use the strategy, model its use, and require students to use the strategy in relation to their content assignments. In short, the purpose of deliberately weaving strategy instruction into content instruction is to teach students "how to learn" and how to gain control over the information they are expected to master.

General education teachers can incorporate into their classes strategies for acquiring, remembering, and expressing course information. By teaching students strategies that are directly relevant to the demands of their courses, they are shifting the instructional emphasis, in part, from just learning course content to acquiring the underlying processes to enable them to independently understand and remember information. When teachers expand their role to include instruction in learning strategies, they alter the dynamic depicted in the right-hand portion of Figure 6.2. That is, they replace part of the time devoted to subject matter acquisition to helping students learn strategies that will improve their literacy competence.

An example of how a general education teacher might incorporate learning strategy instruction into ongoing class activities is as follows. At the beginning of an academic year, a science teacher might explain to the class that being able to regularly ask and answer questions about information they covered in their science text book is an important learning behavior. The teacher would then share the specific steps involved in a self-questioning strategy and model how the students will be expected to ask questions about science information as they are read. Class activities and assignments would, in turn, be structured to require students to practice asking and answering questions related to course content and to use the information generated in the process. Over time, the teacher would expect students to use the newly learned strategy in a host of naturally occurring situations within the course and would provide feedback on students' work.

Level 3: Supporting Mastery of Learning Strategies by Targeted Students

Some students who lack literacy skills have great difficulty mastering learning strategies within general education classrooms under Level 2 conditions. The large number of students involved in the instruction, the limited time available for individual feedback, the small number of opportunities to ask questions for clarification, and other conditions present in these classrooms make learning difficult for some students. Hence, Level 3 interventions may be necessary. In these interventions, students with literacy problems receive specialized, intensive instruction from someone other than the subject matter teacher (e.g., a special education teacher, a study skills teacher, a resource room teacher, a remedial reading teacher).

Continuing with the example cited for Level 2, if the science teacher notices that some student or students in the class are struggling with mastering the self-questioning strategy, support personnel (e.g., the special education teacher or other remedial teacher) would be asked to provide much more explicit, intensive, and systematic instruction in the strategy. An explicit instructional sequence would be followed that ensures students' understanding of each step of the strategy, opportunities to practice the strategy in materials that are at the appropriate instructional reading levels, provision of elaborated feedback after each practice attempt, and generalization of the strategy by students to a broad array of learning tasks and materials (e.g., Ellis, Deshler, Lenz, Schumaker, & Clark, 1991). Such intensive instruction would be provided until the student gains the necessary confidence and masters the strategy at a level of fluency. At that time, the student would apply the newly mastered strategy to assignments in the general education classroom. To increase the probability that this will happen, general and remedial teachers should plan together to ensure that the strategies taught in the remedial setting are relevant to the curriculum demands in the general education class. In addition, the general education teacher should prompt (and expect) students to use their newly mastered strategies in completing work in the general education classroom.

A host of strategies can be employed to enable reading specialists and special education teachers to work with students to provide them with intensive instruction. Some middle schools use "exploratory" or "home room" hours. High schools often develop specialized courses that focus on reading and writing strategies. Typically, these courses are most effective when the student–teacher ratio is not greater than 12–15 students per teacher per period. It is important for teachers to have the opportunity to provide intensive individualized feedback and specialized practice for students. In other schools, class-within-a-class models have been effective. These are classes that are co-taught by a general education teacher and a reading specialist or special educator. Intensive skill or strategy instruction is provided within the context of the core curriculum.

Level 4: Offering Intensive Instructional Options for Students Who Lack Foundational Skills

In most secondary schools, there are several students who cannot respond adequately to the intensive strategy instruction provided in Level 3 interventions because they have not learned the basic, prerequisite skills required to learn the strategies. For these students, teachers need to consider interventions at Levels 4 and 5 on the continuum. While the numbers of students who require interventions at these levels may be relatively small in most school systems (and higher in high-poverty schools), educators need to be aware that these students exist and require a type of instruction that is often not available to them. These are students who have severe learning disabilities; who have specific underlying language disorders in linguistic, metalinguistic, and metacognitive areas; who are English-as-a-second-language learners; or who have had prolonged histories of moving from one school to another. As a result, they lack many of the foundational skills required for advanced literacy instruction.

Students participating in Level 4 interventions learn content literacy skills and strategies through specialized, direct, and intensive instruction in listening, speaking, reading, and writing skills. Reading specialists and special education teachers work together at this level to develop intensive and coordinated instructional experiences designed to address severe literacy deficits. For example, they may implement an intensive reading program for those students who are reading at the first- through third-grade levels. These professionals may also assist content teachers in making appropriate modifications in content instruction to accommodate severe literacy deficits.

Level 5: Offering Intensive Clinical Options for Language Intervention

In Level 5 interventions, students with underlying language disorders learn linguistic, metalinguistic, and metacognitive foundational skills they need to become ready to acquire more advanced skills and strategies. Generally at this level, speech pathologists deliver one-on-one or small-group curriculum-relevant language therapy in collaboration with other support personnel teaching literacy skills. They also assist content teachers in making appropriate modifications in content instruction to accommodate severe language disorders.

Before- and After-School Supports

Adolescents with literacy problems often need support and opportunities to practice learning newly learned literacy skills outside the regularly scheduled school day. Before- and after-school tutoring programs can be an effective component to an overall literacy program (Hock, Pulvers, Deshler, & Schumaker, 2001). When tutoring programs are designed to teach students specific skills in how to learn as well as content knowledge, students' performance can improve to the extent that they earn higher letter grades in general education courses. An example of one such program is the research-based *Strategic Tutoring* program. Strategic tutors within this program teach adolescents the core literacy skills needed to complete high school assignments as well as the associated learning strategies that help students to learn independently and stay abreast of class assignments on their own in the future (Hock, Deshler, & Schumaker, 2000). In order to be effective, before- and after-school tutoring programs must be well organized and research-based, with the major goal being the improvement of students' overall literacy skills.

Foundational to making all levels of the Content Literacy Continuum work in a coordinated fashion is a commitment by key staff to working together in a spirit of joint planning and communication. Strong administrative support is required to make the kinds of scheduling accommodations that facilitate students' programming and teachers' planning and problem-solving work. These efforts of bringing staff together for planning and instructional programming helps to minimize the negative effects of fragmentation that typifies many of the learning experiences for adolescents in secondary schools.

Summary

In short, the Content Literacy Continuum provides a means through which the needs of adolescents with poor literacy skills can be addressed by: (a) the infusion of literacy instruction in all aspects of the secondary curriculum; (b) the involvement of all secondary teachers (not just those who are associated with remedial or special education) in making literacy instruction a top priority; and (c) strong administrative leadership to ensure optimal conditions for sound literacy instruction (ensuring that the majority of teachers in a secondary school are involved in literacy instruction, with the expectation that quality instruction be provided at all five levels); and (d) the availability of a broad continuum of literacy instruction, including provisions for intensive, small-group or one-on-one literacy instruction for the students who are most deficient in literacy skills.

INSTRUCTIONAL PRACTICES THAT IMPROVE STUDENTS' PERFORMANCE

University of Kansas Center for Research on Learning (KU-CRL) researchers have found that the teachers who achieve the greatest gains with students with literacy deficits are those whose instruction is consistently responsive, systematic, and intensive. These factors are central to much of what is embodied in effective instruction, regardless of whether a student is being taught subject matter content or a learning strategy to facilitate the learning of subject matter content. The paragraphs that follow will define and elaborate on three instructional domains: responsive instruction, systematic instruction, and intensive instruction (Lenz & Deshler, 1999).

Responsive Instruction

Responsive instruction is a way of making teaching decisions in which a student's reaction to instruction directly shapes how future instruction is provided. Responsive instruction involves making key moment-to-moment as well as long-range teaching decisions about the unique learning characteristics of students. To do so, teachers need to know a lot about their students, especially those with special learning needs. At-risk students often process information differently from their normally achieving peers. Specifically, students can have great difficulty in acquiring, remembering, and retrieving information, as well as in conveying what they know. Similarly, these students often lack much of the necessary background information and prior knowledge required to understand what is being taught. Teachers who adhere to the principle of responsive instruction regularly do three things during their teaching: (a) they continuously assess students' learning; (2) they make specific instructional accommodations to meet students' needs; and (3) they provide elaborated feedback.

Continuous Assessment. Continuous assessment is an element of responsive instruction in which the teacher regularly monitors students' performance to determine how closely it matches the instructional goal. Ongoing assessment enables students to learn most quickly. For at-risk students, daily assessment probes are best; they are usually informal and are done using classroom materials. They should provide information about what the student is learning and which instructional procedures need to be changed altogether or adapted to make the instruction more effective. As instruction progresses to skill practice, assessment should be regularly embedded throughout to determine whether instructional procedures and sequences are working.

In addition, students should be asked how well the methods the teacher is using seem to be working and whether they have any feedback to give to the teacher to help improve learning for them. Although it may be difficult for some students to articulate what is working for them, involving the student to the greatest extent possible can give him or her a strong sense of commitment and ownership in the learning process and is very important. One tactic that some teachers have used is having students keep a journal to record observations about how a newly learned strategy is working, thoughts they have for generalizing or modifying the strategy, and how they feel they are changing as a learner as a result of the new strategies and skills they are being taught.

Instructional Accommodations. Instructional accommodations make up another element of responsive instruction in which changes in instructional groupings, materials, or teaching techniques are made to increase students' performance. Instructional accommodations are often made on the basis of the unique information-processing characteristics of the students being taught.

Instruction can become more responsive in a variety of ways through the use of accommodations. First, the size and nature of groups in which students work can be changed. Regrouping, for example, can increase the amount of time that can be spent practicing needed skills at the pace and level appropriate to the student. Second, to maximize the benefits students can receive from instruction and practice activities, placing students as close to their instructional level as possible is also critical. This may mean selecting materials that are different from materials that other students are using. It may also mean that some materials will have to be adapted or altered. Selected materials need to be appropriate for both teaching the skills or strategies necessary to reach the instructional goal and enriching the students' background knowledge and information. Third, instruction can be adjusted to increase students' understanding. This often involves making the necessary accommodations to reduce or eliminate the impact of information-processing difficulties on learning. For example, if a student has the opportunity to process information in multiple ways and venues (e.g., visually, auditorially), learning may be enhanced.

Elaborated Feedback. Elaborated feedback is an element of responsive instruction in which the results of a student's performance on a practice task are shared with him or her to help the student understand what was done correctly and what specific things need to be targeted for improvement during subsequent practice attempts. At-risk students generally require that feedback be detailed or elaborated in order to learn. A teacher should focus on doing five things during elaborated feedback. First, the teacher should help the student see and categorize the errors made during the practice attempt so the student can better understand how he or she is performing. Second, the teacher should select and reteach one of the error types at a time. This reteaching may involve modeling the appropriate skill or strategy for the student, as well as explaining the relevant concepts in new ways. Third, the teacher should have the student practice using the new skill that has been learned and watch the student perform it. As the student practices the skill, feedback should be given. Fourth, the teacher should ask the student to paraphrase the main elements of the feedback (this steps helps the student better understand and internalize the change that needs to be made). And fifth, the teacher should prompt the student to set goals for performing the targeted skill or strategy correctly during the next practice attempt.

Systematic Instruction

Systematic instruction is a way of organizing instruction so both the teacher and the student follow and continuously review a dynamic plan related to how new content will be learned and how that new content relates to past and future learning. Systematic instruction involves deliberately planning what and how different skills, strategies, and content are taught to students. Generally, the most effective lessons are those that are well planned in terms of the information to be taught, the sequence of the instruction to be followed, and the various activities and materials to be used. Good teachers recognize that effective instruction is dynamic because it must continuously vary along a continuum from explicit instruction (more teacher-guided or -directed) to implicit instruction (more student-guided or -directed). Generally, early in the instructional process, when students lack knowledge and confidence, instruction should be more explicit and directed by the teacher. As students gain fluency and confidence, responsibility for guiding their learning should be turned over to them so they can become independent learners and performers. Systematic instruction is typically: (a) structured; (b) connected; (c) scaffolded; and (d) informative.

Structured Instruction. Structured instruction is a way of teaching in which information to be learned is divided into smaller segments or steps and sequentially taught through a process that involves direct explanation, modeling, and practice. Instruction is "structured" when information is divided into pieces that are manageable for the student to learn. At-risk adolescents often have difficulty processing large amounts of information, especially when that information involves complex concepts or multistep procedures. Such complex information should be broken into smaller "chunks" or steps; these chunks should then be taught in sequential stages designed to promote mastery at each level. Teaching methods that emphasize unstructured explorations, discussions, or group investigation during the early acquisition of new skills or information are not likely to be successful.

Connected Instruction. Regularly helping students understand the connections between the different parts of information that they are learning is another way to make instruction more systematic. Instruction is "connected" when teachers deliberately show students how information is linked together and related. As noted earlier, breaking information into manageable chunks is an important part of systematic instruction; helping learners see how each chunk of information relates to others that have been learned, as well as to the overall body of information being learned, is equally important.

An effective tool for helping students see how information is connected is a unit map (Lenz, Bulgren, Schumaker, Deshler, & Boudah, 1994). Unit maps can show students the big picture of the various pieces of information to be learned and how these various pieces relate to one another and fit together. In short, such a teaching tool provides students with a road map for what has been learned and what will be learned. When this map is constructed and expanded with the students' help, it can be used to draw attention to connections among pieces of information that have been learned. It can also be used to review and discuss progress. Teachers often post unit maps at the front of the room, or students can keep copies in their notebooks for easy reference. By using these maps, students not only can see the sequence of instruction that the teacher will be following; they can also see how the various strategies are related and join together to promote learning.

Scaffolded Instruction. Scaffolded instruction, or scaffolding, is a systematic teaching method in which the teacher provides a significant amount of support to students early in the learning process in the form of modeling, prompts, direct explanations, and targeted questions, as well as easy learning tasks. Instruction during this phase is primarily teacher-guided. Then, as students begin to acquire mastery of the targeted objectives, direct teacher supports are reduced, and the major responsibility for learning is transferred to the student (student-guided learning). In addition, learning tasks become more and more difficult until the student is performing well with tasks that are similar to those he or she will encounter in general education classes.

Good teachers provide well-designed supports to assist students in mastering new information. Initially, they provide considerable support or scaffolding. As the students become proficient with the new skill and gain confidence, fewer and fewer supports are needed until the students finally master the skill and can use it independently. Scaffolded instruction uses what the learner already knows as a guide to determine the next step for instruction. Knowing how much support to provide to students during the learning process requires careful judgment by the teacher. The goal is to provide just enough, and not too much or too little. Obviously, the amount of scaffolding required varies from student to student and from one type of skill to another. Scaffolding is providing just the right amount of support to enable students to complete a task that they could not do on their own. As students become more proficient, the scaffolding or support is reduced until the students are doing the tasks on their own.

Informative Instruction. Informative instruction is a teaching method in which the teacher ensures that students understand how they are learning, how they can plan and control their own learning at each step of the learning process, and why this is important. Instruction is "informative" when the teacher informs students about how the learning process works, what is expected during instruction, and what specific things the students can do to improve their learning and performance. At-risk adolescents often have not developed the necessary self-monitoring and self-evaluation strategies to track their learning progress, so they do not know how much progress they have made or what goals they should be trying to reach.

Therefore, these students must be kept informed of when, how, and under what conditions learning or performance will occur. They must also be prompted to set goals and monitor their progress toward reaching those goals. Periodically, they should be asked to reflect on their progress. Having students look back at where they were and how much they have improved can motivate them to continue to put forth effort to become better learners.

Intensive Instruction

Intensive instruction is a way of directing students' attention in which sufficient time is spent in teacher-guided interactive learning activities characterized by a high degree of goal-directed student engagement that leads to student mastery and generalization. Intensive instruction involves helping students maintain a high degree of attention and response during instructional sessions that are scheduled as frequently and consistently as possible. In other words, key factors that affect learning are the amount of time in instruction and the effectiveness with which each instructional moment is used to engage students in activities that contribute to their learning.

Sufficient Time. Sufficient time is an element of intensive instruction in which interactive teaching and learning experiences are sustained until the critical information has been mastered, maintained, and generalized by the student. Once a commitment is made to achieving an instructional goal in reading, for example, it must be taken seriously. Classrooms often hold a host of competing demands, and many of them can distract teachers from working on the instructional goals that they have set for their students. Teachers must continually weigh these competing demands on their time and their students' time, and they must not lose sight of the fact that any time taken away from targeted and well-focused instruction in reading can be very difficult, if not impossible, to make up. For students who struggle with learning, the loss of these instructional minutes can take a significant toll.

Practicing a skill only once or twice a week is rarely enough for students learning to read. Practicing something new on a very limited or sporadic schedule, especially in the early phases of the learning process, is like learning it over again every time. Thus, one of the key dimensions of intensive instruction is committing the necessary time on a consistent basis for instruction and practice opportunities.

High Engagement. High engagement is an element of intensive instruction in which each instructional moment is maximized through the use of activities that keep students' attention focused on critical learning outcomes. Since the overall amount of instructional time is so limited and the challenges facing adolescents who struggle with literacy are so great, each instructional session should be exceedingly well planned. Instruction should demand a high degree of learner attention and response, as well as statements of high expectations to students and feedback for their responses. Intensity during instruction is achieved by progressive pacing, frequent question–answer interactions, and activities that require a physical response (for example, pointing, writing, raising hands, repeating, etc.). Intensity can also be achieved through reflective or open-ended questions if the activities are focused on an outcome that engages interest and maintains the student's attention. Another effective instructional tool for increasing the instructional engagement is student goal setting. When students are knowledgeable about what the teacher is trying to accomplish instructionally and are actively engaged in setting goals that they want to work on during each instructional session, their engagement increases.

MUSKEGON HIGH SCHOOL: ONE IMPLEMENTATION OF THE CONTENT LITERACY CONTINUUM

An example of one secondary school in which staff members have tried to improve the literacy performance of adolescents by implementing programs within the Content Literacy Continuum is Muskegon High School, in Muskegon, Michigan. A brief description of how the first three levels of the continuum have been implemented will be provided in this section, along with resulting student outcomes.

Level 1: Ensuring Mastery of Critical Content in All Subject Areas

All of the physical science teachers at Muskegon High School decided to infuse several Content Enhancement Routines (Schumaker et al., 2002) into their classes. Content Enhancement Routines have been the target of research efforts by KU-CRL staff for nearly 20 years. These routines are designed to be used by general education teachers within subject matter classes to teach critical content to academically diverse classes.[1] The four routines incorporated into each unit of their instruction were: the Unit Organizer Routine (Lenz et al., 1994), the Concept Comparison Routine (Bulgren et al., 1995), the LINCing Vocabulary Routine (Ellis, 2000), and the Recall Enhancement Routine (Schumaker, Bulgren, Deshler, & Lenz, 1998). The teachers examined each of the state science benchmarks in relation to information they covered in readings and lectures to identify information that was in alignment with state outcome measures. They then included this information in the graphic devices that they drafted to be used during instruction. The teachers also developed a test for each unit that assessed students' knowledge of the information that they deemed critical for students to pass the state competency exam. These unit tests included many application level-questions as well as two constructed-response questions per unit.

On average, students' test scores improved by one letter grade when the teachers used the Content Enhancement Routines in comparison with when the teachers did not use them. The average test scores on the units in which teachers did not use Content Enhancement Routines were 65%. These same students scored an average of 74% on unit tests when their teachers used the routines to create more "student-friendly" learning conditions. Low-achieving students (including those with disabilities) improved from 62% to 71%, and students who were not at risk improved from 65% to 73%. Not surprisingly, as the teachers continued to use these instructional routines, students' performance on tests continued to improve. On the final unit test, the average score for low-performing adolescents (including students with disabilities) was 75% and for students without disabilities was 83%.

These data suggest that when subject matter teachers deliberately take steps to select critical content and transform it in such a way as to make it easier to understand and remember, the performance of students from low-, average-, and high-achieving groups within an academically diverse class, including those who have the greatest difficulty in learning because of literacy problems (i.e., students with disabilities), can improve.

Level 2: Weaving Learning Strategy Instruction Within Rigorous General Education Classes

While the kinds of instructional modifications described under the first level of the Content Literacy Continuum are helpful for many students in a subject matter class, for some students these instructional modifications are not sufficient. Many students struggle to master the subject matter content because they have not mastered those learning strategies that are most directly tied to the demands of the curriculum. For those students, teachers integrate strategy instruction into their ongoing instruction. For example, the English faculty noted that many students were performing poorly on the state writing competency exam and that they were unable to complete written assignments. The teachers decided to systematically integrate instruction in three written expression strategies within their English classes during the 9th, 10th, and 11th grades: the Sentence Writing Strategy (Schumaker & Sheldon, 1985), the Paragraph Writing Strategy (Schumaker & Lyerla, 1988), and the Error Monitoring Strategy (Schumaker, Nolan, & Deshler, 1985).[1] As a result of weaving instruction in this array of writing strategies into the general education curriculum, the statewide assessment administered at the end of the 11th-grade year showed that 94.1% of the students in this high school passed the written assessment portion of the exam, compared with 74.5% of the students in similar-size schools with the same socioeconomic status and ethnicity composition. The overall statewide pass rate for all high school students was 85%. These data underscore the power of literacy instruction that is well coordinated across teachers and years in school. When instruction on targeted learning strategies that are centrally tied to key outcomes is coordinated and delivered with fidelity, student outcomes can improve.

Level 3: Supporting Mastery of Learning Strategies for Targeted Students

As in many secondary schools, Muskegon High School has a subgroup of adolescents who require more intense instruction in key learning strategies than can be given in general education classes. Thus, in this school, all entering ninth-grade students are administered a reading screening test to determine their ability in word recognition and reading comprehension. Students who score four to five grade levels below placement are provided with intense learning strategy instruction to improve their ability to cope with grade-level materials. Two programming options have been developed: one to teach word recognition strategies, and one to teach reading comprehension strategies.

Students who receive scores in decoding that are two or more grades below grade level are taught a word recognition strategy called the Word Identification Strategy (Lenz, Schumaker, Deshler, & Beals, 1984) during their first year of high school in the following configuration. In cooperation with the ninth-grade English teachers, students are sent to a reading center to work in small groups (one-teacher-to-five-students ratio). They attend these remedial sessions five days per week, 50 minutes per day. Students receive intensive instruction in the Word Identification Strategy with many instances of teacher modeling and feedback and ample opportunities for practice. Students set and work toward goals. Data are kept by both teachers and students to help monitor students' progress. To the extent possible, content materials from the students' English classes are used for reading practice exercises.

For the past seven years that this program has been in operation, students' grade-level gains in word attack skills have been encouraging. In one comparison study the following results were achieved: students with disabilities, from 5.4 on the pre-test to 8.5 on the post-test; male Latinos, from 5.7 on the pretest to 8.5 on the post-test; African American males, from 5.3 on the pre-test to 9.1 on the post-test; total group performance, from 6.1 on the pre-test to 9.1 on the post-test. Students in comparison schools performed at the 6.1 grade level on the pre-test and at the 6.1 level on the post-test. The instructional time that the Muskegon High School students were involved in this intense learning strategy instruction ranged from 15 to 40 days.

For students who score more than two grade levels below ninth grade in reading comprehension (or who have been referred by English teachers), a semester-long class has been created. This class, called Strategic Reading, meets daily for 50 minutes and is taught by English teachers who stress the development of reading comprehension and the enjoyment of reading through the use of three comprehension strategies: the Visual Imagery Strategy (Schumaker, Deshler, Zemitzsch, & Warner, 1993), the Self-Questioning Strategy (Schumaker, Deshler, Nolan, & Alley, 1994), and the Paraphrasing Strategy (Schumaker, Denton, & Deshler, 1984). These strategies give students a framework for comprehending a wide variety of fiction and nonfiction text. Enhancing students' vocabulary building through strategies for memorizing vocabulary and constructing meaning in text is also emphasized. Students express their comprehension through written work and by sharing perspectives with others to help construct an understanding of the text.

Results across four semesters in which students have been taught the three strategies are consistent. On average, students gain 1.5 grade levels in reading comprehension during one semester. However, this finding is somewhat misleading because some of the students' tests indicate that they make no gains, while others make large gains. The students who show gains when their post-test scores are compared with their pre-test scores make an average gain of 2.5 grade levels in reading comprehension in one semester (from the 5.6 grade level to the 8.1 grade level). Some students are reading at or above the ninth-grade level at the end of the semester course. Why some students make gains, according to their post-test results, and others do not remains unclear. The practice results of the students who make no gains, according to their post-test scores, indicate that they have made gains during instruction.

CONCLUSION

Successful programs for improving adolescent literacy will vary dramatically from one secondary school to the next because of school size, staff and student characteristics, and administrative commitment. Research with dozens of secondary schools, however, has convinced researchers at the KU-CRL that the most successful schools in addressing the needs of adolescents with literacy problems are the ones who share these four attributes:

1. Administrators who have as one of their top priorities literacy improvement and as such will make the tough decisions required to shift resources to those instructional areas that directly affect literacy outcomes;
2. Teachers, regardless of their role and area of specialization, who see themselves as having responsibility for improving the literacy performance of all students in their classes. (While roles to accomplish this may vary across teachers, none see themselves as being exempt from playing an important role in the overall program of improving literacy outcomes);
3. Coordinated instruction across teachers, classes, and grade levels that results in a critical mass of instruction focusing on literacy improvement; and
4. A heavy reliance on the use of research-validated instructional practices and programs that are appropriate for students' needs.

If these attributes are in place, students with literacy deficits are likely to learn the skills they need to succeed in high school, earn standard high school diplomas, pass competency tests, and proceed to some sort of postsecondary education.

NOTE

1. For descriptions of the various KU-CRL research-validated content enhancement routines and learning strategies, see http://www.ku-crl.org/downloads/. Click on "Strategic Instruction Model Handouts."

REFERENCES

Bulgren, J. A., Lenz, B. K., Deshler, D. D., & Schumaker, J. B. (1995). *The Concept Comparison Routine*. Lawrence, KS: Edge Enterprises.

Bulgren, J. A., Schumaker, J. B., Deshler, D. D., Lenz, B. K., & Marquis, J. (2002). The use and effectiveness of a comparison routine in diverse secondary content classrooms. *Journal of Educational Psychology, 94*(2), 356–371.

Deshler, D. D., Schumaker, J. B., Lenz, B. K., Bulgren, J. A., Hock, M. F., Knight, J., & Ehren, B. J. (2001). Ensuring content-area learning by secondary students with learning disabilities. *Learning Disabilities Research and Practice, 16*(2), 96–108.

Ellis, E. S. (2000). *The LINCing Routine*. Lawrence, KS: Edge Enterprises.

Ellis, E. S., Deshler, D. D., Lenz, B. K., Schumaker, J. B., & Clark, F. L. (1991). An instructional model for teaching learning strategies. *Focus on Exceptional Children, 24*(1), 1–14.

Hock, M. F., & Deshler, D. D. (2003). Adolescent literacy: Ensuring that no child is left behind. *Principal Leadership, 13*(4), 50–58.

Hock, M. F., Deshler, D. D., & Schumaker, J. B. (2000). *Strategic tutoring*. Lawrence, KS: Edge Enterprises.

Hock, M. F., Pulvers, K. A., Deshler, D. D., & Schumaker, J. B. (2001). The effects of an after-school tutoring program on the academic performance of at-risk and students with learning disabilities. *Remedial and Special Education, 22*(3), 16–23.

Hock, M. F., Schumaker, J. B., & Deshler, D. D. (1999). Closing the gap to success in secondary schools: A model for cognitive apprenticeship. In D. D. Deshler, J. B. Schumaker, K. R. Harris, & S. Graham (Eds.), *Teaching every adolescent every day: Learning in diverse schools and classrooms*. Cambridge, MA: Brookline Books.

Lenz, B. K., with Bulgren, J. A., Schumaker, J. B., Deshler, D. D., & Boudah, D. J. (1994). *The unit organizer routine*. Lawrence, KS: Edge Enterprises.

Lenz, B. K., & Deshler, D. D. (1999). Principles of teaching reading to students with learning disabilities. In B. K. Lenz & B. Ehren (Eds.), *Teaching reading to students with disabilities: Online academy*. Lawrence, KS: University of Kansas Center for Research on Learning.

Lenz, B. K., & Ehren, B. (1999). Strategic content literacy initiative: Focusing on reading in secondary schools. *Stratenotes, 8*(1), 1–6. Lawrence, KS: University of Kansas Center for Research on Learning.

Lenz, B. K., Schumaker, J. B., Deshler, D. D., & Beals, V. L. (1984). *The Word Identification Strategy: Instructor's manual*. Lawrence: University of Kansas Center for Research on Learning.

Schumaker, J. B., Bulgren, J. A., Deshler, D. D., & Lenz, B. K. (1998). *The Recall Enhancement Routine*. Lawrence, KS: Edge Enterprises.

Schumaker, J. B., Denton, P. H., & Deshler, D. D. (1984). *The Paraphrasing Strategy: Instructor's manual*. Lawrence: University of Kansas Center for Research on Learning.

Schumaker, J. B., Deshler, D. D., Bulgren, J. A., Davis, B., Lenz, B. K., & Grossen, B. (2002). Access of adolescents with disabilities to general education curriculum: Myth or reality. *Focus on Exceptional Children, 35*(3), 1–16.

Schumaker, J. B., Deshler, D. D., & McKnight, P. (2002). Ensuring success in the secondary general education curriculum through the use of teaching routines. In G. Stover, M. R. Shinn, & H. M. Walker (Eds.), *Interventions for achievement and behavior problems* (pp. 791–824). Washington, DC: National Association of School Psychologists.

Schumaker, J. B., Deshler, D. D., Nolan, S. M., & Alley, G. A. (1994). *The Self-Questioning Strategy: Instructor's manual*. Lawrence: University of Kansas Center for Research on Learning.

Schumaker, J. B., Deshler, D. D., Zemitzsch, A., & Warner, M. J. (1993). *The Visual Imagery Strategy: Instructor's manual*. Lawrence: University of Kansas Center for Research on Learning.

Schumaker, J. B., & Lyerla, K. (1988). *The paragraph writing strategy*. Lawrence, KS: Edge Enterprises.

Schumaker, J. B., Nolan, S. M., & Deshler, D. D. (1985). *The Error Monitoring Strategy*. Lawrence: University of Kansas Center for Research on Learning.

Schumaker, J. B., & Sheldon, J. (1985). *The sentence writing strategy*. Lawrence, KS: Edge Enterprises.

PART II

Addressing the
Literacy Achievement Gap

Promising Practices

PART II offers actual examples of exemplary practices from field-based research, urban schools, and school districts that demonstrate success in closing the literacy achievement gap. Drawn from a broad cross section of school districts throughout the country, each chapter demonstrates the value of collaboration among practitioners and researchers. Each also provides encouraging examples of how the implementation of sound literacy instruction and the systematic work of professional development teams can make a difference in the academic and personal lives of youth caught up in a web of poverty and low expectations.

Christy Falba and **Ralph Reynolds** describe an instructional intervention for use with students having difficulty in reading. Teachers and administrators in Clark County, Nevada, learn to access students' literacy strengths and areas of need and provide targeted instruction to help them attain essential reading and writing strategies and skills.

Fred Carrigg and **Margaret Honey** share the success story of the Union City, New Jersey, public schools, in which a locally developed model for successful English language acquisition and proficiency in reading in English is described. They tell the story, beginning with the city at its lowest point in 1989, with a state takeover looming, and describe its transformation from one of the lowest performing urban districts in New Jersey to one of the top performing ones in 2002. **Douglas Fisher** and **Nancy Frey**, university professors, and **Douglas Williams**, principal of Hoover High School in the city of San Diego, California, describe their collaboration on a school-wide literacy initiative that moved Hoover High from the lowest performing school in the city of San Diego and among the lowest performing high schools in the state to the high school with the highest gain on the state accountability test.

The success story of an urban middle school is told by **Tamara Jetton** and **Janice Dole**. Spearheaded by a professional development program that made use of a reading coach who worked with language arts teachers in Ogden, Utah, while they were simultaneously taking graduate courses in reading, this effort led to a dramatic increase in students' reading achievement over a three-year period.

Project CRISS (Creating Independence Through Student-owned Strategies), which focuses on content area learning, is described by **Carol Santa**. Project CRISS has been used successfully in Montana and elsewhere throughout the country, and research indicates that students in content classes where teachers have collaborated in the project are able to remember more information and use a greater variety of learning strategies than students in classrooms where teachers have not had an opportunity to collaborate.

Working collaboratively as researcher and classroom teacher, **Cynthia Greenleaf** and **Cindy Litman** (researchers) and **Willard Brown** (classroom teacher) also focus on content area learning. Their chapter illustrates one knowledgeable science teacher's work to integrate reading apprenticeship into inquiry-oriented science teaching in Oakland, California. The model has been shown to be effective in raising underserved and underachieving secondary students' scores on a standardized reading measure. Just as important, it enhances their belief in their own abilities to be successful as students in rigorous academic settings.

A team of researchers and practitioners, **Elizabeth Birr Moje**, **LeeAnn Sutherland**, **Ronald Marx**, **Phyllis Blumenfeld**, and **Joseph Krajcik**, of the University of Michigan, and **Deborah Peek-Brown**, science coordinator of the Detroit public schools, are collaborating in a long-term systematic reform effort to engage students in the discourse of science and scientists, distinguishing scientific literacy from everyday literacy and engaging the students in more thoughtful interactions around the phenomena and scientific concepts.

James McPartland, **Robert Balfanz**, and **Alta Shaw** developed the Talent Development Literacy Program for Poorly Prepared High School Students. A comprehensive high school reform package developed at Johns Hopkins University, the program has been implemented in secondary schools throughout the country. The Talent Development Literacy Program involves extra instructional time for a highly specific sequence of courses that focus primarily on fluency and comprehension issues in reading and on the stages of good writing for different purposes.

In the final chapter, **Nora Hyland** provides a collection of activities for use with *Bridging the Literacy Achievement Gap, Grades 4–12*. These activities can be used in pre-service teacher education, in-service professional development, and graduate-level studies, and by teacher study groups.

7

Strategies to Accelerate Reading Success (STARS) in the Middle Grades

Christy J. Falba and Ralph E. Reynolds

Key Points

- A district–university partnership was formed to provide professional development to middle grade teachers.
- A systematic program featuring in-classroom intervention and reading comprehension had a direct, positive influence on the nature and quality of instruction in the classroom.
- Analysis of student performance showed a significant difference favoring STARS students over a comparison group.

There is a growing understanding across the United States of the importance of teaching all children to read. The recent publication of *Preventing Reading Difficulties in Young Children* (Snow, Burn, & Griffin, 1998) and the report of the National Reading Panel (2000) underscore this understanding. These two volumes are compilations of what scientifically based reading research says about the nature of reading and best practices for reading instruction. The primary emphasis of these works is on helping children become successful readers by the end of third grade. What is not covered in great detail in these reports is how to intervene with children who do not read well after they have passed the third-grade level. Yet this population is large and presents unique challenges for successful reading instruction.

The purpose of this chapter is to discuss a program that has been shown to be effective with these older children (specifically, students in third, fourth, and fifth grade). This program, Strategies to Accelerate Reading Success (STARS), was developed in 1997 by a partnership of teachers, district specialists, and university professors. The program is based on a small group tutoring model and includes extensive professional development for teachers; however, the model is not static. As more and more has been learned about reading instruction, aspects of the program have been updated. Indeed, continuous refinement and development of the program continues today.

A second purpose of the chapter is to discuss the formation, contributions, and maintenance of the partnership among district personnel, teachers, and university professors. In this instance, this partnership involves Clark County School District (CCSD) personnel and teachers, and professors from the University of Nevada–Las Vegas (UNLV). Over time, some of the members of this group have changed, but the basic elements of the STARS program and the commitment to collaboration have remained constant.

PROGRAM DEVELOPMENT

Project STARS began in 1997. CCSD had just implemented a new early intervention program for the primary grades (K–3) called Project LIFE. With Project LIFE ongoing, it did not take teachers long to begin asking about what should be done with students who are struggling readers in the upper grades. About the same time, district administrators were becoming aware of high numbers of students being recommended for special education testing based on below-grade-level reading scores. It was clear that many of these students did not need special education services; they just needed better initial reading instruction and, in some cases, additional reading instruction. In response to these issues, Martha Tittle, director of academic services (now assistant superintendent of the Curriculum and Professional Development division), initiated a discussion regarding the need for a reading intervention program in the intermediate grades.

Also at this time, UNLV faculty members were in the process of revising the pre-service reading and language arts methods courses contained in their pre-service teacher education (certification) programs. Reading Methods, Writing Methods, and Reading Remediation were combined into two courses, Reading Assessment I & II. Literacy specialists in academic services, who were teaching classes for UNLV as adjunct faculty, were included in the conversations as the new reading courses were created.

CCSD personnel sought assistance from UNLV literacy faculty in identifying research related to intervention models for intermediate grades. Programs for older students were sparse, so little research was available. The next step was to look at components that programs had in common. As a group, the literacy specialists and university faculty began to examine components and read literature on early and intermediate programs.[1] They found that commonalities included rereading, word attack skills, guided reading (direct teaching of comprehension strategies), and written responses. The group also looked at issues of reading motivation and studied the negative effects on at-risk children in other academic subjects (Stanovich, 1986).

The culmination of six months of brainstorming sessions was a clear statement of goals for the STARS project (Smith, 1999). The goals remain the same today:

- To reinforce student literacy strengths and to provide opportunities for mastery of skills and strategies needed to become fluent readers and writers.

- To improve students' motivation and self-confidence in reading through use of high-interest and low-readability materials.
- To provide training and support for intermediate teachers in the implementation of effective literacy intervention instructional strategies.

Some alignment to the UNLV courses was sought. For example, materials being used at UNLV, such as the *Reading Inventory for the Classroom* (Flynt & Cooter, 2001) and *Words Their Way* (Bear, Invernizzi, Templeton, & Johnston, 2000) textbooks, were incorporated into the STARS instructional materials.

THE STARS PROGRAM

Intervention programs are often structured as pullout or remedial programs, involving individual students or small groups of students working with a reading specialist. Remedial reading programs frequently follow a philosophy of slowing down the teaching of basic skills, a philosophy that can lead to students' falling farther behind their peers (Stanovich, 1986). Pikulski (1994) described a systematic, fast-paced, structured plan of instruction, one that includes decoding skills in the context of daily reading, strategic analysis of words, explicit instruction on comprehension strategies, and increased reading time in the classroom (Cooper, 1997). Given this information, one goal of STARS became intervening with children in ways that did not involve slowing them down; hence, some elements of Pikulski's model were incorporated into the project.

Through STARS training, teachers acquire knowledge of the reading process and gain awareness of literacy challenges that students may encounter. Teachers assess students, identify individual learning needs, and provide daily 30-minute Project STARS lessons in small group settings in their classrooms. Lessons place emphasis on the understanding of word patterns, comprehension skills, reading and writing fluency, and student independence and confidence in reading.

Professional Development for Teachers

Project STARS is designed as a 45-hour, three-credit course. It is simultaneously an instruction and implementation model in which strategies are introduced to teachers, applied in the classroom, and discussed the following class. Course instructors provide ongoing support through weekly discussions, feedback on written assignments, and classroom observations of STARS lessons. Usually, the course is delivered over 14 consecutive weeks.

1. *Session One* of the STARS course provides background and a brief review of related reading intervention research, the components of a STARS lesson, an overview of assessments included in the STARS model, and detailed instruction on administering an Informal Reading Inventory (IRI). Assignments the first week include reading pages 9–15 in the *Reading Inventory for the Classroom*

(Flynt & Cooter, 2001) and the journal article "Assessing Motivation to Read" (Gambrell, Palmer, Codling, & Mazzoni, 1996). Teachers are assigned the tasks of selecting three to five students who are struggling readers in their classes, setting up testing packets for each student's IRI, and administering the IRI to each student prior to the second class session.

2. In *Session Two,* participants share IRI testing experiences and concerns and discuss the IRI Results and Summary Sheet. Next, the Motivation to Read Profile (MRP) (Gambrell, Palmer, Codling, & Mazzoni, 1996) and the Qualitative Spelling Inventory (QSI) (Bear, Invernizzi, Templeton, & Johnston, 2000) are explained. The Small Group Profile, a table for recording students' scores and levels on the QSI, IRI, and MRP, is discussed. Areas of strength and instructional goals are also noted on the Small Group Profile. The article "Blue Jays Win! Crows Go Down in Defeat!" (Wuthrick, 1990) is read during class time and discussed. Assignments for the following week include completing the IRI Assessment and Summary Sheet, administering the MRP and the QSI, and completing the Small Group Profile.

3. Results of the MRP, the QSI, and the Small Group Profile are discussed at the beginning of *Session Three.* Characteristics of readers are described, including emergent, early, transitional, and fluent readers, as well as strategies to use with each of these stages (Taberski, 2000). This session includes an explanation of and practice with procedures to determine reading levels of texts and a discussion about classroom libraries. Teachers are given the assignment of pulling their STARS groups and matching text to reader. They are asked to read "A Case Study of Middle School Reading Disability" (Morris, Ervin, & Conrad, 1996) for the following class.

4. *Session Four* begins with a discussion of the reading process. Approaches to reading that include modeled, shared, guided, and independent reading are described with a focus on teacher and student responsibilities. The main topic for this class is guided reading. Essential components of guided reading as outlined by Fountas and Pinnell (1996) are emphasized. Creating a literacy environment and establishing the classroom structure are also discussed. Assignments include conducting a guided reading lesson with a STARS group and reading "Literature Discussions in the Primary Grades" (Jewell & Pratt, 1999).

5. The topic of guided reading continues in *Session Five.* Directed Reading-Thinking Activity (DR-TA) is described, as is Rereading and Familiar Reading. Development of a guided reading lesson plan is also delineated. These topics become the assignments for the week as teachers pull their STARS groups for instruction. The assigned reading is "Sometimes the Conversations Were Grand, and Sometimes . . ." (Roller & Breed, 1994).

6. In *Session Six,* the guided reading continues with a focus on nonfiction. Special features and text structures are described, and graphic organizers for organizing thinking and for prewriting are discussed. Response to literature is

introduced through reading "Introducing Response Logs to Poor Readers" (Sudduth, 1989). Grand conversations (Roller & Breed, 1994) and retelling strategies are also described. Assignments for the week include working with the STARS group on rereading of familiar text, guided reading, and response. In addition, teachers read the first chapter of *Words Their Way* (Bear, Invernizzi, Templeton, & Johnston, 2000).

7. Topics for *Session Seven* include a review of guided reading and an introduction to cueing systems, running records, and retrospective miscue analysis. Participants watch a video about running records that illustrates the conventions used, and they spend time practicing. Emphasis is on building understanding that running records inform teaching, document strengths as well as needs, and provide information that is essential in designing Project STARS lessons. The importance of conferencing with the child is discussed, including feedback on what the child did well and one or two teaching points. Assignments include *Words Their Way* (Bear, Invernizzi, Templeton, & Johnston 2000) readings, gathering samples of students' writing and QSI, and adding running records to the STARS group.

8. Time to discuss and practice running records is built into *Session Eight.* *Words Their Way* is the main topic, with an introduction of orthographic levels and sequence of instruction. Spelling stages as categorized by Bear and colleagues are described. Participants analyze the students' writing they brought and discuss consistencies and inconsistencies with the results from the QSI. The assignment for the week is to read the fourth chapter in *Words Their Way* and to add word study to the STARS group.

9. Practice with running records and reflection on the process continues in *Session Nine.* Word sorts and games, developing the weekly plan, and the lesson plan are described. Time is spent doing a variety of word sorts and games, explaining the rationales behind each activity. A correlation of *Words Their Way* developmental spelling levels to the district curriculum is examined. Participants are asked to read "Using Think Alouds to Enhance Children's Comprehension Monitoring Abilities" (Baumann, Jones, & Seifert-Kessell, 1993) before the next class.

10. *Session Ten* includes additional practice with running records and a discussion of proficient reader strategies. Participants read "Reading Comprehension: What Works" (Fielding & Pearson, 1994) and "Modeling Mental Processes Helps Poor Readers Become Strategic Readers" (Duffy, Roehler, & Herrmann, 1988). Other topics include metacognition, think aloud, and prior knowledge. Assignments for the week include completing the running record and analysis and reading "The Method of Repeated Readings" (Samuels, 1997).

11. *Session Eleven* focuses on questioning strategies and on reading fluency. Question–Answer Relationships (QAR) (Raphael, 1982) and reciprocal questioning are described. Participants read and discuss "Fluency Beyond the

Primary Grades: From Group Performance to Silent, Independent Reading" (Worthy & Broaddus, 2002). Emphasis is on a key point made by Worthy and Broaddus that reading fluency "develops over time through modeling and instruction, and guided and independent practice in a variety of texts" (Worthy & Broaddus, 2002, p. 337). This week's assignment is to complete a STARS lesson plan.

12. The importance of reassessment is discussed in *Session Twelve*. Reading workshop, literature circles, and small group rotations are described in detail. At this point, classroom structure is revisited and discussion revolves around issues and potential solutions. Assignments for the week include beginning reassessment and a complete Project STARS lesson plan.

13, 14. *Sessions Thirteen and Fourteen* allow for participant self-reflection of practices, ongoing discussion of STARS components, and review of text comprehension instruction as outlined by the report of the National Reading Panel (2000): (a) monitoring comprehension; (b) using graphic and semantic organizers; (c) answering questions; (d) generating questions; (e) recognizing story structure; and (f) summarizing. Reassessment results are shared and discussed in the last class, as are guidelines for when to discontinue children in STARS.

Assessment and Instruction

Assessment is fundamental to the STARS model, and through the practice and implementation of assessment procedures teachers gain expertise in matching students with appropriate texts, skills, and comprehension strategies (Smith, 1999). Administration and scoring of the IRI, the Reading Inventory for the Classroom (Flynt & Cooter, 2001), occurs within the first two weeks of the Project STARS course. Independent, instructional, and frustration reading levels are estimated from the IRI. Other assessment procedures include the Qualitative Spelling Inventory (Bear, Invernizzi, Templeton, & Johnston, 2000), the Motivation to Read Profile (Gambrell, Palmer, Codling, & Mazzoni, 1996), running records, and anecdotal records. These assessments were selected based on what was being taught in the university reading methods classes at the time STARS was designed. Teachers determine appropriate instruction by using a combination of these measures and readminister them at the end of the STARS course to identify reading and listening comprehension levels, word knowledge, spelling, writing skills, and students' self-confidence in reading.

Teachers trained in Project STARS plan and implement instruction in a structured, 30-minute, small group lesson. Components of the lesson include rereading of familiar text, running record, word study, and guided reading. The purpose of rereading of familiar text is to build fluency and comprehension. Rereading selections may be taken from previous reading assignments or journal entries. During this component of the lesson, the repeated reading strategy may be used. Running record is employed to analyze a student's oral reading miscues in order to provide appropriate instruction. Word study builds and accelerates students' orthographic knowledge. The purpose of guided reading is to provide a structure in which students use appropriate level materials and strategies to support reading growth. Following the 30-minute small group lesson, students work on independent reading and participate in authentic writing experiences or meaningful dialogue about the text.

Rereading of Familiar Text. Many struggling readers in upper elementary grades have mastered the basic skills necessary to read but have not mastered the ability to apply these skills automatically. With this in mind, the Project STARS model includes a focus on rereading to gain automaticity. Rereading is intended to help students shift the focus from the printed page to reading for comprehension. In addition, the Repeated Reading Strategy (Samuels, 1997) is used to build reading fluency. Students are timed as they reread short passages of 100–200 words, with the end goal of reading 100 words in approximately one minute.

Word Study. The concept of word study came from the work of Morris (1982). Word study procedures such as word sorting are intended to help students master and internalize patterns of words. A word sorting strategy can help students make analogies from known to unknown words and refine both decoding and encoding skills. The QSI (Bear, Invernizzi, Templeton, & Johnston, 1996), one of the assessments given near the beginning of the Project STARS intervention, places students at the appropriate orthographic knowledge level: preliterate, letter name, within word, syllable juncture, or derivational constancy.

Guided Reading. Fountas and Pinnell (1996, p. 2) describe guided reading as "a context in which a teacher supports each reader's development of effective strategies for processing novel texts at increasingly challenging levels of difficulty." Through guided reading, students use and develop strategies with teachers' assistance, allowing them to focus on constructing meaning. Use of independent reading strategies is the ultimate goal of guided reading.

A guided reading lesson is brief and explicit, with a focus on comprehension strategies. It includes introduction of the text, demonstration of the strategy, opportunities for reading the text and practicing the strategy, and a reminder to the students to practice the strategy as they read independently. Texts are at the instructional levels of the students as determined through the use of the Reading Inventory for the Classroom (Flynt & Cooter, 2001). As students do the silent reading, the teacher works individually with one student. This provides ongoing opportunities to work with the strengths and needs of each student.

Fountas and Pinnell (1996) describe roles during guided reading for both the teacher and the student. These roles include before, during, and after the reading. A lesson plan template is provided in the Project STARS manual for teachers to use in guided reading. During a guided reading lesson for a short text structure, the teacher first provides a pre-reading activity, such as making predictions. Next, the teacher sets the purpose for reading (e.g., "Read to find out if . . ."). Students read the text, requesting assistance when needed. After the reading, students respond to the story and may be guided by the teacher to return to part of the text. Teachers' records of guided reading are important and may include books read, running records, and notes on reading behaviors.

Reading Comprehension Strategies. Several comprehension strategies are described in Project STARS, including DR-TA (Stauffer, 1976); ReQuest (Manzo, 1969); Retelling (Beaver, 1997); Think-Alouds (Keene & Zimmerman, 1997); Graphic Organizers, Question-Answer Relationships (QAR) (Raphael, 1982); Collaborative Strategic Reading (CSR) (Klingner & Vaughn, 1999); and Generating Interactions Between Schemata and Text (Anderson, Reynolds, Schallert, & Goetz, 1977).

Directed Reading-Thinking Activity (DR-TA). Stauffer (1976) described DR-TA as a strategy to help students develop the ability to determine a purpose for reading in order to extract, comprehend, and make decisions based on information gained from reading. During DR-TA, students are involved in three steps: (a) predicting as defining a purpose for reading; (b) reading and selecting relevant data; and (c) evaluating and revising predictions using the information they acquire.

ReQuest. A reciprocal questioning technique in which the teacher models questioning behavior for the students is the basis for ReQuest. The student and teacher begin by silently reading and exchanging questions on a sentence-by-sentence reading of the material. Teacher and student continue until the student can make a logical prediction of what is going to happen in the rest of the story.

Retelling. The purpose of retelling is to help determine a student's ability to comprehend text and stories, sense of story, and language complexity. Important elements of a story are recalled or reconstructed with the retelling procedure. After reading a text silently or listening to the teacher orally read a text, students are asked to retell the story in their own words without referring back to the text. Retelling can also be done in writing or through pictures. Teachers support students through the explicit instruction of story elements.

Think-Alouds. Teaching students to verbalize their thoughts as they are reading can assist in illuminating strategies they use to understand text. The think-aloud strategy can also provide a way for teachers to model their thinking as they read, pointing out strategies they are using to process text (Keene & Zimmerman, 1997).

Question-Answer Relationships (QAR). Raphael (1982) described a systematic means for analyzing task demands of different types of questions to enhance students' ability to answer comprehension questions. Question types that students are asked to identify include "Right-There" questions where the answer is explicitly stated in the text, "Think and Search" questions where the answer is located in the text but requires the integration of textual material, and "On My Own" questions where the answer is not in the text but in the student's knowledge base.

Collaborative Strategic Reading (CSR). Klingner and Vaughn (1999) combined reading comprehension strategy instruction and cooperative learning. Cooperative groups are made up of students of mixed reading and achievement levels. The focus is on four reading strategies: (a) *preview,* recalling prior knowledge and predicting; (b) *click and clunk,* identifying difficult words and concepts in the passage; (c) *get the gist,* restating the most important idea; and (d) *wrap-up,* summarizing and generating questions. Studies of the effectiveness of CSR with English language learners have had positive findings.

Written Response to Literature. Written response is emphasized in STARS to foster reflection. Response to literature provides an important link between reading and writing. When students write about their reading, they think about elements of plot, characterization, and setting. Students may retell portions of the text, summarize ideas, express their analysis of the text through analogy, or generalize about the work or theme (Applebee, 1978).

TESTING THE EFFECTIVENESS OF THE STARS PROGRAM

With input and review from the advisory panel, a large-scale evaluation of the STARS project was undertaken using a quasi-experimental design that included a true comparison group.[2] What follows is a brief description of how this evaluation study was carried out and a summary of the relevant outcomes.

School and Student Selection

A sampling plan was created to help ensure the greatest comparability between the schools and the students selected. Three variables were considered as guidelines in selecting schools for participation in the study.

1. *Similar reading scores:* The overall fifth-grade reading scores across all the schools on the previous year's Terra Nova had to fall within five percentile points of each other.
2. *Similar transience rates:* Transience rates across all the schools had to be within five percentage points of each other.
3. *Participation:* Each school's principal and intermediate teachers had to agree to become involved in the study.

These guidelines were used to select seven schools from 172 elementary schools in the school district. Perfect coherence to Guidelines 1 and 2 was not always possible because of Guideline 3. Selected schools could be included only

TABLE 7.1. Mean Reading Scores and Transience Rates

School	Mean reading score on Terra Nova test (percentile)	Transience rate (percent)
Alpine	53	28
Beaumont	31	37
Canyon	49	36
Dampier	45	31
Echo	45	33
Franklin	48	31
Goddard	51	23
AVERAGE	46	31

if the principal and teachers agreed. Table 7.1 shows the selected schools (names changed) and values for the two quantitative selection guidelines.

The data used in this study came from teachers trained in the first semester and their students. A second group of teachers, who had elected to be trained in STARS during the second semester, formed the comparison group.

Students were selected for participation in the study by their teachers. Each teacher was asked to identify three to five students "in need of remediation in reading." These students could not be English language learner- or special education-eligible. Students were selected using this criterion in both STARS-trained and non-STARS-trained classrooms. Table 7.2 shows the number of students in the trained and nontrained samples.

What the Data Showed

Three data analyses were performed to ascertain whether or not a quasi-experiment would support the three major performance goals of the STARS program: (a) a significant improvement in STARS students' reading comprehension, listening comprehension, and spelling performance over the performance of comparison students; (b) a significant increase in STARS students' motivation to read and sense of themselves as readers over the performance of comparison students; and (c) a significant increase in STARS program teachers' knowledge in the areas of reading assessment, word study, and guided reading.

There was a sense among district personnel and teachers that the program was working well and that all of these goals would be supported; however, this sense was based on personal experience and anecdotal information, not actual data. The data used in these analyses came from a pre-test administered before students and teachers started the STARS program and a post-test given about 10 months later.

Student Achievement Data. The STARS intervention's most important impact on students can be seen on the reading and listening comprehension tests. This is not surprising in that the major reason STARS was implemented was to increase reading comprehension achievement for intermediate-grade students. The results on the spelling measure were somewhat unexpected. The word study portion of STARS is built around increasing students' knowledge of letter patterns; hence, one might expect spelling scores to be positively influenced.

- In reading comprehension, the post-test scores showed an improvement of 146% for the treatment group and an improvement of 111% for the comparison group.
- For listening comprehension, the trained students raised their scores by 37.9% over the year, while students in the comparison group showed much smaller gains (13.8%). The reading and listening comprehension test results suggest that the STARS treatment was effective in improving student reading comprehension performance—the first goal of the program. However, it should be noted that the effect sizes for both results were in the small to moderate range.
- For spelling, the post-test scores showed an improvement of 15.5% for the treatment group and an improvement of 3.1% for the comparison group. Although we cannot say for sure exactly why spelling scores improved for the treatment students, it may reflect the relative effectiveness of the word work (word sorts) and writing portions of the intervention. The effect size for this result is in the moderate range.

Student Motivation. The second major goal of the STARS project was to increase students' motivation to read and positive senses of themselves as readers. The Motivation to Read Profile (MRP) was given to all students before

TABLE 7.2. Selected Schools and Participant Numbers

School	Students working with trained teachers	Students working with nontrained teachers
Alpine	31	30
Beaumont	17	36
Canyon	24	0
Dampier	24	16
Echo	0	21
Franklin	0	13
Goddard	12	15
TOTAL	108	121

TABLE 7.3. Project STARS Group Post-Test Scores

Variable	SD	F ratio	p	Eta	STARS Mean	N	Comparison Mean	N
Silent reading	1.76	$F(1, 217) = 17.71$	<.001	.08	3.99	99	3.02	121
Listening comprehension	1.83	$F(1, 217) = 9.46$	<.005	.04	4.71	99	3.91	121
Spelling	1.93	$F(1, 217) = 21.42$	<.001	.09	6.45	99	6.17	121
Value for reading	12.94	$F(1, 218) = 0.012$	.91	0	79.3	99	79.11	122
Self-concept as reader	11.24	$F(1, 218) = 1.06$	.3	.005	71.13	99	71.04	122

and after the STARS intervention. No significant results were found in a comparison of either subtest: Value for Reading or Concept of Self. These findings suggest that the STARS intervention did not raise students' motivation to read; hence, goal 2 of the project was not supported by these analyses. Future research might be done. Perhaps using a more sensitive analysis approach composed of several triangulating measures would reveal an effect on student motivation.

Means and standard deviations for all analyses described earlier can be found in Table 7.3.

Teacher Knowledge Data. Goal 3 of the STARS program was to significantly increase teachers' knowledge of three critical areas in reading instruction: reading assessment, word study, and guided reading. Teachers were given a knowledge survey before they started the STARS programs and after they completed the training. Questionnaires were not given to teachers who worked with children in the comparison groups.

Analyses were performed on composite scores made up of the average scores from all of the questions that related to the three areas of knowledge. Results showed that post-test scores were significantly higher than pre-test scores in all three areas, suggesting that STARS instruction is effective in increasing teachers' knowledge about how to teach and assess reading. The greatest gains in teacher knowledge came in the area of reading assessment. However, these results describe only internal gains because tests were not given to comparison group teachers; hence, this evidence supports goal 3 of the STARS program but does not prove it.

Another question of interest concerned the reliability of STARS training—that is, whether these results would be obtained at each of the five schools involved in STARS. An analysis of the results showed that STARS instruction was highly reliable in the areas of reading assessment and guided reading; however, four of the five school involved did not show significant knowledge increases about word study. These results were not unexpected. Members of the STARS national advisory panel had suggested that the word study portion of the training was the weakest of the three in the training. The results of the study confirmed their impression. Consequently, future iterations of STARS training will include more substantial information on word study.

In summary, results from the study showed that the STARS program was effective in meeting its first program goal. Implementation of the STARS program raised reading and listening comprehension performance for third-, fourth-, and fifth-grade students identified by their teachers as at risk of reading failure. There was no evidence that implementing the STARS intervention increased students' motivation to read (goal 2). STARS-trained teachers increased their own knowledge about reading assessment, word study, and guided reading, supporting program goal 3. However, this result is not conclusive because knowledge surveys were not given to comparison group teachers. Finally, effects size for all results were in the low to moderate range. This suggests that while projects STARS is clearly on the right path, some small changes may have to be made in future iterations of the program with the goal of increasing the degree to which students benefit from it.

Looking to the Future

Given the dynamic nature of the collaboration surrounding the development and implementation of Project STARS, components of the intervention model continue to evolve. As noted, there is a need for increased word study in STARS, and this is being addressed. Kathleen Brown of the University of Utah was brought in to provide expertise as the word study component was expanded.

A New Word Study Component. Project STARS currently uses *Words Their Way* (Bear, Invernizzi, Templeton, & Johnston, 2000) for the word study portion of the intervention model. Although *Words Their Way* is a wonderful spelling program, teachers who instruct struggling readers often do not have the time to create materials. More important, the short amount of time allotted for *Words Their Way* instruction during the STARS course does not allow teachers to gain enough knowledge to make critical decisions for appropriate word study for their students.

The word study that is being added to STARS is based on *The Howard Street Tutoring Manual* (Morris, 1999). Automaticity of word recognition (fluency to some) is the main focus for this new program addition. Work on decoding automaticity is necessary because many young readers who appear to be poor comprehenders are in reality just slow decoders; hence, instructing them on comprehension strategies alone likely will not help them (Reynolds, Hendricks, & Sinatra, 2004). With the new word study, teachers are given specific word study materials, which are created in class, as well as a specific sequence of instruction. A speed check is used to move children from one level to the next, ensuring accuracy and automaticity. This ongoing assessment gives teachers a greater knowledge of how to best instruct students to assist them with a comprehension deficit. The new word study component will be piloted in two STARS classes in spring 2004.

Expanding the Program. In looking to expand Project STARS beyond the Clark County School District, one course was taught to a group of 14 educators in Washoe School District in Reno, Nevada. This course was offered in fall 2002 and delivered through a combination of traditional face-to-face sessions and six teleconferenced sessions. In addition to teaching the course, one of the CCSD STARS project managers conducted the follow-up classroom observations. Two teachers were selected from the class to become STARS instructors in Reno and the course was expanded to include middle school teachers. Ongoing support was provided during spring 2003, including visits from one of the project managers approximately every six weeks. Many teachers in the Washoe School District have been trained in CELL and EXCELL and commented that the STARS course provided the structure to help them move theory into practice.

We plan to continue the research on STARS as well as examination of the program itself. Classroom observations confirm whether or not teachers correctly implement STARS strategies. These observations occur within the semester that a Project STARS course is being taught, but no evidence has been gathered to determine whether teachers continue to implement the STARS strategies in subsequent years. In addition, longitudinal data on STARS-treated students is needed to examine whether effects hold over time.

CONCLUSION

STARS has provided a vehicle for strengthening the relationship between CCSD and UNLV. It has led to the writing of collaborative grants and the exchange of ideas on district curriculum and university course design. Recently, a research group called the Center for Accelerating Student Achievement (CASA) was formed. It is a formalized three-way partnership that includes UNLV, CCSD, and the Nevada Department of Education.

The real strength of the district–university partnership is indicated in the actions taken around the word study issue. While the basic principles of the initial STARS program remain, the partnership relies on up-to-date research to ensure that the program remains on the cutting edge of what is known about the nature and practice of reading instruction. Another advantage of the partnership is that sophisticated evaluations and studies will continue to be run to make sure that the STARS program is effective. This is necessary if we are to continue to give teachers the best information possible so they can ensure that all students learn to read.

Given the success of the STARS project collaboration, UNLV and CCSD have undertaken numerous other joint efforts in the past two years. We have learned many valuable lessons about, and gained numerous insights from, working together on Project STARS and these new projects. Following, we will share some of what we have learned.

A Tentative Outline for Successful School District–University Collaboration

1. Establish a high level of trust. This normally begins with conversations centered on topics and concerns of interest to both groups. However, it is established by frequent interaction and communication.
2. Work as true colleagues. This means respecting each others views and orientations, not just tolerating them.
3. Establish truly joint goals for projects rather initiating projects that are amalgams of separate goals.
4. Acknowledge the realities of working in schools. In this project, two schools dropped out near the start, and other schools that were willing to participate had to be found. We had to accept that we could not achieve a perfect experimental design.
5. Foster continuous collaboration rather than one-shot partnerships.

STARS is a case study of how preconceived biases and attitudes can be set aside to allow a meaningful focus on student achievement through providing skills and strategies to teachers.

Project STARS was created through an active collaboration between the CCSD and the UNLV College of Education. The program continues to evolve through ongoing and expanded collaboration, which now includes reading experts from other universities. Through this collaboration, Project STARS exemplifies a program that continuously seeks to improve—and more important, that is viewed as a program that is dynamic and research-based.

NOTE

1. The original STARS intervention program design team included three literacy specialists from CCSD: Annie Amoia, Sue Hendricks, and Chelli Smith. These three individuals collaborated with the UNLV College of Education faculty members Thomas Bean, Marilyn McKinney, and Maria Meyerson. As the STARS model was refined and revised, the extended design team included additional CCSD literacy specialists: Caroline Gaynor, Joan Lombard, Meg Nigro, and Christine Venturis. Christy Falba and Ralph Reynolds have joined the STARS team in the last two years. Currently, Meg Nigro serves as the STARS project manager in the district.
2. The study contained three between-group factors: school (seven schools participated), grade (third, fourth, fifth), and treatment (STARS-trained vs. comparison). There were five dependent measures: the listening comprehension subtest and the silent reading test from the Reading Inventory for the Classroom (Flynt & Cooter, 2001), the Qualitative Spelling Inventory (Bear, Invernizzi, Templeton, & Johnston, 2000), the Value for Reading and Concepts of Self as a Reader subscales from the Motivation to Read Profile (Gambrell, Palmer, Codling, & Mazzoni, 1996). Analysis of covariance (ANOVA) using student pretest score as the covariant was performed on all post-test data.

REFERENCES

Anderson, R. C., Reynolds, R. E., Schallert, D. L., & Goetz, E. T. (1977). Frameworks for the comprehension of discourse. *American Educational Research Journal, 14*(4), 367–381.

Applebee, A. N. (1978). *The child's concept of story: Ages two to seventeen.* Chicago: Chicago University Press.

Baumann, J. F., Jones, L. A., & Seifert-Kessell, N. (1993) Using think alouds to enhance children's comprehension monitoring abilities. *The Reading Teacher, 47*(3), 187–199.

Bear, D., Invernizzi, M., Templeton, S., & Johnston, F. (2000). *Words their way: Word study for phonics, vocabulary, and spelling instruction* (2nd ed.). Upper Saddle River, NJ: Merrill.

Beaver, J. (1997). *Developmental reading assessment resource guide.* Parsippany, NJ: Celebration Press.

Cooper, J. D. (1997, May). *Project SUCCESS.* Paper presented to the annual meeting of the International Reading Association, Atlanta.

Delphi Research of Nevada, Inc. (2003). *Project STARS: Interim evaluation report.*

Duffy, G. G., Roehler, L. R., & Herrmann, B. A. (1988). Modeling mental processes helps poor readers become strategic readers. *The Reading Teacher, 41*(8), 162–167.

Fielding, L. G., & Pearson, P. D. (1994). Reading comprehension: What works. *Educational Leadership, 51*(5), 62–68.

Flynt, S. E., & Cooter, R. B. (2001). *Reading inventory for the classroom* (4th ed.). Upper Saddle River, NJ: Merrill Prentice Hall.

Fountas, I. C., & Pinnell, G. S. (1996). *Guided reading: Good first teaching for all children.* Portsmouth, NH: Heinemann.

Gambrell, L. B., Palmer, B. M., Codling, R. M., & Mazzoni, S. A. (1996). Assessing motivation to read. *The Reading Teacher, 49*, 340–355.

Jewell, T. A., & Pratt, D. (1999). Literature discussions in the primary grades: Children's thoughtful discourse about books and what teachers can do to make it happen. *The Reading Teacher, 52*(8), 842–850.

Keene, E. O., & Zimmerman, S. (1997). *Mosaic of thought: Teaching comprehension in a reader's workshop.* Portsmouth, NH: Heinemann.

Klingner, J. K., & Vaughn, S. (1999). Promoting reading comprehension, content learning, and English acquisition through collaborative strategic reading (CSR). *The Reading Teacher, 52*, 738–747.

Manzo, A. (1969). The ReQuest procedure. *Journal of Reading, 13*, 123–127.

Morris, D. (1982). Word sort: A categorization strategy for improving word recognition ability. *Reading Psychology, 3*, 247–259.

Morris, D. (1999). *The Howard Street tutoring manual: Teaching at-risk readers in the primary grades.* New York: Guilford Press.

Morris, D., Ervin, C., & Conrad, K. (1996). A case study of middle school reading disability. *The Reading Teacher, 49*(5), 368–378.

National Reading Panel (NRP). (2000). *Teaching children to read: An evidence-based assessment of the scientific research literature on reading and its implications for reading instruction.* Washington, DC: National Institute of Child Health and Human Development.

Pikulski, J. J. (1994). Preventing reading failure: A review of five effective programs. *The Reading Teacher, 48*(1), 30–39.

Raphael, T. (1982). Question-answering strategies for children. *The Reading Teacher, 36,* 186–191.

Reynolds, R. E., Hendricks, L., & Sinatra, G. (2004). *Teachers' perceptions of word callers.* Manuscript submitted for publication.

Roller, C. M., & Breed, P. L. (1994). Sometimes the conversations were grand, and sometimes. . . . *Language Arts, 71*(7), 509–515.

Samuels, S. J. (1997). The method of repeated readings. *The Reading Teacher, 50*(5), 376–381.

Smith, M. M. (1999). The influence of an intermediate intervention model on two teachers' literacy practices (Doctoral dissertation, University of Nevada, Las Vegas, 1999). UMI Dissertation Abstracts Microform 9932598.

Snow, C. E., Burns, M. S., and Griffin, P. (Eds.). (1998). *Preventing reading difficulties in young children.* Washington, DC: National Academy Press.

Stanovich, K. E. (1986). Matthew effects in reading: Some consequences in individual differences in the acquisition of literacy. *Reading Research Quarterly, 21,* 360–407.

Stauffer, R. (1976). *Teaching reading as a thinking process.* New York: Harper & Row.

Sudduth, P. (1989). Introducing response logs to poor readers. *The Reading Teacher, 42*(6), 452.

Taberski, S. (2000). *On solid ground.* Portsmouth, NH: Heinemann.

Worthy, J., & Broaddus, K. (2002). Fluency beyond the primary grades: From group performance to silent, independent reading. *The Reading Teacher, 55*(4), 334–343.

Wuthrick, M. A. (1990). Blue Jays win! Crows go down in defeat! *Phi Delta Kappan, 71*(7), 553–556.

8

Literacy as the Key to Academic Success and Educational Reform

Fred Carrigg and Margaret Honey

Key Points

- The Union City Public Schools established the use of authentic literature, an alignment of textbooks with state outcomes, and the requirement of an ESL or bilingual certificate for tenure.

- Schools implemented thematic teaching, cooperative learning, and activities designed to stimulate higher-level thinking.

- New practices were supported by ongoing professional development, a flexible evaluation system, and professional development support positions.

If you believe that all children can learn, then anything is possible. Consider the story of Union City Public Schools, a majority minority school district (where a majority of residents are part of an ethnic minority) that rescued a generation of schoolchildren and an educational system from the brink of collapse.

In 1989, economic woes and disjointed school structures, curriculum, and practices saddled Union City Public Schools with a dubious distinction: failure in 44 of 52 indicators set by the New Jersey State Department of Education (NJDOE). The district was given one last opportunity to "fix" itself or face the same fate as its neighbors—Paterson, Jersey City, and Newark—which had been taken over by the state.[1]

Five years later, the *New York Times* called the system "an inspiring example for troubled districts elsewhere" (*New York Times*, editorial, August 1995). By spring 2002, students finished first in each New Jersey Grade Eight Proficiency Assessment (GEPA) test and subtest when compared with the state's 12 largest Abbott districts (a set of approximately 30 poor, urban school districts grouped by 30 years of dialogue, litigation, and New Jersey court decisions). Union City students were approaching or exceeding state averages on the Elementary School Proficiency Assessment (ESPA) and GEPA, the state's fourth- and eighth-grade tests, respectively. What guiding principles and key changes led to this dramatic turnaround? Hard work and common-sense practices:

believing in children, trusting teachers, adapting reforms to the community, showing patience in judging and scaling change, and embracing literacy as the cornerstone for learning. These were the ingredients that enabled the reforms to succeed.

BACKGROUND: THE LOWEST POINT

By the late 1980s, the Union City, New Jersey, public school system was deep in crisis. The state's reliance on locally based property taxes to finance its schools had resulted in such severe underfunding that broken windows in classrooms often went unrepaired, students shared outdated books, and class sizes of 30 or more were commonplace.

At the same time, the district experienced an acceleration of a "Latinization" trend that was transforming the city as a whole and the district's student body. What started as a Cuban chain migration 20 years before had evolved into a massive influx of Cuban, Puerto Rican, Peruvian, Ecuadoran, Salvadoran, Dominican, and other Latin populations dispersed almost equally throughout the nine-school district. As a result, Union City Public Schools became majority minority enrolled institutions, with Latino students approaching 90% of the district's student body.

The district's de facto academic structure focused on dividing students into homogeneous groups based primarily on English language ability and to a lesser extent math ability, as measured by book publishers' level tests and the districtwide summative test, the California Achievement Test (CAT). This system established four unique and separate instructional paths for students to follow. The bilingual/ESL program, with its language ability groupings, accounted for approximately a third of the 8,000 public school students; the special education program accounted for 12% to 15%; the gifted and talented (G&T) program accounted for 5%; and the general education program (GEP) accounted for the rest (approximately half). The GEP also operated by its own tiered system, with classes where remedial students would be pulled out and classes where students were on "level." Teachers with no "pull outs" and on level were considered the lucky or favored ones.

The curricular model reflected the de facto structure of the schools. There were four systems of curriculum and instruction, each with a unique system of leveled books, assessments, and entry–exit criteria. The GEP used a nationally popular basal system with level tests, teaching and re-teaching materials, workbooks, supplements, dittos, and so on used by most elementary teachers and the pull-out Title 1 teachers. The G&T program, which had its own bilingual/ESL subcomponent, used some of these materials but had more resources, smaller class sizes, and a much more child-centered approach, featuring mini-courses on authentic literature and "specials" such as photography that were not available to the general population. Special education was "localized" to each building. It used and adapted whatever was available, attempting to adhere to the two larger programs, the GEP and bilingual/ESL program. The State of New Jersey in its accountability system monitored only the test results of the GEP in its evaluative procedures and ranking of school districts in the approval continuum (and continued to do so until the No Child Left Behind Act of 2001). By 1989, results from the "monitored" grades were dismal, reflecting the disjointed structures, curriculum, practices, and economic woes.

After a series of monitoring visits, the NJDOE delivered its final report in spring 1989. The district was given one last opportunity to "fix" itself. Within a year, the administration would have to present a Corrective Action Plan (CAP) addressing all 44 deficiencies, obtain state approval, and succeed by spring 1994. Failure to do so would lead to a state takeover of the school system.

A NEW BEGINNING

The school board naturally preferred to retain local control and therefore began a drastic reformation of the entire educational system. It turned to those supervisors whose departments had not been cited for violations: Tom Highton, principal of the Gifted and Talented School, and Fred Carrigg, director of Bilingual/ESL Education. Highton and Carrigg were given the titles of superintendent and executive director for academic programs, respectively, as well as new responsibilities.

Guiding Principles

Highton and Carrigg strongly believed in several guiding principles that would serve as the core philosophy behind the district's radical transformation. They included:

All Students Can Learn. The reformers crafted a new district mission statement that clearly communicated an important belief—that all children can learn. It acknowledged that various school structures and attitudes often made children feel deficient. And it recognized that when children feel excluded from the mainstream (by being unable to pronounce certain words, by being pulled out of class, by the low expectations of their teachers), they begin to feel like failures and their learning is inhibited. The reforms were designed to stop making students feel inferior. The vast majority of the staff in Union City believed in the statement, genuinely liked their students, and had respect for Latino culture, the community, and the Spanish language. Given that staff believed the children were not the problem and could succeed, this allowed for a fundamental assumption that change was possible. The questions became what to do and how to do it.

Teachers Must Be Part of the Process. The reformers set goals and offered guidance and time for change but in general did not force teachers to institute new methods. Rather, they rewarded teachers for experimenting with ways to achieve the goals. The central administration operated from the first day with great respect and appreciation for the teaching faculty and staff and made every effort to include them in the plans and implementation of change. It was not a top-down imposed model. The district weighted reform committees with teachers to demonstrate to all district personnel their commitment to teachers' input. Furthermore, teachers were not penalized if their students' test scores declined while they worked out new practices (the original nonpenal trial period was two years).

Research Must Begin at Home. The reformers did not unquestioningly accept conventional thinking but persistently conducted their own research about basic teaching issues and tailored their responses to local conditions. It became apparent that no external replacement model, no matter how successful somewhere else, could be superimposed on Union City. It would fail. Whatever was learned from research would have to be localized and adapted to the particular population and organizational structures at the district, school, and classroom level. It would have to be Union City's model.

Reform Is a Long-Term Process. The reformers quickly acknowledged that they could not do everything at once and gave themselves five years to achieve results. In addition, they instituted annual reviews of curriculum and methods to ensure a process of continuous reform. Careful thought was given to how best to communicate their commitment to substantial change as well as practical strategies for making it happen.

Organizational Structures for Reform and Planning

With less than a year to produce a plan to avoid state takeover, the district immediately formed the CAP committee to coordinate the entire reform plan. To do this, it set up 10 predominantly administrative subcommittees (e.g., a School to Work Committee, a Safe and Clean Environment Committee, a Reduction of Class Size Committee). Many of these dissolved as soon as their objective was achieved. The committee that dealt with the core of teaching and learning, the Primary Literacy Committee, however, was designed to be self-perpetuating because its subject was basic curriculum and how to teach it. It eventually became the Elementary Standing Curriculum Task Force.

Teachers were a heavily weighted majority so that no one could question where the ideas had come from. This makeup had the added benefits of helping to attract a wide base of support from a variety of groups among the teacher population and to signal confidence in their abilities.

Because Highton and Carrigg had worked in Union City for nearly 20 years, they knew the community intimately and chose committee members with great deliberation. In the past, policymaking committees too often had included only teachers from traditional classrooms, ignoring the large numbers of students assigned to special programs. The new leadership made sure that the members of the committee included representatives from all the major groups in the school system (monolingual English only, bilingual/ESL, special education, Title 1). They sought individuals marked by energy and open-mindedness. Their selections were a clear signal to the community that the voices of teachers—in all their diversity—would be heard and that life in Union City would be very different. The ability of the new leadership and committee members to speak for and to many groups would prove essential to the process of reform.

Long-Range Thinking

With the district's failings so overwhelming and with a very short time to produce improvements, the CAP committee wanted to plunge into change immediately. However, it resisted the temptation to make that plunge and instead made its most critical and difficult decision: to allow a year for educational research to develop a district-level educational philosophy. The committee felt that the district's educational philosophy consisted of platitudes—"each student succeeding to the best of his abilities"—without substance and concrete reality. To articulate a philosophy and means to enact it would take time and require acceptance from the very top level to be effective.

During that year, the reformers realized that they could not tackle the entire system at once because it was too immense and complex. They decided instead to acknowledge that change would be a long-range process and planned for a five-year implementation. The first year was spent conducting research and planning for the subsequent years of implementation. In addition, pilots were set up at the K–3 level involving different materials, strategies, and techniques and keeping most classes in the existing program as a control group. In year two (1990–91), the reform curriculum would be fully implemented for grades K–3; in year three, for grades 4–6; and in year four, for grades 7–8. In year five, the committee would begin planning for change at the high school level. This meant that no student schooled in the new methods would enter a new grade only to face old-style instruction. Further, it meant that the reformers were able to take the lessons learned from each successive implementation and apply them toward easing the transition in subsequent years.

Localization

The committee examined the specific circumstances of Union City. It had an urban school system with aging buildings and no extra space to build new facilities. The student body was 93% minority, 90% Latino; 75% did not speak English at home; 33% were limited English proficient (LEP) or bilingual/ESL; 14% to 17% had been in the country for less than three years, and many of these students lacked reading and writing skills in their own language. The vast majority of the students enrolled in the general education program were exited as bilingual/ESL students. The mobility rate was 44%—that is, only about half the students in any class in June had been there the previous September.

LITERACY AS THE FOUNDATION

Children are driven to learn language, not for its own sake, but because of their natural curiosity about the world.
    —*Union City K–3 Communications Curriculum (1990)*

To develop a philosophy of education pertinent to local circumstances, the Primary Literacy Committee turned to research, ranging from Bloom's (1956) taxonomy to Krashen's (1973, 1981, 1985) and Cummins's (1979, 1980) theories of second-language acquisition to a variety of pieces on whole language and reading (Goodman 1973, 1982; Graves 1983; Krashen & Terrell 1983).

Based on research and the demographics of its student population, the Primary Literacy Committee decided to base systemic reform on literacy. Its members believed that literacy is the key to all other learning, and therefore that all efforts in the entire district would be aligned with the goal of advancing literacy. (In 1989, literacy as the foundation was an innovative idea; today, it is accepted by the mainstream education establishment.)

Next, the reformers focused on constructing a literacy curriculum that would help develop thinking, reasoning, and collaboration skills. Teachers and students would be encouraged to explore new ways of learning. In particular, students would learn by doing—demonstrating proficiencies by writing research papers and carrying out projects.

Before reform, separate curricula governed GEP, special education, ESL/bilingual, and Title 1 students. The reform strategy was to produce one inclusive, seamless guide that represented real diversity and did not single out any group. This was not merely an idealistic notion. The different guides led to anomalous results. For example, when a student left the bilingual program for the GEP, the levels test (based on basals) focused on specific, prescribed vocabulary words, not the skill of reading, so that many bilingual students were too often held back when in fact they were able to read at a more advanced level. (Conversely, a student could know the vocabulary of the basal but not be able to read.) The reformers wanted to rationalize the outcomes.

Again, the Primary Literacy Committee conducted basic research. First it examined the way that American schools were traditionally organized and concluded that virtually the entirety of American education is based on the following concepts about the development of reading skills:

- K–2 students work on decoding how to read (phonics skills).
- Middle elementary students learn to read for meaning (e.g., main idea, inferences, and author's intent).
- Upper elementary students (6–8) learn to read for content (information and in content areas).
- High school students diversify their uses of reading. They read for new information and usable knowledge and to develop their own creativity and their writing skills.

The Union City committee felt that the traditional basic outline of the American organizational structure of education was sound but decided to dig further into how educators went about achieving these goals. They looked at the state-mandated lists of skills and achievement levels; they also surveyed the Union City teachers on what they considered necessary skills for students and when to teach them. The committee then combined these two lists and opened up new ways of achieving the desired results.

Using Children's Literature

The traditional unspoken guidelines stipulate mastering initial consonants, then final consonants, and then medial vowels in first grade. Instead of working from the phonetic sound system and covering the alphabet starting with *A* and ending with *Z*, the reformers suggested that elementary teachers work from authentic children's literature with obvious initial consonants. Students would read these selections aloud in class. This served the multiple purposes of phonemic awareness, vocabulary, and building background knowledge of Anglo-American culture and motivation (the clear meaning of the stories and the usefulness of the underlying message in the students' lives). Today, the *read-aloud* is widely accepted as the beginning point for literacy. For example, the committee selected Eric Carle's *Very Hungry Caterpillar* to teach the initial *H* sound, which in Spanish is silent and therefore particularly a challenge for Spanish speakers to master. Similarly, "Three Little Pigs" teaches /p/ with repetitions of the words *pig* and *puff,* final /f/ with repetitive *huff* and *puff,* medial /I/ with *big, pigs(s), little,* etc. The work ethic is a moral in the story—the third little pig works a long time to build a house to withstand the wolf's attempt to blow it down (clear meaning on the value of hard work). By reading these stories, children have an opportunity to practice listening and speaking while repeating phrases as well as to see how letters are used, all while enjoying a story that captures their imagination. All these concepts are commonly shared practices today (*repetitive, decodable language*).

In addition, the committee suggested using a personal alphabet book (same letters but in different order and with different examples). Teachers were asked to keep records of what they covered so that they could be sure they eventually worked through the entire alphabet in a way that built on the students' familiarity with various sounds without a prescribed order based on English language background assumptions. This was a common practice among the district's special education teachers. Their students would create a book of high recognition words and pictures that was personalized for each student to remind him or her of the initial consonant sound. Hulk Hogan was a ubiquitous character for the initial *H* at the time. This technique, called the Language Experience Approach, was shared with all teachers.

Choosing Texts

Next, the various committees (literacy, math and science, fine arts) conducted an in-depth examination of the textbooks and materials that claimed to teach state-mandated skills. They called publishers to deliver K–3 materials, spent three months analyzing content and methods, and discovered little educational congruency between the desired skill outcomes and the actual materials. That is, many textbooks were not designed to achieve the state's mandated outcomes.

The Primary Literacy Committee looked at the entire inventory of textbooks in Union City and decided that the existing texts should be demoted from core materials to supplementals. Not only did the texts not achieve what was wanted, but, further, the reformers noted a dearth of children of color in the texts and in the illustrations. For a 93% minority school district, these texts had little relevance. This aspect of the research reinforced the committee's idea that the whole system had to be reconceived.

Creating a Pedagogy

The system that emerged in Union City was a clear hybrid. It uses embedded phonics instruction with centers (balanced literacy approach) and direct, explicit phonics instruction after the letter sound correlations have been introduced through authentic literature. (The phonics books did not disappear, but they were relegated to practice and homework.) Whole language was used to signal a major shift away from English language background basals. Many whole-language assumptions were based on common sense, although the reformers felt that for their particular population, where many parents were not native English speakers, literacy would not naturally "emerge." Instead, in the Union City version of whole language, literacy would be deliberately nurtured or encouraged by specific activities such as reading genuine stories (read-alouds, shared reading, choral reading), a lot of discussion that introduced new vocabulary words (background knowledge; what I know, what I want to know [K-W-L]; think-alouds), all designed to promote oral development. In addition, the committee noted that parents at home did not pick up basals to read aloud. They read authentic children's literature, which is written by writers who want to communicate a story.

The committee focused on building its phonics acquisition system on teachers' professionalism and knowledge through the use of children's literature and deep knowledge of Spanish–English transfer of phonemes and phonological awareness (phoneme–grapheme relationships). To do this, the Union City Board of Education (UCBOE) adopted a resolution requiring all teachers to get an ESL or bilingual certificate before they would receive tenure. (This was actually an extension of a less prescriptive resolution adopted in 1978 that already paid 100% of the cost for graduate-level bilingual/ESL courses.) It took the average teacher four years to get the certificate.

In the interim and as immediate guidance, the district released the K–3 Thematic Unit Handbook to every primary teacher. The handbook has explicit guidelines for the teaching of phonics and subskills in a child-centered curriculum that aligns materials, strategies, and techniques with outcome expectations and assessment through performance suggestions (very similar to today's concept of mapping). This freed teachers from the problems arising from the English language background-dependent cumulative subskills model, which had proved ill matched to the needs of the population. In addition, the committee decided to institute the reforms throughout the district to address the problem of mobility. The reformers also knew that teachers needed training to successfully negotiate the transition from using basal readers to the unique emerging model of literacy in Union City.

MEETING STANDARDS

After deciding to key everything curricular to literacy, the next step was to determine how to build skills based on state and national acquisition standards. The committee sought out authentic children's literature that could be used to teach the desired skills and decided to purchase multiple copies of a variety of stories for each teacher. The stories were chosen using a system that awarded points for different characteristics, such as teaching medial vowels ("Three Little Pigs" received points for medial /I/, for example, as well as initial /p/), and themes chosen by the teachers.

The teachers were polled about themes appropriate to different grades. Themes would unify teaching across a grade and within a classroom. The first-grade teachers opted for cats, dogs, precious pets, and friends. One subtheme cut across all grades—conflict resolution, an issue particularly pressing in the all-too-familiar climate of violence in America. The idea of resolving conflicts through words was covered directly in workshops with the students and in the curriculum guides developed by the committee. Similarly, books depicting verbal resolutions were given extra points as a way to reinforce clearly the idea of using words instead of violence or brute force. *Charlotte's Web* was one choice—a novel in which serious differences among the animals were negotiated by words and reason. In this way, then, the district built up banks of authentic materials, genuine children's literature, based on themes identified as important by the teachers who would use the books. Each teacher across the grade received up to 30 copies of a core book or books and five or six copies of at least four related titles per marking period. Today, elementary rooms all have classroom libraries containing many hundreds of books.

Assessment

While the committee retained the basic outline of reading skills, it adapted the particulars to suit its homogeneous Spanish-speaking community. For first grade, for example, the committee chose to delay assessing for medial short vowels until midyear because some English vowel sounds don't exist in Spanish (e.g., the short a, the /æ/ sound). These sounds are thus more difficult for Hispanics, and teaching them first virtually guarantees initial failure with reading skills. *Most English Language Background systems do this immediately in first grade.* (The final consonant sound /s/ is also dropped in oral speech and thus is more difficult for many Caribbean Spanish speakers; the committee strongly urged that assessing for final /s/ be postponed until later in the year.) To give students a positive first experience, the curriculum began in the fall with initial and final consonants that were similar in both languages. Traditional classrooms begin teaching reading with the letter *A* and its corresponding /æ/ sound because the letter *A* opens the alphabet. Union City strongly urged teachers to detach the letter-learning process from reading. To give students a sense of success, teachers were encouraged to begin with /m/ and /n/, for example, or any other high-transfer initial consonants in September and October. Skeptical about this approach, traditional classroom teachers were reassured that they would still cover the whole alphabet in first grade but in a different order. Students were to create their own alphabet books of words that were meaningful to them. The most important thing was to move away from teaching methods that make children feel like failures on day one to teaching methods that make them feel that success is possible. The committee believed that instilling that sense in students was essential to their ongoing academic accomplishments.

Two Systems at the Same Time: Literature and Basal Readers

The committee wanted ultimately to replace basal readers with authentic literature, but it also knew it had to approach change gradually and offer guidance to those charged with front-line practice. The committee provided structure for the teachers by designing activities and suggesting strategies that would replace the pedagogy of basals.

Success in learning to read is based on prior knowledge—in particular, two aspects of prior knowledge: (a) oral language development (i.e., an adequate background in grammar and vocabulary, because people learn words from context); and (b) familiarity with the dominant culture. Native-born Americans acquire prior knowledge by living in the United States; they pick up associations such as "red" means "danger," whereas in Latin cultures, "red" may suggest "celebration." Children whose families are new to this country, and who often arrive with limited economic resources and limited formal education in their native countries, face a documented nexus of obstacles when negotiating the American educational system.

These students' parents often work multiple jobs, are not fluent in English, and are not familiar with the American system of education. These factors all hinder the ability of immigrant parents to provide the kind of background support (especially vocabulary and grammatical structure in English) that children need to succeed academically. The reformers had worked with Union City students for years and knew that the school system would have to support children in acquiring a core of foundational skills in English. The committee therefore chose to concentrate on training elementary grade teachers to conduct general preparatory pre-reading activities (e.g., reading many stories, extended conversation). The overall objective was to increase the students' oral English, especially vocabulary. Teachers were to create language-rich environments in the classroom by developing oral associations to the stories the children were going to read. To help teachers do this, the committee listed the words that needed to be discussed and suggested techniques that help children acquire essential vocabulary (e.g., talk circles, semantic mapping).

All of these ideas (e.g., vocabulary lists, extended conversation, talk circles) were enumerated in complete detail in guidebooks on how to achieve skills acquisition. The guides, printed in large format, correlated texts, page numbers, suitable activities, proficiencies, and state standards (mapping). They presented as much information as possible in one place, helping teachers plan their activities, and simultaneously stating the desired outcome. The underlying question for teachers behind all the reading activities was: "What does a student need to know to understand this story?"

The reformers, however, did not force radical change on the teachers. They gave them the option of using both systems (authentic literature as well as the basal) at the same time. The dual system was expensive but served as a necessary, useful transition: It showed teachers how to teach skills using both systems. Today, basals have disappeared from the classrooms (voted down by the teachers themselves), and the core materials consist exclusively of good stories.[2]

Curriculum represents the philosophy of a school district and governs what actually takes place in the classroom. The reformers wanted a curriculum that led to student-driven, inquiry-based learning. They further believed that curriculum should not be fixed but must respond to changing circumstances and feedback from practitioners. To embody this belief, they institutionalized a process of examining curriculum every year to seek out opportunities for improvement—in materials, methods, scheduling, and any other area that made sense to change. In practice, new editions of the guides are reissued about every three years.

RESULTS OF THE PLANNING YEAR

The focus on literacy and adoption of its own version of a whole-language approach to learning generated major change throughout the Union City district. Many of these changes addressed seemingly intractable problems in education such as teacher isolation, inertia, and lack of systemic support.

The whole-language approach, as modified by Union City, reorganized the power structure among teachers and broke down barriers that had been in place for years. One third of all Union City teachers were bilingual/ESL. Before reform, they often felt like second-class citizens, underbudgeted and frustrated by placements of exited bilingual students. Another third of the Union City teachers were certified bilingual/ESL as a result of the 1978 Union City Board of Education policy. Thus, fully two thirds of the Union City teachers were already trained in phonological awareness and familiar with research-based literacy techniques (such as the key role of oral language development). Once reform was instituted, the traditional teachers began to perceive the bilingual/ESL teachers not only as equals but also as resources full of useful experience and advice.

The use of curricular themes also provided tremendous cohesion in many areas. The themes were deliberately broad to allow great variation. But the thematic approach also meant that all teachers in one grade—traditional classroom, special education, bilingual/ESL—were teaching the same themes at the same time. Again, this broke down barriers between groups of teachers within a school. The unification provided by themes was particularly important across schools because of the high rate of mobility among students: It meant that a fifth-grader could change schools and still be studying the same subject. Within the classroom, the teachers found that themes made teaching easier. If the subject was "whales," for example, they could assign anything from *Moby Dick* to *Amos and Boris,* depending on the reading level of individual students. This made small groupings easier; it encouraged whole-class discussion, as well.

Literacy is about communication. An additional benefit of themes is that students go home and tell their parents, "I learned about parrots today." Themes invite parents into children's school life in a way that subskill strategies in basal readers never do. Themes were and are the unifiers from K–12. No unifier had existed before, and this change was a great advance for the Union City schools. There is now one curriculum guide per grade instead of four or five.

During the following four years (1990–94) of restructuring, the summer was used to plan the implementation of the next year's reorganization and curriculum for successive grades. The second year of the five-year plan focused on implementing the new K–3 curriculum; the third year, on 4–6; the fourth year, on pilots and reorganizing grades 7–8; and the fifth year, on implementing the new curriculum for grades 7–8, piloting reforms, and developing new curricula for grades 9–10. A second five-year planning process, begun in 1994, focused on comprehensive reform at the high school level.

RESULTS OF THE REFORM

The reform efforts in Union City have dramatically improved students' academic performance across all grade levels. At the elementary and middle school level, students' performance on state-mandated standardized tests exceeds their urban counterparts and is equal to or approaching state average. At the high school level, 80% of the students are passing New Jersey's High School Proficiency Assessment in Language Arts Literacy. The high schools have also had substantial increases in the number of students enrolled in advanced placement courses. In 1994, 25 students were enrolled in advanced placement classes, and 20% of them passed. In 2000, the number enrolled increased to 146, with 38% of the students passing. In addition, the district has witnessed a fivefold increase in the past four years in the number of students gaining acceptance to first- and second-tier colleges and universities.

One thing that sets Union City apart from other reforms in urban schools is this phenomenon. Most urban reforms see their pinnacles of success occur at the lower elementary level. Union City achieves its highest pass rates at the eighth-grade level, continuing the growth begun in the lower elementary grades. This remarkable pattern has been sustained for years, and Carrigg attributes it to the district's focus on literacy.

Seven Key Areas of Simultaneous Implementation

The Education Development Center's Center for Children and Technology has collaborated with Carrigg to identify key reform strategies integral to the success of the Union City school district (Honey, Culp, & Carrigg, 2000).[3] Once literacy was established as the pathway for transforming the district, reformers recognized not only the fundamental changes they needed to enact but also the need for these changes to occur simultaneously to ensure effectiveness. They identified the following seven areas in need of change:

1. Time and structure
2. Pedagogy and cooperative learning
3. Ending pullouts
4. Evaluation/supervision
5. Professional development
6. Physical environment
7. Administrative and professional development support positions

1. Time and Structure. The first major change was in the use of time. The old, classic bell schedule and ability grouping style allotted the teacher 20 minutes for each homogeneous reading group, with the remainder of the class, who had not been pulled out by Title 1, doing seat work such as workbooks or dittos. This was not suitable for the new Union City model, which depends on sustained silent reading, paired reading, authentic writing, proficiency-based research, and hands-on activities. It also contravened the idea of inclusion and one curriculum for all; the reformers considered a heterogeneous group design necessary for the academic success of all children. Literacy skills needed to be taught through a variety of activities (reading, discussion, themes, personal alphabet, use of literacy centers, etc.). It was evident to reformers that literacy skills could not be effectively acquired under the old bell schedule and that at least all the language arts literacy subject areas—speaking, reading, and writing, needed to be pulled together to reinforce learning from different perspectives. This produced a 111-minute block of time known as the "whole language uninterrupted block of time" or the "communications period." With the implementation of a new schedule in the mid-1990s, this block became 120 minutes in primary classes.

The Committee further stipulated that no child could be pulled out of class (discussed further under change #3). Thus, classroom teachers were guaranteed that they would have all their students together at one time for 111 minutes. They could use this period to establish classroom knowledge and thus be sure that everybody knew certain things about the day (group assignments, morning message, establish core concepts like story mapping, etc.). Within this block, teachers were told what to accomplish—to cover reading, writing, and

speaking on the pertinent theme—but not how to do it. They were to organize the time as they saw fit. Planning was changed from daily to weekly goals
and objectives to reinforce the new use of time to delve deeper into ideas. If
two students could work productively without direct adult intervention, they
should be allowed to do so. The teacher would be free to work with students
who needed more guidance. For the first time, teachers were asked to provide
instruction in accord with individual needs rather than the homogeneous
basal groups. This was a radical change (in 1990) that offered teachers unprecedented power and increased their sense of professionalism. It was also a change
that was key to the success of the reform.

Most veteran teachers responded with enormous enthusiasm and energy.
Novice teachers needed tremendous support and training in practical strategies and techniques on cooperative learning and managing time—training not
provided by schools of education. Principals and administrators were alarmed
at the movement in classes and the talking among students. The reform committee recognized that the concomitant of choice is responsibility, and that
the district needed to help teachers and administrators understand the new
environment and accomplish the new goals. In response, they devised a tiered
system of professional development and peer coaching (described later).

The new block of time also allowed an interdisciplinary approach to
flourish. Themes that emerged as part of a historical period of study were also
covered in literature, the arts, and the sciences. For example, seventh-grade students learning about the Civil War not only studied political and social issues
but also began to analyze primary source materials (e.g., personal journals and
art from the period) and read contemporary novels about the war (e.g., *Red
Badge of Courage*) to enrich their understanding of the human experience of
ordinary people during that time. They created bar and pie graphs to visual-
ize advantages and disadvantages of the North and the South.

2. Pedagogy and Cooperative Learning. Cooperative learning is a critical component of making education for Union City students more relevant to
work and life in the real world. Its premise is that very few people are solely
responsible for an entire body of work from goal setting to final result. Instead,
they work in teams and are accountable to different departments and demands.
What students and teachers alike need to learn are the skills of cooperative
learning: goal setting; dividing work into various units; negotiating differences
in skills, temperaments, and schedules; and synthesizing the work of different people into a coherent whole. Various models of cooperative learning were
explored and the choice of the model was left up to each school and grade
level. For the middle elementary grades and higher, successfully implementing a cooperative learning model was a prerequisite to the student-centered
responsibility and accountability system that was emerging. (For more on
cooperative learning, see Johnson & Johnson, 1975, 1998; Slavin, 1986.)

One salient fact about the Union City student population is that every
year, 20% of the students are new entrants into the school system. Teaching
skills acquisition in a linear format was virtually impossible, and the linear

model had led to district failure. The reform committee decided it made more sense to base the system on strategies that help students *learn how to learn* rather than on cumulative discrete skill acquisition. Students would be engaged in contemplating big ideas and questions even if they hadn't completely mastered all the conventions of reading and writing. In communicating meaningful messages to others, individual attention would be given to the student's progress in speaking, reading, and writing. This meant mastering the objectives generally referred to as "Bloom's Taxonomy": learning to remember, comprehend, apply, analyze, synthesize, and evaluate. Cooperative learning became the vehicle to accomplish this. As part of embracing this approach, the reformers worked on replacing the model of the teacher as owner of all knowledge with the model of both teachers and students as active members of the learning process.

For seventh-grade history, for example, a class might be divided into groups of four and read different texts or authentic resources, depending on ability, but each group is asked the same question: "What were the real causes of the Civil War? Write them in priority order and cite the page number where you found the information." The task is *not* "Answer the questions at the end of the chapter." With only four or five in a group, all the students must read and talk together; no one can get away with skipping the work because his or her peers know and disapprove. The students are asked to prioritize and defend their list (a higher-order thinking skill), and recording the citations prepares them to write research papers. Students debate among themselves the list of causes and then compare with other groups, eventually arriving at a class decision (with astute guidance from the teacher) as to the major causes of the Civil War based on research rather than memorization.

Literacy skills (reading for information, details that support the hypothesis, outlining, persuasive-argumentative, speaking, writing, etc.) are all developed in a student-centered effort to communicate meaning and message.

3. Ending Pullouts. The most significant outcome of this change in philosophy was the elimination of pullout services as a means to help all students acquire foundational knowledge. Prior to the reforms, about 80% of the elementary students were in some type of pullout programs. It was difficult for teachers to determine where their students were in the learning process. It was easy not to accept responsibility for the pullout students. They were someone else's responsibility. In addition, as articulated by the CAP committee, "separated, segregated learning contravenes thematic planning" and labels students "remedial." It is tremendously important that children feel accepted as part of the group. When they are pulled out, especially for remedial work, they are often aware that "something is wrong with them and must be fixed," and this by itself impedes their progress. With the wholehearted support of the supervisor of Basic Skills Improvement, the Committee eliminated all pullout programs. (There is one exception: A few students who cannot read at all are pulled out to be given one-on-one attention.) Concomitantly, and for the same reasons, the district eliminated the word *remedial* from its vocabulary and refers to students as *emergent readers* to describe where the students are in the process rather than to label them as deficient.

To replace pullouts, the district instituted co-teaching (team teaching), whereby resource and support teachers no longer required students to come to them in a separate location. Instead, they went to the different classrooms to provide the classroom teacher and the students with extra help. Implementing this philosophy was a major struggle. Co-teaching meant that both specialists and traditional classroom teachers had to learn a new set of skills that would enable them to work together to determine which instructional practices would best meet the needs of individual students. As a result, some teachers quit, left the district, or retired. It was not easy changing a lifetime of habit. However, the ESL/bilingual teachers had co-taught for years, some with teachers who didn't even speak the same language, much less use the same styles. They knew co-teaching would work.

It took at least a year of teetering before the central administration knew whether this element of the reform would be effective or disruptive. The administration was heartened, however, to see teachers circulating among groups to give personal attention to those who needed it; and over time, it saw more team-teaching going on. Now co-teaching is second nature to the Union City teachers.

4. Evaluation/Supervision System. Union City reformers understood, as a classic management paper puts it, "the folly of rewarding A, while hoping for B." Innovation is defeated when the reward system punishes failed experiments and honors old levels of achievement. However, experimentation must be tethered to reality and the likelihood of success. Union City tested various methods of evaluation. Of the traditional criteria, it retained those on classroom management, cleanliness, and routine reporting of information. It added observable strategies and techniques to the teacher evaluation form ("conducts read-alouds," "maintains student portfolios"). Professional development workshops were held for principals, supervisors, and other administrators on how different methods would look and what strategies and techniques were appropriate in the new order. Ultimately, however, the administration developed a very simple test as they visited classes: "Tell me what this group is doing and how it supports how to learn." Any teacher who was trying new materials and could answer this question persuasively would not be penalized if students' test scores dropped. This freed teachers to try new methods and materials without fearing that they would be held accountable for fledgling efforts at new techniques.

5. Professional Development. Union City considers staff development a process, not an event. The district learned a great deal from the early years of restructuring, particularly during the massive staff in-service retraining in the philosophy of literacy acquisition (1989–93). Training increased from fewer than 8 hours a year to more than 40 hours a year, with many more opportunities available for voluntary staff development.

The training included differences in teaching styles so that teachers would understand and respect what others were doing. The district used a five-stage model to support teachers as they worked toward proficiency in the new educational paradigms: awareness; practice; sharing; peer coaching; and mentoring, keeping records of what training faculty had participated in.

- *Awareness.* In this stage, broad or new core concepts are introduced to large groups of faculty. Often state or national figures conducted these sessions. During the first in-service session of each new year, revised curriculum guides are presented and discussed with grade-level or department-level faculty. This continues to today. Hundreds of teachers attended training sponsored by professional groups, out-of-district workshops, and state and national conferences. The district began a Midsummer Conference that attracted hundreds of Union City teachers.
- *Practice.* During the second stage, specific basic strategies and techniques are introduced and practiced in smaller groups or for a specific age level, for example, how to create a "Wall Story." A single story is made up by an entire class over time. One group starts drawing a picture on the wall (on paper) and writing accompanying text. A second group continues both the picture and the story. The result is the product of the entire class. Each student feels a part of it, and the lesson communicates that many small contributions can add up to one unified whole. Teachers actually do, in a workshop atmosphere, the intended practice. This stage has also proved particularly effective for computer orientation. Basic computer skills (e.g., Beginner Macintosh, Internet Explorer) are introduced and practiced over several sessions. Practice sessions may take place over several days, a weekend, or for longer periods of time. Teachers gained "refresher" credits or opted for pay.
- *Sharing.* In collegial meetings, practitioners of new approaches discuss their experiences, both successful and not so successful. At least two half-day grade-level sessions were conducted every year during the initial plan from 1989 to 1993. Teachers from across the district convened by grade to discuss different structures. At each session a different school would set the agenda and lead the discussion, giving ownership to the teachers.
- *Peer coaching.* In response to the need for extensive training for the new system of teaching, Union City developed a two-tier mentoring system. The first approach was peer coaching for new teachers. A new teacher is paired with an experienced, confident colleague who teaches the same grade level or academic area. In the beginning of the year, the pair will work together and co-teach in class. The peer coach observes, models, and provides suggestions and ideas on successful practices. They spend two to five days going over the curriculum guide and co-teaching. After the initial period, the peer coach returns and

meet with the new teachers for consultations. Originally, peer coaches were half-time coaches, half-time teachers. This system of one-on-one individualized support was so popular among teachers that the coaches became full time. The number of peer coaches varies from year to year.

- *Mentoring.* As an extension of peer coaching and as required by the state, Union City has a system of mentors, with every new teacher having a mentor at the building. New teachers can consult these mentors on a one-to-one basis for any reason, academic or bureaucratic issues on a classroom, school, or district level (from filling in lunchroom forms and attendance sheets to insurance payments) over the entire year.

District-led professional development decreased as each school set its own agenda for model implementation. The goal was for the faculty to become knowledgeable of each school's own, separate model which did not transfer well to district-sponsored grade-level efforts focused on classroom practices. Cross-school workshops on classroom-level practices, strategies, and techniques were discouraged in favor of each building developing its model implementation. However, much of what is cited earlier survived. By the 2000 academic year, the district-level professional development cycle reappeared, focused on academic achievement and bringing together teachers from across the district on the same grade levels, as did the Midsummer Conferences. Practice-level workshops have begun to reappear focused on academic achievement. Peer coaches are reappearing as literacy coaches at the school level.

6. Physical Environment. Basic refurbishment of the buildings took place in 1992 with funding from the Union City bond initiative. Windows were replaced, classrooms and hallways were painted, and the buildings were made graffiti-free. The district insisted that in grades K–3, every classroom have a reading center, which it considered essential to basic literacy. But rather than mandate that teachers redesign their entire classrooms, the district chose to reward those who were willing to embrace the new curriculum with refurbished classrooms. Teachers who agreed to try the reform approach were allowed to purchase cooperative learning tables, classroom libraries, and often computers. Further, for teachers willing to implement instructional changes, the district offered to buy furniture for more centers—whether for listening (tapes), a community center (focusing on community workers such as firemen, social studies), science, math, or art. Computer centers were mandated in 1995. Over the years, the classrooms slowly added one center at a time, and now most elementary classrooms have multiple centers. Today, instead of static rows of desks facing front, cooperative learning tables are the *norm* at elementary and middle schools and are becoming increasingly common in the high schools. Teachers are encouraged to make their teaching station a part of the new physical environment and not locate it in the traditional spot in front of the blackboard at the front of the classroom.

7. Administrative and Professional Development Support Positions.
In addition to the creation of peer coaches, two other administrative support
positions were in place to guide the changes in classroom practice: the ESL head
teacher and the curriculum resource teacher. The ESL head teacher had existed
since the early 1980s. Her role was to oversee the language ability testing of
the LEP students, to maintain the longitudinal data, and to make recommendations for intra-bilingual/ESL program placements and entry–exit recommendations. Essentially, ESL head teachers were making data-driven assessment
recommendations. As students moved from one building in the city to another,
the data followed, because the ESL head teachers shared the information with
one another. By the mid-1980s, this system was computerized and maintained
initially on Lotus spreadsheets and then moved to Excel. They were also a primary source at each building for the course sequence necessary for bilin-
gual/ESL certification. All of them were master teachers in their own right and
further served as resources on classroom practices, especially grouping, management, strategies, and techniques. As the system moved away from level tests
based on the basals to student-centered performance-based assessment, their
expertise became critical at the school level.

In 1990, the existing position of helping teacher was abolished. This
position had been created in 1970 to "help" new teachers in each building
learn the routines and materials, to assist the principals in bureaucratic functions, and to oversee inventories of books and supplies. The new position of
curriculum resource teacher (CRT) was created, and existing helping teachers,
like anyone else, had to apply. The change in title was not cosmetic. The new
CRTs' primary responsibility was to guide all staff in the implementation of
the new curriculum in the classroom. Since they were not supervisors, teachers felt more at ease in requesting their help. Some of the helping teachers
applied and enthusiastically welcomed the change; others did not. Each school
now had a local expert on the reform agenda. Regular meetings were held
among the CRTs to discuss the stages of implementation of all of the structures cited earlier. They were critical in the building of classroom libraries, in
support for cooperative learning, in providing resources for teachers in strategies and techniques, and in making recommendations for scheduling the
blocks of time and maintaining the heterogeneous groupings of students.

With the imposition of the whole school reform (WSR) models mandated
by the court in all Abbott districts beginning in 1998, both of these positions
have been phased out. The CRTs have been replaced with additional assistant
principals at each elementary school and a WSR facilitator whose mission is
quite different. ESL head teachers have also been phased out and replaced
with support services chairpeople.

Perhaps the most significant and far-reaching decision made by the reformers, one that made these strategies possible, was to give themselves time to
think about what they wanted to do. The seven strategies listed earlier emerged
out of an understanding of the particular population served by the district, an
acceptance of a long-term process approach to reform, an awareness that learn-

ing involves many interrelated components that need alignment to achieve change, and a commitment to communicate ideas and objectives to teachers and students (not only with words, but also through rewards and incentives). The cumulative effect of these seven interlocking elements was to change the teachers' assumption that "different is deficient" to "everyone can learn." This was probably the most radical, most seminal change in the district. This embracing and optimistic attitude on the part of teachers paved the way for decisions to key all K–3 teaching to the goals of advancing literacy and to create an inclusive curriculum that addresses the diverse instructional needs of all types of learners, including English language learners. Together these changes not only sparked improvements in elementary teaching and learning but also ignited greater reforms and greater achievement gains in grades four through eight and beyond, transforming the lives of a generation of urban youth as well as a school system.

NOTES

1. The material in this paper and the full story of the reform effort can be found in "The Transformation of Union City: 1989 to Present," CCT Reports, August 15, 2000, published by the Education Development Center's Center for Children and Technology, supported by a grant from the Jerry Lee Foundation and the National Science Foundation (#REC-9554327).
2. To comply with Reading First, the district was required to adopt its first basal comprehensive reading program since 1989 in the summer of 2002. However, the curriculum clearly lists it as a teaching material in the system of books and alignments.
3. Additional details on each of these areas can be found at the Union City website, http://www.unioncity.k12.nj.us/curr/1-4humanities/index.html

REFERENCES

Bloom, B. S. (Ed.). (1956). *Taxonomy of educational objectives. The classification of educational goals. Handbook I: Cognitive domain.* New York: Longmans, Green and Co.

Carrigg, F., Honey, M., & Thorpe, R. (In press). Putting local schools behind the wheel of change: The challenge of moving from successful practice to effective policy. In C. Dede & L. Peters (Eds.), *Scaling up success.* San Francisco: Jossey-Bass.

Cummins, J. (1979). Linguistic interdependence and the educational development of bilingual children. *Review of Educational Research, 49,* 222–251. (Reprinted in National Dissemination and Assessment Center, *Bilingual Education Paper Series,* September 1979)

Cummins, J. (1980). The cross-lingual dimensions of language proficiency: Implications for bilingual education and the optimal age issue. *TESOL Quarterly, 14,* 175–187.

Education Development Center. (1995). *1993–1994 summary report: Union City interactive multimedia education trial.* New York: EDC/Center for Children and Technology.

Goodman, K. S. (1982). *Language and literacy: The selected writings of Kenneth S. Goodman,* Frederick V. Gollasch (Ed.). Boston: Routledge & Kegan Paul.

Goodman, K. S., & Burke, C. L. (1973). *Theoretically based studies of patterns of miscues in oral reading performance*. (Final Report.) (ERIC Document Reproduction Service No. ED079708)

Graves, D. H. (1983). *Writing: teachers and children at work*. Exeter, NH: Heinemann.

Henríquez, A. (1999, fall). "The appropriate technology." *Blueprint*, 63–64.

Honey, M., & Andrés, H. (1996). *Union City Interactive Multimedia Education Trial: 1993–95 Summary Report*. New York: EDC/Center for Children and Technology, April 1996.

Honey, M., Carrigg, F., & Hawkins, J. (1998). Union City online: An architecture for networking and reform. In C. Dede & D. Palumbo (Eds.), *ASCD Yearbook* (pp. 121–140). Alexandria, VA: Association for Supervision and Curriculum Development.

Honey, M., Culp, K. M., & Carrigg, F. (2000). Perspectives on technology and education research: Lessons from the past and present. *Educational Computing Research, 23*(1), 5–14.

Johnson, D., & Johnson, R. (1975). *Learning together and alone: Cooperation, competition, and individualization*. Englewood Cliffs, NJ: Prentice-Hall.

Johnson, D., & Johnson, R. (1998). *Circles of learning: Cooperation in the classroom*. Edina, MN: Interaction Book Company.

Krashen, S. (1973). Lateralization, language learning and the critical period: Some new evidence. *Language Learning, 23*, 63–74.

Krashen, S. (1981). *Second language acquisition and second language learning*. Oxford: Pergamon Press.

Krashen, S. (1985). *The input hypothesis: Issues and implications*. London: Longman.

Krashen, S., & Terrell, T. (1983). *The natural approach: Language acquisition in the classroom*. Oxford: Pergamon Press.

Slavin, R. (1986). *Using student team learning*. (3rd ed.). Baltimore, MD: Johns Hopkins Team Learning Project.

9

Five Years Later

The Outcomes of a Schoolwide Approach to Increasing Achievement in an Urban High School

Douglas Fisher, Nancy Frey, and Douglas Williams

Key Points

- The first step toward increased achievement at Hoover High School was the identification of instructional strategies to be used in all content areas.
- The Professional Development Committee presented and modeled the strategies, and administrative personnel evaluated their use.
- The reading lab was replaced with in-class tutoring, Sustained Silent Reading was revitalized, and the curriculum was aligned with standards.

The "ghetto school" was the phrase most commonly associated with Hoover High School in San Diego, California. Students, their families, and teachers all knew the reputation of this urban school that serves over 2300 students. The reputation was so widely known that higher-performing schools recruited "academically talented" students of color from Hoover with the promise of a safe, caring place to learn. The fact was, Hoover was the very lowest-performing school in the county and among the 20 lowest-performing high schools in the State of California.

The average Hoover student in grades 9–12 read at a 5.9 grade-level equivalent, according to the Gates-MacGinitie reading assessments. The majority of students at Hoover scored "far below basic" on measures of their academic knowledge in math, science, and social studies. California uses an official accountability score, the Academic Performance Index (API), to evaluate the performance of students within the school. Hoover students scored a 444 (out of 1000) the first time this assessment was used. Again, Hoover was in very last place in the county. In addition to the numeric score, the API provides comparison data. Using the API number, schools are ranked in deciles (1–10) and then ranked according to similar schools, a second number between 1 and 10. The first year, Hoover received a statewide rank of "1," meaning that the students' performance was in the lowest 10% of the state.

On the similar-schools score, Hoover received a "2," meaning that the student performance was in the lowest 20% when compared with schools that had similar demographics.

Beyond the student achievement issues, the campus was regularly the target of graffiti artists, teachers' morale was low, and turnover was high. Teachers regularly bid out of Hoover when they could, to avoid the poverty and crime associated with working there. Campus security was regularly supported by the San Diego Police Department due to the number of gang fights and race-motivated hate incidents. The entire student population at Hoover qualified for free lunch, 46% of the students were classified as English language learners who spoke a total of 39 languages, and 96% of the students were members of "ethnic minorities." In other words, every student in the school could have been considered "at risk"—or, as one of our consultants reminded us, "at promise."

This is not to suggest that there wasn't a core group of teachers who worked hard every day to reach the adolescents at Hoover, or that the teachers at Hoover didn't care. They did. Unfortunately, their efforts were not coordinated, and far too many students failed to develop academic proficiency.

Then, in 1998, Hoover partnered with faculty from San Diego State University and two other public schools to create the City Heights Educational Collaborative. The goal of this partnership was to significantly alter the historical performance of students and ensure that each and every one of them had a chance to attend college. Our goals were ambitious, and we knew we needed an action plan that was developed and agreed on by the whole faculty.

"MAKING A DIFFERENCE MEANS MAKING IT DIFFERENT"

One of the partnership's first responses to the poor performance of students at Hoover was to elect a literacy leadership team composed of teachers, administrators, and university faculty. This team met over several months and drafted the first schoolwide literacy plan. The plan was presented to the school governance team for approval and then to the whole faculty for ratification. In addition, the principal identified a Professional Development Committee and charged its five members with creating an implementation plan. Figure 9.1 provides a diagram of the work done at Hoover.

Schoolwide Literacy Instruction

The original literacy plan called for the identification of an unspecified number of instructional strategies that could be used by every teacher within the school. The literacy leadership team established two criteria in its original document: The instructional strategies should (a) have a strong research base, and (b) be appropriate for all content areas. The team's rationale, as presented to the school governance team, was to allow students to get to know instructional

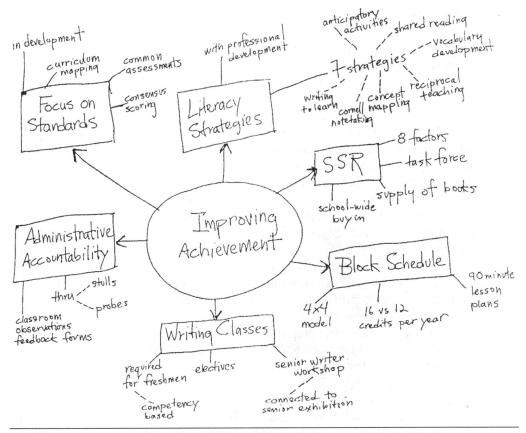

FIGURE 9.1. Graphic organizers of Hoover efforts.

strategies and not have to learn new methods for accessing text and talk each time they entered a new classroom. As one member suggested, "Students need transportable skills so that they spend more time on content and less time on figuring out the strategy." The team also noted that the selected instructional strategies should not limit teachers who wanted to use content-specific instructional strategies or more strategies than the school could agree on.

The final ratified document contained seven instructional strategies that all teachers agreed to use, including anticipatory activities, graphic organizers, note taking, read-alouds and shared readings, reciprocal teaching, vocabulary instruction, and writing to learn (see Fisher, Frey, & Williams, 2002, for more information).

Once these strategies were approved, the Professional Development Committee designed an implementation plan. While the committee worked, it remembered the words of a teacher who did not believe that this would be a long-term focus of the school: "I've been around long enough to know that this too shall pass. You'll do a few stand-and-deliver sessions and then be on to something else." The first phase that the Professional Development Committee wrote contained 18 sessions spread over two years. Teachers would be required to attend professional development sessions during their prep period once per month. Given that the school operated on a block schedule of 90 minutes, teachers had more prep time than was required in the contract with the district. Thus, the governance team deemed it reasonable for the administration to ask them to attend a professional development session once per month.

During the first year, each of the instructional strategies was presented and explained. Teachers who had used the strategy were asked to share their successes and implementation challenges with other teachers during the session. Given that teachers attended these sessions during their prep periods, every teacher received the information on the same day, but this was accomplished in small groups. Each period, 25% of the faculty (or about 28 teachers) attended the professional development session. While this required that the presenter share the same information four times, the groups were smaller and thus more accountable for participation.

The second year of implementation focused on demonstration lessons during prep-period professional development sessions. In other words, teachers shared an example of their implementation of one of the seven strategies with their peers during the prep-period sessions. The Professional Development Committee often videotaped teachers and asked them to share video clips and discuss the use of the strategy in their classrooms.

Since 1998–99, the Professional Development Committee has continued to focus attention on the implementation of the seven instructional strategies agreed on by the staff. Several teachers have commented on their knowledge of these instructional strategies, including a math teacher who said, "I basically knew how to use the seven strategies the first year and thought we should move on. I'm glad we didn't. My skills have really developed, and I am a much better teacher than I ever was. This year, with collegial coaching, I get to meet with another teacher and compare implementation of the instructional strategies. We keep cycling around, getting better all the time."

While there has been significant consistency in the use of professional development time for improving implementation of these strategies, some time has also been devoted to additional initiatives that augment the school's literacy plan. For example, the revitalization of Hoover's Sustained Silent Reading program was accomplished by apportioning time in the professional development calendar to this schoolwide effort. In addition, sharing data analyses of the school's test scores led to a curriculum alignment process that has involved every department.

Schoolwide Sustained Silent Reading

Building on the strategic teaching and learning strategies that were implemented schoolwide, the literacy leadership team turned its attention to the amount of time that students read. Understanding that students are not required to read a great deal during the school day and that reading volume has a strong relationship with vocabulary knowledge, comprehension, and future reading habits, the group undertook the implementation of a school-wide Sustained Silent Reading (SSR) initiative.

Over a series of months, agreement was reached on an SSR policy. If approved, the policy would require that time each day be devoted to free, voluntary reading. The committee recommended that all students be scheduled into a 20-minute class at the same time. The governance team approved the policy, and a daily period was created during which all students read independently the books of their choice.

This schoolwide plan met with mixed success. Over the first two years, we saw increased numbers of students on campus during this time, maybe going to a counselor or walking to the restroom. The period was scheduled immediately after lunch with the goal of easing students back into academic thinking. However, far too many students left campus after lunch due to our block schedule. We also saw teachers grading papers or answering e-mail and not reading during SSR. The committee finally decided to meet and address this issue again when we noticed content area instruction creeping into the SSR time.

The committee conducted a self-study of teachers to determine the factors that would require attention for the school to be successful with the SSR initiative. Pilgreen (2000) identified several factors associated with the success of SSR programs, including staff training, book appeal, follow-up activities, environment, direct access to texts, nonaccountability, distributed time for reading, and encouragement. On a 5-point Likert-type scale, teachers rated each of the factors. The data suggested that we needed to increase access to texts, improve text appeal, and reduce the accountability associated with SSR time. This last factor was somewhat controversial because it meant that students would not be asked to keep reading logs or write book reports. The committee revised the SSR policy and presented it to the governance team. In addition to addressing each of the issues from the survey, the committee recommended that the reading period be moved earlier in the day and that school be "closed for reading."

The policy was approved, and teachers received $800 each to buy books for their classroom libraries. These funds came from a combination of Title 1, English language learner support, and grants. In addition, students were asked about texts that they would like to see in classrooms, and the list was provided to all teachers. Further, the Professional Development Committee identified texts that should be available in every classroom for students, including DMV manuals, short motivational stories such as *Chicken Soup for the Teenage Soul* (Canfield, Hansen, & Kirberger, 1997), magazines, e-books, audiobooks, and graphic novels, and purchased enough for each teacher.

In addition, the governance team approved the request to close the school during the SSR period. That meant that administrators, counselors, secretaries, custodians, security guards, and other adults joined a classroom and read during the period. The phones were switched to automatic answering, and one person staffed the front office (while reading), directing visitors to select a magazine and read during SSR.

One-to-One Reading Tutoring

Understanding that the schoolwide initiatives would take some time to close the achievement gap, the literacy leadership team also focused on individualized instruction for students who performed significantly below grade level. Hoover had employed a reading specialist for many years. In 1998, the reading specialist operated a small computer reading lab that students were scheduled into based on their reading scores. When students were scheduled into the reading lab, they could not take an elective. The reading lab was a homogenous group of the poorest readers and operated counter to the professional knowledge base about ability grouping and tracking. Further, at Hoover, there was no evidence that the reading lab was effective. Reviewing this data, the team recommended that the lab be closed and that teachers and students use the computers in classrooms.

Unfortunately, the reading specialist took this as an affront and transferred out of the school. Over the next year, the literacy leadership team discussed the needs of the most struggling readers and noted that the most effective interventions were individualized.

Using Title 1 funds, English language learner support funds, and a grant from the State of California for underperforming schools, the team developed an intervention program operated during school hours under the direction of a new reading resource teacher. This teacher hired 10 new staff members who were each assigned to 11 ninth-grade students for a term. They each tutored their 11 students daily in their English classrooms rather than as pullouts or in self-contained classes. Thus, 220 ninth graders received 30 minutes of daily, individualized reading instruction for 90 days. The reading resource teacher supervised the intervention program and observed the reading intervention tutors on a daily basis as they implemented their instruction.

As expected, the achievement results were significant. The average reading achievement change for these students was two years on the Gates-MacGinitie assessment. More surprising was the change in the structure of the English classrooms. The introduction of a reading intervention tutor provided the catalyst for the English teachers to create learning centers, small group instruction, and individualized activities. The English teachers understood the need for individualized tutoring but did not want specific students tutored in the back of the room. Thus, they structured their 90-minute class time so that there were reading and writing workshops in which all students worked alone, in small groups, on the computer, or with the teacher. The reading intervention tutors, then, were not conspicuous in their teaching of individual students. For more information on reading intervention tutors, see Lapp, Fisher, Flood, and Frey (2003).

Curriculum Alignment

Content and performance standards in each discipline guide what is to be taught. In some states, these standards are also used for accountability. In California, for example, the state accountability system has moved from standardized tests (norm-referenced) to standards-based assessments. This means that at the end of a course, students should be able to demonstrate mastery of the content.

In reviewing the achievement data for students at Hoover, the literacy leadership team noted significant differences based on specific classes. They could not believe that the same students could score so differently between social studies, science, English, and math. They hypothesized that the data reflected a mismatch between what was taught and what was tested and not poor teaching. As one of the English teachers reported, "I teach mythology because it's in the standards. I didn't realize, however, that my focus on Chinese mythology wasn't getting them anywhere on the test that requires an understanding of Greek mythology."

In response, teachers met in course-alike groups (e.g., Algebra I, World History, ninth-grade English, etc.) to examine the state standards and determine pacing guides appropriate for students at Hoover. In addition, these course-alike groups determined which standards were either not assessed or infrequently assessed and thus could be minimized in class. These test blueprint materials were available from the state (at http://www.cde.ca.gov/statetests/star/resources/blueprints.html) and proved to be very helpful in guiding these conversations. The discussions during this process were intense. One teacher suggested that the state was "controlling our teaching." Another commented, "I can teach whatever I want; it just depends on if I want students to do well on the state assessment." As one of the vice-principals noted, "There are so many standards, too many to be covered humanly. So, if you're going to pick, why not pick the ones that will allow students to demonstrate to the world that they have developed mastery in the content?"

Thus, the curriculum matrix was created (see Figure 9.2 for a sample). This document provides teachers with information on pacing their classrooms to ensure that they have addressed the key standards. It also provides administrators with information about the focus of each course and the content that should be covered in the course. Importantly, teachers—not the state department or district administrators—created these documents. As with other initiatives at Hoover, teachers are encouraged to develop plans that they believe will close the achievement gap; *then* administrators hold them accountable for implementing them.

Administrative Accountability

As people have come to visit Hoover and ask questions about its success in raising achievement, they often note that the schoolwide focus and plans that have been put in place have mixed results in other schools. They ask why this combination has worked at Hoover. We have a few answers. First and foremost, teachers created the initiatives, and the initiatives were implemented schoolwide. In far too many places, "schoolwide" means a core group of teachers, often representing less than one third of the teaching staff. We wish we could

Department: **Course:**

Standard	Unit of Study	Practices/Activities/Strategies	Assessments	Timeline

Vocabulary development (target and concept words)

Accommodations for special education and English language learners

FIGURE 9.2. Curriculum matrix and pacing guide.

say that we had 100% participation, but that would not be accurate. It is reasonable to suggest that over 90% of the teachers at Hoover participate in the schoolwide plans that have been developed. Part of the reason for this is the system of administrative accountability that has been created.

It is important to note that the Hoover administrative team does not hold teachers accountable for initiatives in their early stages. Instead, the administrators are supportive and complimentary when teachers try to implement part of the schoolwide literacy plan. Over time, however, teachers are evaluated based on the plan. Figure 9.3 is the first page of the observation tool used by the administrators at Hoover. Each of the instructional strategies is noted, and administrators can monitor their implementation. This process accountability is as important to the administrators at Hoover as the outcome accountability that the state reports (see Fisher, 2001).

In addition, the administration holds teachers accountable for participation in professional development. No one wants to receive an invitation to visit the principal to explain an absence from a required prep-period meeting. Interestingly, while the administration has created an accountability system, it is not based on threats or coercion. Over the past five years, we have learned a lot about the role of the administrator in leading an urban school to close the achievement gap. Specifically, we have learned five lessons about leadership at Hoover (adapted from Fisher & Frey, 2002).

Lesson 1: "Put Your Body in the Places You Care About." The most obvious and notable difference between Douglas Williams and other princi-

A Note from _____   Subject _____

Teacher _____   Date _____

Period _____ From ____ to ____

Today I observed:

Observation

Standards-based Instruction

- ☐ Students understand what/why learning
- ☐ Students know what makes good work
- ☐ Lesson/activities related to the standards

Instructional Techniques

- ☐ Previewing text, passages and/or content
- ☐ Activation of prior knowledge
- ☐ Purpose set/purposeful, focused activities
- ☐ Connection to the curriculum
- ☐ Anticipation guides
- ☐ Shared reading/Read aloud
- ☐ Vocabulary development/Word study
- ☐ Graphic organizers/Semantic maps
- ☐ Predictions
- ☐ Clarifying/Organizing ideas
- ☐ Questioning
- ☐ Summarizing
- ☐ Structured note-taking
- ☐ Direct instruction
- ☐ Teacher modeling
- ☐ Think aloud
- ☐ Structured small group work
- ☐ Guided practice
- ☐ Directed student discussions
- ☐ Independent group work
- ☐ Independent work time
    - ☐ Centers
    - ☐ Teacher conferencing
- ☐ Sharing
- ☐ Directed/Structured writing activities
- ☐ Assessment of student understanding

Print-Rich Learning Environment

- ☐ Variety of books accessible to students
- ☐ Text/content support materials used

Learning Environment

- ☐ Student work displayed
- ☐ Consistent and appropriate discipline
- ☐ Environment of respect/fairness
- ☐ Engagement of all students/On task
- ☐ Academically rigorous student expectations
- ☐ Clear instructions given
- ☐ Monitors students/students' work
- ☐ Provides feedback to students
- ☐ Validation of student responses/success
- ☐ Effective use of instructional time
- ☐ Use of assessment to guide instruction

Reinforcement

Refinement

FIGURE 9.3. Administrative accountability.

pals with whom we have worked is where he spends his time. Mr. Williams seems to be all over the campus—in the quad, at math department meetings, and at staff development. As we have noted, the 4 × 4 block schedule has allowed for monthly prep-period staff development sessions. Mr. Williams attends these professional development events not once or twice, but for the entire school day. He is an active participant in each of the four presentations, demonstrating to teachers that the content of the professional development is important. If someone misses the day, you can be sure that person will receive a note in his or her mailbox with an invitation to see Mr. Williams about the content of the training.

In addition to his attendance and participation in professional development, Mr. Williams spends an average of two hours per day in classrooms. He observes lessons and interacts with students daily. His feedback is succinct, and he specifically looks for evidence that teachers are implementing the strategies they learned during professional development events (see Figure 9.3). To accomplish his schedule of classroom observations, he has empowered a group of professionals in his office to manage some of the routine tasks. He talks with these people before or after school, when students and teachers are not engaged in teaching and learning.

The biggest and perhaps most controversial decision Mr. Williams has made in terms of where he puts his body and mind has been his participation in district-level events. He does not like to be away from campus and rarely attends meetings that take him away from school during the day. While he acknowledges that this creates a longer work day, he prefers to attend administrative meetings that are held after school hours.

Lesson 2: "Be the Teacher You Want to Hire." Mr. Williams models reading during the daily 20-minute independent reading period. He models trash pick up. He models his interactions with students in front of the campus security and school police. In addition to this type of modeling, Mr. Williams also believes that dress is important in setting a tone and establishing the culture of the school. While there is no formal dress code for teachers, it is made very clear that the teachers at Hoover should look like professionals. Mr. Williams models this daily: He wears slacks and a tie or school spirit clothes each day.

But more important than all those other forms of modeling is his instructional modeling for teachers. Mr. Williams models lessons in front of teachers and students on a regular basis. He does this to demonstrate the "instructional" part of his leadership. These model-demonstration lessons allow him to have conversations with teachers—reflective conversations about the quality of instruction and high expectations. These lessons also reinforce his credibility and keep him focused on the complexities of teaching at Hoover.

Lesson 3: "Talk with Students Often, and Talk About Things That Matter." Most principals like to take time to talk with students—after all, that's why we all went into this business. Of course, principals often have to talk with students during less than positive circumstances (e.g., suspensions, academic failure, not getting scholarships). However, this shouldn't be the only time that the instructional leader has the opportunity to interact with kids. Mr. Williams talks with students daily. The most impressive are student accountability talks before state assessments. Mr. Williams meets individually with each 9th, 10th, and 11th grader to discuss his or her performance on the most recent standardized test. He reinforces areas in which the student has done well and asks for a commitment to do better this year. In addition, he asks the student to tell him how her or his improvement will happen. For example, Mr. Williams was overheard talking with Malik, a ninth grader:

> *Mr. Williams:* You did really well on the math section. You must get good grades in math.
> *Malik:* Yeah, they okay. I do okay in math.
> *Mr. Williams:* What can you do to score even better?
> *Malik:* I gotta remember the formulas. I gotta figure out a way to remember those. They trip me up.
> *Mr. Williams:* What about your English scores? What can you do to get better scores there?
> *Malik:* I need to finish faster. My teacher said that I better read first and find ones that are easier for me. I should read the questions first. But I gotta remember to mark the answers in the right place. Then at the end, I guess I should fill in answers and not leave the paper blank.
> *Mr. Williams:* And you should read every night. Reading will help you a lot through your life. Read whatever you want, but read.
> *Malik:* Yeah, I better get back to class, we're reading *To Kill a Mockingbird* and my teach really likes that book.

Imagine the effect that this conversation has on Malik and the other students at Hoover. Every one of us who has worked in urban settings knows that students often don't take the standardized test seriously. Mr. Williams spent six weeks meeting with students so that they would understand that the test mattered, that they could do well on it, and that they had strategies to apply when they weren't certain of the answer.

Lesson 4: "Surround Yourself with Good People, Then Get Out of Their Way." The demands on an urban secondary principal at a large school are extensive and diverse. Even the most energetic administrator would be hard-pressed to accomplish these tasks alone. Mr. Williams has cautioned his vice-principals that micromanaging can be a fatal error in a large organization. He has also made it clear to staff that he needs each of them to ensure that Hoover's positive trajectory is maintained. Toward this end, he has sought faculty members who show leadership and collaboration skills. For instance, the Professional Development Committee is composed of classroom teachers, the peer coach, and a vice-principal. They have the authority to propose, design, and deliver professional development and advise the administrative team on classroom accountability. The school's SSR Committee—a group of teachers—was charged with setting policy for the 20-minute-per-day Sustained Silent Reading program. In addition, the special education department and another vice-principal have been working for the past year to create more inclusive practices for students with disabilities. They recently proposed a restructured department that will assign special education teachers to each department in the school—English, mathematics, social studies, science, and electives—in order to design and deliver curriculum accommodations and modifications. Other special education teachers will operate an innovative "lab class" where students with and without disabilities can receive specialized support such as individualized reading instruction and assistance with homework. They have also adopted an advocate teacher model for supporting families and writing individual education plans. Importantly, this team not only researched alternatives and proposed the department restructuring, it also did budget projections and a professional development needs assessment, and created an accountability structure. Mr. Williams meets with all of these teams to keep abreast of progress, answer questions, and marshal resources. He has told us that it's not enough to delegate work to others: We must also give them authority to get the work done. It is also vital to ensure that a reporting structure exists. "When I've got good people, I don't need to be there every step of the way. But I do need to stay in touch with the work as it progresses," says Mr. Williams. Call it "freedom with responsibility." We like to think of it as the true definition of shared decision making. The Western Association of Schools and Colleges apparently agreed. It recently awarded Hoover an unprecedented six-year accreditation for the depth and breadth of the collaborative work among faculty and administrators.

Lesson 5: "Nurture Partnerships, Especially Those That Benefit the School." During the time we have spent with Mr. Williams, we have learned a number of valuable lessons about instructional leadership. Interestingly, he tells us that there are many things that he just doesn't get to in a given day. We know, however, that he has created a system to ensure that budgets are monitored, the bells ring on time, and supplies are ordered. We have also learned that Mr. Williams has developed a number of partnerships that ensure his school operates efficiently. For example, Hoover is an old school—more than 70 years old. While many see this as a problem, Mr. Williams realized that there were literally thousands of alumni. Tapping the resources of the alumni with just the cost of a few dinners and some space on campus resulted in new construction, alumni scholarships for current students, and scads of volunteers providing needed services such as mentoring and evaluation of senior exhibition projects. When a new state language assessment was required in 2001, Hoover was faced with the challenge of administering the tests to 1,000 students in six weeks. Enter alumni and retired Hoover teachers, who participated in required training and then assisted staff in assessing all the students within the testing windows. "I don't know how we would

TABLE 9.1. Changes in Achievement in San Diego City High Schools: Academic Performance Index Summary

School	1999	2002	Growth
Lincoln	477	485	+8
Gompers	476	497	+21
Hoover	444	506	+62
Crawford	537	528	–9
San Diego	538	529	–9
Madison	601	575	–26
Clairemont	595	590	–5
Kearny	557	605	+48
Morse	604	633	+29
Serra	665	669	+29
Mira Mesa	719	719	0
University City	707	722	+15
La Jolla	812	795	–17

Source: California Department of Education.

have done it without them," remarked Mr. Williams. We don't, either, if the principal didn't already have an ongoing relationship with the school's alumni. In addition to the alumni, Mr. Williams has developed a number of business partnerships. These partners have provided intern sites for seniors and funds for computers, crime prevention, graffiti patrol, and books for the library.

Outcomes: Does This Focus Matter?

As noted, Hoover High School was the lowest-performing school in the city of San Diego and among the lowest-performing high schools in the State of California. In 2000, Hoover met its state accountability target for the first time in 15 years. Hoover students have increased their reading achievement by an average of 2.4 years (Gates-MacGinitie), and Hoover has the highest gain in the city on the state accountability test (see Table 9.1).

Importantly, measures of achievement are rising while the student body has remained stable. In addition, the expulsion rate has been reduced by two thirds, and the dropout rate has declined each year. Teachers at Hoover are especially proud of the recent published independent review of the changes at the school, written by a former Hoover teacher and current State Department of Education employee (see Figure 9.4).

NEXT STEPS AND LINGERING ISSUES

As with each previous year, we remain unsatisfied with the achievement. As the principal says, we'll be happy when "Hoover High School is the model school for all schools," not just for urban schools with exceptionally poor and excitingly diverse student populations. Thus, the literacy plan and professional development initiatives have been regularly revised. At this point, the literacy leadership team is considering several efforts that will complement the schoolwide focus on student literacy achievement.

In 1988, Hoover High School in San Diego was a tough place to go to school. It had a huge dropout rate, many incidents of violence, low academic achievement, and low teacher morale. But what a difference a decade makes, and what a difference a new benefactor and an innovative articulation plan can make.

Hoover High School is now one of four schools involved in the City Heights Education Pilot, a consortium of feeder schools and foundation schools that comprise a K–16 continuum. The consortium, initiated by local businessman Sol Price, works to ensure that the initiatives mandated in No Child Left Behind are met. San Diego State University has partnered with the feeding elementary, middle, and high school to create a model system of accountability and support that is based on content literacy.

Literacy is a focal point at Hoover High School where students speak 39 languages. All students are assessed in reading three times per school year. Students who are one-and-one-half years behind in reading must take a reading development class in addition to their English-language arts classes. This means that half of one's day could be spent in English-language arts and reading; this also means that students have opportunities to succeed more quickly in other content areas. Once students are close to grade-level, they may leave reading development classes and choose other curricular options. A 4 × 4 block schedule makes this possible.

Almost everything at Hoover revolves around student literacy: content standards, professional development, collegial coaching, horizontal articulation, teacher performance evaluations, and student support programs. Student support programs may take place during the school day in the form of tutorials; ten tutors are responsible for the success of the 200 most at-risk students. A state-of-the-art library, student incentives, "attendance advocates," AVID, an extended school day, major stakeholder meetings, common standards-based assessments, and on-campus teacher training help bolster an already student/teacher-friendly environment.

Hoover High School's programs are shaping into a model of holistic reform. Although test scores will surely follow, it is clear that this reform effort has already changed a school culture. Hoover High School is still a tough place to be, but the toughness is all academic.

—Adam Berman, *California Department of Education*

FIGURE 9.4. A focus on literacy: Hoover High School in San Diego. *Source:* California High School Newsletter.

Strategy #8—Questioning

Over several months during 2003, the literacy leadership team discussed the need to consider questioning and classroom discussion as part of the literacy plan. Too often, teachers ask literal questions in an "initiate–respond–evaluate" (IRE) format (Cazden, 1988). For example, the teacher asks, "Name one cause of World War II," and calls on one student, who responds, "Hitler." To this, the teacher responds, "Good. Can anyone add to this?" This style of classroom discourse, while not prevalent, does exist. Thus, after five years of focus on seven instructional strategies, the literacy leadership team would like permission to focus on an eighth. One idea currently being explored is to frame questioning within each of the existing schoolwide strategies. For instance, what is the role of questioning in writing to learn? In anticipatory activities? It would seem that this view of questioning is beginning to evolve into the more complex notion of inquiry.

Elective Class on Writing

The focus of the schoolwide literacy plan has been weighted toward reading. In fact, only two of the strategies (note taking and writing to learn) require student writing. In addition, Hoover teachers have not focused systematically on process writing. However, the literacy leadership team is aware that literacy means more than reading and that students must demonstrate their writing skills in order to pass the high-stakes High School Exit Exam. As the team has been reminded several times by Professor Leif Fearn during training, "You can read and not know how to write, but you can't write and not know how to read." Toward that end, the school has received a supplemental grant to develop and implement a ninth-grade writing class for all students. The course would begin at the sentence-writing level and progress through independent writing prompts. This approach emulates a gradual release of responsibility model (Pearson & Fielding, 1991). For information on the early work on this class, see Fisher and Frey (2003).

Test-Taking Skills and Test Prep

Given the fact that many of the students at Hoover are poor test takers and that the current accountability systems require performance on multiple-choice and essay tests, the literacy leadership team has begun conversations about schoolwide test-taking skills and test-prep materials. While concerned about using instructional time on these areas, the team hopes that infusing these skills throughout the school day and school year will provide students with skills to demonstrate their knowledge in class (see Langer, 2001, for a discussion of test preparation that is infused).

In response to this need, the Professional Development Committee has developed a series of after-school sessions for teachers that focus on several areas of test readiness, including attitude, general test-taking skills, direction words, multiple-choice questions, and skills for reading passages. In addition, the literacy leadership team has created a poster that is displayed in every classroom. The title of the poster is "Hoover High Scorer!" and it says:

You too could become the next High SCORER!

S = Schedule your time while taking the test.
C = Use Clue Words to help answer questions.
O = Omit difficult questions at first.
R = Read questions carefully.
E = Eliminate unreasonable choices.
R = Review your responses.

Each of these test strategies is accompanied by demonstration lessons developed by the departments so that these skills can be taught to students, not merely "told." As classroom teachers have become better able to recognize opportunities to model them in their own lessons, students are increasingly experiencing test preparation that is infused into the curriculum—an important feature of the schools that Langer (2001) identified as highly effective.

Collegial Coaching

Over the past five years, the Professional Development Committee has initiated a transfer of responsibility for in-services from their own group to other classroom teachers. Early in the process, the committee invited teachers to provide demonstration lessons during the prep-period sessions. It also began videotaping teacher volunteers and facilitating conversations about strategy use. In one of the prep-period meetings in 2002, groups of four teachers used their prep period to observe a colleague teach and then met with a professional facilitator who guided a discussion about strategic teaching and learning.

In the near future, the Professional Development Team hopes to fully implement collegial coaching. In this model, each teacher will have a partner either selected or assigned from another content area. Every teacher involved both coaches and receives coaching support from his or her partner. The teachers will use some of their prep-period time (partners will have different prep periods) to observe their collegial coaches and meet after school to discuss the lesson. Given that each member of the partnership teaches a different content area, the conversations will not focus on the content but, rather, on the ways in which the teacher engaged his or her learners and the ways in which strategies were used to ensure that all students participated in the lesson and could access the text and the talk. This evolution will allow the teachers to develop increased skills focused on the core seven (or perhaps eight) instructional strategies adopted by the school.

CONCLUSION

The teachers at Hoover High School have begun an important journey. They have assumed responsibility for the achievement gaps of students that come to them. They have banded together to identify specific schoolwide structures that they believe will help all students develop mastery across content areas. They have also provided students with distributed time to learn and access to supplemental reading tutoring as needed.

The outcomes to date have been positive and noteworthy, but they have not advanced far enough yet. However, the faculty and students at Hoover have been inspired by their early success and are eager to experience more in the future. There seems to be a parallel between teacher development and student achievement. Whether adult or adolescent,

all learners need multiple opportunities to apply strategies in a variety of contexts;
all learners benefit from collaboration with peers;
all learners need an opportunity first to be taught, then to teach others; investment in learning pays dividends in future accomplishments; and success breeds success.

At Hoover High School, we can hardly wait for the next five years.

NOTE

For more information concerning National Association of Secondary School Principals (NASSP) services and/or programs, please call (703) 860-0200, or visit http://www .principals.org.

REFERENCES

Canfield, J., Hansen, M. V., & Kirberger, K. (Eds.). (1997). *Chicken soup for the teenage soul: 101 stories of life, love and learning.* Deerfield Beach, FL: Health Communications.

Cazden, C. B. (1988). *Classroom discourse: The language of teaching and learning.* Portsmouth, NH: Heinemann.

Fisher, D. (2001). Trust the process: Increasing student achievement via professional development and process accountability. *NASSP Bulletin, 85*(629), 67–71.

Fisher, D., & Frey, N. (2002). Five lessons for leaders. *Principal Leadership, 3*(3), 53–55.

Fisher D., & Frey, N. (2003). Writing instruction for struggling adolescent readers: A gradual release model. *Journal of Adolescent & Adult Literacy, 46,* 396–405.

Fisher, D., Frey, N., & Williams, D. (2002). Seven literacy strategies that work. *Educational Leadership, 60*(3), 70–73.

Langer, J. A. (2001). Beating the odds: Teaching middle and high school students to read and write well. *American Educational Research Journal, 38,* 837–880.

Lapp, D., Fisher, D., Flood, J., & Frey, N. (2003). The dual role of the reading specialist in urban schools. *Journal of Staff Development, 24*(2), 33–36.

Pearson, P. D., & Fielding, L. (1991). Comprehension instruction. In R. Barr, M. L. Kamil, P. Mosenthal, & P. D. Pearson (Eds.), *Handbook of reading research* (Vol. 2, pp. 815–860). New York: Longman.

Pilgreen, J. (2000). *The SSR handbook: How to organize and manage a silent sustained reading program.* Portsmouth, NH: Boynton/Cook.

10

Improving Literacy Through Professional Development

Success and Sustainability in a Middle School

Tamara L. Jetton and Janice A. Dole

Key Points

- Reading achievement at Mound Fort Middle School was improved in part by facilitating the use of instructional strategies before, during, and after reading.

- Both professional development and strategy instruction with students consisted of modeling, guided practice with feedback, fading, and independent practice.

- Effective components of the literacy education project were: committed teachers, a clear vision of literacy, a supportive and effective administrator, an effective reading coach, coursework and study groups, and books for students.

In 1996, the Utah State Office of Education (USOE) designated several hundred thousand dollars for a three-year project designed to improve the reading achievement of several low-achieving schools in the state. The Literacy Education Advocacy Project (LEAP) was designed to provide a high-quality, research-based literacy program to selected schools scoring in the bottom 30% of the nation on standardized tests. Several elementary and middle schools were selected to be a part of the project. The USOE successfully assisted some schools in improving reading achievement over the course of the project, but it was not successful with all schools.

This chapter focuses on the most successful school in the project, Mound Fort Middle School in Ogden, Utah. Mound Fort is a middle school of sixth-, seventh-, and eighth-grade students located in an urban area. Unlike the typical image of Utah, this district has a high level of poverty and a significant number of minority students.

In this chapter, we describe the model of literacy developed for middle schools by LEAP and the program's implementation at Mound Fort. We focus especially on the staff development process and on the role of the reading coach at Mound Fort, Tamara Jetton, as she worked with teachers at the school.

THE LEAP MODEL OF LITERACY

In order to ground the project in a common framework and understanding of literacy, USOE staff and consultants developed a model of literacy. Our model included a definition of literacy as well as a conceptual framework that involved a delineation of the literacy process and literacy instruction.

Definition

As we began to implement LEAP, we believed that teachers needed a common understanding of how those involved in the project defined literacy. We defined literacy as *knowing how to read and write well enough to function in a literate society and to apply this knowledge whenever needed* (adapted from Anderson, Hiebert, Scott, & Wilkinson, 1985). We also identified several key characteristics of literacy that are relevant to students' lives, especially in middle school.

Definition of Literacy

- *Literacy is constructive.* Readers use their existing knowledge to construct an understanding of text; likewise, writers use what they already know to construct meaningful text.
- *Literacy is fluent.* Readers and writers master the basic processes to the point where these processes become automatic.
- *Literacy is strategic.* Readers and writers are aware of their purpose for reading and writing, the nature of the materials, and whether what they read and write makes sense. Based on this awareness, readers and writers have strategies or plans to help them solve problems while reading or writing. These strategies occur before, during, and after they read and write.
- *Literacy is motivated.* Readers and writers have goals for learning, they are interested in and informed by what they read and write, and they believe that they are capable of reading and writing to communicate effectively with others.
- *Literacy is a lifelong pursuit.* Readers and writers continuously practice, develop, and refine their reading and writing.

Conceptual Framework for Literacy Processes and Instruction

Another goal of LEAP was to provide teachers with conceptual frameworks for reading and writing processes and reading and writing instruction. As shown in Figures 10.1 and 10.2, we constructed conceptual frameworks that provided teachers with overviews of literacy processes that were then used to identify literacy instruction. In the following sections we discuss the three areas of focus for the conceptual framework; the reader/writer, the text, and the processes of reading and writing.

The Reader/Writer. We wanted teachers to understand that there are factors within the reader and writer that are crucial to their literacy development. Readers use their prior knowledge in order to connect what they already know with the ideas in the text. Readers do this, for example, by integrating ideas in the story they are reading with existing ideas they already have or with other stories, or by challenging the text in light of their own experiences and knowledge. Likewise, writers use their prior knowledge to construct convincing and

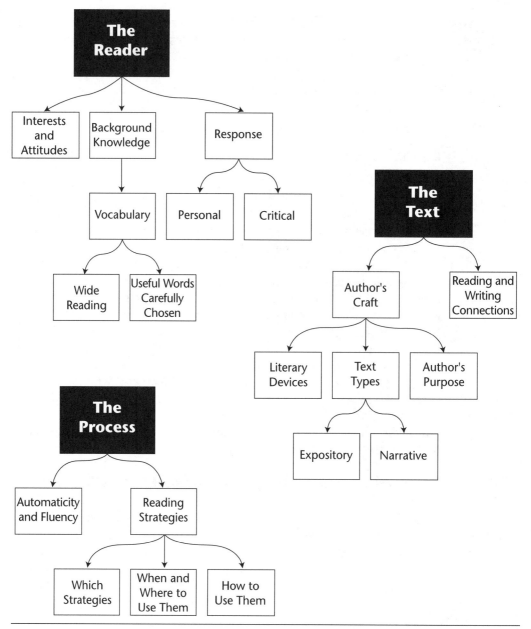

FIGURE 10.1. The reading process: Conceptual framework.

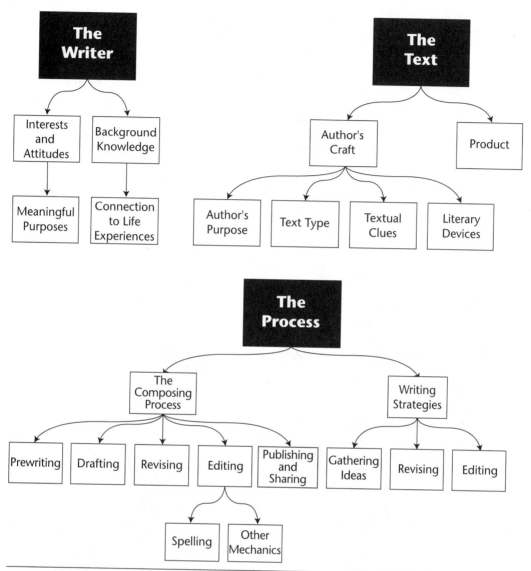

FIGURE 10.2. The writing process: Conceptual framework.

elaborate texts in a variety of genres. Through wide reading of a variety of texts, readers and writers are able to expand their background knowledge through the vocabulary and knowledge they acquire.

Another very influential factor is readers' and writers' attitudes or interests in reading. Readers' and writers' interests are strong when students have a goal or purpose for reading and writing, when they have sufficient prior knowledge, and when they can connect the text to their own lives. Their attitudes are most positive when they believe that they can be successful at reading and writing, and when they feel that they are supported in the community, home, and school environments. To generate interest, teachers need to give students time to read and write, ownership of what they read and write, and opportunities for personal and critical response to what they read and what they and their peers write.

Finally, students need opportunities to respond to text both personally and critically. Their personal responses allow them to integrate ideas in the text with their own feelings, emotions, images, and associations. Critical responses allow students to stand apart from the text and analyze, synthesize, and evaluate the author's ideas.

The Text. The text plays a critically important role in reading and writing processes. Readers and writers must understand that there are many functions for language that operate within texts and that there are a variety of text genres that include stories and informational texts. Students must possess a clear understanding of the authors' purposes for constructing particular texts and of how these different texts are organized. They must also understand how authors craft texts through the literary devices they employ. In turn, an understanding of these devices enables students to critically analyze and evaluate the quality of the texts they read and compose. Finally, writing and reading are related in that writing is an important tool for a reader to use in conveying his or her understanding of the text and responding to the text. Through writing, students gain a deeper understanding about the literature they read. Explicit lessons focus on the differences between text genres and their structures and the literary devices that the author uses to craft text.

The Processes of Reading and Writing. Teachers must also understand the essential processes involved as students read and write. While reading, students must develop the automaticity to recognize words and read them effortlessly and with expression while showing their understanding of what they read. To increase their understanding of what they read, they employ strategies for comprehending the text that include activating prior knowledge, predicting, paraphrasing, inferring, and monitoring their reading. In becoming a strategic reader, students come to understand which strategies they need to employ at a certain time and place and how to use those strategies effectively to increase comprehension.

Writers must learn to compose with automaticity so that their writing becomes effortless and fluent in expression. Writers employ a process for composing that includes prewriting, planning, drafting, revising, editing, and publishing or sharing. Through this process, writers employ such strategies as gathering and organizing ideas to enhance the quality of their writing.

During reading and writing instruction, teachers should utilize a variety of modes of reading that include teacher reading in which students hear models of fluent reading; reading in which student practice fluent reading with knowledgeable others; reading in which the teacher guides the students through the reading by modeling reading strategies that increase word recognition, fluency, or comprehension; and independent reading in which students practice reading on their own. Likewise, teachers employ several modes of writing that include modeling their own writing with the students and providing opportunities for students to share their writing with peer groups. Teachers model writing to teach strategies for improving writing quality. Students are given ample time to write independently in order to increase writing fluency. Teachers and students also participate in lessons designed to explicitly teach students about reading strategies for increasing word recognition, fluency, and comprehension.

THE EVOLVING ROLE OF THE READING COACH

The pivotal and changing role of the reading coach was critical to the success of LEAP in Mound Fort. Tamara began her assignment as a reading coach for the school with little more than a general vision of what she was supposed to do. She helped develop the LEAP conceptual framework, so she knew the conceptual orientation to the literacy process and to literacy instruction. Having taught at the secondary level, she knew adolescents, and she knew their literacy needs.

Over the course of the project, however, Tamara's role as a coach evolved based on the evolving needs of the teachers. Tamara's work could be called "responsive instruction" because she constantly adjusted her role and her instruction based on the strengths and needs of the Mound Fort teachers.

As Reading Instructor

When Tamara first entered Mound Fort Middle School as the reading coach, she knew no one at the school. She began her work by creating experiences that developed a level of trust between her and the teachers and administrators. This trust needed to include trust that she had a deep knowledge about literacy, trust that she would be able to provide teachers with knowledge about literacy processes and instruction, and trust that she could help them meet the literacy needs of their students. She also wanted to get a sense of the school and classroom cultures in which she would be participating. Who were the students with whom she was dealing, and what were their strengths? Who were the teachers in the school, and how did they interact with the school?

Semester 1. In trying to secure trust and understand the culture of Mound Fort, Tamara decided that during the first two months she would slowly develop a rapport with the teachers by visiting their classrooms to observe their practice. While she was observing, she wrote each teacher a personal note in which she gave each of them positive feedback regarding the literacy practices she observed that supported the LEAP framework. These classroom visits also gave Tamara the opportunity to understand the culture of the students at Mound Fort and their relationships with the teachers.

Tamara also chose to socialize with the teachers, counselors, and principals during the lunch hour. Through their lunch discussions, she began to suggest ways that she could help the teachers with their classroom instruction. She wanted them to see her as an additional resource that they could use in order to meet their literacy needs. She also wanted them to begin to see her as one of them, a former teacher who had battled with the same issues they confront with reading and writing instruction.

After the first two months, Tamara asked teachers to fill out a questionnaire in which they identified particular reading and writing issues about which they wanted to learn more. The questionnaire also asked them to identify topics for which they wanted to see classroom demonstrations, such as comprehension instruction or response group discussions. Based on this questionnaire, Tamara began to make appointments with the teachers to demonstrate literacy lessons in their classrooms on the topics they chose. Her goal in doing the classroom demonstrations at this time was to build their trust in her knowledge about literacy and her ability to apply theory to practice. She conducted several lessons that focused on chunking and sorting big words (Cunningham, 1999), making big words (Cunningham, 1999), and reciprocal teaching (Palincsar & Brown, 1984). After each classroom demonstration, she met informally with the teacher either during lunch or after school to debrief about the lesson. She used the debriefing sessions to convey the theory behind the activity. For example, when she taught a reciprocal teaching lesson, Tamara talked about the metacognitive strategies that readers use as they read and comprehend texts. The teachers, in turn, made comments and asked questions about the activity.

By the end of the first semester, teachers were comfortable with Tamara and excited about the lessons they saw during her classroom demonstrations. Tamara's next goal was to emphasize that they needed to plan a more formal schedule for implementing the LEAP framework in the school.

During an after-school meeting, the assistant principal, Mr. Anderson; the teachers; and Tamara planned the second semester. Tamara suggested that they take university coursework with her (which later became part of their reading endorsement). That way, she could directly tie the topics of the coursework to her classroom demonstrations of the following week. So, for example, one week she introduced a literacy topic, and she and the teachers discussed the theory and how it might be implemented in practice. The next week she could directly demonstrate how that topic translated into practice in the classroom.

Semester 2. During the following weeks, Tamara conducted classroom demonstrations of lessons pertaining to each topic discussed in the university coursework. For example, teachers knew their students needed help with word recognition. Most of their students struggled when they encountered multisyllabic words. Tamara devised lessons based on the work of Ehri (1991) and Gaskins, Gaskins, and Gaskins (1992). She taught students how to make big words by using prefix and suffix chunks and to decode by analogy. She also had students practice sorting words according to their common prefix, root, and suffix chunks (Bear, Invernizzi, Templeton, & Johnston, 2003). All of these lessons were conducted within the context of the adolescent literature that the students were reading. For example, as a pre-reading lesson, Tamara might ask students to skim through the chapter that they were about to read and find some big words that they did not know. Tamara would put the words on the board, and together she and the students practiced decoding the words by analogy.

Tamara also worked on fluency with students in a number of ways. First, she modeled read-alouds that gave the students the opportunity to hear adolescent literature read at a good rate, with accuracy and expression. Students were also given time to practice reading aloud on their own. In addition, Tamara asked students to perform repeated readings in which they read over and over a small piece of text. Students also had opportunities to use reader's theater with adolescent fiction. All of these activities were designed to give students repeated practice with text in order to increase their fluency.

Tamara also focused on developing conceptual understandings of words as part of comprehension instruction. Through their university coursework, teachers learned about the principles and practices of vocabulary instruction. Then Tamara modeled teaching vocabulary words in the stories that students read. Tamara selected several useful and unknown words from a story that students were reading (Beck, McKeown, & Kucan, 2002) and assisted students in understanding what the words meant and how they might be used in sentences. After reading, she might ask students to write the words in different sentences. As a class, they would then discuss the meanings of the words in different contexts.

Of course, a large part of the curriculum for the first year focused on comprehension instruction. Through the coursework, Tamara taught teachers the reading strategies that readers use to comprehend text (Alexander & Jetton, 2000; Wood, Woloshyn, & Willoughby, 1995). These strategies are noted in Figure 10.3. She introduced these strategies through the framework of pre-reading, during reading, and post-reading (Alvermann & Phelps, 2002). For example, before readers begin to actually read the text, they set a purpose for reading and preview the text. In previewing the text, they begin to activate their prior knowledge and think about their interests or lack thereof. They also have a task in mind as they begin to read. As students read, they determine whether information is important or not. They also think about how interested they are in the information. They attend to the organization or text structure to help them determine importance. They also ask questions about information that is confusing, and they predict future events in the story. They monitor their understanding by trying to determine whether the text is making sense. If not, they apply fix-up strategies to help them solve their confusion with the text.

Tamara modeled for teachers how to teach students to employ several instructional strategies before, during, and after reading. In Figure 10.3, we note several of these instructional strategies. For example, when Tamara wanted to show students how readers access prior knowledge, she might choose to teach the know–want to know–learned (K-W-L), the list-group-label, or an anticipation guide (for a good resource on these and other strategies, see Tierney & Readence, 2000). In K-W-L, students write what they know and what they want to know about the text before they begin reading. During list-group-label,

Reading Strategies
(Student Knowledge)

Teaching Strategies
(Teacher Knowledge)

B E F O R E	Setting a Purpose
	Activating/Building Prior
	    Knowledge
	Consider Interest
	Preview the Test
		Brainstorming
		List-Group-Label
		PreReading Plan
		    (PReP)
		K-W-L
		Advanced Organizer
		Analogies
		Semantic Maps
			Journals
			Anticipatory
			    Questions
			Anticipation Guide
			Text Preview
			Guided Imagery
			Discussion

D U R I N G	Activate/Build Prior Knowledge
	Actively Construct Meaning
	Clarify Words/Sentences/Paragraphs
	Ask Questions
	Summarize
	Predict/Verify Predictions
	Determine Important from
	    Unimportant Information
	Determine Important Versus
	    Interesting Information
	Analyze Text Structure
	Monitor Progress
		Analyzing Text
		    Structure
		Graphic Organizer
		GRP
		Summary
		Think-Alouds
		Anticipation Guide
			Build Knowledge
			Reciprocal
			    Teaching
			Request
			Directed Reading
			    Thinking Activity
			    (DR-TA)
			Learning Logs
			K-W-L

A F T E R	Activate/Build Prior Knowledge
	Summarize/Integrate Keys
	Confirm Predictions
	Generate New Questions
	Extend Learning to New Situations
	Identify Gaps in Learning
		Graphic Organizers
		Journals
		DR-TA
		Anticipation Guide
		Response to
		    Literature
			Discussion
			K-W-L
			Question-Answer
			    Relationship
			    (QAR)
			Learning Logs
			Jigsaw

FIGURE 10.3. Reading and teaching strategies. *Source:* Tamara L. Jetton, James Madison University.

students access prior knowledge by listing everything they know about a topic. Then they group their ideas into categories and label those categories. Finally, an anticipation guide consists of a set of statements to which the students respond. In responding to the statements, they are pulling from their prior knowledge.

Likewise, particular instructional strategies can be used during reading to facilitate students' use of strategies. For example, Reciprocal Questioning, or ReQuest, is an instructional strategy that encourages students to ask questions as they read. Guided Reading Procedure, or GRP, helps students realize the importance of monitoring as they read (see Tierney & Readence, 2000).

The central component of Tamara's teaching and demonstration was based on two instructional frameworks: explicit instruction and scaffolding

(Pearson & Dole, 1987; Pearson & Gallagher, 1983). At the beginning of the university coursework, she introduced these instructional models. Consistent with the models, the teacher first assumes full responsibility for using a strategy—say, a comprehension strategy such as visualizing—by modeling the strategy so students can see what it is and how it is used during the reading process. The modeling is followed by several opportunities for guided practice with feedback. During this stage, the teacher facilitates students' use of the strategy by working with students to use the strategy introduced. As the strategy is used, the teacher assists students as they practice with it and provides them with feedback on their performance. She provides the amount of scaffolding necessary for students to be successful—sometimes a lot, sometimes a little. As students become more proficient in using the strategy, the teacher gradually fades her instructional support, allowing students to assume more control over their strategy use. Finally, after a period of days or weeks, depending on the difficulty level of the strategy, students are able to apply the strategy to their reading independently and without support and assistance from the teacher or their peers.

Tamara and the teachers adopted this scaffolding framework for the delivery of all the explicit instruction they gave. Thus, when she modeled with students how to decode by analogy or how to summarize a text segment, she used the explicit instruction model and scaffolded her instruction to do it.

Tamara and her teachers spent most of the second semester of LEAP demonstrating instructional strategies through the explicit instruction and scaffolding models. After demonstrations were completed, Tamara and the teachers then team taught the lessons as they applied their newly learned skills to their own classrooms.

Semester 3. During the second year of LEAP implementation, Tamara shifted her instructional focus to writing based on a needs assessment of her teachers. Teachers expressed anxiety about the writing process and instruction framework of LEAP. In discussing the writing process with teachers, Tamara focused on two ways in which teachers could use writing in their language arts classrooms. First, teachers could ask students to write to respond to their reading. Writing about what is read aids readers in clarifying, summarizing, and remembering ideas. So Tamara introduced writing instructional strategies such as response logs, journals, quick writes, data retrieval charts, and letters. Once again, as she modeled lessons on these instructional strategies, she used the explicit instructional model to assist her.

Second, Tamara wanted her teachers to provide students with opportunities to use writing as a process for expressing their ideas. Thus, she and the teachers focused on the writing process and the instructional strategies facilitating the process with students. Teachers learned about prewriting strategies to increase students' abilities to generate ideas for writing and planning strategies to create well-organized prose written for an appropriate audience. Tamara also discussed strategies for revision and for adding clarity and coherence, as well as specific editing strategies for improving the mechanics of students' writing.

Notice that Tamara followed the explicit instruction and scaffolding model as she worked with teachers and demonstrated the instructional strategies for writing. First, she taught teachers information about the writing process and writing instruction during the university coursework. Then she modeled writing lessons both during the university coursework and in teachers' classrooms as they observed and took notes. After they had observed Tamara, teachers began to plan together to teach writing lessons for their students. Over time, she faded her support so that teachers conducted lessons on their own.

A Professional Development Model

As the reading coach, Tamara began to realize that she was using her own adapted form of explicit instruction and scaffolding as she worked with Mound Fort teachers. We came to realize that the adapted model of instruction could become a useful model for professional development, as well.

According to the adapted model, Tamara worked with teachers much as she hoped her teachers would work with their students. Basic to the explicit instruction professional development framework were the concepts of *modeling, guided practice with feedback, fading,* and *independent practice.*

With each instructional strategy that she wanted to teach her teachers, Tamara began in the university coursework by *modeling* the reading process and the strategies that readers use to access print and understand text. She also modeled instructional strategies that teachers could use to teach the reading process. During the school day, Tamara modeled the instructional strategies again with the Mound Fort students not only so teachers could see them modeled through their coursework, but also so they could see how the instructional strategies worked in the classroom with their students. After watching Tamara model the strategies, teachers had the opportunity to debrief about the lessons with Tamara. They discussed how Tamara went about planning for the lessons, why she chose to use a particular strategy with a specific text, and other ways that she could have structured the lesson.

After several weeks of the modeling both in the coursework and in the classrooms, Tamara moved to *guided practice with feedback* for the teachers. She began asking teachers to teach the instructional strategies, with Tamara as their team teacher. Tamara and the teachers met together and planned lessons with the adolescent literature that they were currently using. These planning sessions provided opportunities to problem solve the issues with which the teachers were most concerned. For example, some teachers were still teaching whole-class reading lessons. Through the planning sessions, Tamara was able to show the teachers how to teach the instructional strategies as mini-lessons and have students practice the strategies while reading different novels. Other teachers had already implemented small-group instruction in their classrooms. They needed to know how these instructional strategies fit within that framework. As a result, teachers began to realize the benefit of including explicit instruction as part of small-group instruction.

Once Tamara and the teachers had conducted several team-teaching lessons, Tamara began to *fade* her support. She gradually let the teachers practice the strategies with their students and moved from a team teacher to an observer in the class. Afterward, Tamara and the teacher would debrief about the lessons by talking about the parts of the lesson that went well and other parts that they could have structured differently to have more success. In this way, over time, Tamara removed her support completely, allowing teachers *independent practice* of the newly learned strategies.

We believe there are several benefits of our adapted instructional model for professional development. First, the model is consistent with Joyce and Showers's (1995) identification of necessary elements in staff development. These researchers identified guided practice with feedback and coaching in classrooms as key elements in a professional development model that make the most difference in teachers' abilities to apply their newly learned skills in their classroom routines. The adapted instructional model includes this guided practice with feedback and coaching as critical components of the instructional process for teachers.

EFFECTIVE COMPONENTS OF LEAP FOR MOUND FORT

What made LEAP effective at Mound Fort? We identify and discuss six components of LEAP for the middle school (in no particular order):

1. Deeply committed teachers who saw themselves as learners.
2. A vision of literacy that was effectively conveyed to teachers.
3. A highly effective administrator to support the project and remove barriers to its implementation.
4. An effective reading coach.
5. University coursework and study groups.
6. A flood of books for students.

Deeply Committed Teachers

Jan Dole's first impression of the Mound Fort teachers stands out among that of all the teachers in the seven original LEAP schools. As she held her initial meeting with them, the group generated enormous enthusiasm about LEAP. While other teachers at other schools were polite but noncommittal, the Mound Fort teachers radiated energy and enthusiasm about the project immediately. They asked Jan, "When can someone come into my classroom and observe me? When can we start taking classes? When can we order the books?" While other schools needed to think about whether they wanted to be involved in the project, the Mound Fort teachers immediately responded that they did.

The Mound Fort teachers continued to maintain a high level of enthusiasm and energy throughout the project. Each August on the three-year project, they were the first to call the USOE and ask, "When do we get our money for books? When will the reading coach begin? Who will come out and visit us?"

Where did the teachers get their energy? From the very beginning, it was obvious that they had positive attitudes, and we believe that these positive attitudes were a key to their energy and success. They told us that they had known for several years prior to LEAP that their language arts instruction was not meeting their students' needs. Students' scores on standardized tests reinforced those beliefs. Their eighth-grade students were scoring typically in the 20th–30th percentile. They knew that many of their students came to them already struggling with reading. Some of these students were struggling to learn English as a second language—thereby exacerbating their difficulties in reading in English.

However, teachers did not blame the students; nor did they blame themselves. One teacher said, "It's not about the kids. It's not about you. I know these kids. I know they are capable of doing more." The teachers looked at their students and said, "We can't keep passing the buck to someone or something else. We had to take responsibility. We had the attitude that something had to change." One teacher said, "We were not afraid to say to ourselves, 'This is not working.'"

Mound Fort teachers appreciated the fact that their administrators did not blame them for their students' reading difficulties. One teacher explained, "What was pivotal for us was that our district didn't shove anything down us. They didn't say, 'We are here to correct you.'" Their principal had already established reading as a high priority in the school, and he had reduced class size in an attempt to help teachers in their daily instruction. The principal had also assisted teachers in creating reading classes in an attempt to help the Mound Fort students. In addition, the teachers had the continuing support of their assistant principal, who provided a significant amount of assistance both in getting LEAP into the school and removing barriers to its effective implementation.

Vision of Literacy Effectively Conveyed

A second critical component of success for the Mound Fort teachers was their ability to get a sense of the vision of literacy that the project conveyed. As we began LEAP, questions that repeatedly came up among almost all teachers were, "Just what are you talking about here? What is the project supposed to be? What does an effective LEAP classroom look like at the middle school level?" It is important to remember that in 1996, when LEAP began, exemplary laboratory sites of classrooms were few and far between. So we had no way to show teachers a living LEAP classroom that did the things we were espousing in the project.

To convey a sense of LEAP, Jan and other USOE consultants developed conceptual and instructional frameworks for reading and writing. At the beginning of the project, teachers attended a week-long workshop at the USOE to learn about the LEAP framework. Teachers participated in sessions in which they learned about reading and writing processes and instruction for language arts. They each received a booklet with the frameworks shown in Figures 10.1 and 10.2, as well as additional frameworks that focused on the instruction itself.

However, most teachers in the project did not see the vision right away. At Mound Fort, it was Tamara who assisted teachers in creating the vision for themselves. One teacher remarked, "Tamara gave us the vision of what it was supposed to be and what it was supposed to look like. She would model for us. She would say, 'This is what you are supposed to do.' And you could see instantly that the strategies she used would work."

Highly Effective Administrative Support

All teachers identified the assistant principal, Mr. Anderson, as a significant factor in the success of LEAP at Mound Fort. He was instrumental in bringing the project to Mound Fort as he saw the project as an *opportunity* for rather than a *burden* to the school. A former English teacher, Mr. Anderson immediately saw the vision for literacy presented in the frameworks. This was significant because it enabled him to generate and maintain enthusiasm for the project himself and to provide his total support for it. It also gave him the incentive to assist teachers as they implemented the project.

In addition to his vision of the project as one that was right for the school, in his role as assistant principal, Mr. Anderson had the means and resources to make things happen for the project that teachers were unable to do themselves. For example, he saw the need for a place to store the large quantity of books that teachers began to purchase. He freed up an old storage room for these books. When teachers decided that they wanted to take graduate classes to receive their reading endorsements, Mr. Anderson helped pay the tuition for the teachers through district reimbursement and negotiated with a local university to bring the classes to the teachers. During faculty meetings, Mr. Anderson shared specific reading strategies with all the content area teachers based on his own learning of them from Tamara and the teachers. He was a key negotiator with the USOE in all plans and activities for LEAP. When teachers had ordered about $300 in books above the amount the USOE gave the school, Mr. Anderson came up with the extra money for the books through district reimbursement.

Mr. Anderson's personality was also relevant to the success of the project. He was a gregarious, enthusiastic, and energetic man who had positive effects on the teachers. Teachers remarked that he was the kind of person who always made them feel like they were doing their best. He was able to inspire them and motivate them. As one teacher summarized, "Mr. Anderson talked *to* you, and not *at* you."

An Effective Reading Coach

Mound Fort teachers saw Tamara as instrumental in their professional growth as reading and writing teachers. As they began LEAP, they delighted in the many books they received through USOE funding, and they intuitively knew that these books were a critical part of their improved instruction. But they also knew that books alone were not going to make things better. They argued that Tamara gave them the "vision" and the strategies for implementing that vision in the classroom through the books they had purchased. The specific before-, during-, and after-reading strategies taught by Tamara gave them a framework for understanding how to teach reading to their students. The university courses gave teachers the understanding of why the strategies were useful and how to implement them in their classrooms. Tamara worked with them not only on how to use different strategies, but also on how to pick specific books to use to teach the strategies.

A particular instance that teachers identified as an "ah-ha" experience was when Tamara taught them that if they wanted their students to get better at reading, they would have to make sure students read a lot. Teachers came to realize that they actually had their students do very little reading in their classrooms. So they changed their instructional time block to include two sequential blocks of 45 minutes a day as language arts class. During this time, teachers made sure students read for at least three quarters of their time in class. Tamara taught teachers how to use different methods of reading—group reading, choral reading, buddy reading—so that students had many different varieties of reading experiences.

University Coursework and Study Groups

The Mound Fort teachers were unique in that they were uniformly interested in obtaining a reading endorsement, and they were very willing to take classes outside school to receive the endorsement. Teachers began their coursework with a class on adolescent literature. As part of that class, teachers were assigned to read, research, and select high-quality adolescent literature to buy for the school. Teachers also participated in a foundations of reading and writing course in which they learned about theories of reading and writing. A central assignment for this course focused on formulating a personal philosophy of literacy at the beginning of the course; they were then given the opportunity to revisit their philosophy at the end of the semester and make changes based on their participation in the course, LEAP activities, and their classroom experiences.

It is also significant that Tamara taught many of the reading classes that teachers took. In her dual role as university professor and coach, Tamara was able to tailor the university classes to meet the unique needs of the Mound Fort teachers. In addition, she was able to observe and provide feedback to teachers as they implemented particular strategies that she taught in the courses. Her observations of teachers teaching in their classrooms provided her with the feedback she needed to adapt and change her instruction during the university coursework.

In addition to the coursework in which teachers participated, Mound Fort teachers began weekly study group sessions in which they read professional books about literacy. All teachers read the same book and attended sessions in which they discussed topics and issues within the books (for example, Allington & Walmsley, 1995: Atwell, 1987; Cunningham & Allington, 1999). During the first year, teachers led the study group discussions themselves. Discussions usually focused on classroom applications of the theoretical ideas within the texts. Teachers also formulated questions to explore. These questions were often the topic of discussion during the after-school university coursework in which Tamara could provide further research and information.

A Flood of Books for Students

Each school participating in LEAP was given a total of $30,000 over three years to spend on books. However, we found that some schools did not want to purchase books—they began ordering Weekly Readers, bookshelves, plastic baskets, games, computer programs, and so on. The USOE then provided a list of the types of print materials that were acceptable for purchase.

The Mound Fort teachers, in consultation with the assistant principal, right away decided to spend all their money on books. They had two goals for purchasing books for their school. First, they wanted to buy a variety of adolescent literature for teachers to store in their individual classrooms. These books were used as part of their independent reading time. Second, they wanted to buy class sets of adolescent literature that could be used for whole-class or small-group instruction.

Teachers spent considerable time researching book titles, ensuring that books were ordered at a variety of reading levels. They also ordered several books in Spanish. When these books were ordered, the titles, authors, and reading levels were entered into an Excel spreadsheet. The teachers jointly determined which titles would be used for particular grade levels, so they would not be teaching the same book at every grade level. After the first year of the project, students voted on their most and least favorite books for the year, and they voted on books that they would recommend to other students. These were placed on a special list for teachers.

As the second year began, teachers took a close look at their classroom library to determine the additional resources that were needed. The USOE provided the school with $10,000 to order materials during the second year. The classroom library at Mound Fort was already full of high-quality text sets of adolescent fiction. The teachers expressed comfort in using the fiction to practice integrating word study, fluency, and comprehension instruction. Tamara noticed that the teachers had not ordered nonfiction titles. Thus, their task for the second year was to order nonfiction titles in a variety of content areas that teachers would use both in their individual classroom libraries and in the classroom library for the school. Teachers did indeed purchase nonfiction texts in different subject areas—science, social studies, history, math, and so forth.

SUCCESS AND SUSTAINABILITY OF LEAP
AT MOUND FORT

LEAP came to Mound Fort because it was a high-poverty, low-achieving school that needed assistance and support in improving literacy instruction. An ever increasing number of minority and non-English-speaking students were moving into Mound Fort in the mid- to late 1990s and continuing well into 2003. Standardized test scores in reading had been hovering between the 20th and the 30th percentile.

Often, it takes several years for teachers to learn new forms of instruction, incorporate them into their classroom routines, and then see an effect of that instruction on students' achievement. However, Mound Fort teachers changed their instruction almost immediately. Changes were reflected in the students, as teachers pointed out that students began to fight over the books they wanted to read. Changes were reflected in the teachers as well. A new level of energy and enthusiasm came over teachers. One teacher began LEAP not liking to read at all, but through the project she became an avid reader. Now she enjoys the adolescent novels as much as her students do. Another teacher remarked, "I used to test instead of teach," and a third teacher said, "I reversed the before, during and after parts of reading. Most of what I did came at the end instead of up front."

Teachers noted that LEAP gave them a new way of thinking about teaching. There was a common vocabulary that everyone could use. One teacher remarked, "You change your way of speaking." Another pointed out that LEAP gave a kind of continuity to teachers' instruction. Yet another said, "I can feel an iceberg moving with reading" as her instruction and students' responses changed.

The changes that teachers described were, indeed, reflected in changing reading test scores (see Table 10.1). From 1996 to 2000, reading test scores at Mound Fort leaped to reflect the new influx of assistance and support. In 1996, before LEAP began, standardized test scores in reading hovered at the 30th percentile. In 1997 and 1998, after the first two years of LEAP, scores jumped to the 59th percentile. In the last year of LEAP, 1999, scores increased a bit, to the 61st percentile. These numbers reflect the kinds of changes we can see in test scores when instruction has changed dramatically.

However, these initial gains were not maintained over time. In 2000, the first year after LEAP ended, reading test scores decreased to the 53rd percentile. In 2001, scores took a decided drop to the 36th percentile. The latest test scores, in 2002, plummeted and remain in the 26th percentile.

Why have reading scores plummeted over the past few years? We can only speculate on this question. When we asked the chair of the English department, an accomplished and dedicated teacher, she mentioned several changes that had taken place in addition to the loss of the LEAP project. Assistant Principal Anderson had retired, and there had been turnover in the teaching staff. Teachers who were involved in LEAP kept the vision, but, of course, those who were

TABLE 10.1. Mound Fort Reading Test Scores—SAT-9

1996	1997	1998	1999	2000	2001	2002
29%	59% LEAP	59% LEAP	61% LEAP	52%	36%	26%

new never had it. Because of a series of unforeseen circumstances that included budget constraints, long-term substitute teachers had been hired in reading classrooms. This further eroded the vision of LEAP. The department chair also mentioned that there had been some appropriate grouping of students, the results of which she was unsure. She also mentioned that the team does not meet as regularly as it had when LEAP was in the school. Finally, there had been some addition of non-English-speaking students to the school, and she was uncertain whether teachers were meeting their needs appropriately.

CONCLUSION

As it played out at Mound Fort, LEAP represents the best of what outside support and assistance can do for classrooms, teachers, and students. The project came into the school and breathed new life into teachers and students. Enough financial and human resources were provided to support a group of dedicated and diligent teachers in changing their instruction. The group knew that what they had been doing was not working, but they did not have the means and knowledge to know what else to do. LEAP provided them with both. Changes in students' achievement were immediate based on LEAP. Students' test scores rose almost 30% and remained there for three years. In the fourth year, as LEAP left, scores declined a bit. However, in the fourth and fifth years—years with no outside help—scores plummeted back to where they were before LEAP.

The LEAP story at Mound Fort presents an important cautionary tale for educators interested in reform in low-achieving schools. When Jan visited the LEAP teachers recently, it was apparent that they sorely missed the support and assistance with which they had been provided. They remained enthusiastic and a good working team, but they missed Tamara and her instructional leadership. And they missed LEAP.

In recent efforts toward systemic reform, educators consistently point out the importance of a three- to five-year cycle that is necessary to sustain reform over time. In many ways, Mound Fort represents the ideal school in which to work—dedicated and talented teachers, strong leadership, an effective reading coach, sufficient time and resources. Yet after LEAP left, progress did not continue.

We know that change is difficult and takes time. This is so even in the best circumstances. Mobility of teachers and administrative leadership make it extremely difficult to sustain change.

LEAP at Mound Fort shows that success is possible and even likely, given a set of good circumstances. More needs to be learned about how to sustain that success over time when support goes away.

REFERENCES

Alexander, P. A., & Jetton, T. L. (2000). Learning from text: A multidimensional and developmental perspective. In M. L. Kamil, P. B. Mosenthal. P. D. Pearson, & R. Barr (Eds.). *Handbook of reading research* (Vol. 3, pp. 285–310). Mahwah, NJ: Erlbaum.

Allington, R. L., & Walmsley, S. A. (1995). *No quick fix*. New York: Teachers College Press.

Alvermann, D. E., & Phelps, S. F. (2002). *Content reading and literacy: Succeeding in today's diverse classrooms*. Boston: Allyn and Bacon.

Anderson, R. C., Hiebert, E. H., Scott, J. A., & Wilkinson, I. A. G. (1985). *Becoming a nation of readers*. Washington, DC: National Institute of Education.

Atwell, N. (1987). *In the middle*. Montclair, NJ: Boynton/Cook.

Bear, D. R., Invernizzi, M. Templeton, S., & Johnston, F. (2003). *Words their way: Word study for phonics, vocabulary, and spelling instruction* (3rd ed.). Upper Saddle River, NJ: Merrill.

Beck, I., McKeown, M. G., & Kucan, L. (2002). *Bringing words to life: Robust vocabulary instruction*. New York: Guilford.

Cunningham, P. M., & Allington, R. L. (1999). *Classrooms that work: They can all read and write* (2nd ed.). New York: Longman.

Ehri, L. C. (1991). Development of the ability to read words. In R. Barr, M. L. Kamil, P. B. Mosenthal, & P. D. Pearson (Eds.), *Handbook of reading research* (Vol. 2, pp. 383–417). New York: Longman.

Gaskins, R. W., Gaskins, J. C., & Gaskins, I. W. (1992). Using what you know to figure out what you don't know: An analogy approach to decoding. *Reading and Writing Quarterly, 8,* 197–221.

Joyce, B., & Showers, B. (1995). *Student achievement through staff development* (2nd ed.). White Plains, NY: Longman.

Palincsar, A. S., & Brown, A. L. (1984). Reciprocal teaching of comprehension-fostering and monitoring activities. *Cognition and Instruction, 1,* 117–175.

Pearson, P. D., & Dole, J. A. (1987). Explicit comprehension instruction: A review of the research and a new conceptualization of instruction. *Elementary School Journal, 88,* 153–167.

Pearson, P. D., & Gallagher, M. C. (1983). The instruction of reading comprehension. *Contemporary Educational Psychology, 8,* 317–344.

Tierney, R. J., & Readence, J. E. (2000). *Reading strategies and practices: A compendium* (5th ed.). Boston: Allyn and Bacon.

Wood, E., Woloshyn, V. E., & Willoughby, T. (1995). *Cognitive strategy instruction for middle and high schools*. Cambridge: Brookline Books.

11

Project CRISS
Reading, Writing, and Learning in the Content Subjects

Carol M. Santa

Key Points

- Through explanation and modeling, Project CRISS teachers help students become strategic, active, and metacognitive learners in their content subjects.

- Project CRISS teachers have students use background knowledge, read purposefully, organize information, and write and talk about what they are learning.

- Workshops can be effective when they encourage interaction, emphasize the importance of turning CRISS principles over to students, and encourage teacher research.

roject CRISS began, like most important ideas in education, in a teacher's lounge. Jim Scalf, a social studies teacher, started the conversation: "Students don't read my assignments. They come to class totally unprepared. I have to cover everything again. My reading assignments are becoming a waste of time!" His words struck a cord with others sitting around that table. Don Neu, a science teacher, joined in: "My students don't have a clue about how to study. I spend most of my time lecturing and telling them what to learn. They don't write very well, either!"

These concerns were the beginnings of Project CRISS (Creating Independence Through Student-Owned Strategies)—a teacher development program which has since spread from teacher to teacher across this country, into Canada, and to several European countries. Who would have thought that a lunchroom conversation, held more than 20 years ago, would end up touching the lives of so many teachers and their students?

Project CRISS began in Flathead High School, a school of about 1,500 students in Kalispell, Montana, a small isolated community nestled in the shadows of Glacier Park. The conversations continued during the spring of 1979. Soon the principal and several teachers met with the curriculum director to write an ESEA Title IV-C grant to do something about the problem of students' poor reading, writing, and learning skills. Six months later, I was hired to direct the project.

THE BEGINNINGS

During that first year (1979–80), eight teachers (two each from the content areas of mathematics, science, social studies, and language arts) volunteered to work with me in developing the project. We met at noon and during release time to read and talk about research in comprehension and learning.

We began questioning our own teaching. Why don't our students have the skills for lifelong learning? Might the problem rest more with us than with our students? Could our teaching models be wrong? We began to realize that our standard teaching model was giving lectures, assigning readings, and evaluating students' performance with multiple-choice tests. We taught like our own teachers had taught us. Yet this flat, boring methodology began to feel degrading to our own vitality and curiosity. More important, it seemed degrading to students. Such a passive teacher-directed paradigm started eating away at our common sense and conflicting with our growing knowledge of theoretical principles about how students read, write, study, and learn.

From our discussions and professional reading, we started to evolve an initial philosophical framework to guide our change efforts. For example, we began to see relationships between organizations in learning and text structure. We also knew that our instruction should involve students as a more active learners capable of integrating formation with existing knowledge. The research literature helped us begin to see why we should teach students a variety of organizing strategies and help them internalize principles of metacognition or self-monitoring procedures. Once we had identified some of these preliminary principles, we started to try out ideas as part of classroom investigations.

Teacher Research Studies

We devised a series of simple research studies in mathematics, social studies, and science classrooms. In the beginning, none of us realized the power of this approach—how it would evolve into a sensitive and successful way to change teaching. Involving teachers in planning and carrying out experiments turned out to preserve ownership and provided convincing evidence motivating change.

The first area we investigated had to do with background knowledge. I noticed that most content teachers spent little time developing schema or background knowledge before asking students to read, view a video, or listen to a lecture. Typically, they would say, "I want you to read pages 25–30 for tomorrow," without any thought given to what students might know or need to know about the topic beforehand. Although our study group had read several professional articles about the role of background knowledge in reading comprehension, most participants remained skeptical about its relevance for learning and felt unsure about specific ways to ensure its use. Classroom-based experiments laid the groundwork for change.

During one of our lunchroom discussions, I asked: "I wonder if eliciting and developing background knowledge before students read their mathematics or social studies assignments would make a difference in learning?" We set up two research studies, one in mathematics and the other in history classes.

Two Math Classes. Cheryl Plettner used two of her geometry classrooms. The class that consistently performed better on her chapter quizzes became the control, and the lower-achieving class became the experimental group. The rationale behind this was that if her lower-achieving class could do as well as or better than her higher-achieving one, she could be fairly confident that a particular approach worked to improve learning.

Cheryl assigned her control class to read a chapter on indirect proofs and study the sample problems. The students were free to ask questions during and after reading. Following the reading she presented a short explanation of indirect proofs and went over the example problems.

For the experimental group she taught basically the same lesson, but the emphasis was different. Before assigning the reading, she wrote key vocabulary on the board and asked students to brainstorm what the words might mean. She summarized their comments and next asked them to list two or three ideas they hoped to gain from the selection before reading it. Following discussion and rereading, she went over the example problems, just as she had done with the control group. Both experimental and control classes did the same problems at the end of the chapter as a test.

The experimental group, in which Cheryl emphasized background knowledge and purpose setting, answered more of the problems correctly than did the control students. She then shared this finding with all of her classes. "Why do you think this class did the best on this lesson?" As Cheryl explained her different methodologies, her students also began to understand the value of pre-reading strategies.

Two History Classes. Jim Scalf did a similar study in his history classes. He used two classes. Students in his experimental class (his lowest-achieving class) brainstormed what they knew about the topic before reading, developed purposes for reading, and took time afterward to talk about new information they had learned. Students in the control condition (his highest-achieving class) simply read without doing any pre-reading brainstorming and purpose setting. A brief quiz the following day confirmed what Jim had suspected: The pre-reading group outperformed the control group. He, too, shared his findings with his students. "What does this study show you about background knowledge and setting purposes for reading?"

Both Cheryl and Jim touched on something that ended up being critical for the project's development. Notice how they both had process conferences with their students as part of their research. "How did this approach work for you? Why?" Students were encouraged to share their reactions. When asked to describe their study processes, students often became aware of them for the first time. From the start, both Cheryl and Jim saw the need to begin turning knowledge about learning over to their students.

In the meantime, I arranged for "research chats" over lunch, where Cheryl and Jim presented their data to other project teachers. They also decided to write up brief descriptions of their research in a staff newsletter, which they slipped into everyone's mailboxes. Soon, other teachers, not just those originally working on the project, began similar investigations. Pre-reading activities started to become standard practice in the content classrooms.

Expansion Within the School. These initial studies led to a surge of classroom investigations pursuing a variety of research questions. For example, Don Neu, a biology teacher, examined the effects of pre- and post-reading journal entries. Before students read a selection, he asked them to write about several key concepts. After reading, students checked their pre-reading entries for misconceptions and wrote revised post-reading journal entries. One week later, Don administered a quiz on the concepts that students had written about in their journals. More students in the experimental group showed a better understanding of these concepts than did students in normally higher-functioning control group. Again, both students and teacher started seeing the value of the experimental strategy and began to understand the importance of including more informal writing as part of learning.

Our lunchroom conversations and newsletters describing our research began to infiltrate throughout the school. In fact, we started a series of research studies with teachers who were not originally part of the project. The shop teacher wondered whether writing about procedure, such as defining the steps in maintaining a car's exhaust system, would help students better learn them. A social studies teacher questioned whether or not asking students to convert concepts into pictures might help them integrate and remember important ideas. The principal also joined in by reducing the business portion of his staff meetings so teachers could talk about their research findings. Our school took on a new professional energy. Our ideas began to spread throughout the district— even to the elementary schools.

To the District, State, National, and International Levels. Other districts wanted to know about our work. Kalispell teachers did workshops for surrounding districts. After each workshop, we came home rejuvenated with new ideas, which we added to the project. In 1983, Project CRISS became a state demonstration site, and in 1985, after doing an extensive research validation demonstrating that we could export Project CRISS to other districts, we became part of National Diffusion Network (NDN). We received funds to disseminate Project CRISS throughout the country. Over the past 15 years, we have had the good fortune to work with teachers throughout the United States, Canada, and Western Europe. Each time we do workshops, we learn from teacher participants and continue to update and revise our work.

Over the years we have also gathered additional data from various adoption sites. In each case students who learned CRISS strategies as part of regular classroom instruction performed better on the reading and studying evaluations than did students in control classrooms who did not have a CRISS strategy focus. We continually update and revise the project and have just completed the third edition of the CRISS book, *Project CRISS: Creating Independence Through Student-Owned Strategies* (Santa, Havens, & Valdez, 2004), which we use as part of our staff development program.

So with this history in mind, let's turn to some of our discoveries about ways to help students become more competent readers, writers, and learners. Our central question continues to be: How can we insure that students leave our classrooms with the skills needed for lifelong learning?

PRINCIPLES AND PHILOSOPHY

The logical place to begin this discussion is with our belief system and with practical ways that this belief system plays out in our teaching. This philosophical framework provides a backdrop for examining our teaching and for our students to reflect about their learning. It integrates work from cognitive psychology, social learning theory, and neurological research about how our brain learns. It includes these overlapping principles:

1. *Background knowledge and reading purposefully* are powerful determinants of reading comprehension.
2. Effective learners are *actively involved* while listening and reading.
3. Students need many opportunities to *talk* with one another about what they are learning.
4. Good readers know a variety of ways to *organize* information for learning.
5. Students need many opportunities to *write* about what they are learning.
6. Effective learners are *metacognitive.* They are goal directed and know how to use strategies to create meaning.
7. Teaching involves *explanation* and *modeling.* Teachers need to teach students how to learn. The most effective way to do his is show them and then support that with explanation and feedback.

In this section, I describe these principles and provide some examples of classroom practices that help clarify them. To provide a context for the practical portion of this discussion, I refer to Steve Qunell's social studies classroom. Steve is a teacher at Montana Academy, a private high school for troubled teens, where I currently work as director of education. The timing for writing this chapter is perfect. Steve has just completed a rich thematic study of the 1920s and '30s. Students read literature from this period, such as *The Grapes of Wrath* and *The Great Gatsby,* did studies on music (jazz) and the Harlem Renaissance, and read and wrote about the political, economic, and cultural events of this era.

Background Knowledge and Reading Purposefully

Teachers involved in Project CRISS constantly talk about background knowledge in their classrooms. We help students understand that integrating new information with prior knowledge lies at the heart of comprehension. The richer our background, the richer our comprehension. The more we bring to a reading situation, the more we can take away. This conclusion is documented not only by masses of research studies (Pearson & Fielding, 1991; Pressley, 2002) but also by neurological research, particularly that on selective attention (Jensen, 1998). We are far more likely to learn new information when we have some previous knowledge or mental priming about the upcoming topic. In order to take something into memory, we have to attend to it. But we have difficulty paying attention to something when we know nothing about it or have no opportunity to think about it before hearing or reading about the topic.

We warn students, "Don't just start reading. Take time to 'prime' your background knowledge. What might you already know about the topic?" We also remind them to preview the assignment and develop several purposes for reading. Frequently, we have to be quite directive with purpose setting: "After reading this selection, you should be able to . . ." or "After viewing the video, you should be able to identify. . . ."

Steve used a variety of pre-reading strategies with the students throughout his 1920–'30s thematic unit. Two examples are mind-streaming and double-entry journals.

Mind-Streaming. Mind-streaming prompts students to use their background knowledge. Content teachers like to use this strategy because it doesn't take much time away from their teaching of content. In this example, Steve's students worked in pairs discussing what they knew or thought they knew about the 1920s and 1930s. If they knew little about this era (the situation for most of his students), he told them to ask questions about what they might want to learn. Here is a summary of his directions:

> Divide students into pairs.
> Student A talks for one minute about what he or she knows about
>   the 1920s. Include questions as part of your discussion.
> Student B listens and encourages student A but doesn't talk.

After one minute, the roles reverse:

> Student B talks for one minute about the topic.
> Student A listens and encourages the speaker.

After these paired discussions, students participated in a whole-class discussion about what they knew or thought they knew about this era. They also generated a list of questions about what they wanted to learn, most of which became individual topics for research. Mind-streaming also works effectively as a post-reading/listening strategy in which students do one-minute paired re-tellings of what they have learned from a reading assignment, video, or lecture.

By 1929 the U.S. stock market was at an all-time high. Many economic analysts and business executives felt that the stock market was the key to prosperity and urged American citizens to invest as much as they could.	This reminds me of:
Some crooked inside investors purposely inflated the value of a company's stock in order to make a quick profit. Outside investors would then discover that the company was not as profitable as they had speculated, and their stock was worth far less than they had paid for it.	the current time we now live in. Many people's eyes are bigger than their brains. Material possessions are more important than the things that come for free; love, family, friendship. If we thought more about how we could improve our relationship with the people we care about we would be just as rich, maybe even more so.

FIGURE 11.1. Julia's journal response.

Double-Entry Journals. Pre-reading double-entry journals provide students with a brief preview of upcoming content and inspire them to start making some connection with their background knowledge.

On the left side of the paper, Steve lifted quotes, comments, or summary statements from the text and asked his students to use the space to the right for making connections (see Figure 11.1): "Before we begin reading this assignment, let's take a moment and read these quotations taken from your next reading assignment. What do these quotations about the 1920s remind you of? What connections can you make to present-day events? Write your ideas in the right-hand column."

Teachers like Steve continually think about ways to ensure that students connect new learning to their own background knowledge. He keeps certain questions in mind as he teaches.

- How can I help students figure out what they know or don't know about a topic?
- How can I help students assess the accuracy of their background knowledge?
- How can I help them use this knowledge to guide their own comprehension?
- What knowledge do my students need before they read? Or what misconceptions need to be changed before students read?
- What do I want students to focus on during this assignment?
- How can I help them read and listen selectively, focusing on portions of text and content most relevant to their goals?
- How can I help students understand why background knowledge and setting purposes are so critical to their learning?

This last question is most important. It is not enough for us, as teachers, to understand why background knowledge and purpose setting are so powerful. Ultimately, theoretical principles must become a part of our students' understanding of how reading and learning works. We can't keep these important principles to ourselves.

Active Reading, Listening, and Learning

In order to learn, we must be actively involved. None of us can sit back and simply let learning happen. Our brains don't work that way. Neural connections are made when we act on incoming information and do something with it. Research in cognitive psychology provides documentation of this activity principle. Learning happens when students actively process information through writing, talking, and transforming by using a variety of organizing strategies (Keene & Zimmerman, 1997). Many students, particularly those who struggle in school, don't understand the difference between active and passive learning. They think learning means glossing through text or passively listening to a lecture. As part of our teaching, we constantly show students how to become more actively engaged. Here are some examples from Steve's classroom.

Read and Say Something. While reading an article about the people of the 1920s, Steve divided students into pairs and asked them to stop after three or four paragraphs and say something to their partners about what they were reading.

Read and Retell or Read and Ask a Question. In other situations he was a bit more directive: "Read this page; turn to your partner and retell important information from the page. Or read and ask a question that comes to mind while you read."

Read and Write Something. Steve gave each student a packet of sticky notes. As they read, he asked them to stop after several minutes and write down one or two words on sticky notes about their reading. After completing their reading, he asked students to discuss in small groups what they had written on their sticky notes.

The Two-Minute Pause. After lecturing for about 10 minutes about the economic situation during the Great Depression, Steve's students took a two-minute pause, generating several questions about what they heard. He continued to intersperse the two-minute pause for the rest of his lecture.

Each of these strategies helped students become more actively engaged in their reading and listening.

After students experienced a particular strategy, Steve led a process conference about what it means to be an active reader and listener. For example, he asked: "How did reading and saying something help you untangle meaning from the text? How did pausing during my lecture inspire you to process the information more actively?"

We always talk process as part of our teaching. "What did you do in this lesson to grapple with meaning? What did I do as a teacher to help you become more actively engaged? Why did this strategy work better for you than just listening or simply reading the assignment?"

Conceptualizing the student as an active strategist has led to changes in our approaches to teaching. We aren't on stage very much, giving our lectures or asking hundreds of questions. Instead, we assist our students to become engaged in their learning. In the process, they learn about learning and consequently understand and remember course material more effectively.

Discussion and Instructional Conversations

Learning is both an active, constructive process and a social, interpersonal process. Students create meaning by transforming information, by building their own connections. Discussion is essential to these constructive processes. We live in a social world and learn by interacting with others. Each of us comes to the learning situation with some knowledge, but by pooling our understandings and talking about what we might know, we develop deeper understandings. Teachers who emphasize one-sided lecture methods as their primary mode of teaching not only discount key principles drawn from cognitive and social psychology but violate important principles of our brain. Discussion is critical, as we are biologically wired for language and communicating with one another (Jensen, 1998).

So we work hard in our classrooms to involve students in discussions about what they are learning. Students plan lessons, lead group discussions, and actively participate in class. For example, when Steve asked students to read and say something, everyone talked—not just the teacher. This view of discussion is quite different from situations where the teacher remains the authority figure, with students reciting answers to teacher-directed questions. When discussion is viewed as recitation, little interaction occurs among students, little learning takes place. We help students understand that it is their talking, their oral grappling with meaning, that leads to deeper understanding. They, not the teacher, need to do the processing.

Organization and Learning

We also teach students about the power of organizing or transforming information. We tell them about the past 30 years of research in cognitive psychology and more recent research about brain physiology documenting that learning and memory depend on acting on and organizing information. We explain that the average adult can remember from five to nine discrete units of new information at once. Our short-term memories have limitations. However, our ability to remember increases dramatically when we transform information by clustering discrete bits into categories, by developing hierarchical relationships, and by converting information into charts or pictures. The more organized, the better remembered.

We show students flexible ways to organize information. They learn how to take notes, to underline selectively, and to structure information into hierarchies of meaning. We demonstrate, model, and show students how to organize what they are learning from their reading, from video presentations, from lectures, and from laboratory experiences. Once students understand a variety of ways to transform information, we start harping: "You have to do more than just read this assignment. Think about what organizing structure might work here. What organizing scheme are you going to use to transform it, to make it meaningful to you? Choose one that makes the most sense given what you need to learn."

In Steve's classroom, students learn a variety of ways to transform information. As a review, he challenged them to select an organizing strategy to review key concepts. Beforehand, he reminded them about the importance of processing and transforming information so knowledge becomes personally meaningful. "You have to do more with information than just read or read and underline. You have to change it, to transform it so that it becomes your own. How will you do that?" He divided his class into small groups and challenged each group to come up with its own transforming or organizing strategies, several of which are described next.

Content Frames. One group decided to do a content frame to organize and compare information (see Figure 11.2). This organizing strategy helps to define interrelationships of ideas. In this case, a content frame provided students with a structure for comparing the 1920s with the 1990s.

	Economics	Stock Market	Culture/People	Morality
1920s	Farmers in terrible shape; had to sell land Real estate prices going higher Rich getting richer Poor getting poorer	Went up and up; everyone thought they'd get rich!	Flappers Al Capone Scandals Smoking cigarettes Jazz music	Bootleggers Prohibition Flappers Speak-easys
1990s	Farmers selling land—can't make it! Real estate—huge houses; million-dollar houses Rich—very rich stock market	Record gains over 10,000 Lots of people putting money in stock market! Thought they would get rich!	Rap music Divorce common Moms are working Yuppies	Drugs Short skirts Sexual revolution Abortion

FIGURE 11.2. Example content frame.

Conclusion	Evidence
People lacked principles	Supported bootleggers
	Bought stocks on borrowed money
	Chicago and other big cities had gangsters—organized crime
	The most famous people are athletes and movie stars!
People had strong principles; highly moral	Most worked hard to make money for their families
	Most supported prohibition
	Most weren't gambling on Florida real estate and the stock market
	Had strong family values—very few divorces; much less than today

FIGURE 11.3. Conclusion-proof notes.

Conclusion Support. Another group selected conclusion support notes as a way to analyze and review different points of view about the people of the 1920s (see Figure 11.3). This organizing approach stresses critical thinking skills with both expository and narrative text. Students write down their thesis or conclusion in the left-hand column and use the space in the right-hand column for recording evidence. After they form an opinion or come to some conclusions, they find support in their reading. They then use their notes to develop persuasive written arguments.

Writing and Learning

Writing is integral to all learning and to every aspect of Project CRISS. Writing is a way of knowing. If we can explain things to ourselves and others we can claim knowledge as our own. Writing helps each of us make personal sense about what we are learning. We cannot write about something we do not understand. Writing forces us to make choices about meaning. It lets us know what we know.

Writing forces organization. As we write, we begin to see clusters of information and hierarchies of ideas to make new information our own. Writing also encourages active involvement in learning. It is impossible to remain passive as a writer.

Students write constantly in Steve's classrooms. Most of the strategies described so far involve writing. Steve gives a brief lecture and asks students to write about what they have just learned. He begins each day with writing activity. On his white board, he has several statements or questions that students write about. The "quick writes" might be about a previous day's reading or a background knowledge question about a topic they are about to study.

We can never start our life over again. Our memories of the past will always stay with us whether it is a burden or a help. Our life creates a story which we can not go back and delete. We can, however, move on and gain wisdom from the past.

Paige

FIGURE 11.4. Paige's journal response.

On one occasion, he listed a series of quotations from *The Grapes of Wrath*:

> The moving, questing people were migrants now. . . . Behind them more were coming. . . . The movement changed them; the highways, the camps along the road, the fear of hunger and the hunger itself, changed them. The children without dinner changed them, the endless moving changed them. . . .
>
> Maybe we can start again, in the new rich land—in California, where the fruit grows. We'll start over. But you can't start. Only a baby can start. You and me— why, we're all that's been. . . . This land, this land is us; and the flood years and the dust years and the drought years are us. We can't start again.

After reading the quotations, students wrote freely about their feelings (see Figure 11.4). Many of these informal writings become fodder for longer assignments. For example, Steve would ask his students to reread their journal entries. "Do you find any ideas here that you could expand into a longer paper?"

Students also did more formal writing projects. In a collaborative project with an art teacher, Steve required students to write books about the 1920s and to bind them in their art class so they could be catalogued in the library. One group wrote an illustrated book about racial and sexual prejudice during the '20s. Another wrote about the Great Depression and life in migrant labor camps.

Metacognition and Strategic Learning

The concept of metacognition and strategic learning is at the heart of Project CRISS. In fact, our central goal is the development of expert, strategic readers. Students who achieve well in school have a heightened metacognitive awareness and a repertoire of self-regulatory behaviors. They know when they have understood, and they know how to employ a variety of strategies to attain meaning (Pressley, 2002).

We teach our students about the concept of *metacognition*. We usually begin this discussion with an explanation of differences between effective and less effective readers. Good readers are in control as they energetically attack the problem of making sense from their reading. They sort through the author's meaning to fit with their own background experiences and knowledge. They set learning goals and know how to use a variety of strategies to meet these goals. They have flexible reading strategies and know how to revise their plans to reach their goals effectively. They know how to reread, to self-question, and to organize information. They constantly assess their own learning progress. Do I understand this point? Do I need to reread? Should I write this idea down? Is the author making this clear, or do I need additional information? In other words, successful students are metacognitive and have strategies they can deliberately apply to their reading and learning to gain understanding. They know when they have understood, and they know how to employ a variety of strategies to attain meaning.

We contrast this profile with the research about poor readers (Paris, Wasik, & Turner, 1991). Poor readers are not metacognitive. They aren't in control. They don't understand the need for setting goals and have no flexible plans for comprehending. Often they do not know whether or not they have understood a selection. They may read through a selection once without knowing their comprehension has failed. They lack flexibility and deliberate plans for correcting comprehension. Poor readers respond with helplessness. Good readers attack the problems; poor readers shut down and give up. They know they have failed, but they do not know why.

Given that successful students know when they know and when they don't know, Steve shows his students ways to monitor their own learning. For example, he asks them to develop notes about important concepts, showing them how to write main ideas in the left-hand column and details to the right (see Figure 11.5). Then he uses his notes to model how to self-test: "Cover the information on the right. Use the left-hand column as a quiz. Test yourself.

Main Topic	Details
1920s—Time of Transition	Mass production—Automobiles, airplanes, radio
	Era between wars
	Really not much different than other times
People	Some—Hated prohibition, played stock market, went to speakeasys, danced Charleston
	Most—Hard working families, strong, supported prohibition, didn't buy stock
Economy	Workers' income up 40 percent—times good
	Overproduction
	People using credit
	Rich very rich; poor very poor
	Factories—Assembly lines
	Farming—Not doing well; loss of exports

FIGURE 11.5. Sample two-column notes.

It's only you who knows what you know. Check your own comprehension. See how much you remember. The responsibility rests with you. If you can answer your own questions, you will be able to answer mine."

We also help students become more metacognitive by demonstrating and talking about learning processes as part of teaching and learning. "How can you bring your own background knowledge to this learning situation? What active strategies will you use to learn the information? How can you transform or organize the information to make it your own? How can you use writing and discussion as tools for your own learning?" Our goal is for students to internalize these questions so that they can consciously apply these principles to their own learning.

In fact, Steve has the following questions printed on a large chart in his classroom:

Self-Questionnaire

What do I need to do to prepare myself for this reading assignment? What do I need to learn from it?
What active strategies will I use during reading to make sure I am understanding what I read?
How am I going to transform the information? What strategies will I use?
How am I going to make sure that I understand and remember it? How will I self-test?

The "how" of learning always holds equal weight to the "what" of learning. We want our students to leave our classrooms confident in ways of knowing that will carry them through a lifetime of learning.

Teacher Modeling and Explanation

Our final theoretical principle has to do with our own teaching. Students learn to think strategically when we demonstrate processes through explanation and modeling as part of our instruction. Our demonstrations are particularly critical for struggling readers. Most have no clue about how to learn. We have to show them how.

When introducing a new strategy, we take center stage, showing, telling, modeling, demonstrating, and explaining not only the content but the process of active reading (Duffy, 2002). As students learn, we gradually release responsibility to them. Steve doesn't assign note taking, underlining, or an essay exam without first showing his students how to do these skills. For example, before asking his students to underline a piece of text, Steve made a transparency of the assignment and demonstrated how he would underline important information in the selection.

Our strategy instruction involves two overlapping steps. First, we explain what the strategy is and why students should use it to improve their learning. If students do not know why they are performing an activity, they rarely repeat the behavior on their own (Duffy, 2002). Next, we demonstrate and talk about procedures for doing the strategy. We discuss, demonstrate, and think aloud while modeling. Then students practice under our guidance and feedback. Throughout, we ask students to talk about strategies they find personally effective. We constantly think about ways to help them become metacognitive.

Thus, the principles and philosophy of Project CRISS provide the context for strategic instruction. Even though this is the case, our philosophical stance always remains fluid as we learn new ideas from our students, from our colleagues, and from our own research. Articulating and rearticulating our belief system was and still is vital to the development of Project CRISS. We have a theoretical framework not only for developing the program but for continually evaluating and modifying it. The framework provides us with a way to think about how a particular lesson may or may not reflect what we now know about teaching and learning. It provides a mirror for reflection not only for us, but for our students.

A LINGERING ISSUE

Yet, as with any innovation in education, there are always lingering issues. Figuring out ways to deal with these issues also keeps us moving forward. The major issue that haunts us is a big one: Many teachers and administrators don't really understand Project CRISS.

They see the project more as an organized bundle of strategies than as a philosophical shift in what it means to teach. When we think about it, the particular strategies teachers use are not what is really important. Instead, it is their understanding of CRISS principles and philosophy that matters. CRISS isn't about assigning students to take notes or do a concept map. Instead, it involves a change in the definition of what it means to teach. Teachers who don't understand often ask, "How can I incorporate Project CRISS into my science, history, or math class? I have too much content to cover." Those that do understand will respond, "Yes, content is important, but teaching students how to learn content holds equal weight. Knowing how to learn is what will carry them through life, not the specific details of my content. Just as I have internalized CRISS principles and philosophy in my own teaching, so, too, have my students in their own learning. They know about the power of background knowledge, the need to be active learners, the importance of writing and talking about what they are learning, and why it is essential to transform information into a variety of note-taking schemes. My students are also metacognitive. They know when they understand, and when they aren't getting it, they know what to do about it. They take charge of their own learning and leave my classroom with new confidence in what it means to be a student. That's what CRISS is about. It is not about assigning two-column notes."

Understanding CRISS means changing attitudes about teaching—not an easy task. One thing is for sure: Changing attitudes takes more than a two-day CRISS workshop. It took us a while before we learned that lesson. Even though we still have no definitive answer for helping teachers and administrators build a deep understanding of CRISS, we have uncovered several procedures or processes that start jimmying the door open. Here are some of our discoveries.

1. *We guide districts in their implementation of the project.* Changing views of teaching can't happen alone. It's too hard. When we agree to do a two- or three-day CRISS workshop in a district, we start asking questions. How many teachers will be involved? It works best if several teachers from the same content area attend. The ideal scenario occurs with a series of workshops, where all teachers in a school become involved. Are teachers volunteering to participate? (Forced attendance practically never works.) Who will take charge of facilitating the project—a content teacher, a reading specialist, a principal? Will the principal attend? You know how difficult is for teachers to change if the principal has no clue about what's involved. Who will be responsible for continual follow-up? Will teachers have opportunities to meet and to share ideas with one another? Who will coordinate a project newsletter featuring ways teachers have implemented the project?

2. *We keep our workshops interactive.* This way, participants begin to see the power of background knowledge, transformation, active strategies, written response, discussion, and metacognitive understanding with their own learning. When introducing specific learning strategies, we take time for reflection. How did this approach engage your background knowledge? Did you write, talk, and transform the information? Describe how you were metacognitive. Did this work better for learning than simply reading the chapter and answering the questions? How would you adapt these approaches in our own classroom?

3. *We talk about how to turn CRISS principles and philosophy over to students.* It's not enough that we, as educators, understand these principles. How might you help students understand how this philosophy works for their own learning? The heart of CRISS is turning over the project to the students. It is not enough that teachers understand our teaching philosophy. It is not enough that teachers remain the experts in the various learning procedures.

4. *We entice participants to become teacher researchers.* "How might you investigate different ways of organizing information with your own students? What do you think might happen in your math class if you taught students how to analyze a text, to underline selectively, to write explanations of key terms? Do you think students would perform better in that class compared to another class? Or, how might you do a case study with one or two students in your class?" Involving teachers in examining their own practice through research is a sensitive way to generate change.

Even more important, participants learn what it means to be a teacher researcher, to take on a research approach, to take on an attitude that becomes a process of self-examination, growth, and continuing change. Teacher research becomes a way of teaching, of never really finding the right answer, of seeking ways to do the job even better. It involves maintaining a research attitude that encourages constant examination, growth, and continuing change as opposed to finding the right solution to a problem. Teacher research promotes a dynamic approach to the teaching professional as opposed to maintenance of the status quo. In looking back on the past 20 years, we now know that the real power of Project CRISS lies in its potential for fostering a research attitude among teachers and students.

CONCLUSION

In the end, I guess we don't want definitive answers to our lingering issue about changing something so major as what it means to teach. Instead, our goal is to nourish communities of teachers and students as continual learners about learning. We do know, however, that our thinking will always be under revision. While we now have more trust in our own abilities to construct knowledge for improving our teaching, we won't become stagnant; we'll keep challenging ourselves and our students to become even better clinicians of teaching and learning. Our lunchroom conversations will continue to unfold with new ideas about ways to become even better at what we do. In the end, we want our students to leave our classrooms confident in ways of knowing that will carry them throughout their lives.

REFERENCES

Duffy, G. (2002). The case for direct explanation of strategies. In C. Block and M. Pressley, *Comprehension instruction: Research-based practices* (pp. 28–41). New York: Guilford Press.

Jensen, E. (1998). *Teaching with the brain in mind.* Alexandria, VA: Association for Supervision and Curriculum Development.

Keene, E., & Zimmerman, S. (1997). *Mosaic of thought.* Portsmouth, NH: Heinemann.

Paris, S., Wasik, B., & Turner, J. (1991). The development of strategic readers. In R. Barr, M. Kamil, P. Mosenthal, & P. David Pearson (Eds.), *Handbook of reading research* (Vol. 2, pp. 609–640). New York: Longman.

Pearson, P. D., & Fielding, L. (1991). Comprehension instruction. In R. Barr, M. Kamil, P. Mosenthal, & P. David Pearson (Eds.), *Handbook of reading research* (Vol. 2, pp. 815–860). New York: Longman.

Pressley, M. (2002). Comprehension strategy instruction: A turn-of-the-century status report. In C. Block and M. Pressley, *Comprehension instruction: Research-based practices* (pp. 11–27). New York: Guilford Press.

Santa, C., Havens, L., & Valdez, B. (2004). *Project CRISS: Creating independence through student-owned strategies.* Dubuque, IA: Kendall-Hunt.

12

Apprenticing Urban Youth to Science Literacy

Cynthia Greenleaf, Willard Brown,
and Cindy Litman

Key Points

- Multiple and varied science texts, students' level of academic literacy, and an ambitious curriculum all present challenges in the teaching of science.
- At the core of Reading Apprenticeship is ongoing metacognitive conversation, often resulting in more powerful, academic identities.
- Reading Apprenticeship teachers build a literacy inquiry community by developing routines and structures to support reading and thinking.

The computer monitor at the front of Will Brown's classroom reads:

Think–Write

Last night you read chapter 7 section 1.
What went well for you?
What did not go well for you?
What was the most interesting idea that you learned?

Students are sitting in table groups, named for the chemistry they are learning this year: pH Pals, Solubility Sleuths, Stoichiometry Stars, Molar Majority, Phase Fans, Kinetic Kids. They take out their notebooks and write to the metacognitive prompts on the monitor. While they write, Will checks attendance and then walks around the room, monitoring students' progress.

This metacognitive Think–Write is routine in this classroom. It links the prior day's learning, reading, and homework to the day's work in chemistry and goes by the auspicious name, the "preamble." After a moment, Will says, "Class, please focus here. What happened with your homework last night?" He directs students to share their preamble responses with their table groups "in one and a half minutes, using 5 centimeter voices. Choose a spokesperson for your group. Go, go, go!"

During this period, Will's students are all English language learners, recent immigrants from Hong Kong, Vietnam, Taiwan, Tanzania, India, Mexico, Iran, Pakistan. As in Einstein's physics, time is relative in this class. One and a half minutes lengthens as students share the difficulties as well as the new ideas and concepts they encountered while reading the assigned section of their challenging chemistry textbook. Will moves from group to group as students work together, entering their conversations, probing their thinking, suggesting a different way to look at a problem. At Joaquim's table, for instance, Will stops to comment on an observation Joaquim has made about his reading process: "Yeah. Sometimes you read something and you know, 'Ha, they're going to talk about this next.' It's called 'foreshadowing' and that foreshadowing happens in science. There's a sense of a rhythm to science texts: They talk about this, then they're probably going to talk about the other thing."

As these conversations wind down, Will pulls the class back together so that table groups can share their discussions with the whole class. Lily volunteers, "I learned to write chemical formulas." Will encourages her to say more, "And what was hard?" Lily responds, "All the names of them." Lily's difficulty is one Will has anticipated; today's lesson will focus on learning how to name the chemical compounds. "After today," he promises, "I do not think it will be so hard." Other students speak up. Bao offers her strategy for reading the textbook—taking notes on the chemistry by focusing on the "important words." When asked how she can tell which words are important, Bao says that "the book showed me." With Will's prompting, Bao demonstrates how she uses the bold words in the text and the glossary at the back of the book. But Chang observes, "It was easy for me to look for the bold words and the key words, but it's hard for me to understand the hard words I don't know that aren't bold." Will agrees, "It can still be hard even when they give you the definitions of the key words. The words around the key words can be words you don't know. Did you put some of these down to ask me about?" He then councils, "Start with the word in bold or italics and the sentence it is in. Try to understand that one sentence, work very hard on it, and then look around it in the paragraph. Put most of your energy into understanding the bold words."

Through this metacognitive talk and sharing, students' shared puzzles, problems, and problem solving are linked to the chemistry they are learning as the preamble spills into the day's lesson. In this sheltered chemistry class, as in Will's other chemistry classes, ongoing inquiry into reading and reasoning processes supports students to become stronger science readers and thinkers. Students reflect on their learning, bringing their questions and difficulties with the reading and the chemistry to their tablemates. They are encouraged to think and go as far as they can together before turning to their teacher for help. Often reading is done for homework; sometimes students read together in class through a Team Reading process. But always there is this opportunity to inquire together into science concepts and literacy processes and to collaborate in order to reach fuller understandings.

These routine metacognitive conversations—opportunities to talk about one's own thinking and reading processes—provide an opportunity for Will to access and support students' thinking, and for his students to both reflect on and share their comprehension problems and problem solving. In the urban high school where he teaches, Will has found metacognitive conversation to be a powerful lever to move students' disengagement and lack of interest out of the way of the thinking and learning he wants them to practice. In metacognitive conversation, he creates ongoing opportunities to negotiate with his students new and more successful ways of being in the classroom, helping these young people to rethink their prior conceptions of reading and take on new, more powerful identities as readers and learners.

OUR COLLABORATION: PROFESSIONAL COMMUNITY AND INQUIRY INTO READING IN URBAN SCHOOLS

This is a Reading Apprenticeship classroom.[1] The teacher, Willard Brown, is a member of an ongoing professional learning community in the San Francisco Bay Area of California, where he is working to apprentice his urban students to science literacy practices. Will is one of hundreds of Bay Area secondary teachers integrating Reading Apprenticeship into subject area teaching. This community of teachers is supported by the Strategic Literacy Initiative at WestEd, where coauthors Cynthia Greenleaf and Cindy Litman work as part of a research and development team focused on adolescent literacy. Because Will has taken a leadership role in his school and in this professional community, for the past two years we have worked together as a practicing teacher and as classroom researchers to explore how Reading Apprenticeship might support historically underprepared and underachieving students to see themselves as thinkers, readers, and doers of science.

In this chapter, we introduce Reading Apprenticeship, a model of reading instruction for middle and high school students that embeds powerful instructional routines around reading into subject area teaching in courses such as Will's chemistry class. We illustrate Will's work to integrate Reading Apprenticeship into inquiry-oriented science teaching in an urban high school, offering portraits of classroom practices as well as descriptions of diverse young people making, with their teacher's help, a journey toward more powerful, academic identities. Along the way, we reveal the challenges and dilemmas we face in this work, starting with the challenges that motivate our ongoing collaboration: the complex literacy practices of science that are necessary if students are to participate successfully in the processes of invention, discovery, explanation, and critique that are central to science inquiry and engagement; the school-based literacy proficiencies and experiences of many urban youth; and the goals we hold for equitable participation of all students in the academic enterprise.

THE CHALLENGE OF LITERACY IN SCIENCE EDUCATION

To learn science is to learn not merely a body of scientific knowledge but also ways of participating in scientific exploration and reasoning. Access to the scientific community, and the ability to carry out or evaluate the outcomes of science inquiry, relies on various kinds of sophisticated literacy skills—the ability to make sense of scientific terminology, to interpret arrays of data, to comprehend scientific texts, to use and interpret models and illustrations, and to read and write scientific explanations (Lemke, 1999; Osborne, 2002). Despite this recognition, making the case for reading instruction in science classes is not straightforward, in part because the history of science instruction and reading has been a troubled one.

Traditional science education has been criticized for an overemphasis on acquiring science facts through teachers' lectures or demonstrations, prefabricated laboratory experiences, and reading textbooks. Recent reforms in science education aim instead to engage students in building science knowledge through hands-on scientific explorations (e.g., Bybee, 1997). Sometimes this has meant consigning science textbooks to the dustbin—witness the description of outstanding teaching in *National Science Education Standards*: "Many generous teachers spend their own money on science supplies, knowing that students learn best by investigation. These teachers ignore the vocabulary-dense textbooks and encourage student inquiry" (National Research Council, 1996, p. 12). Often, science educators call for the use of reading materials other than textbooks to increase engagement and add relevance to students' daily lives, pointing out that language, reading, and writing can play a significant role in understanding science and that the process skills of reading and science are parallel and mutually supportive of learning (e.g., Baker, 1991; Manzo & Manzo, 1990; McMahon & McCormack, 1998). Yet many science teachers are not certain how to integrate science reading experiences with hands-on investigations and are keenly aware of students' difficulty comprehending science texts. As a result, in recent years there has been a widespread reduction of reading in secondary science classrooms, precisely as policymakers are raising alarms about the reading proficiencies of adolescents (Rycik & Irvin, 2001).

In Reading Apprenticeship science classes, in contrast, reading plays a prominent role in students' learning. The teachers we work with are encouraged to draw on their own experiences as readers in their disciplines to assist students with complex reading tasks, making apparent both the challenges and the value of such reading. Will's experience as a research chemist has influenced his work with students on reading in science:

> Reading is part and parcel of science inquiry. Scientists must digest huge amounts of science text, yet reading science is significantly different than reading other kinds of literature. Science readers need powerful reading habits and attitudes to comprehend the ideas of science embedded in the various structures and conventions of science texts and language. I want to pass on to my students the joy of figuring things out through science inquiry and through reading science.

The "texts" of the science world and of Will's chemistry classroom are multiple and varied, ranging from traditional, encyclopedic textbooks to trade journals and science reports, numerical equations, visual and physical models of atoms and molecules, and conventional systems for denoting chemical bonding such as Lewis dot structures, chemical equations, and drawings of atomic structures. Even laboratory equipment and the phenomena explored in the lab require "reading" and interpretation. Each of these texts poses a comprehension problem for the science learner. The diverse students in American schools, particularly those from groups who have been historically underrepresented in the sciences, will need help acquiring high levels of reading and literacy proficiency in order to participate more fully in the scientific enterprise. Will recognizes that supporting his urban students' growth in academic reading is key to their growth as science learners and citizens in our science-rich society.

THE CHALLENGE OF ACADEMIC LITERACY FOR URBAN ADOLESCENTS

Will's students, like many of the ethnically and linguistically diverse students we meet in urban secondary classrooms, are *inexperienced, but not beginning* readers. Many of them need the opportunity and instructional support to read varied materials in order to build their experience, fluency, and range as readers. Virtually all middle and high school students—those who struggle academically as well as those who have been more successful—need help acquiring the particular comprehension processes that underlie skilled reading in varied subject areas and academic disciplines (Snow, 2002).

Yet precisely because reading and comprehension processes take place mentally, hidden from view, reading is often mystifying to these young people. As a result, many adolescents hold conceptions of reading that are usually based on their experiences in school, which do not serve them well. They may persist in believing that skillful reading simply amounts to pronouncing the words on the page. They may not realize that all reading involves problem solving, that meaning does not always come to readers automatically, and that there are many strategies proficient readers use to solve the comprehension problems they encounter in text. And they are often unaware that the reading materials of the different subject areas require different kinds of interpretive strategies and can offer dramatically different reading experiences.

By the time they reach middle and high school, many of these same students have built a repertoire of strategies to avoid reading and to hide what they believe to be the secret shame of poor reading abilities. The cumulative effect of years of negative, unproductive, or mystifying school experiences with reading can weigh heavily on young people, shaping their lifelong identities. Many of these adolescents do not see themselves as readers and do not choose to read books in their lives outside of school. Despite this, adolescents are resourceful and strategic practitioners of a variety of literacies outside of school. Many urban, immigrant youth function as culture brokers and language interpreters for their families, demonstrating considerable agency and skill with a range of texts necessary for day-to-day living. Other young people may avidly explore the meaning of song lyrics or pore over computer manuals for help in outfoxing a videogame opponent. In addition to these strate-gic—if not academic—literacy abilities, young people are at a point in their lives when their social identity is highly important to them. Adolescence is the developmental moment when young people begin to explore or try on pos-sible selves, to expand or solidify their visions of who they are and can become.

THE CHALLENGE OF THE AMBITIOUS CURRICULUM

This key developmental task of adolescence takes on yet greater import in light of the fundamental shift in the way educators have come to define learn-ing in the past few decades. Schools and society now hold ambitious new goals for all students, in part because our understanding of what it means to learn has evolved beyond traditional definitions—the accumulation of knowl-edge and skills—to include a growing capacity to participate in particular kinds of conversations and to engage in particular kinds of thinking and doing. We now see learning as a growing ability to participate skillfully—in scientific inquiry, mathematical problem solving, literary conversations, or the weigh-ing of diverse perspectives on historical events. If participating in this kind of complex activity has become a goal for all of our students, then the role of reading in learning has also become both more critical and more complex. Lit-eracy can be either the gatekeeper or the gateway to full participation in school and society.

We know that the students who come to us in middle or high school are often unprepared to participate successfully with the challenging tasks and texts they will encounter. More troubling still, many of these young people—even those in college preparatory classes—have disinvested in learning, resignedly carrying out tasks in the most perfunctory exchange of labor for grades. To help inexperienced or novice readers participate more skillfully in the literacy activities expected and valued in particular academic disciplines, we believe we will have to go beyond a reading specialist model to integrate reading instruction across the curriculum. And we will need to address more than content area reading strategies to help disaffected urban youth reinvest themselves in reading and learning. In this critical time in young people's lives, how can subject area teachers reengage students in reading, and partic-ularly in the discipline-specific modes of thinking and reading that support learning? How can teachers more successfully engage adolescents in the kind of literacies that will sustain them as lifelong learners and knowledgeable par-ticipants in a democratic, information-based society?

ADDRESSING THE CHALLENGES: THE READING APPRENTICESHIP INSTRUCTIONAL FRAMEWORK

In response to these questions, we in the Strategic Literacy Initiative have developed and continue to refine the Reading Apprenticeship instructional framework, in the company of a growing network of middle and high school subject area teachers (Schoenbach, Greenleaf, Cziko, & Hurwitz, 1999). Reading Apprenticeship draws both on what subject area teachers know and do as discipline-based readers and on adolescents' unique and often underestimated strengths as learners. The model draws on earlier research characterizing effective teaching for naïve learners of complex mental tasks as cognitive apprenticeship. In a Reading Apprenticeship classroom, the teacher serves as a "master" or proficient reader of subject area texts to student "apprentices." This instruction takes place in the process of teaching subject area content.

Reading Apprenticeship takes well-researched practices in reading instruction into a coherent instructional framework, engaging students in extensive reading, integrating explicit teaching of comprehension strategies into the reading of curricular texts, establishing relevance and making personal connections to reading materials and curriculum activities, drawing on the out-of-school language and literacies of culturally diverse students, identifying and using a variety of language and text structures to support comprehension, and supporting collaborative sense-making activities with written materials. Although Reading Apprenticeship includes strategic reading instruction, it aims higher: to shift students' misconceptions of reading, of their own reading ability, and of the purposes of reading in school and society, thereby reengaging them in the academic enterprise. The instructional model involves teachers and their students as partners in a collaborative inquiry into reading as they engage with subject matter texts.

Metacognitive Conversation: Demystifying Subject Area Reading

At the center of the Reading Apprenticeship instructional model is an ongoing metacognitive conversation, a conversation about the thinking processes teachers and students are engaged in as they work with course materials and readings. In this model, new knowledge, strategies, and dispositions develop in an ongoing conversation in which teacher and students think about and discuss their personal relationships to reading and learning, larger issues of literacy and power and the social environment and resources of the classroom, their cognitive activity, the structure and language of particular types of texts, and the kinds of knowledge required to make sense of academic materials and ideas (see Figure 12.1). This metacognitive conversation is carried on both internally, as teacher and students individually grapple with course materials and reflect on their own mental processes, and externally, as they share their knowledge resources, motivations, interactions with texts, and affective responses to literacy tasks.

A good deal of research has documented positive outcomes in student achievement when teachers engage students in subject area work through classroom conversation (e.g., Nystrand & Gamoran, 1991), including talk about *how* we read in subject areas (Duffy et al., 1994). Despite this, authentic discussion is a rare occurrence in classrooms (Snow, 2002). In Reading Apprenticeship classrooms, however, teachers implement a variety of meta-

SOCIAL DIMENSION

Creating safety

Investigating relationships
between literacy and power

Sharing book talk

Sharing reading processes,
problems, and solutions

Noticing and appropriating
others' ways of reading

PERSONAL DIMENSION

Developing reader identity

Developing metacognition

Developing reader fluency
and stamina

Developing reader confidence
and range

Assessing performance and
setting goals

COGNITIVE DIMENSION

Getting the big picture

Breaking it down

Monitoring comprehension

Using problem-solving
strategies to assist and
restore comprehension

Setting reading purposes and
adjusting reading processes

**KNOWLEDGE-BUILDING
DIMENSION**

Mobilizing and building
knowledge structures (schemata)

Developing content or topic
knowledge

Developing knowledge of word
construction and vocabulary

Developing knowledge and use
of text structures

Developing discipline- and
discourse-specific knowledge

GOAL: To help students become more active, strategic, and independent readers by:

1) supporting students' discovery of their own reasons to read and ways of reading
2) modeling disciplinary ways of reading in different subject areas and genres
3) guiding students to explore, strengthen, and assess their own reading

FIGURE 12.1. Dimensions of Reading Apprenticeship®. *Source:* Strategic Literacy Initiative, 2/03. WestEd 2003. All rights reserved.

cognitive and conversational routines to engage students in discussion about *how* we read and *why* we read in the ways we do, as well as *what* we read in subject area classes. These routines offer students ongoing opportunities to consider how they are trying to make sense of texts, how well their strategies and approaches are working for them, and how others (including the teacher) are approaching course reading. Over time, students can see that academic reading is always characterized by problem solving, that reading proficiency continues to develop for all readers over a lifetime, and that their own reading abilities are not fixed. This understanding can free young people to reinvest effort in reading and, ultimately, in learning.

Promising Outcomes: Studies of Reading Apprenticeship

Our studies of the impact of Reading Apprenticeship suggest that this approach to reading instruction can produce powerful and positive outcomes for the reading proficiencies and engagement of adolescents. An initial study demonstrated increased reading achievement and academic engagement across a diverse group of 216 ninth graders enrolled in an Academic Literacy course in an urban, low-SES high school (Greenleaf, Schoenbach, Cziko, & Mueller, 2001; Schoenbach et al., 1999). These initial results have been replicated in several additional studies of sites with diverse student and teacher populations (http://www.wested.org/stratlit; Killion, 2002).[2] Further, as Bay area middle and high schools have taken Reading Apprenticeship schoolwide, test scores in underperforming schools have begun to rise, especially for those student populations that have historically fared poorly in these schools (see Petrocelli, 2003).[3] Taken together, these studies suggest that Reading Apprenticeship results in significant gains in reading proficiency for students across varied grade levels and subject areas.

Yet more important than these gains on standardized achievement tests are the changes we have witnessed and documented in students' literacy identities, shifts from disenfranchised to empowered readers with a range of strategies for gaining access to the forbidding codes and conventions of academic literacies. This shift takes place as teachers invite their students into the core thinking and reasoning processes of their disciplines by creating a collaborative classroom inquiry into reading course materials and texts. By demystifying academic literacy practices, teachers succeed in opening gateways for students into engaged learning and encourage their students to reinvest energy in the work of comprehending complex ideas and texts.

The preponderance of research in secondary classrooms illustrates that very little teaching of how to read academic materials is actually done, even though teachers may know content area reading strategies (Alvermann & Moore, 1991; Snow, 2002). An important part of our research agenda, therefore, has focused on studying the impact of professional development in Reading Apprenticeship on teachers' attitudes, beliefs, and classroom practices (Greenleaf & Schoenbach, 2001). The research we have carried out in Will's classroom builds on our prior studies examining both students' reading development and changes in teachers' conceptions and classroom practices. In the current study, conducted in 11 different subject area classrooms across a range of academic subjects and secondary grade levels, we are exploring the relationships between teachers' professional development experiences, their classroom practices (i.e., the learning experiences they provide for students), and their students' engagement and success with subject area reading. As part of this study, over the past two years we have interviewed Will and observed his participation in professional development settings; observed and recorded his science teaching weekly; and collected students' work, reading assessments, grades, and interviews. In the remainder of this chapter, we draw on these data to illustrate how one science teacher works to apprentice his urban youth to science literacy.

IMPLEMENTING READING APPRENTICESHIP IN CHEMISTRY AT AN URBAN HIGH SCHOOL

Will teaches chemistry at Skyline High School in Oakland, California. Designated an "underperforming high school" by the California Department of Education due to low standardized test scores, Skyline recently was granted status as a Title I school, making increased resources and academic support available to its diverse students. These students are diverse in many ways. Ethnically, the student population is about 50% African American, 25% Asian American, 15% Latino, and 10% Caucasian. Nearly 40% of the students qualify for free or reduced lunch. Nearly 60% of the students test below grade level in reading, language, math, and science, according to the California state standardized tests. And while 700 freshmen enter Skyline in the ninth grade, only half of them graduate. This alarming attrition rate attests to one of the primary challenges faced by Skyline's faculty: to hold high standards and expectations for all students while simultaneously giving the degree and type of support needed for students to reach these standards. For the past few years, the administration and faculty have focused schoolwide on increasing the success of underserved populations of students at the school.

For example, district and school equity initiatives, coupled with the work of Skyline's counseling staff, have increased the number of African American and Latino students enrolling in college preparatory courses. The science department at Skyline, chaired by Will, has developed open enrollment requirements for honors chemistry to promote equity and to usher more of Skyline's African American and Latino students into the more rigorous science classes. Over the past few years, Will and a fellow science teacher have also worked concertedly to create an enrollment pipeline from biology to chemistry and successful learning experiences for these students who are underrepresented in the higher sciences nationwide.

Will has taught honors chemistry, regular college preparatory chemistry, sheltered chemistry for English learners, and introduction to chemistry, including a summer session of the course for students who failed it during the school

year. In Will's experience, the students in the sheltered chemistry and introduction to chemistry courses typically face the greatest language and literacy
challenges in science. However, the effort toward greater inclusiveness in honors chemistry means that these classes also contain students with different
degrees of preparation for the rigorous work of the honors curriculum. Some
enter honors classes as relatively skilled readers, while others struggle with academic text, with standardized reading achievement scores as low as the 6th
percentile. It's not surprising that Will believes virtually *all* of his students
need instruction and support in the processes of reading science to successfully meet the demands of reading science texts. He was motivated to take up
Reading Apprenticeship as a means of providing this needed reading instruction because in his professional development experiences he saw that it as res-
onant with his goals for his students' inquiry learning in science.

Building a Literacy Inquiry Community

The spirit of inquiry is a common thread binding literacy and science in Will's
classroom. As he says:

> The heart of science is science inquiry. In science inquiry instruction,
> students explore phenomena, form questions and hypotheses, design
> and implement experiments, draw inferences from observation, and
> refine their understanding of science concepts. In Reading Appren-
> ticeship, collaborative inquiry is the primary mode of engaging in
> reading and is resonant with science inquiry; they support each
> other. Students make sense of science research and laboratory experi-
> ences through discussions in which they test their ideas and appro-
> priate others' ways of thinking about science. Students develop their
> science reading habits through the metacognitive conversation in
> which they share their reading experiences and appropriate others'
> ways of reading. The transition between the two forms of inquiry is
> seamless.

Will begins the year by establishing routines and structures that nurture
and support a collaborative, inquiry learning environment. Early in the school
year, Will talks explicitly with students about the ideas behind Reading Apprenticeship and invites students to explore their science literacy histories—the
experiences that have shaped their current attitudes and motivations toward
science reading. This brings students' conceptions of reading, of science, and
of themselves as learners into the classroom where they can inform Will's
instructional decisions and become resources for student learning. As new
reading opportunities arise in the classroom, Will models his own sense-making processes by thinking aloud as he works to make sense of a reading or
chemistry problem. By making his own reading and reasoning processes—the
confusions, clarifications, and connections—visible, Will demonstrates mental engagement and problem solving as the hidden work of comprehension.

His willingness to take the risk involved in showing his students how he actually *works* to comprehend texts helps students realize that it is strategic effort and not magic that is involved in comprehension.

Throughout the year, Will gives students ongoing opportunities and responsibility to reflect on their own thinking and learning through metacognitive reflections such as the preamble that prefaced this chapter. As students read multiple types of science texts and carry out laboratory experiments and explorations, they are asked to reflect on and share their thinking and learning. As in the literacy history inquiries, this sharing brings students' individual reading and thinking into the wider classroom community. Will's classroom is structured to promote collaboration, with students placed in table groups that change membership periodically throughout the year. Many assignments are done by "expert groups," a structured group-work routine in which each table group responds to a different open-ended prompt about a topic-related problem. After working on the problem as a team, expert groups present their solutions to the class and solicit their peers' feedback and assistance.

Will notes that having students work together on a problem is very powerful:

> I think students know that their ideas and contributions are valued by the design of our lessons, where teams often have to report back to the class what they've learned, or what their ideas are. Expert groups are one of the things students felt most positively about this year. Teams taking responsibility for one or a certain fraction of the assignment, presenting their thoughts back to the class, clarifying. They felt safe doing that. It was okay to make mistakes, you saw that people did, but they also got mistakes corrected and questions answered. And if you had a question, you had an opportunity to ask about it.

Will describes his own important role during this group work as that of "itinerant mentor." His mentoring begins with listening:

> If they're asking a question, I have to hear it, understand what they're saying, decide how much I'm going to answer, or whether I'm going to ask them a few questions to figure out where they are and what they already know. Even if they didn't call me over, I listen just the same.

To promote students' thinking and confidence in their ability to do challenging work, Will avoids giving students answers to their questions. Rather, he tries to guide them to answer as many questions as they can by themselves or with the help of their classmates:

> I may leave them with a question that will just help them organize their information so they can go on and answer their own question. Or I may propose an idea to them and let them respond and let

them talk for a while. I want to reinforce the idea that they're the learners and can learn. I want them to actually practice learning and practice figuring things out and know that they are the ones who are doing it.

To support students' development as science readers and learners, Will focuses explicitly on science literacy throughout the year, emphasizing ways of reading, thinking, and talking that are particular to science. Over the course of the year, he introduces a variety of high-leverage comprehension strategies to help his students develop a repertoire of comprehension problem-solving tools. But no one particular strategy or mix of strategies seems to provide the optimal leverage for increasing students' engagement with academic texts. Rather, the climate of the classroom community in which inquiry into reading and chemistry becomes a shared conversation is key to engaging individual students in the reading and reasoning processes of science. Will notes that as his students work together on increasing their understanding of their reading in science, they develop not only a sense of community, but a sense of responsibility for their own and each others' learning. Slowly, even initially resistant students begin to ease into new roles as science learners with the modeling, challenge, and support offered in this classroom. Thus, unlike approaches that focus exclusively on cognitive strategies, Will notes that nurturing changes in students' academic engagement necessitates strategically engaging the social and personal, as well as the academic, dimensions of classroom life.

The following vignette illustrates Will's mentoring—his gentle insistence that students abandon the role of passive learners to engage actively as thinkers and doers of science.

Will's honors class is engaged in an team exploration aimed at exploring the bonding characteristics of carbon and connecting the names and structures of organic molecules during a unit on organic chemistry. Surrounded with modeling kit, textbooks, their reading logs, and sheets of hand-drawn molecular structures, teammates Crystal, Suzanne, and Tisha leaf randomly through the textbook's baffling array of Lewis structure and computer-generated representations of organic molecules, looking for a clue that will help them construct a model of 2-pentanol. They believe they have exhausted all resources. Tisha flags down Will and explains their problem: "The only one we could find was pentanol. I guess we're supposed to make it up by knowing what the different forms are. None of us knows how to figure it out." Will's response—"Not *yet,* anyhow"—reveals his confidence that the three can solve the problem. "Tell me what you *do* know," he says. While her teammates continue their haphazard search through the textbook, Tisha ventures, "Penta- means five."

With Will's support, Tisha makes progress puzzling out the structure of 2-pentanol, leveraging what she does know to tackle this new molecule. Aware that something worthwhile is transpiring, Tisha's teammates pause in their random page turning to join the conversation. Will explains to the three of them, "Now you just need to identify what the -an and -ol is." Will listens for a while to the ensuing burst of conversation, then summarizes what he hears and prompts, "So -ols are alcohol. Where is the -ol group going to be?" Tisha ventures, "Around the carbons?" Will pushes for greater specificity: "Where in that five-member carbon chain?" Although another short conversation among teammates does not yet produce consensus about the exact location of the alcohol, Will indicates his confidence that the three can solve this problem on their own and identifies the remaining piece of the puzzle: "Well you know *what* that is, and you know it goes *somewhere*. So what part of the name have you not dealt with?" When Tisha says, "The 2," Will agrees and tells the reenergized and refocused team, "So you have to figure out what the 2 tells you, then you'll know how to build it."

As team members discuss carbon chains and double bonds, informed by now purposeful forays into the textbook, Will steps back. But he doesn't leave the group yet. He listens in, reentering the conversation twice, once to articulate a general principle that the team has vaguely apprehended and once to ask a question that moves the discussion forward. Before moving on, Will tells the team, "So you just need to figure out how to number the chain; then you'll know where to put the alcohol."

As this vignette makes clear, Will engages students in comprehending traditional, encyclopedic textbooks as well a rich array of trade journals and science reports, computer visualizations, Lewis dot structures, laboratory procedures, and experimental equipment and phenomena. When students read the chemistry textbook, which is frequent, reading and working to clarify understanding does not begin and end with the assigned textbook reading. After the initial reading, which often happens as homework, the text resurfaces as students attempt to deepen their understanding of a specific phenomenon or solve a specific problem. Dog-eared tables and charts and a range of student-created texts are constant companions as students engage in science inquiry. Will explains his rationale for the recursive nature of reading in his class:

> The first reading of the text, even when it is a close reading, does not result in immediate and universal comprehension. Revisiting the text in the context of classroom investigation of the same ideas discussed in the text can result in deep understanding of the phenomena.... Students harboring misunderstandings not clarified through the text reading can revise their thinking through the inquiry process.

To build deeper comprehension of the chemistry, Will therefore intentionally blurs the boundaries between science investigations and reading.

Routines and Structures Supporting Reading Apprenticeship in Chemistry

In Will's classroom, a small set of classroom routines supports students' reading and thinking about chemistry. In the following pages, we describe a few of these routines—reading logs, conversational routines, and science investigations—in more detail and illustrate the process of negotiating new understanding, new relationships to reading and learning, and new identities as science students that these metacognitive conversations make possible.

Reading Logs. One routine that helps students become better science readers is the reflective reading log, a double-entry journal in which students record important, interesting, or confusing ideas from the assigned reading in the left column and their own thoughts about, connections to, and questions about the text or their reading processes in the right. The structure of the reading log encourages close attention to both content and students' own reading processes. Reading logs are commonly used as a homework routine. In addition to promoting individual inquiry and reflection, however, reading logs support collaborative meaning making in the classroom, where they serve as a resource during class and lab work, a study tool to prepare for tests, and a springboard for metacognitive conversation. Will encourages students to revise or add to their own entries in the log when classroom discussion or other activities extend or clarify the content. Students also share their reading logs with one another so that they can notice and appropriate classmates' reading strategies and expertise.

However, promoting genuine participation in reading logs and related sharing routines requires labor and patience. Students who are unaccustomed to thinking about their reading may see little value in keeping a reflective reading log. Often, doubt and discomfort surfaces in the form of complaints—about having to write a log, about the length or difficulty of the reading, or about the dullness of the material. Will responds to these complaints by listening, then attempts to redirect students' attention to the task. When a student complains that the reading assignment is too long, Will acknowledges the student's diligence and encourages the student to persevere. When a student complains that the reading is too hard, Will asks the student to identify a part of the text that needs clarification. Clarification then becomes a small group or whole class activity.

Early in the year, Will attends almost exclusively to the right-hand column of students' reading logs to gauge the degree of their interactions with the text and begin to shape their reading and science reasoning processes. As a result, the flavor of students' notes and reflections evolves over the course of the school year. In the fall, students tend to fill the left column of the double-entry journal with notes copied directly from the text. The right column, with students' reflections, is limited to general comments about whether they like or understand the reading. As Will gradually introduces specific reading processes—such as clarifying, questioning, making connections, summariz-

TABLE 12.1. Reflective Reading Log Rubric

Students receive the grade for the category most descriptive of their work. Students who receive the "trainee" grade should improve their reading log and resubmit for a new grade.

Nobel Laureate 100%	Research Scientist 90%	Lab Technician 80%	Trainee 40%
Reading log is completed on time	Reading log is completed on time	Reading log is turned in late	Reading log is turned in late
The left column contains plentiful essential information from each section of the text	The left column contains most essential information from each section of the text	The left column contains some essential information from each section of the text	The left column contains little essential information from each section of the text
Correct page numbers accompany each entry	Correct page numbers accompany most entries	Correct page numbers accompany some entries	Correct page numbers accompany few or no entries
The right column contains reflections for each entry that clearly show thoughtful reading	The right column contains reflections for most entries that show thoughtful reading	The right column contains reflections for some entries that show thoughtful reading	The right column contains reflections for few entries that show thoughtful reading

ing, predicting, and using science-specific text features—through think-alouds and reading inquiries, he begins to insist on deeper demonstrations of "thoughtful reading." With practice and guidance, left-column entries transition to paraphrasing the text, and students' reflections deepen from personal to more cognitive and content-related responses.

Reading logs are graded using a rubric that rewards effort generously, and rewards prior knowledge stingily (see Table 12.1). Students who are struggling with content are rewarded for clearly identifying the ideas they want clarified and asking cogent questions. Students who bring more prior knowledge and initial understanding to the text are rewarded for exploring ideas more deeply through questioning. Responding in writing to students' reading logs provides Will with an arena for negotiating students' motivation and use of comprehension strategies. His written feedback provides support and encouragement, recognizes and celebrates progress and effort, and allows him to monitor and assess students' comprehension of vocabulary and chemistry concepts and problem-solving skills. Will uses information from reading logs to apportion class time and activities to address areas of demonstrated student need and to flag students who need additional encouragement and support.

By providing a record of students' thoughts and reading processes, reading logs and their associated activities contribute significantly to both disciplinary knowledge and shifts in perceptions about reading and schooling. For example, at the beginning of the year, when Eduardo learns that students may use their reading logs during tests in Will's introduction to chemistry class, he blurts out, "That's cheating." By spring, the reading log is Eduardo's constant companion, and when he spontaneously consults it to clarify a point while tutoring a classmate on functional groups, it is clear that he sees himself as the proprietor of his own reading, eager to use his reading log in the service of his own learning and the learning of others.

Eduardo earned poor grades in the first grading period, largely due to incomplete assignments, including the reading logs. In an interview, he describes how Will's ongoing support and the collaborative learning environment of the chemistry classroom turned him around academically:

> When I had my first [reading log] and I tried it, you know, I did it
> with Ben in class, you know. And he helped me realize it wasn't
> hard, you know. And one day, I came during lunch, and Dr. Brown
> helped me with what you're supposed to do, so from there, from
> both of their help, you know, I tried it at home, and it came out.
> I got an A on it, you know. . . . When he told me I can get my grades
> up, I tried it, and I seen it go up, so then I thought, from there on
> I said, you know, "If I can do that, I might as well try harder." And
> I started trying harder in school, in all my classes.

Over the course of the year, Eduardo developed a preference for reading science text. He explained that he enjoyed reading science texts more than literature, and that he wanted to become an engineer. This change was reflected in timely completion of all reading assignments during the second semester, for which he earned an A. Moreover, Eduardo's change of attitude, the new expectation that he could do science, influenced the whole class. He encouraged classmates to come to class and do their work and tutored his peers when he finished his work early. The frequent conversations throughout the fall semester that focused on the thinking processes of reading and science inquiry supported Eduardo in rethinking his relationship to science and learning. He came to see that he had the capability to succeed in class through simply working at it, thereby experiencing the intrinsic rewards of learning the chemistry that Will conveyed with such apparent enthusiasm.

Yet the rewards of reading and learning can be fragile, in need of a teacher's ongoing support. One day in late May, Will enters his sheltered chemistry class with feedback on the students' homework assignment. They were to have written a gas law and its meaning in their reading logs. He begins, "Recently I asked you to write a gas law and its meaning. There were four original papers, and then there were duplicates. Copies. Which became less and less accurate. People copied as though it were a picture, and everything got less accurate." Will explains that it is everyone's responsibility to focus on learning: "My recommendation is to read and think for yourself. Those of you who had original papers, to help someone, don't give them your original papers." Appealing to a student who runs track for the high school, he offers an analogy: "James, when a friend asks you, 'Hey, can you help me? Can you write down a faster time?' it doesn't help them run faster when they get to the meet, does it?" Underscoring the similarities for thinking and learning chemistry, Will reminds his students, "There is a skill of reading that your peers need experience doing. They don't need experience copying. Don't give your work to your friends. Ask them what is hard for them and give them *real* help."

Conversational Routines. Among the routines that support students' growth as science readers and learners are the many opportunities Will offers his students to discuss the ideas and texts of chemistry. In Will's classroom, conversational routines include the preambles and expert groups already described, as well as Team-Reads. These conversational routines generally begin with individual reflection, then move to small-group and whole-class discussion before returning to the individual, providing opportunities for students to revisit, revise, and deepen comprehension and content knowledge as well as to practice and refine discipline-based thinking and reading processes. Topics of these conversations are wide-ranging—students may grapple with a difficult concept or operation, connect new ideas to prior knowledge, or discuss real-life applications of chemistry in a preamble; synthesize and consolidate information and ideas from multiple sources in an expert group; or tackle a particularly challenging section of text in a Team-Read—but they nearly always involve reading and text of some kind.

While many conversational routines involve reading and learning from previous lessons or homework, Will also occasionally provides extended in-class opportunities for "on-line" conversations about reading through Team-Reads. During Team-Reads, students alternate between reading a small section of text individually while making notes about their reading and thinking processes and discussing the section with three teammates. In both the individual reading and small group conversations, students practice four cognitive processes: clarifying, questioning, summarizing, and predicting (see Figure 12.2). Based on Reciprocal Teaching (Palincsar & Brown, 1989), Will's Team-Reads integrate thinking processes particular to science inquiry. As teams share their reading experiences, supported by role cards that structure students' facilitation of the conversation, formerly invisible reading and thinking processes and understandings become visible for public scrutiny and use. Through this cycle of reading and talk, Will's students practice discipline-based reading skills and gain stamina for challenging reading as well as knowledge of the chemistry content.

The benefit of recursive metacognitive conversation—moving from the individual to small group to whole class and back to the individual—is apparent in the following incident.

In early January during a Team-Read of an article on acids and bases, Erika, an student whose native language is Punjabi, complains that reading is boring. While probing her dissatisfaction with the reading, Will recognizes signs that Erika comprehends little of the text, which

- The Clarifier helps team members find parts of the reading that are not clear, and asks the team to help find ways to clear up these difficulties
- Science Reading Strategy Reminder
  —Look for the parts of a text that are confusing and use fix-up strategies such as rereading, scanning ahead, thinking back, identifying vocabulary words, chunking words or phrases, and prior knowledge
  —Look for the author's ideas, hypotheses, and evidence
- Discussion Prompts
  —Which parts were confusing or unclear as you read?
  —What can we do to understand this?
  —What strategies did you use to clarify this part of the reading?

- The questioner helps team members ask and answer questions about the text and categorize questions as *right there, pulling it together, author and me,* and *on your own.*
- Science Reading Strategy Reminder
  —Ask questions to build interest, comprehension, and memory.
  —What evidence supports the author's ideas?
  —What science themes do I see: energy, evolution, patterns of change, scale & structure, stability, systems & interaction?
- Discussion Prompts
  —Which questions did you have or wonder about as you read?
  —Can anyone help us answer that question? Who?
  —What kind of question was that?
  —What did we do to find the answers?

- The summarizer helps team members restate the main ideas and key facts in the reading in their own words
- Science Reading Strategy Reminder
  —State the main ideas (hypotheses, laws, theories, research methods, and evidence) in your own words. Summaries are formed by the reader, not found in the text. Summarizing helps us remember what we read.
- Discussion Prompts
  —Can you use your own words to state the main idea in one sentence?
  —Which parts to you have to understand to be able to retell this part in one sentence? Which parts could be left out and still get the point across?
  —How can we combine ideas into one summary?

- The predictor helps the team connect sections of the text by reviewing predictions from the previous sections. The predictor helps the team to ask what they will read next by using clues in the reading.
- Science Reading Strategy Reminder
  —Ask what will happen next and guess, using information from the reading. Predictions help us to check our understanding and keep us engaged.
- Discussion Prompts
  —What were the predictions about the section we just read?
  —Were any of them correct?
  —How were you able to guess? What information did you use?
  —What do you think we will read about next?

FIGURE 12.2. Team-Read discussion leader prompts.

contains unfamiliar chemistry vocabulary and challenging general vocabulary, formulas, diagrams, and chemical symbols. In response to Erika's complaint, Will initiates a whole class conversation about what makes reading boring. Among the answers Erika and her classmates offer is that the text doesn't make sense. Because Erika's lack of interest (and that of many of her classmates) arises from her struggle to make sense of the text, Will encourages her to return to the text, writing questions and comments in the margin to identify places where she needs the help of the class. As Erika and her classmates share their confusions, understandings, and reading processes, the class sorts out ways to make sense of the text.

As the Team-Read continues, the text becomes yet more challenging, but Erika also becomes more visibly engaged. She goes on to make quite a bit of sense of the article. During the week following the Team-Read, she continues asking questions about the text, still working through the meaning of it, often coming into class with a question that demonstrates her ongoing curiosity about the topic. She is no longer bored but now willingly engages in the ongoing processes of reading and sense making. The capstone of this story comes three months later. On the afternoon after the California achievement tests are given, Erika arrives in class early to proudly tell Will that she was able to answer a question on the test correctly because she remembered the information from the acid–base Team-Read.

Erika's experience underscores the role of metacognitive conversation for helping students navigate academic texts. However, like many underserved and underachieving students, students in Will's classes have little prior experience with instructionally focused conversations, particularly conversations about science. Because he sees these conversations as essential to developing the scientific reasoning and literacy skills he wants for his students, Will invests considerable effort in ensuring their success. Just as he makes reading processes visible to students, Will purposefully and strategically mentors students in the language and protocol of scientific discourse. He shapes students' discussions over the course of the year by deliberately sequencing metacognitive prompts to deepen their focus on key concepts in the chemistry reading and on particular science reading and reasoning processes. In addition, he works to ensure everyone's participation in class discussions.

In early September, when no volunteers come forward to share responses to a preamble with the whole class, conversation is nurtured by having students share with a partner or by having teams negotiate and share a consensus response. As the year progresses, Will continues to use pair-shares to increase students' participation. With norms of participation well established, however, Will doesn't hesitate to supplement bona fide volunteers with "volunteers" whom he calls on at random. Likewise, Will explicitly structures conversations to oblige students whose radar is initially attuned exclusively to the teacher to listen to and value one another's contributions. During classroom discussions, he ensures that students not only share their own ideas but also respond to the contributions of the classmates who have spoken before them. Through the guided practice of these conversational routines, Will finds that much of the awkwardness around these discussions dissipates, and participation becomes more spontaneous and universal.

In addition to this explicit mentoring and support for metacognitive conversation and collaborative work, Will works to make the benefits of collaboration apparent to his students. In an interview late in the year, Joaquim admits that his table group in the sheltered chemistry class sometimes divided group projects into four subtasks to carry out individually rather than engaged in joint work. As "itinerant mentor," Will coaxes his students into more authentic collaborations, in part by demonstrating the value of each student's contributions and in part by the way he structures group work and class conversation. Joaquim notices the difference: "I feel like if we do all the things together, I understand better. That's better because we can help each other, and we can figure out the things he say to figure out more easy." Well-ingrained if unproductive school behaviors present Will with a constant challenge, which he addresses by remaining engaged himself in the structures and routines and conversations of the class. He knows that once he succeeds in capturing students' buy-in to reading and learning routines, he must remain alert for the lassitude or discouragement that may resurrect old habits.

Science Investigations. Another prominent routine in Will's classroom, science investigations offer important opportunities for Will to apprentice his students in the inquiry thinking and reasoning at the heart of science. To begin this apprenticeship, Will starts the year focused on developing in students the habits of observing and questioning. He helps them acquire a language for identifying common types of science questions (attention focusing, measuring and counting, comparing, action prompting, problem posing, values reasoning) and coaches his students to see the connection between these question types and the types of research that will be needed to investigate them, an analogue to Question–Answer Relationships (Raphael, 1982).

Will offers his students a variety of science inquiry experiences, including team investigations of chemical problems and phenomena, "cookbook" labs, open-ended laboratory inquiries, and student-generated laboratory explorations designed to answer student-generated questions. He coaches students to develop and carry out research plans for both teacher- and student-designed questions. Finally, Will assists students in writing lab procedures to carry out the investigations they have designed. Through this inquiry cycle, teams share their inquiry questions with the whole class; later, they share their research plans and their results.

These inquiry activities make visible the ordinarily invisible processes of students' conceptual change. Through ongoing reflection and collaborative inquiry, students share their ideas, tests, data, and inferences with one another and apprehend others' ways of thinking about the subject of inquiry or the inquiry process itself. These inquiry conversations also give Will the opportunity to coach students through the otherwise invisible thinking processes of science. Just as Will engages students in ongoing metacognitive conversations about how, as well as what, they read, science investigations provide rich opportunities to engage students in ongoing conversations about science processes—how we do science—as well as science content.

Laboratory procedures, like other science texts, are a mix of words, symbols, equations, figures, diagrams, and new vocabulary for lab equipment, procedures, and topics. This mixture of symbol systems must be negotiated nonlinearly and recursively as students carry out the inquiry and develop their understandings of the chemistry under investigation. Students work in collaborative teams as they read lab instructions, propose inquiry questions, design research plans, conduct experiments, make observations, draw inferences from data, and revise their understanding. Team conversations assist students in reading the texts that pervade laboratory work. Will notes: "Without support in reading science texts, lab investigations can be entertaining yet obscuring excursions rather than inquiry leading to discovery and refinement of thought."

Will uses role cards parallel to the Team-Read cards to establish team roles and encourage teams to work together effectively during laboratory investigations. Each team member has a special role in the team: facilitator, reader, editor, and resource person. Each manages a certain aspect of the teamwork, making sure that the team works effectively in the area of his or her responsibility. The reader, for example, coaches teammates' close reading of the procedural and informational texts associated with the lab investigation, leading a team discussion to clarify the texts' meaning and redirecting the team to the text to clarify comprehension problems and to refine questions.

As they work in labs, students keep lab journals that assume the familiar structure of double-entry reflective reading logs. Here students record laboratory procedures, measurements, observations, calculations, and responses to laboratory questions in the left column (loosely labeled "I Saw"), and reflections, thoughts, connections, procedure questions, and questions about the observations and data in the right column (labeled "I Thought"). As in the reading logs, Will emphasizes that the right-column entries, where students work through their own thoughts, are more important than the left.

As in other conversational routines, a recursive cycle of metacognitive inquiry and conversation is built into labs. Students begin a lab investigation by making a mental inventory of their team members' thoughts and questions regarding the subject of inquiry using the traditional reading and reflection activity K-W-L. Students end the lab report with an account of what they learned and what questions linger. The recording of prior thoughts and questions signals respect for students' intelligence and curiosity. It sets a context by establishing that students have some background knowledge and are bringing questions they want answered to the investigation. Finally, it allows them to test their own ideas against experimental evidence.

In carrying the routines of Reading Apprenticeship into laboratory investigations, Will observes: "The heart of Reading Apprenticeship is reasonably the heart of excellent science instruction. Here, the object of inquiry includes physical materials and phenomena as well as written text." In Will's class, science investigations, including laboratory experiences, are therefore designed to emphasize and encourage the interaction between hands-on inquiry and science literacy. By revisiting the ideas of the text through laboratory investigations, and by recursively consulting the text resources as they do so, students build deeper understandings of the science content. And in this linking of science reading and science investigation, Will's students are continually invited and challenged to figure out how the information catalogued in the textbook came to be known and to pose and investigate questions that begin at the point of their understanding and move them beyond the book and into their own scientific inquiries.

ADDRESSING THE CHALLENGES TO STUDENTS' ENGAGEMENT IN SCIENCE LITERACY AND LEARNING

As we have described the learning environment in Will's chemistry classroom, we have pointed to several of the challenges Will attends to as he works to integrate reading and science instruction. Inevitably, as Will invites his students' authentic responses and understandings into classroom conversations, the challenges of helping these students to become stronger readers and learners of science emerge. In these pages we have described the work Will does, and engages his students in doing, to address these challenges. Here, we return to three of the most thorny dilemmas facing any subject area teacher attempting to increase students' reading proficiency while also teaching a core curriculum: the challenge of the course texts, the challenge of time, and the challenge of engaging inexperienced adolescent readers in rigorous reading and learning.

The Challenge of the Texts

The challenging chemistry textbook is a resource that Will chooses to use, and to help his students use, as one support for students' science learning. Just as the reading and comprehending of the text is not finished once the reading log assignment is done, the science text is not expected to stand alone in science learning. Rather, science inquiry and reading and comprehending in chemistry work together and stretch over time. Will helps negotiate students' work with the textbook by adjusting their expectations about their experience of reading it. "Reading this textbook will be hard work but work that you can do," he advises. The metacognitive conversation and classroom routines ensure that students will not undertake this hard work on their own; rather, they will have support and encouragement.

We have described the many varieties of science texts that offer students comprehension challenges and learning opportunities in Will's classroom. In addition to the textbook, Will writes directions and prompts to guide students' inquiries and brings current science articles into the classroom for Team-Reads. Choosing texts that the wide range of readers in the class will find approachable is always difficult, and for Will it is always in tension with the demand for accuracy in the science presented. In addition, Will recently decided that shorter and more frequent reading experiences would better serve his introduction to chemistry students' needs. Selecting texts wisely, ensuring accuracy, and providing needed support require Will's ongoing professional attention, yet Will finds that extensive science reading enriches the inquiry environment of the classroom in several ways. He finds that science reading provokes students' questioning and informs their hypotheses and experimental designs for their own inquiries. Reading science material also provides some of the language experience and models that students need to explain their own discoveries to peers and wider audiences. And while he admits that supporting students to become stronger readers of the many texts in a science classroom takes effort, Will is convinced that helping students learn to use these texts productively is his responsibility and, further, that it supports his students' learning of the science content to do so.

The Challenge of Time

As a science department chair and as a teacher concerned with the historical inequities that result in the underrepresentation of his diverse, urban students in the scientific fields, Will often finds himself in the position of advocating to his science colleagues the need to integrate reading instruction into science teaching. The pressure to cover an ever widening curriculum haunts every secondary teacher, and this pressure seems all the greater when teachers begin to integrate support for students' reading into the curriculum. Supporting students' discipline-based reading does take time, particularly if teachers take an apprenticeship approach, helping students to learn *how* to grapple with texts to gain understanding of the content.

However, as teachers such as Will see their students gain confidence and become more willing to struggle with challenging academic texts, they become more certain that the time it takes to model and engage students in metacognitive inquiry into reading is well spent. Many teachers have told us that, by slowing reading down at times to model productive comprehension processes, students develop the capacity over time to read challenging texts more independently and successfully. Will's experience makes this point concretely:

> In the fall semester my class progresses less quickly through the textbook than some of my colleagues' classes that are not using Reading Apprenticeship or the like. By spring, we have caught up or passed by because my students are reading and learning more independently.

The Challenge of Engagement

While the complexity of course texts and the press of content coverage pose clear challenges to subject area teachers, the most pressing challenge in our urban high schools is often the students' own prior conceptions of reading, of learning, and of the purposes of schooling. As we have worked and studied in urban subject area classrooms, we have come to understand the work of apprenticing students to discipline-based literacy practices as an ongoing negotiation with adolescents who often hold competing conceptions of the value and processes of reading and school-based learning. In classrooms such as Will's, we have witnessed how the metacognitive conversation opens an interactional space in which teachers can help shift these conceptions in more fruitful directions.

In this work of helping young people take on more powerful identities and abilities as readers and learners, teacher endurance is key. In our many visits to his classroom, we have documented how Will maintains and elaborates classroom literacy routines in spite of students' initial resistance and difficulties. Will ruefully admits that reading 150 reading logs in the beginning of the year to begin to reshape students' reading processes takes commitment and confidence on the part of the teacher that this expenditure of time and energy will pay off. Yet he knows that this reading and responding, if only to the "right side" of the log, is what moves students toward more engaged learning with text. Will counsels that teachers need to guide their instruction by indications of students' successes rather than failures and to be ready to redouble their efforts rather than abandon them. Will himself resolves to tackle challenging reading in his chemistry classes more often, not less—particularly in his introduction to chemistry class, where students come into the class with such disparate reading abilities.

From Will's point of view, the rewards of his efforts more than make up for the challenges. From his work to implement Reading Apprenticeship through ongoing mentoring, collaboration, and metacognitive conversation, Will has seen his students take up more effective science reading and learning strategies, while his efforts to teach comprehension strategies to science students in prior years did not have this impact. He has noticed that students of varying reading levels demonstrate progress in reading stamina and greater ownership of the reading and learning process as the year progresses. These trends often mean deep, personal change for individual students, particularly introduction to chemistry students such as Erika and Eduardo, who may be at risk of failing rigorous science courses.

The experiences of these young people in Will's chemistry class bolster our confidence that it is not merely a cognitive repertoire that grows for students in Reading Apprenticeship classrooms; rather, it is a belief in their own abilities to be successful as students and as readers in rigorous academic settings. Many students by this point in their academic careers have heard about and even practiced some cognitive strategies in their prior classes. What is new, however, is that they now choose to use these strategies, and by using them they begin to see their power. They move from a full stop at the first barrier to comprehension, to actually trying to make sense—an increase in their will and stamina for the work and difficulty of navigating academic texts. Through metacognitive conversation, students are also introduced to new cognitive strategies, thereby increasing their strategic repertoire. But it is the shift in their dispositions toward reading that motivates the use of these strategies to begin with. As students' confidence increases, their attitudes toward academic work change, and ultimately their sense of identity, of who they are and can become, expands to new vistas as readers and as learners.

In Will's view, the work he has done to apprentice his urban students to science literacy "empowers adolescents to access the essential texts of science. Students develop the expectation that they will be able to make sense of science text and enjoy doing so. This opens the door to lifelong science learning." For Will, as for us, this work is deeply motivated by a desire to support the participation of diverse, urban youth in the intellectual life of this country:

> Students deserve the right to be able to choose science based on having done science, and to choose academics from a position of skill rather than because they don't think that they can succeed. Students who can read an academic textbook are no longer shut out of aca-

demics as a means for their own professional growth, their own economic well-being. I want them to know that they can do science, and they can use education to their advantage because they know how to read academic material. Then they have the choice of whether they want to participate or not.

NOTES

1. The work described in this chapter would not be possible without the generous support of the Carnegie Corporation of New York, the William and Flora Hewlett Foundation, the Walter S. Johnson Foundation, the W. Clement & Jessie V. Stone Foundation, the Stuart Foundations, the Stupski Family Fund, WestEd, and, of course, the many adolescents, teachers, schools, and districts in the Bay area and around the country that contribute to our work. The statements made and views expressed are solely the responsibility of the authors.

2. For the 216 diverse ninth-grade students enrolled in the Academic Literacy course, the average reading level was equivalent to the national norming population at late seventh grade, or 50 DRP Units, in October. By May, these ninth graders' average reading level had reached the national population's average reading level at late ninth grade, 54 DRP Units. As a group, they gained in average independent reading level from books similar in difficulty to *Charlotte's Web* to books similar in difficulty to *To Kill a Mockingbird*. These ninth graders moved from the 48th to the 50th percentile nationally. A follow-up study during their 10th-grade year showed these gains not only holding, but accelerating, as students increased their reading scores to 58 DRP Units and their national percentile ranking to 53 by spring. In another study, DRP test data were also collected on 478 middle and high school students from diverse, urban schools where teachers were embedding Reading Apprenticeship ideas and strategies into content area teaching. Students in these classrooms made statistically significant, greater than expected gains from pre- to post-test. As a group, middle school students in these classrooms made a statistically significant 3-point gain in normal curve scores, moving from the 44th to the 47th percentile nationally. As a group, high school students started out higher performers but still made a statistically significant 2-point gain in normal curve scores, moving from the 50th to the 52nd percentile nationally. As a group, English Language Learners started out scoring lower but also made greater gains over the school year. These and other study data are available online at http://www.wested.org.

3. For example, Westlake Middle School, an urban middle school in Oakland Unified School District, has been implementing Reading Apprenticeship schoolwide since 1999. At Westlake, the California Department of Education's accountability, or Academic Performance, Index (API)—a composite score based on standardized test performance, especially for targeted populations of underperforming students—has risen steadily since 1999, from 518 to 645, greatly exceeding the state's mandated improvement targets each year. At Dixon High School, a rural high school with a high migrant population where Reading Apprenticeship has been implemented across the curriculum, the API has risen from 606 to 664 since 2001, with the performance of low-SES students and Hispanic students rising even more steeply (from 479 to 568 and from 481 to 583, respectively). These and other study data are available online at http://www.wested.org and on the California Department of Education website, http://www.cde.org. Similarly, in Durham, North Carolina, middle schools implementing Reading Apprenticeship reached 80% and 90% reading proficiency for the first time.

REFERENCES

Alvermann, D., & Moore, D. (1991). Secondary school reading. In R. Barr, M. L. Kamil, P. Mosenthal, & P. D. Pearson (Eds.), *Handbook of reading research, Vol. 2*. New York: Longman.

Baker, L. (1991) Metacognition, reading, and science education. In C. Santa & D. Alvermann (Eds.), *Science learning: Processes and applications* (pp. 2–13). Newark, DE: International Reading Association.

Bybee, R. W. (1997). *Achieving scientific literacy: From purposes to practices*. Portsmouth, NH: Heinemann.

Duffy, G., Roehler, L., Sivan, E., Rackliffe, G., Book, C., Meloth, M., Vavrus, L., Wesselman, R., Putnam, J., & Bassiri, D. (1994). Effects of explaining the reasoning associated with using reading strategies. *Reading Research Quarterly, 22*, 347–368.

Greenleaf, C., & Shoenbach, R. (2001). *Close readings: A study of key issues in the use of literacy learning cases for the professional development of secondary teachers*. Final report to the Spencer and MacArthur Foundations' Professional Development Research and Documentation Program.

Greenleaf, C., Schoenbach, R., Cziko, C., & Mueller, F. (2001). Apprenticing adolescents to academic literacy. *Harvard Educational Review, 71*(1), 79–129.

Killion, J. (2002). *What works in the high school: Results based staff development*. Oxford, OH: National Staff Development Council.

Lemke, J. L. (1999). "Teaching all the languages of science: Words, symbols, images, and actions." Available at: http://academic.brooklyn.cuny.edu/education/jlemke/papers/barcelon.htm.

Manzo, A., & Manzo, U. (1990). *Content area reading: A heuristic approach*. Columbus, OH: Merrill Publishing.

McMahon, M., & McCormack, B. (1998). "To think and act like a scientist: Learning disciplinary knowledge." In C. Hynd (Ed.), *Learning from text across conceptual domains*. Mahwah, NJ: Erlbaum.

National Research Council. (1996). *National science education standards*. Washington, DC: National Academy Press.

Nystrand, M., & Gamoran, A. (1991). Instructional discourse, student engagement, and literature achievement. *Research in the Teaching of English, 25*, 261–290.

Osborne, J. (2002). Science without literacy: A ship without a sail? *Cambridge Journal of Education 32*(2), 203–218.

Palinscar, A. S., & Brown, A. L. (1989). Instruction for self-regulated reading. In L. B. Resnick & L. E. Klopfer (Eds.), *Toward the thinking curriculum: Current cognitive research* (pp. 19–39). ASCD Yearbook. Alexandria, VA: Association for Supervision and Curriculum Development.

Petrocelli, M. (2003, June 2). "Durham cheers over test scores". *Herald Sun*, A1.

Raphael, T. (1982). Question-answering strategies for children. *The Reading Teacher, 36*, 186–190.

Rycik, J., & Irvin, J. (Eds.). (2001). *What adolescents deserve: A commitment to students' literacy learning*. Newark, DE: International Reading Association.

Schoenbach, R., Greenleaf, C., Cziko, C., & Hurwitz, L. (1999). *Reading for understanding: A guide to improving reading in middle and high school classrooms*. San Francisco: Jossey-Bass.

Snow, C. (2002). *Reading for understanding: Toward a research and development program in reading comprehension*. (Report of the RAND Reading Research Study Group.) Arlington, VA: RAND Corporation.

13

Explaining Explanations

Developing Scientific Literacy in Middle School Project-Based Science Reforms

Elizabeth Birr Moje, Deborah Peek-Brown, LeeAnn M. Sutherland, Ronald W. Marx, Phyllis Blumenfeld, and Joseph Krajcik

Key Points

- Science literacy reform was embedded in project-based science units, with a focus on helping students construct scientific explanations.
- The reform initiative also focused on the teaching of skills for collecting, representing, and analyzing data in investigations.
- Interactive reading materials were created so that they could be closely integrated with the activities of the curriculum units.

In this chapter, we report on our work within the Center for Learning Technologies in Urban Schools (LeTUS) to develop scientific literacy in a systemic science education reform initiative.[1] Begun in 1997, LeTUS was launched to promote inquiry-based science and technology learning at the secondary school level. In the LeTUS collaboration, teachers, curriculum developers, and administrators in the Detroit Public Schools have partnered with University of Michigan researchers, teacher educators, and curriculum developers to develop, enact, and study "project-based science" curriculum units in more than 20 middle schools across Detroit. In the remainder of the chapter, we will focus on describing project-based science (PBS) and our efforts to embed scientific literacy reform in PBS units.[2]

PROJECT-BASED SCIENCE

Project-based science (or any project-based curricula) frames and motivates student learning by real-world questions that are of interest to real people in real places. For example, our units revolve around questions such as, "What affects the quality of air in my community?" (air quality—chemistry); "Can good friends make you sick?" (communicable diseases—biology); and "What is the water like in my river?" (water quality—chemistry and ecology). The features of PBS curricula include

1. Driving questions anchored in real-world problems.
2. Investigations and artifact creation.
3. Collaboration among students, teachers, and others in the community.
4. Use of technological tools (Krajcik, Blumenfeld, Marx, Bass, & Fredricks, 1998; Singer, Marx, Krajcik, & Clay-Chambers, 2000).

Each LeTUS PBS unit is constructed with these features, as well as with the state standards and district benchmarks, in mind. We also continually consider the language and form of the state testing program as we develop various activities (both print and non-print) so that students will experience activities that are consonant with the testing program. The results of this work have been encouraging, with analyses of nearly 5,000 students' test scores demonstrating statistically significant increases for each year of participation. Moreover, the strength of the effects grew over the years, as shown by increasing effect size estimates across years (Marx, Blumenfeld, Fishman, Krajcik, & Soloway, 2001).

Until recently, the curricula have focused primarily on developing electronic technology tools and have not looked as closely at the language and literacy tasks embedded in the curriculum (and within the technology) or at the demands those tools make of students and teachers. We are particularly interested in questions of language and literacy because, although students have made gains, the gains tend to be highest at a basic knowledge level of science content learning. Gains are less strong when it comes to process questions or more cognitively demanding assessments, in which students must read data tables and graphs as they produce short-answer responses to questions about fictional investigations (Marx et al., 2001). In addition, a number of questions and challenges raised by teachers in professional development meetings, together with the Detroit Public Schools' systemic commitment to the improvement of content area literacy learning, has led us to focus a substantial aspect of our current systemic reform efforts on the development of scientific literacy. Our research in these classrooms (e.g., observations of students struggling to read questions or to record data during investigations) supports and informs this new emphasis in our efforts to develop project-based science.

Literacy in Project-Based Science

Although project-based science provides opportunities for students to engage in dialogue and collaboration around investigations of real-world problems, it can make extensive demands on students and teachers (Moje, Collazo, Carrillo, & Marx, 2001). In particular, as teachers attempt to engage students in real-world investigations, they struggle with the role that various print materials—from curriculum worksheets to electronic databases—should play in supporting and extending these investigations. Both teachers and curriculum developers in our current efforts recognize that scientists use print texts extensively in their work. Moreover, the teachers in Detroit are committed to engaging students in reading and writing texts in ways that support students' investigations. And yet, many of their students either struggle with basic reading and writing processes or with the technical and interpretive demands of science text. Most students require support in comprehension, composition, and meaning making or application of science texts (Goldman, 1997; Lee & Fradd, 1998; Nicholson, 1985). Unfortunately, the constrained time periods for doing science during a typical school day make it challenging for teachers to *teach* students how to use print texts to engage in inquiry.

In addition, science learning requires students to bring skills of prediction, observation, analysis, summarization, and presentation to their science reading, writing, and oral language practices (Lee & Fradd, 1998). These scientific literacy and language practices are even more important in project-based science in which students search for and synthesize information across texts and other people (Blumenfeld, Marx, Patrick, & Krajcik, 1997; Goldman, 1997). At the secondary school level, in particular, young people are expected to apply previously learned language, literacy, and technology skills to the comprehension, interpretation, and application of disciplinary knowledge even when not engaged in project curricula.

In addition, PBS presents a bit of a paradox in terms of language and literacy: Because project-based curricula engage youth in textual and experiential inquiry about authentic questions, the curricula can be considered discourse *enabling* and thus represent an excellent way to learn science, as students are engaged in communicating science (National Research Council, 1996). At the same time, however, the extensive discursive demands of the inquiry activities in the curricula can be difficult for students because science discourse and practices are new to them (Krajcik et al., 1998; Merino & Hammond, 1998) and they do not yet have facility with the language of science. As Lemke (1990) has illustrated, the language of science represents a specialized system of language that is based on *thematic formations* or assumptions about what counts as scientific inquiry, which are well understood by scientists who have apprenticed and practiced in the profession for years. For example, scientists know that they must not only report data collected in an experiment but also explicitly articulate their reasoning about the data as they explain findings and draw conclusions about the phenomena, even when the findings, on the surface, may appear self-evident. Scientists recognize that their articulation of logical connections among phenomena is as important as the statistical or observational analyses that they make, for it is in these explicit, articulated interpretations that knowledge is produced and shared among the members of the science community. Becoming a member of the science discourse community, however, can be challenging for any student. For many, the assumptions of science are not explicit, which can lead to confusion as students encounter new ways of thinking, talking, reading, and writing in their science classrooms

(Hicks, 1995/1996). Thus, even fluent readers and writers of narrative or general knowledge texts can struggle with reading and writing science texts simply because they have not yet taken up the assumptions and corresponding practices of science.

Finally, many students in Detroit schools live in homes where mainstream English is not a dominant language. The importance of an emphasis on language and discourse in the curriculum is heightened for children in dual language or dialect schools. As Cummins (1984) argued, students proficient in the English necessary for social interactions are not necessarily prepared to engage in academic and disciplinary discourse. Similarly, Wong-Fillmore (1982) demonstrated that two basic language skills are required for the learning of academic subject matter: an understanding of the spoken language of instruction and an understanding of the language of textbooks. The discourse of science—that is, the thematic formations or assumptions that shape the ways people speak, read, and write with the science community—represents a challenge to understanding the language of instruction and text even for English-dominant students (Goldman, 1997); what is it like for students whose first language is not mainstream English? In other words, English language learners face a triple challenge: They must learn not only the English language but also the language of academic discourse and of the discourse of science. Thus, the discourse-*dependent* aspect of the curriculum may be especially challenging and, without some scaffolding, may constrain learning opportunities for these students.

In our last six years of developing, enacting, and researching project-based curricula in Detroit, we have come to recognize these language and literacy demands as a central dilemma for science teachers and students. As a result, we have developed and piloted a number of strategies and materials without adding to teachers' and students' already overwhelming set of classroom tasks. We also have been studying how these skills shape students' opportunities to learn. In this chapter, we describe just a few of these strategies and present some findings on our initial efforts in the systemic reform of scientific literacy education at the secondary school level.

The Reformers and the Learners

Approximately 75 middle school science teachers in approximately 200 classrooms throughout the Detroit Public Schools (numbers vary from year to year) enact the PBS curriculum units. The schools in Detroit are populated primarily by African American students (91.1%), followed by Latino/a students (4%), European American students (3.7%), Asian and Pacific Island students (0.9%), and American Indian students (0.2%). The average percentage of students eligible for the free or reduced lunch program throughout the district is 70%, although the percentage of eligible students is higher in most of the LeTUS schools. The teachers who participate in LeTUS represent a mix of ethnic, racial, and social class groups, but the teachers in the subset represented in this paper are all African American and Latino/a in racial and ethnic background.

Achievement scores on the state testing program show 13.6% of all students in the district meeting state standards in science, 55% in writing, and

33.2% in reading in 1999. These percentages illustrate that there is a gap between students' achievement in science and their achievement in general literacy proficiency (although the literacy scores also demand improvement). Consequently, our focus on literacy in science learning seems merited not only by our observations of the challenges students and teachers face as they engage in reading and writing in their science classrooms, but also by the disjuncture we have observed in achievement scores. These scores, combined with research on the role of oral and written language in learning science, suggest that a focus on helping students understand and access the language and processes of inquiry in science may support their developing understanding of and achievement in critically important science concepts and processes.

The literacy work that we describe in this chapter is being piloted in 16 science classrooms of four teachers. At the schools in our pilot, a range of 0.8% to 72% of students have met state science standards. Reading scores at the pilot schools range from 19.1 to 61.9% of the students meeting state standards, and in the eighth-grade writing assessment, 28.4–100% of the pilot school students meet state standards. Again, the disparity between science achievement and general literacy achievement seems vast, even in the school in which achievement scores are high. What accounts for this disparity? Is it the amount of time spent on science instruction in the earlier grades? Is it students' lack of scientific literacy skills, which may impede their demonstration of achievement on print-based achievement tests? Could more time be dedicated across the grades to teaching literacy skills as embedded in content area learning? This last question taps into our goals for this systemic reform initiative.

Methods of Enactment and Research on the Reform Efforts

All teachers who participate in LeTUS attend monthly professional development activities, often led by more senior LeTUS teachers. In addition, the teachers, researchers, and curriculum developers involved in the pilot work meet for bimonthly professional and curriculum development work. As a team, we videotape in classrooms and collect students' and teachers' work, which serve as artifacts of students' learning over time. Students' learning is also measured via pre- and post-unit tests on science content and process knowledge, as well as on several performance tasks administered throughout the unit. Finally, at the conclusion of each unit, we interview a subset of students in each target classroom on their content knowledge, attitudes about and toward science, and strategies for sense making in the curriculum. Each of these measures is used to inform our curriculum development and to generate research findings.

EXPLAINING OUR PRACTICE AROUND EXPLANATIONS

Our reform efforts in scientific literacy development follow several different trajectories. Due to space constraints, we will report on only three of these interrelated efforts: (a) a focus on teaching the conventions of scientific communication or discourse, focused particularly on how to construct *scientific explanations*; (b) a focus on the teaching of skills for *collecting, representing, and analyzing data* in investigations; and (c) the creation of *interactive reading materials* that support the development of skills required in points (a) and (b). Although we will discuss our practices in all three areas, we will focus our discussion of findings on the teaching of explanation writing because explanations have been a central aspect of our work and because we continue to collect and analyze data in the other two areas.

Scientific Explanations

In project-based science, students conduct investigations for which they must represent their data visually (e.g., chart or graph), represent their interpretation, and use the data interpretation to write an explanation of phenomena. In our recent work with teachers and students, we have focused on explicit instruction in and repeated practice around writing explanations of actual investigations. When we use the term *explicit,* we refer to an approach in which teachers and students make specific distinctions among different kinds of explanations of real-world phenomena. Such distinctions include the everyday explanations of their experiences that they make to friends and family and the scientific explanations that they make after conducting a controlled experiment in the classroom. This engagement with the discursive conventions (e.g., making hypotheses and claims about hypotheses, providing data to support claims, explaining one's reasoning, arguing, etc.) and practices of different discourse communities, we argue, is the key to developing thoughtful literate practices in the content areas.

As teachers and students engage in inquiry around phenomena, teachers help students learn the literate practices required to make scientific investigation meaningful. Together with students, the teachers and researchers have constructed, tested, and refined criteria for producing scientific explanations that include

1. Making a claim.
2. Providing multiple pieces of evidence drawn from experimentation or from others' research.
3. Reasoning how it is that the evidence links back to the claim.
4. Writing in precise and accurate scientific language that someone who understands or cares about science, but who is not familiar with the particular investigation, can understand.

We use these criteria in the classroom teaching and in our analysis of classroom data.

This practice follows a certain pattern each year. At the beginning of our first curriculum unit (which is typically the air-quality unit), teachers ask students to read sample explanations, written by actual students, and to evaluate the explanations. The teachers do not necessarily introduce the criteria before asking students to evaluate, with the goal of engaging students in generating criteria that they will apply to their writing of evaluations throughout the year. The teachers, of course, have in mind the criteria that we generated (from just such a process) in Year 1, and they may guide students to frame the criteria in similar language, but they nevertheless take their students through the process each year because they recognize the value in asking students to assess samples and to induce criteria, rather than simply being presented with a list of criteria.

Throughout the unit, the teachers and students work through a series of investigations and electronic text searches that allow them to practice writing explanations both of empirical investigations and of information they must synthesize from multiple texts. As a group, we have also worked out a scheme for thinking about what each criterion means.

Making a Claim. For example, a *claim* is a statement of one's understanding about a phenomenon or a situation, about the results of an experiment, or about other data. If the claim is made in reference to an empirical investigation, then the claim must relate to the hypothesis or the research question. In addition, when drawing a conclusion from an experiment, the claim must show how the dependent variable and the independent variable are related to one another (if there *are* dependent and independent variables in the investigation).

Providing Evidence. To *provide evidence* for the claim, a student may use observations, a controlled experiment, or other sources, such as a review of research already conducted. We remind students that not all data one collects are important to the original question asked or to a particular hypothesis. A good explanation uses only information that relates to the original idea.

Finally, if possible, students should use multiple pieces of evidence in an explanation based on an experiment.

Linking Evidence to a Claim. Often, the most difficult aspect of explanation writing to teach revolves around encouraging students to articulate their reasoning for a claim that they have made. We find that once students realize that they need to use data drawn from their investigations or from data tables provided for them, they tend to simply restate the data without explaining how they have made sense of the data to answer their questions or test their hypotheses. We also find this difficult to teach. Teachers have worked on modeling reasoning, making clear to students that reasoning involves explaining *how* the evidence supports the claim. This "reasoning" aspect typically answers, "How do you know that?" (e.g., I know this because . . .).

Writing a Scientific Explanation. We also encourage the use of precise and accurate scientific language. For this criterion, we emphasize that a good explanation is *focused* on a particular phenomenon. A good explanation is also thorough. It includes all necessary details and no unnecessary details.

We not only hope to see students using technical terms appropriately, but we also look for students' use of specific indexical terms (e.g., "when the temperature increased" rather than "when it got hotter," since the "it" in the second phrase could refer to any one of the objects in the experiment). Teachers have found it helpful to have students think in terms of how a scientist might write the same explanation. We also hope eventually to have students experiment with how different groups of people might write an explanation of the same phenomena, thus emphasizing that the language and literacy conventions and practices of science are only one set of possible conventions and practices they might take up. We also hope to move, eventually, to engaging students in critique of those conventions. To engage in critique, however, requires some facility with the conventions themselves.

The teachers also engage the students in thinking about what each of the criteria mean. What, for example, is precise language that someone who is not familiar with an investigation could understand? One teacher suggested taking students through a direction-writing activity, in which the students gave directions for accomplishing some simple task (e.g., making a peanut butter sandwich) while she attempted to follow their directions to the letter. Through such activities, students began to see what it meant to spell out the objects being studied and analyzed, the details of procedures used in investigations, and how data relate to a particular claim. Some of the examples of student explanations pre- and post-unit that we provide later in the chapter illustrate the students' growth in this area.

Collecting, Representing, and Analyzing Data

In this aspect of our work, we are striving to better support students' mediation of understanding across multiple forms of representation. As inquiry approaches have gained more currency in secondary school science classrooms, students have found themselves faced with actual data from actual investigations. Unfortunately, most students have little experience with developing appropriate questions and hypotheses for investigations and designing studies (i.e., choosing controls, eliminating confounding variables) to carry out the investigations. Far fewer have had experience with the process of collecting, representing, and analyzing the data that they collect in investigations. Our curricula in the past have included explicit scaffolds to support students in planning and designing investigations (e.g., rubrics for good questions and hypotheses, a teacher modeling strategy that we call the "eyeglass model"), but we have not developed as many strategies to support the mediation of understanding across many different forms of representation. Given our emphasis on developing strong and accurate scientific explanations, we decided to simultaneously attend to supporting students' work with the data that they would ultimately need to explain. Our work on meaning making across multiple forms of representation involves four areas that precede the writing of explanations: collecting data systematically and rigorously, representing what one observes in data collection, translating first-level representations into other forms of data representation, and interpreting and synthesizing data from different representations.

Collecting Data Systematically and Rigorously. The focus on data collection includes making explicit the importance of seemingly mundane and obvious requirements that are necessary to clean data collection in science. For example, in the bacteria growth investigation conducted as part of the communicable disease unit, students are reminded of such things as the need to record and maintain the location of a Petri dish and what the conditions are of the location, to check the Petri dish regularly, to make notes about the same qualities of the bacteria under study for each observation (e.g., do not note color on one occasion and size of the colony on the next). We emphasize that such skills can be modeled by teachers even if schedules do not allow students to conduct their own investigations over lengthy periods of time.

Representing What One Observes in Data Collection. This aspect focuses on what teachers should model for students about how they could record their data in any given investigation. We encourage teachers to provide students with several different options, from drawing pictures to making tables. Teachers ask their students to think about whether it is better to represent a phenomenon with numbers, with words, or with shapes. Teachers ask students to think about the kinds of changes they might look for and to think carefully about what is worth recording, all in relation to one's research questions and hypotheses. The teachers talk with students about how their data representation choices depend in part on the nature of the data (drawing bacteria colonies in the communicable disease unit may be most useful, but drawing the cases of people who have syphilis would not be), *and* they model what such representations might look like in each instance. Depending on schedules, some teachers ask students to try to come up with their own systems for recording the data, often in small groups, and then groups share the different methods with the whole class.

Translating First-Level Representations Into Other Forms of Data Representation. In this phase, teachers provide students with opportunities to work across a number of data representations, explaining that scientists (both natural and social) often do this because it allows them to think about the data differently. These representations, then, are tools that help them make sense of the data. The teachers also help students recognize that people use tools like this all the time in life. We draw pictures of things we want to remember, then we redraw them into some other kind of representation, perhaps with words, with numbers, on a chart, or on a graph. Then the teachers can ask students what they think they could do to represent the pictures differently, or they can walk students through three other forms: verbal (a written description), tabular, and graphic.

It is also important for teachers to help students see that certain forms are often used by scientists and journalists to report data because they can show complicated concepts in a small amount of space. Such conversations about how writers choose different ways of representing their ideas helps students begin to see that print, while important and useful, is not always the best way to represent ideas. In addition, students can come to see that people use different representational forms for good reasons, not just to make their writing look interesting. And finally, students can start to see that different forms of representation, from print to drawings to graphs, can work together to communicate some concept that is deeper and more all-encompassing than any single form of representation can communicate.

Interpreting and Synthesizing Data From Different Representations. This aspect of data analysis leads into writing a formal scientific explanation. The students have to draw conclusions about what their data say *in relation to their hypotheses.* They may have to look across multiple representations they have made (from a graph to a table to a drawing to words), or they may have to look across the data sets of multiple groups of "researchers." This work comprises opportunities to talk about what the different representations might mean and then to focus on trying to make some claims, use data from different representations, and reason through the data to turn the data into evidence that supports their claim(s). Teachers have engaged students in what the teachers call "museum walks" in which they examine the representations of other groups and then engage in constructive peer critique. Maintaining the constructive focus but encouraging thoughtful critique is the most challenging aspect of this practice, and the teachers in our group continue to refine this strategy to scaffold students' critiquing skills and their ability to make the best use of helpful critiques.

Interactive Reading Materials

We have sought to develop student reading materials that are tightly integrated with the everyday activities of the curriculum units (in a way that a general textbook could not be) and that both draw from and lead into new ideas introduced in each lesson. To support our pilot work on developing students' abilities to make scientific explanations, we are currently weaving into the reader opportunities to explain findings of investigations, concepts learned from literature searches, and everyday experiences with the physical world.

In addition, we have identified different text forms that students may encounter in and out of school: (a) *constructed expository text* (such as one might find in a textbook or science journal); (b) *constructed narrative text* (such as case studies); and (c) *real-world texts* (such as one might find in a newspaper or citizen's action group publication). We work from the stance that, for students to learn optimally from text, texts must be *considerate.* That is, they must (a) present clear organizational patterns; (b) make relationships among ideas clear; (c) contain only the most relevant information; and (d) be sensitive to the knowledge base of the imagined reader (Anderson & Armbruster, 1984). In addition, print texts of any type need to include other forms of representation (e.g., graphs, icons, models) that illustrate, highlight, or present concepts that cannot be clearly explained in print form.

We are working from the hypothesis that constructed narratives—or case studies—can support students' literacy development and science learning as they provide a link between real-world texts and constructed expository texts. That said, however, case studies alone cannot provide the depth of information that expository texts can provide, nor do they represent the real world of students' experiences as do real-world newspaper texts. Students need many different kinds of texts for optimal learning. They need considerate expository texts from which to glean content information, and they need real-world texts that are situated in actual community and world events to fully contextualize the science concepts. They need constructed narratives, or case study texts, to link the other types of texts together. What is more, students need to develop strategies for navigating many different types of science text. If carefully sequenced and linked to classroom inquiry activities—particularly to our scientific explanation activities—as well as to students' real-world experiences, these three text types can function as a unit to promote conceptual understanding, the development of process skills in inquiry, and the development of scientific literacy. Although we have been using reading materials that we have developed according to the guidelines for considerate expository text, we are only at the beginning stages of developing multiple-genre readers that draw from the real-world, popular cultural texts that students use daily in sophisticated ways.

Materials That Support Our Work (Samples in Appendix)

As illustrated in the Appendix, teachers, researchers, and curriculum developers have worked together to develop materials for teaching and research purposes. A sample of each of the materials described is included in the Appendix.

Rubrics for Writing and Scoring Explanations. One of our primary tasks was to develop rubrics to assess the explanations that students produce from each investigation. The scoring rubrics in Figure 13.1 are directly tied to the criteria that teachers and students generate together at the beginning of the semester. The teachers in the pilot work use the rubrics holistically to make regular assessments of students. That is, they rank the explanations from a high of 3 (accurate, complete with evidence and reasoning, and clearly written) to 1 (inaccurate, lacking evidence and reasoning, or poorly written). In addition, our team (teachers, developers, and researchers) reviews the students' explanations using the rubrics in order to determine next steps in our curriculum development and ways to enhance the day-to-day enactments. Finally, we use these scoring rubrics to analyze the growth over time in students' scientific literacy development.

Student Sheets. For each lesson set in each unit, we develop sheets that give students opportunities to practice their scientific literacy and process skills. For example, the student sheets included in the Appendix provide a scaffolded space for students to carry out an investigation on how much oxygen is in air (see Figure 13.2) and to practice writing a scientific explanation of their findings (see Figure 13.3). This sample comes early in the first curriculum unit. As we move throughout each unit, we eliminate more and more scaffolding so that by the end of the unit, students are addressing the questions and activities without reminders and supports. The most important aspect of these sheets is that they are not intended to be used as seat work or even as homework. Instead, they are intended to support the work of students and teachers—as individuals or in groups—as they move throughout the curriculum units. For example, as illustrated in the sample provided in the Appendix, these student sheets provide guidance during investigations that students carry out during class time. And in this particular example, students begin by making predictions in small groups, working in small groups to carry out the investigation and record observations, writing claims as a whole class, and, finally, writing individual explanations with the scaffolding provided on the student sheets.

Reading Materials. Readers are provided for each curriculum unit that LeTUS produces. To date, our only reader that includes multiple text genres is the reader that accompanies the communicable disease unit; however, all of our other readers include constructed expository text that seeks to integrate the readers with classroom inquiry activities and provide a space for students to interact with the concepts discussed in the readers. We continue to develop multiple-text-genre readers according to the design principles described earlier, and we have planned an experimental study for the fall and winter of 2003–2004 in which we will test different versions of the reader in different classrooms. Two pages from the communicable disease curriculum reader are included in the Appendix as Figure 13.4.

Findings From Research on Our Practice

Findings from our first year of work indicate that although we obtained gains on lower-level content knowledge measures, a majority of the middle school students we work with experience some difficulties with abstract concepts and processes encountered in project-based science. (This pattern was not new to us, as it had been the driving force behind our focus on scientific literacy.) We found that students have difficulties with

1. Science process skills, especially analyzing, interpreting, and reporting data in verbal or graphic representations.
2. Scientific thinking that underlies understanding of these processes, such as causal and analogical reasoning, representation, and explanation.
3. Using scientific discourse to communicate and build understanding of scientific ideas.

These difficulties influenced the degree to which students could benefit from the opportunities to engage in inquiry offered via project-based science.

Explanation Writing. As we have engaged in the systematic teaching of how to represent one's understandings of real-world phenomena according to the conventions of a scientific discourse community, we have observed students articulating their internalization of these conventions in both everyday classroom interactions, on classroom written artifacts, and on formal curriculum post-tests. Initial data analyses of the post-tests and performance tasks from our pilot enactment indicate that the students showed gains in the production of written explanations that met the major criteria of our analytic rubric. Using criterion scoring rubrics based on the categories of the holistic rubric that teachers use in the classroom (see Figure 13.1 in the Appendix), we have found that approximately 50% of students in all classrooms are able to produce more accurate and more detailed explanations at the end of each unit.

Consider the difference in the following explanations offered in response to a written air-quality-unit pre- and post-test question that provided the students with the details of a fictional experiment, together with data presented in tabular and graph form (same data simply represented differently). Students were asked to read the details of the investigation, analyze the data presented in the table and graph, and then explain the data in relation to the hypothesis the fictional class of students had posed. The experiment proposed to investigate whether there was a difference in the amount of particulate matter released by cars produced in different years by using a sock placed over the exhaust pipe. The fictional class's hypothesis is "The age of the car will have no effect on the amount of particulate matter the car releases." The following examples are taken from students at three different schools and represent a range of student ability levels (spelling, punctuation, grammar intact in each exemplar):

Student 1
Pre: The old one is black and when they made the new one it start to get lighter and lighter.

Post: Old cars got more pollution the new cars because the old cars average sock color at end of experiment is black that mean the old cars polluted the air the most. The average car got dark gray average sock color at end of experiment because is also polluted the air but not more pollution then the old cars. The new cars also polluted the air but not as much as the old cars and the average cars.

Student 2
Pre: The age does have an effect on the amount of particulate matter that the car releases.

Post: The older the car the more particulate matter it's going to realease. I know this because according to the charts the old car sock turned black the average turned dark gray and the new turned light gray. The class hypothesis was wrong.

Student 3
Pre: This probably happened because the old cars weren't very up to date. They were regular cars, but they probably ran on something

else or some additional electronics. The new cars were up to date and probably ran on something different that used less fuel than the old cars. The students had a very good guess, but they were completely wrong.

Post: The hypothesis was first of all wrong. When the car was made before 1978 and was old there was more particulate matter released and the sock was black. When the car was made between 1978 and 1989 there was a little less particulate matter released and the sock was dark gray. Last when the car was made after 1990 there was alot less particulate matter released into the air and the sock was light gray. So over all the newer the car the less particulate matter that was released.

We have noted several areas of growth in analyzing responses such as these. First, students appear to be developing a higher degree of facility with scientific discourse. For example, Student 3 shifts from "the students had a good guess" to "The hypothesis was first of all wrong." Similarly, Student 2 refers to the hypothesis in his post-test explanation but not in the pre-test explanation. The same student took up the phrase "particulate matter" in her post-test explanation. Student 1, who uses the least scientific terminology in the post-test, does, however, use more detailed and precise language to explain her accurate claim about the investigation.

These exemplars also illustrate a second pattern that we have observed. In making post-unit explanations, students now tend to marshal the data to be used as evidence to support their claims rather than simply list or restate the data they noted in the tables or graphs (e.g., "the old one is black and when they made the new one it started to get lighter"). This developing ability to use data to provide evidence or warrant for their claims demonstrates the students' developing reasoning practices using data from investigations.

A third pattern in these exemplars and in the larger data set is that students are more likely in post-unit explanations to make some generalizations from the data, and thus are more likely to make claims. In addition, the claims that students make at the end of the unit are more likely than not to be scientifically accurate, even if their explanations are not complete with data.

Finally, students are simply writing longer and more detailed explanations post-unit than they were at the beginning of the units. Even when students came into the unit able to make sophisticated "guesses" as to the answers on pre-tests (as in Student 3), they typically included ideas that appeared to be drawn from their own prior knowledge rather than from the data provided in the charts. By the end of the unit, the majority of students in the pilot used data from the charts and tables they were provided in test questions and were able to provide reasons for using the data to support their claims.

Constructing Explanations Across Discourse Communities. In addition to students' growth in scientific explanation writing, we have seen evidence on post-tests and in classroom practices that students can distinguish between the kinds of explanations they might make for different purposes and different discourse communities. We believe that the ability to recognize the literacy and language conventions and standards of any given community or context is an important skill for the scientifically and generally literate person. For example, in a performance task we designed for the unit on communicable disease, we asked students to analyze data from a hypothetical experiment designed to test a mother's advice that two young women wash their hands for at least 15 seconds in order to reduce bacteria growth. We asked students to write in their conclusions a scientific claim based on the data and to write what they would tell their mothers about their experiment. To do so, students had to read data from charts, synthesize the data, link their findings to the original hypothesis posed, and then write the two kinds of claims. An exemplar from one student illustrates her understanding of *claim* in a scientific explanation. When asked whether "Yes, our mother was right" is a good scientific claim, the student wrote (spelling, punctuation, and grammar intact):

> No it is not. I would improve it by giving 2 pieces of evedence a illustiation and make sure anyone can understand.

This exemplar illustrates what we found in many of the students. That is, they recognized what the criteria were for constructing a good scientific explanation, but they did not necessarily produce such explanations unless coached. When asked what she should tell her mother, the same student wrote:

> They should tell there mom that she was right and they were wrong and they should of believe her in the first place cause mama knows best.

This "everyday" explanation illustrates the difference in the roles that explanations play in students' lives in and out of the classroom, as well as their awareness of the discursive conventions of different communities. This young woman was well aware that a scientific explanation needed to be written in a way that a broad audience of other people interested in the phenomenon could make sense of it (written clearly) and should include a certain amount of evidence and some sort of illustrative example. Her explanation to her mother, by contrast, simply involved confirming her mother's initial claim and reinforcing the adage that "mama knows best." This student saw her everyday explanation to her mother as an explanation embedded in an existing relationship and a mutually understood context, whereas a scientific explanation was one that might be made to relative strangers, across a number of science contexts. Thus, this student was implicitly aware of the different ways that people explain in various communities.

Students also demonstrated similar discursive conventions on the same task, with many echoing the idea that "mama knows best" and that the students should "tell her they were sorry for not believing her, Even know [though] it was a good experiment to test." Some, however, showed evidence of constructing hybrids of scientific and everyday discourse, more often than not, as they made explanations to their mothers, as in this exemplar:

> *Scientific Explanation:* Trisha and Sonya can conclude that their hypothesis was incorrect. The more seconds they washed their hands the less number of bacteria colonies showed up. They can also conclude that as they washed their hands more, the bacteria colonies were not decreasing at a fixed rate. For example, when they washed their hands for ten seconds, the number of colonies decreased by ten, but when they washed their hands for fifteen second, the number of bacteria colonies decreased by two.

> *Everyday Explanation:* Trisha and Sonya should tell their mother that she was correct because when they didn't wash their hands for fifteen second they had a lot of bacteria on their hands. They could also tell their mother that the longer they washed their hands, the number of bacteria colonies decreased. For example, when they didn't wash their hands they had fifty bacteria colonies, when they washed their hands for fifteen second they twenty-eight bacteria colonies.

In one student's response, however, a hybrid of everyday and scientific knowledge was offered in the scientific explanation:

> *Scientific Explanation:* They can conclude that there hypothesis was incorrect, and they should have just listened to there' mother when she told them that bactirea when not cleaned, is harmful if you eat it. The results were there are less bactirea the longer you wash your hands.

> *Everyday Explanation:* They should tell there mother there sorry for not listening to her in the first place. They should say this because they debated with there mother for no reason.

In general, we are encouraged both by the depth of the students' responses, by the distinctions they make across discourse communities—which is a useful literacy and language skill to develop as students begin to move out into the world and enter new and different communities—and by their willingness to weave explanations together when appropriate, drawing from both everyday and school science knowledge to construct explanations, and potentially new understandings, of natural phenomena.

We also see students' growth in their ability to explain as evidence of what they are learning about data collection, representation, and interpretation. In each exemplar given earlier, students were analyzing the procedures carried out in investigations (although not conducting the investigations themselves, because these were paper and pencil tasks), reading and making sense of data tables and graphs, and drawing conclusions that they used to write scientific explanations. Thus, although we have focused more on explanation writing, and we do not have as many direct measures of students' abilities in data collection, representation, and analysis, we are optimistic about their growth in these areas, and we look forward to continued growth across more classrooms as we take our pilot to scale throughout Detroit public middle school science classrooms.

NEXT STEPS FOR OUR REFORM EFFORTS

Our primary goal is to expand this scientific literacy reform effort to full scale in the Detroit Public Schools. We envision two ways to take this work to full scale. First, in 2003–2004, we will expand from our pilot of four teachers (16 classrooms) to more of the middle school science teachers who use LeTUS curricula in Detroit: approximately 30 teachers and 120 classrooms. We eventually plan to expand to even more middle school science classrooms. We also have plans to begin working on high school level curricula.

The challenges of any move to larger scale are numerous. The greatest challenge of moving these literacy practices laterally—that is, across middle school science classes—will be in providing enough professional development to ensure that the data collection, representation, interpretation, and explanation strategies are taught deeply and consistently over time. Teachers involved in the pilot have commented that they feel more confident about the various strategies and can see more rapid growth in their second year of enactment. In other words, it takes some time and practice to become comfortable with these scientific literacy strategies (but it appears to be worth the time and practice). Indeed, many science teachers do not see themselves in the role of literacy teacher, regardless of whether the goal is scientific literacy. Taking on this role requires a shift in one's identity as a science teacher and will require professional development, material and emotional resources (another teacher to debrief with, for example), and patience.

Taking the scientific literacy strategies to scale by moving to the high school level will require similar resources, including time and patience. As the science concepts become more advanced, the literacy and language demands become even greater. Both the use of technical language and the precision of the assumptions and themes of science increase. Ironically, there typically seems to be even less time for literacy teaching in upper-level science classrooms. Giving up what many teachers feel is precious time to cover content will be a difficult challenge.

Another reason that going to greater scale is difficult is that the students bring many different kinds of literacy and language skill into their science classrooms. As illustrated by the reading, writing, and science achievement scores across the district, schools range from well below to well above state standards on these achievement measures. Thus, although many of the students we work with are sophisticated literacy and language users in their everyday lives, they often struggle to read and write with proficiency the academic texts of the classroom—particularly of the science classroom. The range of skill levels and abilities with different types of literate practice present a challenge for individual teachers, and make the production of a districtwide curriculum that strives to meet *all* students' needs and interests even more difficult.

As a result of these challenges, we plan to expand our professional development efforts to model for teachers new to the reform a variety of practices and strategies that can support students' learning to read and write according to the conventions of science. We want to encourage the LeTUS teachers (and other interested teachers) to make use of the University of Michigan's Center for Highly Interactive Computing in Education's online professional development resource, Knowledge Networks on the Web (Fishman, Marx, Best, & Tal, in press; http://know.soe.umich.edu). We hope to use video clips and teacher documentaries to provide novice teachers with specific strategies that they can use to integrate literacy learning with science learning (Fishman, in press).

Another goal is to engage in professional development that increases teachers' awareness of the need to teach students how to navigate across and learn to critique the practices of different communities. Even as our students learn the conventions of science, we hope that they learn that these are human conventions, ones that were produced in certain contexts and for certain purposes, and ones that can be changed.

To support that goal, we also hope to be able to develop a wide variety of curriculum readers that will give students the opportunity to practice scientific literacy skills across many different genres and discourse communities. Because the readers are portable—and, eventually, will be more interactive, as we move toward CD-ROM or DVD versions—they can be used beyond the classroom as homework, support for action projects, or resources for carrying out long-term investigations. More important, once the readers are developed in electronic formats, students will be able to *add to the readers*, thus constructing curriculum reading materials that are current, focused on their interests, and connected to the science they are studying.

Finally, we hope to continue our research on the enactment curricula that support inquiry in science, whether through an empirical investigation or through the use of textual tools. As we continue to develop these curricula as the integration of empirical and textual research, we need to document the processes that teachers and students engage in the classroom, the joys and woes of teaching via these curricula, and the extent of students' learning. We are just beginning in these efforts, and we have developed partnerships with school and university teams in Illinois and North Carolina, working together from similar principles or assumptions about science and literacy learning, while also taking care to make curriculum development efforts responsive to the local and particular communities in which these efforts are embedded.

Given the impact the larger PBS project has had on student learning, and given the enthusiasm of the pilot teachers and the encouraging results of the Detroit pilot data, we believe that this work will have significant and lasting impact throughout Detroit and beyond.

NOTES

1. This material is based upon work supported by the National Science Foundation, under Grant No. REC 0106959 Amd 001. Any opinions, findings, and conclusions or recommendations expressed in this material are those of the authors and do not necessarily reflect the views of the National Science Foundation.
2. Additional information can be found about LeTUS and a related center, the University of Michigan's Center for Highly Interactive Computing in Education (hi-ce), at http://www.hi-ce.org.

REFERENCES

Anderson, T. H., & Armbruster, B. B. (1984). Content area textbooks. In R. C. Anderson, J. Osborne, & R. J. Tierney (Eds.), *Learning to read in American schools: Basal readers and content texts* (pp. 193–226). Hillsdale, NJ: Erlbaum.

Blumenfeld, P. C., Marx, R. W., Patrick, H., & Krajcik, J. S. (1997). Teaching for understanding. In B. J. Biddle, T. L. Good, & I. F. Goodson (Eds.), *International handbook of teachers and teaching* (pp. 819–878). Dordrecht, Netherlands: Kluwer Academic Publishers.

Cummins, J. (1984). *Bilingualism and special education: Issues in assessment and pedagogy.* Boston: College-Hill.

Fishman, B. (In press). Linking on-line video and curriculum to leverage community knowledge. In J. Brophy (Ed.), *Advances in research on teaching: Using video in teacher education* (Vol. 10). New York: Elsevier Science.

Fishman, B., Marx, R., Best, S., & Tal, R. (2003). Linking teacher and student learning to improve professional development in systemic reform. *Teaching and Teacher Education 19,* 643–658.

Goldman, S. R. (1997). Learning from text: Reflections on the past and suggestions for the future. *Discourse Processes, 23,* 357–398.

Hicks, D. (1995/1996). Discourse, learning, and teaching. In M. W. Apple (Ed.), *Review of research in education* (Vol. 21, pp. 49–95). Washington, DC: American Educational Research Association.

Krajcik, J., Blumenfeld, P. C., Marx, R. W., Bass, K. M., & Fredricks, J. (1998). Inquiry in project-based science classrooms: Initial attempts by middle school students. *Journal of the Learning Sciences, 7,* 313–350.

Lee, O., & Fradd, S. H. (1998). Science for all, including students from non-English language backgrounds. *Educational Researcher, 27*(3), 1–10.

Lemke, J. L. (1990). *Talking science: Language, learning, and values.* Norwood, NJ: Ablex.

Marx, R. W., Blumenfeld, P., Fishman, B., Krajcik, J., & Soloway, E. (2001). *Creating usable innovations for systemic reform: Large-scale design research in science and technology for urban schools.* Symposium presented at the annual meeting of the American Educational Research Association, Seattle, WA.

Merino, B. J., & Hammond, L. (1998). Family gardens and solar ovens: Making science education accessible to culturally and linguistically diverse students. *Multicultural Education, 5*(3), 34–37.

Moje, E. B., Collazo, T., Carrillo, R., & Marx, R. W. (2001). "Maestro, what is 'quality'?" Language, literacy, and discourse in project-based science. *Journal of Research in Science Teaching, 38,* 469–496.

National Research Council. (1996). *National science education standards.* Washington, DC: National Academy Press.

Nicholson, T. (1985). The confusing world of high school reading. *Journal of Reading, 28,* 514–526.

Singer, J., Marx, R. W., Kracik, J., & Clay-Chambers, J. (2000). Constructing extended inquiry projects: Curriculum materials for science education reform. *Educational Psychologist, 35,* 165–178.

Wong-Fillmore, L. (1982). Language minority students and school participation: What kind of English is needed? *Journal of Education, 164,* 143–156.

APPENDIX

Teachers, researchers, and curriculum developers have worked together to develop materials to aid instruction and to guide the research process. Included in this Appendix are excerpts of three types of materials used regularly: an Explanation Rubric, for evaluating the quality of students' growth in explanation writing; a two-page excerpt from the Student Sheets that accompany the air curriculum; and a two-page excerpt from the Student Reader that accompanies the communicable disease curriculum.

EXPLANATION RUBRIC FOR EVALUATION

How to write a good scientific explanation:

1. Make a claim about the problem.
2. Provide evidence for the claim.
3. Provide reasoning that links the evidence to the claim.
4. Use precise and accurate scientific language.
5. Write clearly so that anyone interested in science, anywhere, can understand the explanation.

	Level 1	Level 2	Level 3
Makes a claim about the problem.	Does not make a claim, or makes an inaccurate claim.	Makes a claim that reveals *partial* understanding. The claim may include both accurate and inaccurate details, or it may omit important details.	Makes an accurate claim.
Provides evidence for the claim.	Does not provide evidence, or provides inaccurate evidence for the claim.	Provides some accurate evidence for the claim, but not sufficient. (May include some inaccurate evidence for the claim.)	Provides accurate evidence and sufficient evidence for the claim.
Provides reasoning that links the evidence to the claim.	Does not provide reasoning, or provides rationale that does not link the evidence to the claim.	Provides some reasoning that links the evidence to the claim, but the rationale is not sufficient. (May include rationale that does not link the evidence to the claim.)	Provides sufficient reasoning that links the evidence to the claim. (May use linking words like *because, so, therefore* to make the connections.)
Uses precise and accurate scientific language.	Does not use scientific language, or uses scientific language incorrectly.	Uses some scientific language correctly, but some may be incorrect (or imprecise).	Uses precise and accurate scientific language.
Is written clearly. (Anyone interested in science, almost anywhere, can understand it.)	Is not written clearly. Does not provide necessary contextual details.	Is written relatively clearly. (May include only some of the necessary contextual details, or may include both necessary and unnecessary details.)	Is written clearly. Focuses on a particular phenomenon, includes all necessary contextual details (and no unnecessary details).

FIGURE 13.1. Explanation rubric: general.

AIR CURRICULUM STUDENT SHEETS EXCERPT

POE: Is air only oxygen?

Step 1: Predict what will happen when:

1. The jar is placed over a lit candle standing upright in a pan with water.

   What will happen? _____

   _____

   Why? _____

   _____

Step 2: Record your observations:
   —Draw a picture of what you observe before you place the candle over the jar and after you place the candle over the jar.
   —List the properties you observe and any changes you see inside of the jar.

Before:

After:

Properties observed:

_____

_____

_____

_____

_____

Properties:

_____

_____

_____

_____

_____

Changes inside the jar:

_____

_____

_____

_____

_____

FIGURE 13.2. How much oxygen is in air? The investigation. "POE" stands for "Predict, Observe, Explain." The students are taught this acronym early in the curriculum.

AIR CURRICULUM STUDENT SHEETS EXCERPT

Step 3: Explanations—Writing a scientific explanation for "Is air matter"?
(1) *Think* about your observations
(2) *Review* your initial claim
(3) *Write* your explanation using your claim and supporting evidence

---

Think:

1. Summarize what happened to the water level after the candle went out.

   _____

   _____

2. How much volume of air space did you lose to water?

   _____

   _____

   _____

3. Propose a reason for why the water didn't move all of the way into the jar.

   _____

   _____

Review:

4. Does your original claim make sense after making your observations? If not, describe what you would change about it below.

   _____

   _____

   _____

Explanation:

5. Is air only made up of oxygen? Write out your scientific explanation below.

   _____

   _____

   _____

Remember that:

An explanation needs to have:

—A *claim* about the question being answered

—*Evidence* or observations that support your claim

—*Clear* reasons why the evidence supports your claim

—Clear and understandable *sentences*

FIGURE 13.3. How much oxygen is in air? The explanation.

COMMUNICABLE DISEASE CURRICULUM READER EXCERPT

So how do you think a disease can spread?

You are going to be investigating how a disease can spread and what are some of the different ways that you can catch a disease. The unit that you are starting is called "How can good friends make you sick?"

1. Do you know anything about catching a disease? You might want to ask family members how they knew you were sick or had a disease.

_____

_____

2. Who can you catch a disease from?

_____

_____

3. How do you think your friends could make you sick?

_____

_____

What should be done when a friend has a disease?

How many of you have heard of Nkosi Johnson? Or of Ryan White? They are two boys who became famous because they became AIDS victims. But you don't need to be famous to be a victim of a disease. These two boys are just two out of the many millions who are sick or who have died from the disease caused by HIV.

HIV is Human Immunodeficiency Virus—the virus that causes AIDS.

These two boys were famous because they spoke about what it was like to be HIV positive and they fought for disease victim's rights.

You will be learning about HIV as you do this unit.

Here is some of Nkosi Johnson's story taken from an article that first appeared on CNN.com. It will tell you a little about what HIV is and what living with HIV is like.

- -

World's young AIDS fighter may lose his own battle
January 9, 2001
Web posted at: 4:36 PM EST (2136 GMT)

From staff and wire reports
JOHANNESBURG, South Africa (CNN)—For this 11-year boy, being brave enough to declare—then openly discuss—his HIV-positive health status sends a powerful message: AIDS sufferers are very real, very loveable humans.

Nkosi Johnson's struggle for AIDS awareness, however, came closer to tragedy as the child activist remained in a coma. He has been unable to talk since suffering brain damage last week as the deadly disease spread further through his frail body.

"His legacy is that he has taught the world—and more importantly, South Africans—that people with AIDS are very normal people that we need to care for and accept," Gail Johnson, his adopted mother said.

FIGURE 13.4. Communicable disease curriculum reader. _(Continues on next page.)_

Nkosi prompted national soul-searching when he applied to join a primary school in 1997. This caused an uproar among some parents and the school in the Johannesburg suburb where he lives. Now his classmates and friends are among those who wait for word of hope outside the hospital.

"I would like to tell him to come back to school to get well," said Edward Bikie, a classmate and friend. His mother said Nkosi, who could speak and walk normally as recently as a month ago, was now deathly ill.

The small boy became the unofficial spokesman for AIDS in a country where 4.2 million, or one in 10 people, are stricken with the disease. He gained worldwide attention when he stepped to the podium at the opening of the world's biggest AIDS conference in Durban last year and called on the South African President to allow AIDS-fighting drugs be used on pregnant mothers and urged others to change public behavior.

After birth, Nkosi was HIV positive. His mother was HIV positive.

"His greatest contribution was to get public awareness of HIV-AIDS ...," said Daniel Ncayiyana, editor of the South African Medical Journal.

Nkosi "spoke ... with enormous courage and eloquence. He showed that you can hug and love a child without risk to yourself," said Yvonne Spain.

To make sure his legacy is not forgotten, Nkosi and his mother have created a shelter home for HIV-positive mothers and children. Called "Nkosi's Haven," the center is funded by donations.

Johnson said Nkosi's wish for the home was simple, but powerful: "He said to me, 'Gail, the mommies and babies must stay together.'"

----

4. How did Nkosi Johnson get HIV?

_____

_____

5. Did he give it to his friends and family?

_____

_____

6. Do you think anyone can get it?

_____

_____

In this real life story, Nkosi attended a public school and had friends in this school. His friends were concerned about him and his health. His friends didn't seem to worry about getting sick. In fact, the story points out that Nkosi was important in changing how people thought about how you could get sick from HIV.

7. So how do people get sick? Why didn't Nkosi's friends worry about getting sick?

_____

_____

_____

_____

_____

FIGURE 13.4. *Continued.*

14

The Talent Development Literacy Program for Poorly Prepared High School Students

James McPartland, Robert Balfanz, and Alta Shaw

Key Points

- The Talent Development literacy program extended time in English classes to enable students to catch up and to cover the district syllabus.

- Prescribed learning activities included teacher modeling, teacher-directed interactive mini-lessons, cooperative learning activities, and student choice for independent reading.

- Professional development included intensive workshops, in-class coaching, and local supportive networks.

The Talent Development Model is a comprehensive high school reform package that includes a research-based instructional program aimed at gradually closing the literacy gaps of students in high-poverty schools. The Talent Development (TD) literacy program involves extra instructional time for a highly specific sequence of courses that focus primarily on fluency and comprehension in reading and on the stages of good writing for different purposes. The literacy program was not the first reform component developed for the Talent Development Model, but we soon learned that student weaknesses in reading and writing were among the major barriers to high school success.

Starting in 1994 with a major federal grant to establish the Center for Research on the Education of Students Placed At Risk at Johns Hopkins University, a research and development program began to find practical solutions to the serious problems of large nonselective high schools in high-poverty districts. The comprehensive reform model that resulted—the Talent Development High School with Career Academies—is now in 50 large high schools in major school districts across the country, growing by 25% each year. But this model did not begin with the strong emphasis on classroom literacy instruction it now has.

The most obvious first need was to create a safe and serious environment for learning. Student disruptions from frequent class cutting and disrespect toward authorities often set a negative climate where learning was not paramount and teachers were often frustrated and demoralized. In addition, student attendance that fell below 65% on an average day had to be significantly improved for any hope of better learning outcomes. So the initial TD reforms were to reorganize the large bureaucratic structure of the high school into several smaller self-contained units. In these units, better adult control and a more personalized environment could address the school climate and student attendance difficulties.

The TD organizational reforms create a separate Ninth Grade Success Academy where teachers work in teams to help students make a good transition into high school. In addition, there are several upper-grade Career Academies where students choose a college preparatory program with a broad career theme that gives focus and meaning to their studies. When this structure is well implemented so that everyone within the same unit knows each other well and teachers take responsibility to reach out to students with attendance or discipline problems, the climate of a troubled high school can be turned around with newly positive teacher–student relations and more satisfactory student attendance (Legters, Balfanz, Jordan, & McPartland, 2002).

Although it was gratifying to observe many more students with good attendance earning promotion from grade 9 to 10 and the overall climate and attendance rate improving, it quickly became clear that classroom instruction also needed to change if students in high-poverty high schools were to make it through to graduation and pass the high-standards state exams that were expected. Teachers had reported that many of their students were struggling with the textbooks in their advanced high school courses and were often unable to communicate what they might have learned in acceptable written forms. The district had provided some materials to high school English teachers primarily aimed at decoding skills in reading. Research indicated, however, that these were minor problems for teenagers compared with the fluency and comprehension difficulties that required other approaches.

A team of literacy specialists had worked at the same Johns Hopkins University Center for several years on elementary and middle grades instruction. They had been particularly successful at using cooperative learning approaches, with students working in small teams to read selected novels and short stories and discuss comprehension questions. They had found reading materials for early adolescents who needed high-interest content at a level that did not frustrate them. We decided to adapt these approaches in our high school model along with the vocabulary development activities associated with the reading selections and some other instructional activities.

TALENT DEVELOPMENT HIGH SCHOOL LITERACY

We began to develop and evaluate the TD literacy program for grade nine and subsequently added the upper high school grades. At each grade level, TD literacy features:

1. Additional instructional time so both catch-up activities and the local district's syllabus can be covered.
2. A highly prescribed sequence of learning activities to focus on reading fluency and comprehension and the writing processes.
3. Intensive professional development including expert in-class coaches.

Extra Instructional Time

TD high schools use the 4×4 block schedule with two 18-week terms of four extended-period courses (about 90 minutes daily). TD literacy instruction occurs in *both* terms with extended classes, which we have sometimes termed the *double dose*. It is about twice as much instruction as one term of extended periods for one credit, or two terms of English in the conventional shorter period (45–50 minutes).

The first-term course is a new offering developed at the Johns Hopkins University Center to narrow gaps and accelerate reading and writing skills. The second term uses the reading selections and writing goals defined by the district's curriculum guides, supplemented by our materials that continue a focus on reading fluency and comprehension and on writing. In this way, the TD approach should be aligned with state and district standards as we use the required curriculum in the second term. In practice, we usually need to work further with local officials to be sure the required curriculum standards are being met and that students are being well prepared for high-stakes tests.

Learning Activities

We have developed separate first-term courses in grades 9, 10, 11, and 12 to narrow and close gaps in reading fluency and comprehension, and the materials for each of these courses are complete with specific daily lesson plans, so even teachers with little experience in reading instruction will have rich content to guide them. Table 14.1 shows the course titles under the TD literacy program.

A typical instructional day will have four different learning activities: teacher modeling; teacher-directed interactive mini-lesson; cooperative learning activities; and student choice for independent reading (Figure 14.1).

Teacher Modeling. Students can learn comprehension strategies by observing a mature reader verbalizing the thought processes to draw meaning from a selection and by practicing the same approaches with feedback from others. A typical class begins with the teacher modeling various comprehension strategies with a "read aloud–think aloud" presentation. The teacher reads a passage and pauses after every few sentences to report what he or she is thinking. The goal is to demonstrate to students how a good reader is carrying on a mental conversation with the author while checking his or her understanding of the material.

TABLE 14.1. Talent Development High School Literacy Program

Grade	Term 1 TD courses (18 weeks)	Term 2 District courses with TD supplements (18 weeks)
9	Strategic Reading	English 1 with TD supplements Literacy Lab as elective replacement for the weakest readers
10	Reading & Writing in Your Career	English 2 with TD supplements
11	College Preparatory Reading & Writing	English 3 with TD supplements
12	Senior Research Project	English 4 with TD supplements

At appropriate pauses, the teacher will relate the material to his or her own experiences and background to draw a vivid picture of the characters or events; predict what's coming next or reflect on a surprise turn; guess an unknown word from the passage context; notice a writer's techniques such as different print for emphasis or a literary device such as metaphor; or summarize what's been learned up to this point.

The teacher also tells how to monitor understanding and decide how to draw the proper meaning by checking whether he or she is getting lost and deciding whether to keep reading to figure it out, or to go back and reread a bit. The teacher will point out that it is often all right to not be completely clear because it may be the writer's intention to lead the reader along for a while as the story develops.

After observing modeling by a good teacher for some time, students can demonstrate their own "read aloud–think aloud" abilities. Students can practice comprehension strategies either in individual sessions with teachers or in team settings where students can share different reactions as readers.

We have found that teacher modeling of comprehension strategies is a refined instructional technique that requires great resourcefulness and self-confidence, and it may take time to develop. For example, many teachers can read aloud effectively with theatrical voice inflections to create interest but omit the spontaneous think-aloud interruptions that are the core of comprehension modeling. We have sometimes added think-aloud prompts written on Post-Its attached to the reading passage at appropriate points. For example, when a mental picture is called for, we might urge the teacher to "Relate the scene to something in your own experience for a vivid image." Or, when it's a good time for metacognitive monitoring, we might encourage the teacher to "Check yourself for understanding and whether to press on for clarification."

I. **Teacher modeling in "Reading Showcase" (20 minutes)**

Teachers read narrative, poetic, functional/expository text aloud with frequent pauses to give voice to specific reading comprehension and metacognitive strategies. Teachers model stages of the writing process for selected goals.

II. **Teacher-directed interactive mini-lesson, called the "Focus Lesson" (20 minutes)**

Specific comprehension skills and strategies are targeted, appreciation for writer's style and craft is fostered, elements of grammar and sentence structure are reviewed, students learn to utilize reference/resource tools and materials.

III. **Cooperative team discussions using "Student Team Literature" (30 minutes)**

High-interest, low-level novels are read and discussed in cooperative teams using Partner Discussion Guides. Students use new vocabulary and experience authorship with writing activities in response to comprehension questions they had discussed with partners.

IV. **Student choice for independent reading from "Self-Selected Reading & Writing Centers" (20 minutes)**

Students choose from articles/books displayed in an appealing manner for private reading. Student–teacher conferences are conducted. Other centers allow independent student work on word play, research from informational sources, and various writing activities.

FIGURE 14.1. A typical Talent Development literacy lesson.

Teacher modeling of the different stages of the writing process is also an important classroom activity to help students learn the reasoning that should accompany their own writing. Given a topic, the teacher can lead the class in a brainstorming session to list possible ideas and items. Then, by writing on an overhead projector to show how a main theme and outline can bring order and sequence to the initial possibilities, the teacher can demonstrate the next creative activity in a writing assignment. The actual composition of a first draft of paragraphs can also be demonstrated by the teacher's writing on an overhead before the class. Finally, the editing process can be modeled both in terms of rearranging, adding, or removing sections and revising sentences for clarity and directness and paragraphs for coherence and continuity.

Interactive Mini-Lessons. Short lessons can teach how to recognize and handle different types of narrative or expository text (such as appropriate pre-reading activities for nonfiction informational materials); how writers use different literary devices to tell a story (foreshadowing, symbolism, dialect, etc.); and how to apply basic grammar and spelling rules for well-constructed sentences with rich modifiers and lively words. Short lessons can also include reminders of some specific social skills that are useful in cooperative learning tasks.

It's best when the mini-lessons ask students to get involved by following teacher instruction with guided and independent practice and with reflection on the particular skills or strategies. Likewise, a mini-lesson will be more effective when it is connected to the other learning activities of the class that day, such as the material being covered in the read-aloud or included in the discussion questions of the student team activity.

Cooperative Team Discussions.   Students also learn through discussions with peers during which they answer a reading comprehension question in their own words or hear others' opinions on the same topic. Not only will students find the social aspects of cooperative learning attractive, but the opportunity to actively process complex ideas will also increase their chances of understanding and retaining information. To increase student motivation, we have carefully selected novels with high interest to young adults but at a reading level they can handle without a lot of frustration. Sometimes two or more novels will be used with different subgroups in the same classroom at different reading levels.

We found that students' discussions of reading matter without some detailed direction often degenerate into simple reactions without analytic depth or direction. While there is some value in repeated student opinions of which character or event was most appealing and why, discussions that remain on this level are unlikely to raise students' comprehension strategies or sophistication.

To aim students' discussions toward an appreciation of plot development and writer's craft, we have prepared Partner Discussion Guides to accompany each novel, short story, play, or article being assigned. Each guide gives background information about the author and the setting or context for the narrative work, so students come to the reading assignment with some reasons why they might be interested and what to expect in general. For each few pages or chapters, the guide lists the vocabulary words that may be unfamiliar or challenging, to be put into meaningful sentences with the help of the teacher and other students. In addition, it lists comprehension questions for peer team discussions, including the meaning of interactions between story characters, predictions of what may come next, and reflections on how the author developed themes or plots. The guides also provide post-reading activities to follow up with other works by the same author or of the same genre, writing exercises using parallel devices, or book review activities to judge the special qualities of the work.

Students can also read selected passages before the group discussions in different ways. Silent reading during class time is an option, as is reading beforehand as a homework assignment for classes of reliable students. Partner reading can often be the most successful. Pairs of students sit close and trade off reading successive passages aloud to one another. Partner reading usually keeps each student engaged, and partners can help each other with occasional word recognition assistance.

Student Choice for Independent Reading. Instead of concentrating on worksheets for isolated skills, as happens in many remedial reading classes, students gain fluency by extended practice with reading actual books. We equip each classroom with a small library of high-interest books and magazines for students to read at the end of each period for self-selected reading. Each student chooses something to read from the classroom library for about 20 minutes. Some books are also accompanied by audiotapes so a student can follow along as the tape plays. There are also some student learning centers that may offer a writing activity or provide access to a recommended website or other information sources.

When they have finished reading their selection, students are often asked to complete reading logs, summarizing what they have read as well as reviewing the book for their peers.

This time can also be used for teacher conferences with individual students to assess their reading progress and plan follow-up activities while others are busy with their own reading. Also, when teachers find some students who still need decoding instruction, they can be pulled together to work with the teacher while the rest of the class is engaged in self-selected reading.

Teacher Support Systems

The third feature of the TD literacy program is a multilevel system to support teachers who are implementing it. For a strong implementation of the recommended approaches and materials, we have found that it is absolutely necessary to provide teachers with intensive periodic workshops followed by continuous technical assistance from expert in-class peer coaches.

Intensive Workshops. Teachers who will be providing the TD literacy program need to be thoroughly prepared in each of the components. They need to understand why modeling, mini-lessons, cooperative team discussions of novels and plays with vocabulary drills, and self-selected reading will help students develop fluency with effective comprehension strategies, and how to use these approaches successfully in their own classrooms. They need to know how to continuously assess individual students on decoding, fluency, and comprehension skills so they can arrange appropriate pull-out sessions for extra help within the classroom. They need to appreciate the different stages of the writing process for selected goals so that students can be given appropriate "springboard activities" to enliven and motivate each step.

We begin with a two- or three-day initial workshop for TD English teachers, usually held in the late summer close to school opening, when teachers know their course and grade assignments and are ready to focus on the new term. The workshops provide an intensive orientation to each instructional approach led by experienced TD instructors. The participating teachers play the role of students in simulated classroom situations led by the TD instructor so that they will appreciate the student perspective and motivation for each type of activity. These simulations include the mechanics of forming student cooperative learning teams and moving to team activities after whole-class instruction. Also covered are ways to prepare students with specific social skills for different team roles and with proper contexts for self-selected reading and other individual projects. Teachers participating in the workshops also view videos of actual TD literacy classrooms and critique the observed lessons and techniques. Participating teachers take turns demonstrating the instructional approaches for mutual feedback and learning. Finally, the role and functions of the TD in-class coaches with whom they will work throughout the year are explained, stressing that no evaluation information will flow from coaches to school officials so that a collegial partnership of trust can be established and maintained.

After the initial workshop, refresher workshops are held periodically across the school year. TD instructors meet at the school with participating teachers and in-class coaches to discuss successes and problems and to share possible solutions. Usually, these follow-up workshops occur for 90 minutes at the end of a school day—sometimes with a teacher stipend—at four- to six-week intervals. In one district, we organized a course with a local college on Talent Development literacy where TD English teachers received credit useful for employment advancements from participation in the course taught by TD instructors.

In-Class Coaching. Experience has shown that workshops alone do not ensure good implementation of TD reforms. There also must be reliable follow-ups to monitor teacher practices and assist teachers with the new classroom approaches. TD uses expert teacher peer coaches who visit a teacher's classroom at least once per week to support the classroom innovations.

TD usually assigns one full-time TD English coach to two high schools, so two or three days per week can be spent assisting teachers at each site. The coaches are thoroughly familiar with the TD literacy components, having been teachers themselves in a school using the program or having been trained by other experienced TD instructors and coaches. The coaches do not provide information to school officials that could influence evaluations of individual teachers; they are in the classrooms to assist TD teachers in the successful implementation of the recommended approaches. TD coaches may model teach or co-teach a lesson in the classroom with the TD English teacher. TD coaches may give feedback or suggestions on a teacher's use of TD materials and approaches as part of a collegial interchange and mutual feedback. TD coaches also help with the mundane matters of ensuring all needed materials and equipment are available and in working order. For instance, they might replace lamps in overhead projectors and supply enough Partner Discussion Guides.

Local Supportive Networks. We have also found it useful to bring together all the TD English teachers and TD in-class coaches working in a district to form a collegial network. By sharing success stories and exchanging problem-solving techniques, network participants reinforce teachers' enthusiasm for TD reforms and help enrich the detailed methods to reach TD literacy goals.

Evaluation Evidence

Three studies have been completed comparing the learning gains of high school students participating in the TD literacy program with students in matched control schools. The results from four urban districts consistently favor students in TD schools, with statistically significant greater achievement gains on various standardized reading tests, including CTBS, SAT-9, and local state exams (Balfanz, 2004).

Accelerated growth rates are needed to narrow and gradually close the literacy gaps of many students who enter high school three or four years below grade level. In fact, students would have to gain nearly two years for every single year in high school to graduate in four years on grade level and ready for college without further remediation. Some adolescent literary proponents believe the prospects are good for such gains (Balfanz, McPartland, & Shaw, 2002; Curtis & Longo, 1999; Greenleaf, Schoenbach, Cziko, & Mueller, 2001). We have some evidence that such accelerated growth rates can be achieved with the TD literacy program. For teachers with strong implementations of TD literacy reforms, studies show double the student growth rate per time used for instruction. We need to replicate these results for wider sets of teachers and show that the accelerated gains accumulate over multiple high school years in strong TD literacy programs so initial gaps can be completely closed.

LINGERING ISSUES

Three major issues for which we are still seeking better solutions include: (a) differentiated instruction to address student diversity; (b) literacy in the content areas; and (c) scaling up to additional districts.

Differentiated Instruction

Any given high school will have wide range of students in terms of their prior preparation in reading and writing. While the high-poverty high schools in which we do most of our work have mostly students who arrive three or four years below grade level in reading, there will also be some students who are at grade level or above and ready for advanced work. The issue is how to schedule instruction between classes or within classes so each student is participating in literacy learning activities that are appropriate and successful.

One approach is to establish separate classes using reading materials at different levels of difficulty and assign students on the basis of test scores or other assessments. In this case, the comprehension strategies to be learned can be the same in all classes, even though some will be using reading content with lower readability requirements than others. The risks associated with separate classes for students at different starting points are the same as those often attributed to "tracking": The lower classes will get the least experienced teachers and be stigmatized by lower expectations. However, if only a small minority of students needs instruction in early basics but must be taught in a diverse classroom, many other learners in that classroom will be bored as they sit through material they have already mastered.

A second approach is not to separate students with different preparations into separate classes but to differentiate instruction within a widely mixed class. For example, students may all address a common topic but be assigned different novels depending on their reading level. A common lesson on a writer's use of a literary device such as symbolism or on comprehension strategies such as prediction and summarization can be covered with different students using different books. Or students could be taught in small groups within the class on a particular topic they need. However, it takes careful planning and unusual teacher resourcefulness to conduct differentiated instruction within a classroom where several learning activities are going on at the same time matched with various student needs. There may also be so much student diversity within a classroom that differentiated approaches to the same lesson is hardly possible.

At this time, we have decided to offer Strategic Reading as the first-term ninth-grade course to all entering students, regardless of their tested grade level at the outset, and to differentiate learning materials within the classrooms. Under this arrangement, some student cooperative learning teams would work with more difficult novels than others, even though the lesson themes at any time are the same across the classroom. We believe all students need and will profit from the major comprehension strategies taught and practiced in this course, and each student will gain fluency from his or her own starting point over the term. The second-term ninth-grade English 1 course also is not grouped by students' prior tests or grades, and similar efforts are made to differentiate materials within each class. Because the required novels and plays are specified by the district for this course, some teams of students may take more time to complete a work and cover somewhat fewer selections in the term. During both terms, teachers can pull aside selected groups of students who need extra help on a specific topic and provide focused instruction.

The exception for differentiating between English classes in a TD ninth grade is the second-term Literacy Lab that is offered as an alternative to an elective only for the small number of students who still need intensive instruction in decoding. This "triple-dose" added course focuses with smaller class size on decoding skills in ways that have more appeal to young adults than using elementary grade exercises. We have been successful in using rhyming and rapping activities around major word families to assist students with decoding approaches, being careful to emphasize more subtle differences in roots and prefixes that very poor readers often miss. We have also found that some computer-based word games can motivate students to address decoding problems. Computers can also free the teacher for intensive sessions with individual students to address decoding strategies. In some schools, students attend Literacy Lab for only part of the second term and take an abbreviated elective for the rest of the term. This arrangement can be scheduled so that Literacy Lab is experienced one or two days each week, or for consecutive days for several weeks, with the elective course filling the remaining time.

But in the upper high school grades, TD permits some advanced students to replace the first-term course with another English course sequence or advanced placement alternative. Thus, in grade 10, all students who are still one or two years below grade level will take the TD course (Reading & Writing in Your Career) in the first term. We would have no objections to requiring this course for all 10th grades, with some differentiation of materials within each class, because the reading and writing strategies being covered are again of general value to all students. But many TD schools are moving some advanced students right into English 2 in the first term so they can move on to advanced courses as soon as possible. Similarly, we permit differentiation between classes in grade 11, where TD offers another first-term English course to further close gaps, followed by English 3 in the second term. Students who have reached grade level in reading and writing by junior year do not need the first-term course to catch up and may profit more from taking English 3 with another advanced course in the second term.

Another reason for differentiating English courses in the upper grades is the lack of sufficient staffing to provide all students with a double dose in the subject every year. More English teachers will be needed to cover the extra offerings, which would reduce school faculty in other areas. The continuing need for enough teachers to cover foreign language, health, art, music, and career education will constrain the ability to add many more English teachers. Since TD also offers double-dose options in mathematics, requiring more teachers in that subject, the staffing configurations become additionally problematic.

The student skill distributions in a particular high school will also affect how the first-term TD acceleration courses are arrayed across the grades, either as required for all with differentiation within classes or as an option for some with others in advanced alternatives. In any school, we expect to gradually narrow gaps for students who start behind, so the numbers who need double doses should diminish with each successive upper grade.

We will continue to develop approaches and assistance to teachers for within-class differentiation and to evaluate the effects of different TD course sequences for students who enter at different levels. We expect to have guidelines with more evidence for differentiated instruction within the TD materials in the future.

Literacy in the Content Subjects

Being able to read and write well is crucial for students' success not only in English courses but in all other high school subjects. Although the requirements are different for reading textbooks and materials in various subjects, literacy skills are generally not taught for the content subjects. Most English teachers focus on fiction rather than informational texts, and most content teachers in other subjects are not prepared to teach reading strategies. Likewise, the writing requirements to communicate understanding vary by content subject, but instruction rarely distinguishes writing forms or processes for the different high school subjects. We intend to expand the TD literacy program to prepare students with appropriate reading and writing approaches in the major content subjects of the high school curriculum.

The need for more sophisticated reading and writing skills in high school is also being driven by new state and district assessments in the major subjects. These require much more from students than recalling isolated facts or choosing the correct answer to a problem. High-stakes tests are emerging that require students to apply or interpret knowledge for selected situations and to explain how they arrived at a solution or to justify their answers in writing. Students need to read for understanding to be able to make applications or interpretations and to write clearly with appropriate details to demonstrate their true command of a subject.

Content Literacy Taught by English Teachers. English teachers can help their students handle reading and writing in other subjects by expanding their focus beyond fictional narratives and creative writing. In particular, English teachers can give students instruction and practice in the pre-reading, reading, and post-reading strategies useful for deriving full meaning from science, history, social studies, mathematics, and business texts. At the same time, English teachers can provide writing assignments to help students learn to communicate their understanding of topics in content subjects.

For example, the pre-reading activities in informational texts of skimming chapter titles, subheadings, captions, and concluding questions are very useful to establish the mind set and context for careful reading where understanding and retention will be high. The comprehension strategies while reading will also vary for informational texts, including a questioning posture while processing arguments or supporting information and an awareness of the sequence with which facts may flow from either an initial overview or an incremental development of evidence toward a conclusion. The post-reading activities where a reader goes over notes drawn from highlighted sections and reworks them into an outline or mnemonic system can make a great difference in preparing for a test or recalling what was learned. There are many other examples of reading strategies appropriate to different course materials and goals that can be taught in English classes by expanding the reading content used with appropriate instruction.

In the major subjects, writing also takes different forms, which can be taught in English classes. Besides the obvious forms, such as business letters and memos or technical manuals in business or career courses, students need to know how to write critical or persuasive essays in history and social studies and how to explain their solutions for problems in mathematics and science.

Although the same general steps of the writing process often apply—gathering information, organizing it, composing first drafts, and editing for sequence, clarity, and style—practice is needed to be effective for different audiences and goals in each content subject. English teachers can provide a variety of writing assignments to cover each of the content subject requirements.

The links between oral expression of knowledge gained from reading and its application to problem situations can also be used in English classes to develop students' literacy skills in different subjects.

Literacy Taught or Reinforced by Content Teachers. The teachers in high school courses other than English also expect good student literacy skills to handle the textbooks and other materials of their subjects and to communicate their understanding of key topics in the content courses. But when students are struggling to read course materials or have weak writing skills, content teachers rarely are well equipped to help their students with these skills. Poorly prepared students usually wind up with little chance to do well in these classes.

Instead of relying only on English teachers to strengthen students' reading and writing skills for different subjects, it clearly would help to have the other content teachers reinforce and supplement the literacy skills needed in their courses. At the least, this means that content teachers must be aware of the strategies needed before, during, and after reading in their subject that are being covered by English teachers. So it would be ideal if content teachers also knew how to teach relevant reading and writing strategies in their own subjects and had the class time to do so. In this way, students would not have to depend entirely on English courses for appropriate instruction in content subject reading and writing, and they would receive the powerful reinforcement of appropriate literacy approaches in multiple subjects.

We intend to greatly strengthen the TD literacy program across the different high school subjects both by expanding the English course focus to nonfiction materials and by preparing content subject teachers to reinforce and supplement literacy instruction in their own classes. To do so, we will need to develop appropriate instructional materials and work out the professional development and coaching supports for both English and other content teachers.

Sustaining and Scaling Up TD Reforms

Because the TD literacy program depends on excellent support systems for teachers, including well-run workshops and expert local in-class coaches, care must be taken to ensure that such support continues at existing TD schools and is ready for new TD sites. Although we have ways to deal with current demands, it is a lingering issue to be prepared for staff turnover in existing sites and growth to new districts.

Building Local Capacity. To address the inevitable turnover of TD teachers and in-class coaches, we constantly are striving to build local capacity of TD specialists who can take over coaching positions or replace departing TD teachers. We currently identify emerging leaders from newly trained TD teachers in a district to participate in local TD networks and assume some leadership roles. These individuals rise to next in line to become in-class coaches or to internally transfer to a school whose TD English staff has been decimated by retirements or moves elsewhere. Each year, we conduct local training workshops before the start of the new year to prepare new teachers to offer TD literacy program courses. The workshops continue throughout the year to further strengthen new TD teachers in the recommended components.

Adding New Districts. Because we usually require a planning year for TD reforms before they are implemented, we gain lead time for recruiting and training a TD support team. The planning year gives the local staff time to adapt TD elements to local conditions (such as developing the best Career Academy themes) and to earn strong buy-in for the proposed changes. This period gives us time to get a new TD support staff ready so that expert on-site coaching assistance is available when full implementation of TD reforms begins.

When we undertake a new partnership with a major district, we prefer to relocate one or more experienced TD educators to be our lead people there. These individuals are then in charge of recruiting local English educators to serve as TD in-class coaches and TD English facilitators when there are multiple schools. This process of staffing for new districts is a continuing challenge to the TD program as it responds to interest to scale up the TD reforms.

Because of the critical need to provide effective research-based literacy instruction approaches for poorly prepared high school students, we will continue to refine the TD literacy program; evaluate its impact on students' achievement gains under different implementation conditions; and seek solutions to the issues of student diversity, literacy requirements in different subjects, and resources for scaling up successful practices in additional districts.

REFERENCES

Balfanz, R. (2004). "Catching up: Impact of the Talent Development high school's ninth grade instructional interventions in reading and mathematics." *NASSP Bulletin,* in press.

Balfanz, R., McPartland, J., & Shaw, A. (2002). "Reconceptualizing extra help for high school students in a high standards era." *Journal of Vocational Special Needs Education 25,* 24–41.

Curtis, M. E., & Longo, A. M. (1999). *When adolescents can't read.* Cambridge, MA: Brookline Books.

Greenleaf, C. L., Schoenbach, R., Cziko, C., & Mueller, F. L. (2001). "Apprenticing adolescent readers to academic literacy." *Harvard Educational Review 71,* 79–129.

Legters, N. E., Balfanz, R., Jordan, W. J., & McPartland, J. M. (2002). *Comprehensive reform for urban high schools: A Talent Development approach.* New York: Teachers College Press.

15

Sample Activities for Teachers

In Classrooms, Schools, and Communities

Nora E. Hyland

Key Points

- In the classroom—Strategies that relate to specific units of study and are focused on a specific group of students
- In the schools—Strategies that are school-wide initiatives, involving the entire school community: students, teachers, administrators, and other staff members
- In the community—Strategies that reach out to the broader community, including civic leaders, religious community, recreational facilities, and businesses

The activities that follow are designed to expand the knowledge base of the readers of this book and to encourage thoughtful discussion and action about issues of literacy learning for students from low-income communities, immigrant communities, communities of color, and students with special needs. Thoughtfully prepared and carefully led discussions will help to ensure that participants feel free to discuss issues of concern to them and provide opportunities for greater understanding, dialogue, and improved environments for learning.

The activities were designed with three *venues* in mind: (a) in the classroom, (b) in the schools, and (c) in communities. In-the-classroom activities are those that can occur in the college or in-service classroom. These generally are used to further discussion about a topic. These can sometimes be extended to the school and community, as well. The school-based activities are those that teachers may be asked to conduct in their student teaching or teaching placement. These activities provide teachers with the opportunity to interrogate practices in real schools. Finally, the community activities require individuals to enter historically marginalized communities and learn from the families and leaders of the very students that schools are failing to educate. As Carol Lee points out in this volume (see Chapter 5), successful schools take up the literacy experiences of students' home and community and value these as central to school literacy learning. The community activities presented here allow teachers to investigate these literacy practices firsthand.

These activities are also meant as a way to model the kinds of inquiry teaching and learning that takes place in classrooms where students are engaged. They require teachers to think critically about their practice and about the ways in which they engage students.

IN-CLASS ACTIVITIES

Classroom-based activities are designed as a way to stimulate discussion and demonstrate to pre-service and in-service teachers the multiple ways that literacy and language are embedded in larger sociocultural practices that make up teachers' and learners' everyday worlds. These activities vary in terms of their depth: Some are merely activities to stimulate discussion, while others are offered as ways to motivate deeper understanding of issues. The first activity is designed to initiate a discussion about the knowledge and language base that students from historically marginalized communities bring to school and how this specific knowledge base may not be represented in schools or on standardized tests.

As a way to begin to imagine the kinds of knowledge that students from working-class, low-income, or racially marginalized communities bring to school, which may be different from the typical Eurocentric middle-class knowledge base that is valued in school, ask teachers to brainstorm culturally specific "vocabulary," "facts," or "information." For example, many White, middle-class students may not know what a *bodega* is, but a child from an urban Latino community would be quite familiar with the term. Students of color may be very familiar with certain literature, such as the works of Walter Dean Meyers or Ann Cameron, because these authors' books are more culturally relevant to their lives. Students who live in urban areas composed largely of apartment buildings may be familiar with concepts such as *landlord* or *superintendent*, whereas many students living in the suburbs may not.

As teachers brainstorm their lists of culturally specific terms, ask them to work in groups. This may be particularly difficult for a group of teachers who are predominantly White and middle-class themselves. Suggest that they continue to add to their list throughout the semester as they engage with more children and families from historically marginalized communities.

As the list grows, ask the teachers to devise culturally specific test questions based on the list of new terms. For example, questions on a typical standardized test might include, "In what sport would you use bait and tackle?" Most students who have minimal experience with fishing will answer "football" to this question (an answer that is marked as incorrect but is arguably correct). What kinds of questions can be devised from the list generated by the class?

To further demonstrate the cultural bias of testing, share with teachers the article "Black characters depicted as white in tests" (Puch 2000), about a third-grade reading test in Illinois that included excerpts from Ann Cameron's children's book series *The Stories Julian Tells*. These books are commonly used in schools that serve African American children because the main characters are African American. When one of the stories was used on the Illinois state test, the accompanying illustrations depicted white characters. This situation created confusion for many students who were familiar with the book and demonstrates concretely the ways that the dominant cultural perspective can marginalize the knowledge of students of color.

This activity should be followed by a discussion about the kinds of knowledge that are valued in school. How can teachers use culturally specific knowledge (as brainstormed by the class) to engage students? Given the Euro-centric, middle-class bias of school knowledge, how can and should teachers work to incorporate this knowledge of power into the schemas of their students without denigrating the students' own knowledge? Teachers may also want to examine other standardized tests to find instances of cultural bias. (For more information about culturally specific knowledge bases, see Moll, Amanti, Neff, & Gonzalez, 1992; Gonzalez, Moll, Tenery, Rivera, Rendon, Gonzalez, & Amanti, 1995.)

The second activity is designed to initiate a discussion about how teachers' beliefs affect students' learning. Teachers' beliefs about literacy instruction will generally influence how they teach as well as their assumptions about why or how students learn or do not learn. Certain beliefs held by teachers may cause them to rely on a deficit theory of failure when attempting to explain a lower than expected achievement level for certain students in their classes. This activity is a way to generate discussion of reading and literacy instruction and teachers' beliefs about learning and teaching that may help pre-service and in-service teachers interrogate their own assumptions about teaching.

Have teachers rate the extent to which they agree with the following statements (1 = completely disagree; 2 = disagree somewhat; 3 = neutral feeling; 4 = agree somewhat; 5 = completely agree):

- Teachers are the primary people responsible for making sure that every child is literate.
- Some students come to school with less knowledge than others.
- It is the teacher's/school's responsibility to reach out to the families and communities of his/her students.
- It is the family's responsibility to reach out to teachers.
- The school environment (school culture) is critical to students' learning.
- The reading program used by the school/teacher is one of the most important aspects of students' learning.
- Instructional methods are more important than school culture in terms of literacy learning.
- Instructional content is as important as methods in literacy instruction.
- Connecting instruction with the home and community lives of students is among the most important things a teacher should do.
- When students are continuing to have trouble learning to read in the intermediate elementary grades, the teacher should go back to the basics using phonics instruction, basic grammar, and basic vocabulary instruction.
- Regular use of Standard English is a prerequisite to literacy.

- If a child drops an inflectional ending while reading (i.e., *jump*, for *jumped*), he/she should be corrected for the error.
- Teachers should encourage the avoidance of errors while students are reading aloud.

After teachers have answered these questions individually, post the numbers 1–5 around the room. As you read each statement, ask teachers to stand by the number that they selected for that statement. Different numerical groups can then justify their answers. Because it is important to focus the discussion on the information presented in this book, ask teachers to question their assumptions about literacy as they justify their answers. For example, teachers should question their own assumptions about what content schools use and who is represented in that content. They should question the ways that schools and teachers connect to and value or distance and devalue the home communities of students. (For more information about teachers' beliefs in cultural contexts, see Rios, 1996.)

The third in-class activity involves lesson planning. Because inclusive teaching is an essential part of classroom life, ask teachers, in groups of four, to prepare a literacy mini-lesson for the class (vocabulary, a writing skill, introduction to a unit or book, etc.). Each group should prepare the lesson based on certain imaginary class characteristics. They should be given *relevant* demographics of the class, as well as more detailed information about three students who have specific learning needs as represented in Individualized Educational Plans (IEPs). The mini-lesson should then be taught to the class, with particular attention given to the ways that the students with IEPs are being taught inclusively. The instructor (you) should assign three teachers (members of the class) to act as the three students with special learning needs. This activity is geared toward helping teachers recognize the ways in which they can use culturally relevant knowledge when planning literacy instruction for inclusion students with special needs.

IN-SCHOOL ACTIVITIES

The in-school activities presented here are designed to assist pre-service and in-service teachers in identifying the ways that schools participate in (or disrupt) the persistence of the achievement gap. Asking teachers to think critically about in-school practices challenges them to consider alternative school practices and ways of teaching aimed at empowering all students through appropriate literacy instruction. In addition, teachers are encouraged to identify promising school practices as they operate in the real world of schools.

The first in-school activity is focused on building awareness of how literacy instruction is practiced in various school settings. To begin this activity, ask teachers, in groups of two, to visit various schools. They should select their own school placement and be encouraged to think critically about the practices that they observe. They should interview teachers, students, and administrators about how literacy is taught and practiced at the school. Teachers may want to consider what materials are used, how cultural issues are addressed within literacy instruction, what literacy programs are used (if any), how community knowledge is (or isn't) incorporated into the curriculum, and how teachers plan for inclusive education. Teachers should also look at the reading scores of the school and assess the school's reputation in the broader community. As a culminating activity, teachers should prepare a report and present the findings of their investigation. Key issues to consider in discussing the various reports include:

- What specific questions did your group investigate (from those suggested earlier or another question)?
- What are the differences in the schools that serve *mainstream* or middle-class populations versus those that serve low-income communities or communities of color?
- Do all the people interviewed view the literacy program the same way? What are the differences?
- What aspects of the literacy program seem to be working?
- What areas need to be improved?

The purpose of this activity is to identify the many factors that influence schools' decisions about literacy instruction and how these decisions may or may not differentially influence the learning or engagement of students from various racial, ethnic, or socioeconomic groups. For example, in many low-income communities, districts mandate scripted or reductionist reading programs, while more affluent districts have greater freedom to select programs and teaching methods.

The second in-school activity is designed to better understand how schools assess students' literacy development. Begin by asking teachers to collect as many literacy assessment tools as possible from their schools (tests, rubrics, checklists, etc.). Be sure that writing rubrics are collected. These may be tools used by teachers in their regular practice or as part of a standardized or statewide assessment. Also, ask teachers to collect writing samples from students (the names on the writing samples should be omitted). Finally, ask teachers to examine the assessment tools that they collected and identify any cultural or class bias in the tools. They should evaluate how literacy is defined in these tools and whether they agree with the definition inherent in the tool.

Teachers should bring the writing rubrics and writing samples to class. Ask them to identify writing rubrics that they liked, as well as those that are commonly used by their state as part of the formal writing assessment. Ask teachers to trade writing samples with a partner and use the state rubric to assess the writing sample. Have two teachers assess each sample. Allow them to compare their assessments and negotiate any disagreements. Ask them to consider the following: How is "good writing" defined in the rubric? Are there aspects of the students' writing that are not captured by the rubric? How might the students want to change the rubric?

Asking other teachers, parents, and other students to use the rubrics to assess the writing samples can extend this activity. Find out what they think about the writing samples. This activity can be useful in demonstrating that, while writing rubrics are quite useful, they may fail to capture the unique qualities of students' writing. This also gives the pre-service or in-service teacher an opportunity to examine the writing of students and determine the ways that students understand rubrics.

IN-COMMUNITY ACTIVITIES

The number of English language learners in the classroom is growing every day. Few teachers have any concept of what it means to be an English language learner in U.S. schools. Therefore, this first activity is designed to give teachers the opportunity to learn from an English language learner what his or her experience is and how this individual wants to be treated as a learner.

Begin the activity by suggesting that teachers look in their local community resource directory to find a class for adults who are new English language learners. Get in touch with the instructor of the class and set up a meeting of your classes. Each English language student can be paired with a pre-service or in-service teacher. Alternatively, teachers can be asked to go to an organization where newly arrived immigrants are learning English. The idea is for teachers to meet one on one with an adult English language learner and learn about his or her experience. This also provides an opportunity for the adult English learner to practice his or her English. Ask teachers to take the time to consider what they learned from this experience and how it can be translated into their classroom experience. Have the teachers write a reflection about this activity and how it may have an influence on their teaching in the future.

The second in-community activity is designed to bring the literacy worlds of adults and adolescents into closer contact. Young people engage in all kinds of literacy practices, as do adults. In this activity, each teacher should locate an adolescent or preadolescent from a different racial, cultural, or class background than himself or herself. The purpose for doing so is to focus on the knowledge that a learner brings to school literacy practices and how he or she uses that knowledge to engage in school-based literacy. The teacher should interview the child about his or her literacy practices outside school. For example, the teacher might ask why people learn to read, why reading is useful, why people write, and when or where the child reads and writes outside school. Teachers might also ask the child about spelling, poetry, phonics, literature, etc. How does the child define literacy (or "reading" for younger children)? What does she or he like to read? What does she or he like to write about? Does she see herself as a reader and writer? How did she learn to read?

In short, teachers should find out as much as they can about how the child perceives reading as a school subject and how she understands the relationships between reading and her own life. To extend this activity, teachers might do a careful observation of the child during a reading or writing lesson. They might videotape their own lesson for this activity or observe a child in someone else's class. Factors to consider in analyzing the videotape might include the following: How did the child act? What did she or he say and do? The idea is to learn from the student—to really listen and see what a child's perspective can add to the endeavor of teaching. Remind teachers that this should be a conversation, not an interrogation. Teachers should plan to spend adequate time with the child, just talking and sharing. If possible, teachers should collect literacy artifacts from the child. Have teachers consider: What did you learn about how this child has learned to read? What messages does the child have about reading and writing? Do you have any insights into how he or she has been taught? What would you do to teach this child? *Keep in mind that learning about one child can provide valuable insight about the similarities and differences across all children and that one child only represents himself or herself, not an entire community.*

The third in-community activity is designed to build teachers' awareness of the richness of literacy practices that go on daily in the everyday worlds of low-income, immigrant, or nonmainstream families. Every community engages in literacy activities. These activities may be clear examples of print literacy (e.g., reading library books aloud), or they may be oral forms of literacy expression (e.g., speeches at rallies and protests). In this activity, teachers are asked to attend a community event or activity in a low-income or immigrant community or a community of color. These may be ethnic or religious and cultural events that deal specifically with the local community, or they may be more general. The task is to identify the forms of literacy at work at these events.

Teachers are asked to reflect on how the events may relate to classroom literacy. Bear in mind that these should be events that teachers would not normally attend. The purpose is to meet people outside of one's regular social circle. Encourage teachers to find events that challenge typical or mainstream ideas about what counts as literacy. Remind them that when children see that teachers value and incorporate literacy practices observed in events that take place in the children's own communities, students are empowered to see themselves as valuable, and the potential for literacy engagement is increased.

As the teachers participate in the community events, ask them to look for instances in which the presence of literacy practices is clearly visible. Also, ask them to notice how adolescents and preadolescents participate in these community activities (noting particularly their demeanor.) What follow are some general suggestions for sites where community events may entail local literacy practices:

Poetry slams	Art exhibits
Civic meetings	Book signings
Community meetings	Religious events (church services)
Neighborhood school meetings	Political rallies

Critical to the success of this activity is a prior discussion about how to approach the communities that teachers will be visiting. For too long, "outsiders," who are often privileged people, have helped to marginalize certain communities by interrupting their events and misinterpreting their lives. Simply going to "watch" and learn from these events is an exercise in privilege. Teachers should be asked to consider the ways that they are exercising privilege and consider how to approach the community event they wish to attend. Minimally, teachers should contact the leader of the event to discuss their intended visit and to determine whether their attendance would be appropriate.

To summarize, each of the activities listed in the three categories just discussed provide opportunities for thought and critical reflection. It is important that each activity is reflected on in a group setting led by an instructor who can help participants begin to think differently about their pedagogical practices. As an instructor using this book, it is important to remember that many of these activities require teachers to go beyond what they typically do in their work as teachers. They are asked to think broadly about literacy and knowledge and how schools and society privilege some knowledge and marginalize other forms of knowledge. In asking teachers to consider these issues and relate them to their role as teachers of literacy, some teachers may feel threatened or confused. Therefore, it is imperative that one is able and willing to critically reflect on one's own practice and model ways to question the taken-for-granted norms of schooling not by assigning blame to individuals but, rather, by using such opportunities to open up possibilities for greater educational success for all students.

REFERENCES

Gonzalez, N., Moll, L., Tenery, M. F., Rivera, A., Rendon, P., Gonzalez, R., & Amanti, C. (1995). Funds of knowledge for teaching in Latino households. *Urban Education, 29*(4), 443–470.

Moll, L., Amanti, C., Neff, D., & Gonzalez, N. (1992). Funds of knowledge for teaching: Using a qualitative approach to connect homes and classrooms. *Theory into Practice, 31*(2), 132–141.

Puch, D. (2000). Black characters depicted as white in tests. *News Gazette* (Champaign, IL). Available at: http://www.news-gazette.com/story.cfm?Number=021700.

Rios, F. (Ed.). (1996). *Teacher thinking in cultural contexts.* Albany: State University of New York Press.

About the Editors and Contributors

Dorothy S. Strickland is the Samuel DeWitt Proctor Professor of Education at Rutgers, the State University of New Jersey. She was formerly the Arthur I. Gates Professor of Education at Teachers College, Columbia University. A former classroom teacher, reading consultant, and learning disabilities specialist, she is a past president of the International Reading Association (IRA) and the IRA Reading Hall of Fame. She received IRA's Outstanding Teacher Educator of Reading Award. She was a recipient of the National Council of Teachers of English Award as Outstanding Educator in the Language Arts and the NCTE Rewey Belle Inglis Award as Outstanding Woman in the Teaching of English. She has numerous publications in the field of reading and language arts. Her latest publications are *Preparing Our Teachers: Opportunities for Better Reading Instruction, Beginning Reading and Writing; Administration & Supervision of Reading Programs* (3rd ed.); and *Supporting Struggling Readers and Writers: Strategies for Classroom Intervention 3–6.*

Donna E. Alvermann is Distinguished Research Professor of Reading Education at the University of Georgia. A former middle school teacher in Texas and New York, she was principal investigator and co-director of the federally funded National Reading Research Center from 1992 to 1997. A past president of the National Reading Conference and past co-chair of the IRA's Commission on Adolescent Literacy, she currently edits *Reading Research Quarterly.* She has received the Oscar S. Causey Award for Outstanding Contributions to Reading Research and the Albert J. Kingston Award for Distinguished Service, and was elected to the Reading Hall of Fame. Her recent publications include *Content Reading and Literacy: Succeeding in Today's Diverse Classrooms* (3rd ed.); *Reconceptualizing the Literacies in Adolescents' Lives; Struggling Adolescent Readers: A Collection of Teaching Strategies; Popular Culture in the Classroom: Teaching and Researching Critical Media Literacy;* and *Adolescents and Literacies in a Digital World.*

Robert Balfanz is a research scientist and co-director of the Talent Development Middle and High School Programs at the Johns Hopkins University Center for Social Organization of Schools. His recent research has estimated the size and location of the most serious dropout problems in American high schools and evaluated the impact of different approaches to narrowing student skill gaps and supporting high school completion.

Phyllis Blumenfeld is Professor of Education in the Combined Program in Education and Psychology at the University of Michigan. She has conducted research on student socialization, student motivation, and the role of tasks and instruction on student thoughtfulness. Her current research focuses on the design of learning environments, the effect of project-based science on student learning and motivation, and school engagement of urban elementary students. She received her Ph.D. at the University of California, Los Angeles.

Willard Brown is science teacher and department chair at Skyline High School in Oakland, California. He has integrated science reading instruction into chemistry courses for varied populations of urban students and is a participant in the Strategic Literacy Initiative professional development program at WestEd. He has taught a course on reading methods in secondary science teaching at the University of California, Berkeley. He is a member of the National Science Teachers Association and the California Science Teachers Association. His scholarly writing includes publications in *Journal of Physical Chemistry*. He has a doctorate in chemistry from the University of California, Berkeley.

Fred Carrigg is currently on loan to the New Jersey Department of Education, serving in two capacities. As the New Jersey director of Reading First, he coordinates the state's effort to restructure reading programs in the most impoverished districts. He is also a special assistant to the commissioner for urban literacy. In this position, he serves as a senior administrator in the Abbott division for advice on successful literacy policies and works specifically with the poorest districts in the state on curriculum and instruction, policies, and programs to improve urban education. Since 1989, he has been the executive director for academic programs in Union City. His responsibilities include supervising the development and implementation of curriculum for all pre-K–12 programs. Consistent with his other responsibilities is the infusion of the ubiquitous use of technology in the district, which has led Union City to be cited as a national model for seamless integration of technology into the daily curriculum. He has a B.A. in foreign languages from Montclair State University and an Ed.M. in intercultural education from Rutgers University.

Donald D. Deshler, Ph.D., is director of the University of Kansas Center for Research on Learning (KU-CRL). His work focuses on the design and validation of instructional interventions for improving the performance of at-risk adolescents (including those with disabilities). Along with his colleagues at the KU-CRL, he has developed and completed more than $70 million of contracted research on the Strategic Instruction Model (SIM), a comprehensive instruction model for improving outcomes of adolescents in secondary schools. His most recent book is *Teaching Content to All: Evidenced-Based Inclusive Practices in Middle and Secondary Schools*.

Janice A. Dole is Associate Professor of Education in the Department of Teaching and Learning at the University of Utah. She has held positions at the University of Denver, the Center for the Study of Reading at the University of Illinois, Urbana-Champaign, and Michigan State University. She is a former primary grade teacher who has conducted research on comprehension instruction and conceptual change. Her current research focuses on systemic reform in the primary grades, with special emphasis on the professional development of teachers.

Christy J. Falba is director of K–12 Literacy and Elementary Instructional Technology in the Clark County School District, Las Vegas, the sixth-largest district in the country. Her areas of expertise include curriculum development, literacy, technology integration, and teacher education. Her research interests focus on reading intervention strategies for struggling readers and the integration of technology in teaching and learning. She received her Ed.D. from the University of Nevada, Las Vegas, and has served as the school-district liaison for several collaborative university–school district projects. In 2002, she was honored as the College of Education Alumna of the Year.

Douglas Fisher is Associate Professor of Teacher Education at San Diego State University and a teacher at Hoover High School, part of the City Heights Educational Collaborative. His interests center on improving literacy achievement in urban schools, specifically in secondary schools. He has published in numerous journals, including the *Journal of Adolescent & Adult Literacy* and *Educational Leadership*. In addition, he is the coauthor of several books, including *Improving Adolescent Literacy: Strategies at Work*.

Nancy Frey is Assistant Professor of Teacher Education at San Diego State University and the professional development schools coordinator for the City Heights Educational Pilot. Her current research interests focus on grade-level retention policies and providing academic support for students at risk of retention. She is the co-author of *Responsive Curriculum Design in Secondary Schools: Meeting the Diverse Needs of Students*.

Cynthia Greenleaf is co-director of the Strategic Literacy Initiative at WestEd, where her work focuses on addressing the literacy learning needs of diverse urban adolescents. She leads colleagues in designing and carrying out a program of professional development for secondary teachers as well as an integrated program of research focused on student and teacher learning outcomes from this work. Her scholarly writing includes publications in journals such as *Teaching and Teacher Education* and the *Harvard Educational Review*. She has a doctorate in language and literacy education from the University of California, Berkeley.

Deborah Hicks is Associate Professor of Education at the University of Cincinnati. She completed a doctorate at the Harvard Graduate School of Education in 1988. Since that time, she has become known for her interdisciplinary studies of classroom discourse and learning (e.g., *Discourse, Learning, and Schooling,*

Cambridge University Press, 1996). Her more recent scholarship deals with studies of gender, social class, and literacy. Her book *Reading Lives: Working-Class Children and Literacy Learning* (Teachers College Press, 2002) chronicles the home and school lives of two working-class children and draws on histories (memoirs, narratives) of other working-class childhoods. Her current work is focused on the lives and voices of girls growing up in an urban Appalachian community.

Margaret Honey, vice president of the Education Development Center and director of the EDC's Center for Children and Technology, has worked in the field of educational technology since 1981. Her primary research interests include the role of technology in school reform and student achievement, the use of telecommunications technology to support online learning communities, and issues of equity associated with the development and use of technology. In 1992, she conducted the first national survey to look at K–12 educators' use of telecommunications, and in 1993, in collaboration with Bank Street College, she developed one of the first projects to cultivate the Internet as an environment in which to advance teachers' professional development. For more than a decade she has been associated with districtwide school reform in Union City, New Jersey, nationally recognized for its success in incorporating technology throughout its programs. In 1999, she was appointed to the U.S. Department of Education's Expert Panel on Educational Technology.

Nora E. Hyland is Assistant Professor at Rutgers University and was an elementary school teacher in Brooklyn, New York, for eight years. Her work focuses on teaching for social justice; developing anti-racist and anti-oppressive teaching by building relationships between communities and schools; and designing action research with teachers and community members to investigate and improve their practice for liberatory ends. Her research is both participatory and ethnographic and critically analyzes ways that local actions are reflective or disruptive of the broader social and cultural context. She received her Ph.D. in curriculum and instruction from the University of Illinois, Urbana-Champaign. Her work has been presented at numerous conferences and in edited books.

Tamara L. Jetton, Associate Professor of Reading, holds a doctorate in educational curriculum and instruction with a concentration in reading. She was a faculty member in the education studies department at the University of Utah prior to joining the faculty of James Madison University. Before graduate school, she taught language arts in the public schools for 10 years and served as department chair of language arts. Her research focuses on understanding how students learn with text, the strategies that teachers use to help students learn with text, and the language students and teachers use in the form of discussions in the classroom.

Robert T. Jiménez is Associate Professor at the University of Illinois, Urbana-Champaign. He teaches courses on qualitative research methods, second language literacy, and bilingual education. His published work has examined the strategic processing of bilingual Latino readers, and he is now interested in the ways that historical, transnational, and economic factors influence the literacy learning of linguistically diverse students. He is also interested in the potential of alternative literacy practices to promote these students' personal and political goals.

Joseph Krajcik, Professor of Science Education at the University of Michigan, focuses his research on designing science classrooms so that learners engage in finding solutions to meaningful, real-world questions through inquiry. He has authored and coauthored more than 80 articles or chapters and makes frequent research presentations as well as presentations that translate research into classroom practice. His colleagues have recognized his leadership by selecting him President of the National Association for Research on Science Teaching. In 2001, the American Association for the Advancement of Science inducted him as a fellow. Prior to obtaining his Ph.D. from the University of Iowa, he taught high school chemistry.

Carol D. Lee is Associate Professor of Education and Social Policy in the Learning Sciences Program at Northwestern University. She is a former high school English teacher, primary grade teacher, and school principal. Her research focuses on cultural supports for literacy instruction, with a special emphasis on generative uses of African American cultural resources. She is a past president of the National Conference on Research in Language and Literacy.

Cindy Litman is a senior research associate with WestEd's Strategic Literacy Initiative. She was a chief architect of elementary, secondary, and after-school literacy initiatives for more than 10 years. Prior to her work in literacy, she conducted research on parent–child and peer relations during early childhood as a graduate student and postgraduate researcher at the University of California, Davis. She is the author of several books (published by the Developmental Studies Center) and articles in scholarly journals focusing on relationships among social, emotional, and intellectual/literacy development.

Ronald W. Marx is Professor of Educational Psychology and Dean of the College of Education at the University of Arizona. He has conducted classroom-based experimental and observational research focusing on how classrooms can be sites for learning that is highly motivated and cognitively engaging. In the late 1980s, he conducted policy research in British Columbia that led to substantial reform of the province's schools. Recently, he has been working with computer scientists, science educators, and educational psychologists to enhance science education and to develop teacher professional development models to sustain long-term change in science education. He received his Ph.D. from Stanford University.

James McPartland is director of the Center for Social Organization of Schools and Research Professor of Sociology at Johns Hopkins University. For the past

10 years, he has led the team of researchers and practitioners that developed and evaluated a comprehensive reform model for high schools—the Talent Development High School. His current research examines the processes through which smaller high schools with innovative literacy programs for low-performing students become successfully implemented and have impacts on student engagement and learning.

Elizabeth Birr Moje is Associate Professor of Literacy, Language, and Culture in Educational Studies at the University of Michigan, Ann Arbor. Her research interests revolve around the intersection between the literacies and texts youths are asked to learn in formal learning institutions and the literacies and texts they engage outside of school. Moje also studies how youths make culture and enact identities from their home and community cultures, popular cultures, and school cultures. Before Moje received her Ph.D. in Literacy and Language from Purdue University, she taught high school science and history.

Deborah Peek-Brown has been a science teacher for Detroit Public Schools for 22 years. She holds an M.A. in science education from the University of Michigan. Deborah currently works as an instructional specialist for Detroit Public Schools' Center for Learning Technologies in Urban Schools. This NSF-funded center partners the Detroit Public Schools, the University of Michigan, the Chicago Public Schools, and Northwestern University. As instructional specialist, Deborah facilitates professional development, participates in curriculum development, and develops teams of researchers and teachers who integrate technology in Detroit schools to enhance student achievement in science. Deborah is the recipient of many excellence awards in science instruction, including state finalist for the Presidential Award for Excellence.

Ralph E. Reynolds is Professor and Chair, Department of Educational Psychology, College of Education, University of Nevada, Las Vegas. His areas of expertise include attention allocation and use in comprehension, Schema Theory, and figurative language, as well as scientifically based approaches to reading instruction. He has authored or coauthored numerous research articles and book chapters and has won many research and teaching awards during his career. In 1998, he was named as one of the top 20 educational psychologists in terms of publishing in the major educational psychology journals and was elected president of the international Society for the Scientific Study of Reading.

Carol M. Santa is currently co-owner and educational director of Montana Academy, a private residential school for troubled teenagers located on a remote Montana ranch. She has been an elementary teacher, reading specialist, language arts coordinator, and university professor. She is currently co-director of Project CRISS, a program which focuses on reading, writing, and studying across the curriculum. In 1999–2000 she was president of the IRA, a professional organization of teachers, writers, and authors whose goal is to improve literacy.

Jean B. Schumaker, Ph.D., is Professor in the Departments of Human Development and Special Education and associate director of the University of Kansas Center for Research on Learning (KU-CRL). She has spent the past 25 years studying the problems of adolescents and developing educational interventions for them. Along with Donald Deshler and other colleagues at the KU-CRL, she has developed the Strategies Intervention Model. She has also done extensive research in the area of social-skill interventions, describing the social skills of several populations of at-risk youths and reported the development and validation of instructional procedures for social skills.

Timothy Shanahan is Professor of Urban Education at the University of Illinois, Chicago, where he is director of the Center for Literacy. He recently was executive director of the Chicago Reading Initiative for the Chicago Public Schools, a school improvement initiative serving 437,000 children. His research focuses on the relationship of reading and writing, school improvement, the assessment of reading ability, and family literacy. He has published more than 100 books and research articles on literacy. He served on the National Reading Panel, convened by the National Institute of Child Health and Development by the request of Congress to evaluate research on successful methods of teaching reading.

Alta Shaw currently serves as director of Training and co-director of Instruction for the Talent Development High Schools model located in the Center for Social Organization of Schools (CSOS) at Johns Hopkins University. As an experienced secondary teacher of English Language Arts, Ms. Shaw has spent more than 15 years at CSOS serving as an instructional facilitator, curriculum developer, and school reformer. Most recently, Ms. Shaw co-developed *Strategic Reading,* an instructional framework and course designed to provide ninth-grade students who read two or more levels below grade expectancy with a balance of literacy activities during an extended period.

LeeAnn M. Sutherland is Assistant Research Scientist in the School of Education at the University of Michigan. Prior to receiving her Ph.D. in Literacy Education at the University of Michigan, LeeAnn was a high school teacher. She continues to work with adolescents in schools and in out-of-school contexts. LeeAnn's current research focuses on students in urban, middle school classrooms in which curriculum materials, professional development activities, and teacher enactment foster students' scientific literacy. Her research interests include literacy learning and identity construction, particularly as students make sense of school discourse vis-à-vis their everyday experiences.

Allan Wigfield is Professor of Human Development and Distinguished Scholar–Teacher at the University of Maryland, College Park. His research focuses on the development of children's motivation in different areas, including reading. He has authored more than 80 peer-reviewed journal articles and book chapters on children's motivation. He is associate editor of *Child Development.* He is a Fellow of Division 15 of the American Psychological Association. He is currently collaborating with John Guthrie on a study funded by the National Science Foundation of how two reading programs, Concept Oriented Reading Instruction and Strategy Instruction, influence elementary school-age children's reading motivation and comprehension.

Douglas Williams is a former math teacher and current principal of Hoover High School in San Diego. He has led the school to impressive achievement gains and wants to create "the model school for all schools." He is a member of the African-American Educators Association and has written for *Educational Leadership*.

Susan K. Woodruff, M.S., is an educational consultant with 30 years of experience in teaching and working with adolescents and adults with learning problems. She is a national professional developer whose focus is on improving instruction for all students and helping schools develop programs which help all students become strategic learners. She has been a professional developer specializing in SIM strategies and programs in Michigan for nearly 10 years, and more recently nationally, and she is currently working with secondary schools across the country to help facilitate the development of the Content Literacy Continuum within their schools.

Index